Essays in
Money and Banking

IN HONOUR OF
R. S. SAYERS

R. S. SAYERS

Essays in
Money and Banking
IN HONOUR OF
R. S. SAYERS

EDITED BY
C. R. WHITTLESEY
AND
J. S. G. WILSON

OXFORD
AT THE CLARENDON PRESS
1968

Oxford University Press, Ely House, London W. 1

GLASGOW NEW YORK TORONTO MELBOURNE WELLINGTON
CAPE TOWN SALISBURY IBADAN NAIROBI LUSAKA ADDIS ABABA
BOMBAY CALCUTTA MADRAS KARACHI LAHORE DACCA
KUALA LUMPUR HONG KONG TOKYO

PRINTED IN GREAT BRITAIN

PREFACE

IT is fitting that friends and colleagues of Richard Sidney Sayers[1] should join together in a common enterprise to honour him. A happy occasion for doing so is his sixtieth birthday and the completion of twenty years of distinguished occupancy of the Sir Ernest Cassel Chair of Economics with special reference to Money and Banking in the University of London, tenable at the London School of Economics, an appointment that followed his war-time service with the Ministry of Supply (1940–5) and his early post-war work as an economic adviser in the Cabinet Office (1945–7).

Professor Sayers's wide range of interests is reflected in the variety of the contributions here offered. It is not without significance that the main emphasis should be on monetary and banking history, a field in which he has written with great distinction. Indeed, few scholars will leave behind them a more enduring memorial than Richard Sayers, who first achieved recognition (in 1936) as the historian of *Bank of England Operations, 1890–1914*. This reputation as a financial historian was firmly consolidated by a succession of contributions that in later years included the official history of *Financial Policy 1939–45* (1956) and *Lloyds Bank in the History of English Banking* (1957). As an editor likewise, an important part of his work has been devoted to monetary and banking history, as witness his joint editorship (with T. S. Ashton) of *Papers in English Monetary History* (1953) and his own editing of the *Economic Writings of James Pennington* (1963), ably supported as it is by an exploratory essay of the man's life and work. The same care for history is reflected (especially in the title chapter) in the essays collected as *Central Banking after Bagehot* (1957). This interest was maintained in the centenary volume *Gilletts in the London Money Market 1867–1967*. It was no accident that Richard Sayers should be chosen to write the successor volumes to Clapham on the history of the Bank of England.

---

[1] M.A. (Cantab. and Oxon.), D.Litt. (Warwick), F.B.A.; Sometime Fellow of Pembroke College, Oxford; Honorary Fellow of St. Catharine's College, Cambridge; and Honorary Fellow of the Institute of Bankers.

This scholarship has contributed much to our understanding both of the broad sweep of monetary history and of some of its previously less explored corners. It is no secret that Sayers also wrote much of the Report of the Committee on the Working of the Monetary System (Cmnd. 827, 1959) and was a distinguished and highly articulate member of the Radcliffe Committee 1957–9. In this work, he drew on his great historical knowledge; it helped to provide the Committee with the perspective necessary to the performance of its task. It matters little that there were many to criticize; it matters much that the Report provoked discussion and promoted understanding.

The ability to apply scholarship to institutional and practical problems is reflected in *Modern Banking*, first published in 1938 and achieving its seventh edition in 1967. Again, as editor, Richard Sayers led a group mainly of younger men in forming a research team to produce *Banking in the British Commonwealth* (1952) and some ten years later repeated the performance with a somewhat different team to publish *Banking in Western Europe* (1962), in which he also participated as an author.

Finally, he has a facility for distilling his scholarship into simple and lucid exposition. As examples, one might note his little sketch on the *American Banking System* (1948), *Modern Banking* itself, and—more recently—*A History of Economic Change in England, 1880–1939* (1967).

Apart from his public service as a member of the Radcliffe Committee, and a part-time member (with a special knowledge of banking) of the Monopolies Commission, Richard Sayers has given of his time on the Councils of the British Academy, the Royal Economic Society, and the Economic History Society. In 1960 he served as President of Section F of the British Association for the Advancement of Science.

The breadth of Sayers's interests is reflected in journal articles and books—in terms of subject matter, the historical periods covered, and the range of institutions on which he is knowledgeable. It is appropriate therefore that the essays in his honour should have been drawn from friends and scholars on both sides of the Atlantic. They are a tribute to the high professional standing of the man and the esteem in which he is held abroad as well as at home.

In preparing a work of this kind, editors incur many debts

Only one can be acknowledged here. For her unfailing devotion in maintaining lines of communication both between the editors themselves (often when they were far from base) and between them and the other contributors, our sincere thanks go to Miss Paula Malam, Secretary of the Department of Economics and Commerce in the University of Hull. In addition, we express our appreciation to Miss Malam for assistance with reading and checking the page proofs and for preparing the index.

Since several of the contributions to this volume relate to matters that have considerable topicality (and it has not been possible to incorporate all changes or postscripts), the editors have been requested to emphasize that certain chapters were in fact submitted in their final form some months before highly relevant developments took place (such as the devaluation of sterling on 18 November 1967), which authors would have wished to take into account or as a result of which they might have modified somewhat the arguments originally submitted.

C. R. WHITTLESEY
J. S. G. WILSON

7 March 1968

CONTENTS

R. F. G. ALFORD

Bank Rate, Money Rates, and the Treasury-bill Rate

INTRODUCTION

SINCE about 1960 the volume of Treasury bills in the United Kingdom market has tended to decline, while the volume of competing non-marketable assets, particularly local authority loans, has risen greatly. Nevertheless, the Treasury bill has remained a very important short-term marketable asset, and the authorities—broadly speaking, the Bank of England acting on lines agreed with the Treasury—have continued to attach great importance to their ability to influence the Treasury-bill rate. Their most obvious way of doing this is through a change in Bank Rate. But the practice has always been to move Bank Rate in steps of at least half a percentage point and often at considerable intervals of time.[1] Since the relationship between Bank Rate and the Treasury-bill rate is a fairly elastic one, any close management of the bill rate requires some additional means of influencing it, given the level of Bank Rate. Here we shall investigate the means which the authorities use for this purpose and their effectiveness, using data collected for the period 1960–2.

[1] In the twelve years 1955–66 inclusive, Bank Rate was changed twenty-five times, the size distribution of the movements being:

	Rises	Falls
2 points	3	..
1 point	6	2
½ point	1	13

The single rise of ½ point occurred at the very beginning of the period. The general pattern of the changes is evident.

THE MARKET FOR TREASURY BILLS[1]

Treasury bills are tendered for weekly on Fridays, the largest body of tenderers being the twelve discount houses whose tenders, by their own convention, in total approximately equal the total of bills on offer; commonly the discount houses agree a price at which all their individual tenders are made, although sometimes a small proportion may go in at a slightly higher or lower price. Treasury bills are allotted to tenderers beginning with those offering the highest price (prepared to lend to the government at the lowest rate) whose tenders are allotted in full; then those offering the next highest price (next lowest rate) receive their tenders in full, and so on, until the cut-off price is reached—the price at which the sum of tenders exceeds the amount of unallotted bills. The tenderers at this price are allotted the percentage of their tenders which exhausts the bills on offer. Because of the size of their combined tenders, the price agreed between the discount houses invariably becomes the cut-off price and they, and any other tenderers at that price, receive the appropriate percentage of their tenders. Since the Second World War the discount houses have never failed to receive some percentage allotment of their tenders and in the period 1960–2 this averaged about 47 per cent.

In agreeing the price at which they will submit their tenders (or the greater part of them), the discount houses effectively determine the lowest price/highest rate at which the Treasury bills are allotted at that week's tender. They make the market in Treasury bills, which consists primarily of quoting rates at which they will sell the bills they have been allotted at the tender, and in any week they base their selling rates upon the agreed tender rate they paid for the bills at the last tender, which is also the maximum rate at which bills were allotted at that tender. Most commonly their selling rate is around $\frac{1}{16}$ the actual margin having some relationship to the life of the bills they are selling. (On the average, a bill is sold after it has been in the hands of the discount houses for only a very few weeks; not many are held long enough to be sold in their third

---

[1] The institutional arrangements described below refer to the period 1960–2; a very useful source for this period is *The London Discount Market Today*, Institute of Bankers, 1962.

month of life and very few mature in the hands of a discount house.)

When Bank Rate rises, the discount houses for several weeks find themselves selling bills at a higher rate/lower price than they paid for them and, in these circumstances, buyers usually concede to the discount houses something over the normal $\frac{1}{16}$ per cent. margin on the bills they sell, that is, the buyers pay a relatively higher price than normal. Apart from this minor variation, and from the situation in which Bank Rate has changed since the last tender, the preceding maximum tender rate virtually determines the market rates at which the discount houses will sell Treasury bills; bargaining may vary these rates by $\frac{1}{32}$ or $\frac{1}{64}$ per cent., but this is all.

From the point of view of the authorities, therefore, influencing the market rate for Treasury bills means influencing the price, and the corresponding rate, at which the discount houses agree to put in the whole or most of their tenders for Treasury bills on Fridays.

THE STRUCTURE OF RATES

The maximum tender rate for Treasury bills commonly lies between Bank Rate and the average money rate of the discount houses; together these three rates form an important section of the structure of short-term rates of interest.

The key rate in this structure is Bank Rate, the minimum rate at which holders of accounts at the Discount Office of the Bank of England (which means the twelve discount houses only) have the right to borrow for a minimum period of seven days against the security of Treasury bills, short bonds, or approved commercial bills.[1] Rigidly fixed at 2 per cent. below Bank Rate for many years past has been the deposit rate agreed

---

[1] This remains a useful definition of Bank Rate, but while in 1960–2 the Bank of England always made loans on these minimum terms (except for a few loans for eight days), since then the Bank has become more flexible in its practices. It made loans at ½ per cent. over Bank Rate in Mar. 1963, and since mid 1966 it has lent overnight at and below Bank Rate, as well as for seven days or more at Bank Rate. Elsewhere in the discount market also practices appear to have become more flexible since 1960–2.

Bank Rate is also the minimum rate at which the Bank will rediscount approved commercial bills for the holders of accounts at the Discount Office, but this facility is now seldom, if ever, used.

upon by the eleven London clearing banks,[1] while at a small margin above their deposit rate the clearing banks agree a minimum rate for call loans to the discount houses. Since November 1958 this minimum call-loan rate has been $\frac{3}{8}$ per cent. above their deposit rate and $1\frac{5}{8}$ per cent. below Bank Rate. Above this minimum call-loan rate is the fairly stable average rate which the clearing banks expect to earn upon the greater part of their loans to the discount houses—what is often called their regular money; this is not a rate agreed upon between the clearing banks, but there is a natural tendency for some such rate to emerge. Early in 1962 this rate was said to be about $1\frac{1}{8}$ per cent. above their deposit rate, $\frac{7}{8}$ per cent. below Bank Rate.

In the past decade the clearing banks have normally provided more than half of the discount houses' borrowed funds (about 55 per cent. on the average in 1960–2), a high proportion of this lending being regular money at fairly stable rates, given Bank Rate. At the other extreme, rates for overnight money fluctuate freely, with the result that the average money rate of the discount houses—the average cost of their borrowed funds—fluctuates from day to day, but by far less than rates for overnight money. Finally, for our purposes, we come to the Treasury-bill maximum tender rate. This varies, but is most commonly around $\frac{1}{2}$ per cent. above the discount houses' average money rate, allowing them a small margin of profit upon their Treasury-bill holdings. However, when a reduction in Bank Rate is confidently expected, the prospect of gains from the sale of Treasury bills at lower rates/higher prices tends to increase competition at the tender, and this is one influence reducing this profit margin and even making it negative.

THE AUTHORITIES AND THE TREASURY-BILL RATE

Against this background, we turn to the question of how the authorities can influence the maximum Treasury-bill tender rate. The first and most obvious way is through a change in Bank Rate, which will shift the level of the discount houses'

---

[1] At the time of writing (mid 1967), the National Board for Prices and Incomes has just recommended that this rigid link should be relaxed (Report No. 34, *Bank Charges*, Cmnd. 3292).

average money rate by a broadly similar amount. But Bank Rate never changes by less than half a point, and the authorities feel that they can achieve finer adjustment of the Treasury-bill rate, with a given level of Bank Rate, through their day-to-day management of the money position in the market, particularly by their ability to make the discount houses borrow from the Bank of England at Bank Rate. This they see as raising the average money rate paid by the discount houses, which in turn tends to make them raise the rate at which they tender for Treasury bills. The Bank of England's view on this has been expressed very clearly in a number of places:

Committee on the Working of the Monetary System (Radcliffe Committee) *Minutes of Evidence* (HMSO, 1960). Question 421 (July 1957), Mr. O'Brien of the Bank of England:

... If we decide to influence short term rates in one direction or another, given a particular level of Bank Rate, the first rate which is affected is the Treasury Bill rate. Supposing we wanted to make short term rates higher, we should keep money short in the market consistently, and as a result the discount market would be compelled to borrow from us quite heavily and quite often. This would have an effect upon the overall cost of the money which they are borrowing to finance their book of Treasury Bills and short bonds. They would feel for that reason alone that they must put up the rate for the Treasury Bills they buy, in order to retain their profit margin. They would be influenced by the obvious wishes of the authorities to move in that direction. . . .

Commentary, *Bank of England Quarterly Bulletin*, March 1962, p. 5:

... The Treasury Bill rate then rose slightly, as continued borrowing from the Bank began to have a significant effect on the average cost of the funds borrowed by the discount market and so reduced the margin between the cost of money and earnings on Bills. . . .

Commentary, *Bank of England Quarterly Bulletin*, March 1963, p. 4:

... Borrowing from the Bank provides an indication of the Bank's attitude towards short-term rates and affects the average cost of the market's borrowing; if the cost rises, or is expected to rise, the market is likely to seek a higher return on its assets—in particular Treasury Bills, which are the most easily influenced. The Treasury Bill rate will therefore tend to be firmer. . . .

Bank Rate, Money Rates,

'The Management of Money Day by Day', *Bank of England Quarterly Bulletin*, March 1963, pp. 15–16:

. . . The enforcement of such borrowing [at Bank Rate or over] increases the average cost of the houses' total borrowings and is one of the main ways (short of a change in Bank Rate) in which the Bank of England exert an influence on short-term interest rates and particularly on the rate at which the discount houses may be expected to bid for Treasury Bills at the following Friday's tender.

The first quotation appears to allow for some influence of borrowing at Bank Rate being exerted directly upon the Treasury-bill rate and not through the average money rate. But it is clear that in the Bank's view its ability to influence the average money rate of the discount houses does provide an important means through which it can influence the Treasury-bill rate. The next section introduces data which can be used to make some assessment of the magnitude of this influence.

THE DATA

1. *The average money rate of the discount houses*

The average money rate of a discount house is a very important factor in its profitability, and certainly most, perhaps all, discount houses calculate their average money rate as at the close of business each day. Preliminary inquiries made it seem unlikely that any discount house would be prepared to reveal information as confidential as a time series of its average money rate; on the other hand, it seemed that they would have little objection to providing figures of the daily change in their average money rate. Four discount houses were therefore approached; all were most helpful and agreed to provide the information. This produced four series of daily first differences in their average money rates, to three decimal places, covering the period April 1960 to December 1962. Certain observations were missing from these series; in all cases these gaps related to a day when Bank Rate changed, and it seems likely that the work involved did not allow the usual daily average rate to be calculated. When this occurred in a series, one change in the average money rate covered the day on which Bank Rate changed and the following day. In no case did this affect more than a single discount house series for any Bank Rate change, and the missing observation has been interpolated in proportion to the average of the two daily changes in the other three series. Including these interpolations, this provided 840 first difference observations for each of the four series.

From these four series was calculated a weighted arithmetic mean of the daily first differences, using as weights the balance-sheet totals of the four houses roughly centred upon our period. This series was then cumulated from an arbitrary origin of 4·100 per cent. to provide a daily average money rate series, and from this were taken the 144 weekly observations set out in Appendix 2. The starting-point of 4·100 per cent. was chosen as it was a convenient figure which seemed reasonably likely to be in the neighbourhood of the market's average money rate at that time. But clearly there is a considerable degree of arbitrariness in this choice, and it must be stressed that reliance should not be placed upon the absolute level of the average money rate series.

2. *Borrowing from the Bank of England at Bank Rate*

Each day after the close of business, City journalists call at the Discount Office of the Bank of England, where they are given an indication of how the day has gone in the money market from the Bank's point of view. Many people have been aware that the Bank, during these visits, gives a systematic indication of the scale of any borrowing at Bank Rate. This can be seen from the daily money-market reports in *The Times* and the *Financial Times*. In the daily reports in *The Times* over the period 1960–2 seven adjectives are used to describe the scale of such borrowing: *trifling/marginal, very small, small, moderate, fairly large, large,* and *very large.* Each adjective would seem to indicate a size bracket, and it should be possible to make a reasonable estimate of these, provided there is some suitable information available on actual borrowings at Bank Rate.

In fact, there are two sources of such information in the *Bank of England Quarterly Bulletin*. First, there is a table of 'Bank of England advances to the discount market'; this shows the total amount advanced in each 'month' between the make-up dates

of the London clearing banks.[1] Second, the end-quarter figures
for the discount houses show loans outstanding from the Bank
of England Banking Department, which are loans at Bank
Rate. In the period 1960–2 there were three banking 'months'
containing only a single day on which the market borrowed
at Bank Rate, and four end-quarters when loans made on only
one day were outstanding, assuming that these loans were all
for seven days.[2] In Table 1 are the figures for the actual loans
made, or outstanding, at Bank Rate on these occasions, together
with the adjectives used in the related daily money-market
reports.

TABLE 1

	£ million Actual amount	Adjective
Banking 'month'		
March/April 1960	3	Very small
February/March 1961	6	Small
June/July 1961	33	Very large
Discount houses quarterly figures		
15 June 1960	8	Small
21 September 1960	7	Small
20 September 1961	4	Very small
19 September 1962	17	Fairly large

Assuming that *trifling* means the same as *marginal* (the former
was used only between May and November 1960, when *marginal* was not used), the adjectives used in the daily money-
market reports seem to be consistent with the ranges in Table 2.
    This set of ranges was then tested by taking all the 165 occa-
sions in our period when the market borrowed from the Bank
and interpreting each adjective as the magnitude at the mid

[1] It also gives the number of days in each banking 'month' on which advances
were made; these numbers agree over our period with the number of occasions
when borrowing at Bank Rate was reported in the daily money-market reports.
    [2] When borrowing at Bank Rate is very heavy, the Bank often lends a proportion
of the money for eight days or more in order to spread out the repayments. The only
occasion in our period when some loans are known to have been for more than
seven days was on Friday 30 June 1961, when the Bank lent £33 million, some at
least of this being for eight days.

point of the relevant range. This made possible twenty-eight comparisons between our estimates and actual figures of borrowing during banking 'months';[1] in addition, it provided seven comparisons for borrowing outstanding at the end of banking quarters and three for borrowing outstanding at the end of the

TABLE 2

	Range (£ million)			Examples from Table 1 (£ million)
Adjective				
Marginal/trifling	under	1		..
Very small	1 and under	5		3, 4,
Small	5 „	„	10	6, 7, 8
Moderate	10 „	„	15	..
Fairly large	15 „	„	20	17
Large	20 „	„	30	..
Very large	30 and over			33

calendar quarters. It was decided to pool all this data; then, using our estimates to explain the actual figures, in £ million, we have the simple regression result:

$$\text{actual} = 0.353 + 0.919 \text{ estimate} \quad r^2 = 0.983$$
$$33.6 \qquad\qquad\quad t: 45.5$$
$$(3.1)$$

Underneath the dependent variable is shown its mean with the standard error in parentheses, and the t value is shown for the coefficient of the independent variable.

This result seems to be good enough to justify us in using these mid-point-of-range quantifications. On this basis, therefore, a time series of borrowing at Bank Rate was constructed for our period (see Appendix 2). This shows the amount borrowed during each week, and hence the amount outstanding at the end of each week.[2]

[1] Excluding cases in which both actuals and estimates were zero, and the single case of the *very large* borrowing on 30 June 1961, where the actual amount (£33 million) is known, as it was the only borrowing in that banking month, and the relevant range (£30 million and over) was open-ended, so that there was no simple mid-point-of-range estimate.

[2] Two tabulations of borrowing at Bank Rate in our period may be of some interest; these are given in Appendix 3.

3. *The Treasury-bill maximum tender rate*

Here we are concerned with the minimum price/maximum rate at which bills are allotted at each weekly tender; as explained above, this effectively determines the market Treasury-bill rates quoted by the discount houses. In any week the discount houses may acquire a small proportion of 91-day bills at a higher price/lower rate at the tender, or (in November and December in our period) 63-day bills at a rather higher rate; we take no account of this.

The original data used was the lowest price at which tenders were accepted at each weekly tender. Tender prices are to the nearest penny per £100 nominal of bills bid for, and it was found that the bill tables which were readily available did not give sufficient accuracy in the conversion of such prices into rates; new tables were therefore computed for 91-day bills. A number of different definitions of the rate of discount or rate of interest were considered, and it was decided for present purposes to define the bill rate relating to any given price as the equivalent annual rate of return upon the tender price per £100 nominal of 91-day bills held to maturity, interest being compounded continuously. The formula used in the computation was:

$$n = be^{rx}$$

where n is the nominal value of £100, b is the tender price in pounds, e is the base upon which natural logarithms are calculated (= 2·71828 . . .), 100 r per cent. is the bill rate to be found (e.g. if the rate is 5·00 per cent., then 100 r = 5·00 and r = 0·05), and x is the life of the bill in years, in this case $\frac{91}{365}$ (the market convention being that leap years are ignored for such calculations).[1]

The time series of the Treasury-bill maximum tender rate over our period is set out in Appendix 2.

4. *The timing of observations*

Our purpose is to consider relationships between borrowing at Bank Rate, the average money rate of the discount houses, and the maximum Treasury-bill tender rate. The Treasury-bill

---

[1] I have to thank my colleague Mr. N. H. Carrier for the computer programme which was used to construct these Tables.

tender closes at 1 p.m. on Friday, the discount houses having finished the meeting at which they agree their bid half an hour or so earlier. The latest average money rate which the discount houses will know at the time of their meeting is that for the close on the preceding day, Thursday, which will reflect the influence of (*a*) any change in the level of Bank Rate, which most commonly is announced at about 11.45 a.m. on Thursday, and (*b*) any outstanding borrowing at Bank Rate (assuming that such borrowing is for the minimum seven days, this means borrowing done on any day(s) between the preceding Friday and this Thursday, inclusive).

With these considerations in mind, the time series are set out in Appendix 2 in such a form that an observation on each series consists of the following (hypothetical dates are given for clarity):

(*a*) the average money rate of the discount houses at the close of business on Thursday, 9th;

(*b*) Bank Rate at the close on Thursday, 9th;

(*c*) borrowing from the Bank of England at Bank Rate between Friday, 3rd, and Thursday, 9th, inclusive;

(*d*) the maximum rate at which Treasury bills were allotted at the tender on Friday, 10th.

Each observation on the four series is dated to the relevant Thursday, in this case the 9th. There is, however, an exception to this timing. The incidence of the Good Friday holiday means that in one week each year the Treasury-bill tender is held on a Thursday; this has been taken into account in our data, for these weeks the average money rate is that at the close on Wednesday, with corresponding changes in the other series.

SOME ANALYSIS OF THE DATA

As shown above, the view of the authorities has been that, given Bank Rate, they are able to raise the average money rate of the discount houses by making them borrow at Bank Rate, and that in this way they can exert an upward influence upon the Treasury-bill rate. We start, therefore, by testing the single equation hypothesis that, over our period, the average money rate of the discount houses is explained by the level of Bank

Rate and the level of borrowing at Bank Rate. Using least squares multiple regression we then have:

1.
$$A = -0.521 + 0.917\,R + 0.0046\,B$$

    4.412 t: 98.1   6.28

   (0.084)

$R^2 = 0.986$ $r^2_{13.2} = 0.220$ $d = 0.391$

where A is our series for the average money rate, R is Bank Rate, and B is our estimated series for borrowing at Bank Rate. The mean of A is shown underneath A, with the standard error in parentheses. Underneath each coefficient is shown the t value (the ratio of the coefficient to its standard error). R^2 is the unadjusted coefficient of multiple determination; $r^2_{13.2}$ is the partial correlation coefficient between the first and third variables (A and B), allowing for the linear influence of the second variable (R); and d is the Durbin–Watson statistic.

At first sight equation 1 appears to be quite a good result, Bank Rate and borrowing at Bank Rate having the expected signs and together explaining 98.6 per cent. of the variance in the average money rate, the coefficient of each being significant at better than the 1 per cent. level. However, doubt is thrown upon these results by the very low level of the Durbin–Watson figure, which indicates strong positive autocorrelation in the residuals of the equation, and consequent overstatement of the significance of the results.

Looking at the signs of the residuals reveals a very marked pattern, nearly all being negative in the first part of our period and nearly all positive in the second part, with the change-over occurring towards the end of the period of the 7 per cent. Bank Rate. Looking at the graph of the data in Appendix 2, it can be seen that before the 7 per cent. Bank Rate the average margin between Bank Rate and the average money rate was about 1 percentage point, while after it this margin was on the average appreciably less. This change in the average margin appears to account for most of the marked pattern in the signs of the residuals of equation 1. Further, if we divide our period conveniently between observations 77 and 78, in the earlier half borrowing at Bank Rate occurred in 54 per cent. of weeks, with an average for these weeks of £10.8 million, while in the later half it occurred in 80 per cent. of weeks, with an average of

£14·6 million. Thus the more frequent and heavier borrowing at Bank Rate in the later half is associated with a higher level of the average money rate relative to Bank Rate. If we have some good reason for attributing the change in the average margin between Bank Rate and the average money rate to some exogenous change, allowing for this change will lead to a regression equation in which the influence of borrowing at Bank Rate upon the average money rate will be less than in equation 1.

There is one reason for believing that there was such an exogenous change. The latter part of our period was one of widespread, and correct, expectation of reductions in Bank Rate (which, it should be remembered, fell by a further half-point immediately after the end of our period). The discount houses found business unusually profitable (gaining from the turnover of bills at falling rates and improving profit margins on holding bonds, although the profit margin on holding bills was lower), and were thus in a position to concede higher money rates, while lenders of money who were forgoing these gains arising from the fall in rates could be expected to press for some compensation in the form of higher money rates relative to Bank Rate.[1]

Thus the lower margin between Bank Rate and the average money rate in the latter part of our period can be interpreted as having arisen from the fairly consistent, and correct, expectation of a generally falling Bank Rate. At the same time, the more frequent and heavier borrowing from the Bank of England can reasonably be interpreted as showing attempts by the authorities to hold up the Treasury-bill rate in the face of these expectations. This line of reasoning, unfortunately, cannot be

[1] The behaviour of the average money rate during the short period of 7 per cent. Bank Rate can be explained in a similar manner; initially the heavy losses on the sale of bills by the discount houses following the rise in Bank Rate led lenders to concede lower money rates, but as the losses on bill sales ran off, the lenders demanded and got a more normal level of money rates in relation to Bank Rate.

In the residuals of equation 1, out of the four positive ones before the change-over, three occurred together just before the reduction of Bank Rate from 6 per cent. in Oct. 1960. The absence of more marked effects of the type outlined above following the one point rise in Bank Rate in June 1960, and its fall by half a point in Oct. and Dec. 1960, must be attributed, rather unsatisfactorily, to the smaller scale of the rise and to the absence of strong expectations of a large-scale fall in Bank Rate.

objectively tested with the data we have, but it is highly persuasive in terms of market behaviour, and does suggest that the
change-over in the signs of the residuals of equation 1 is a
reflection of this difference in expectations between the two
parts of our period.

In equation 2, therefore, we introduce a dummy variable H,
which takes the value of zero in all weeks up to this change-
over, and unity in all subsequent weeks:

2. $$A = -0 \cdot 672 + 0 \cdot 147 \, H + 0 \cdot 935 \, R + 0 \cdot 0023 \, B$$
$$4 \cdot 412 \qquad\qquad t: \, 17 \cdot 7 \quad\quad 176 \cdot 4 \quad\quad 5 \cdot 26$$
$$(0 \cdot 046)$$
$$R^2 = 0 \cdot 996 \qquad r^2_{14 \cdot 23} = 0 \cdot 173 \qquad d = 0 \cdot 710$$

The introduction of this dummy variable gives equation 2 a
better fit than equation 1, but, as expected, the coefficient of
B falls and the partial correlation coefficient between A and B
also declines. The Durbin–Watson figure is improved, but is
still unsatisfactorily low.

It is possible that there might be some cumulative influence
of borrowing at Bank Rate upon the average money rate; this
was tested by replacing B in equation 2, first by B_2 and then
by B_3, which are the amounts of borrowing at Bank Rate over
the two and three weeks respectively preceding the interest rate
observations. This led to successive but very slight improvements in the fit of the equations, while the Durbin–Watson
figure first improved slightly and then worsened slightly compared with equation 2, and so remained generally unsatisfactory. The partial correlation coefficient between the average
money rate and the borrowing at Bank Rate variable rose
successively, reaching 0·212 in the equation containing B_3. In
the form tested, therefore, the cumulative effect of borrowing
at Bank Rate upon the average money rate was hardly important.

Finally, the relationship between the variables in equation 1
was tested in first differences:

3. $$\Delta A = 0 \cdot 0006 + 0 \cdot 855 \, \Delta R + 0 \cdot 0011 \, \Delta B$$
$$-0 \cdot 0024 \qquad\qquad t: \, 73 \cdot 2 \quad\quad 4 \cdot 64$$
$$(0 \cdot 030)$$
$$R^2 = 0 \cdot 975 \qquad r^2_{13 \cdot 2} = 0 \cdot 132 \qquad d = 2 \cdot 351$$

This equation is satisfactory; the coefficients are significant at better than the 1 per cent. level, R^2 is high for an equation in first difference, and the Durbin–Watson figure is good.

Equation 3 is the only one which is really acceptable by the usual criteria, and shows that, in first differences, borrowing at Bank Rate explained only 13 per cent. of the variance in the average money rate after allowing for the linear influence of Bank Rate. Even if, in the absence of anything better, we were to permit ourselves to take some notice of the admittedly unsatisfactory results of equations 1 and 2, and the versions of the latter using borrowing at Bank Rate over the preceding two and three weeks respectively, the influence of borrowing at Bank Rate is still small. For our period, at least, this must raise some doubts about the effectiveness of borrowing at Bank Rate as a means of influencing the Treasury-bill rate through the medium of induced changes in the average money rate.[1]

We now turn to the factors explaining the Treasury-bill rate. From a series of regressions it was found that using the average money rate as the only independent variable gave an equation with a worse fit than one using Bank Rate alone (R^2 of 0·935 and 0·972 respectively). The change in expectations between the two parts of our period, which was suggested above, could be expected to affect the average margin between Bank Rate and the Treasury-bill rate, as well as that between Bank Rate and the average money rate; some effect of this kind can be seen from the graph of the data, and the dummy variable H was therefore introduced into both these equations. The improvement in the equation using the average money rate was much more marked than in that using Bank Rate, but the latter still had a marginally better fit (R^2 of 0·970 and 0·977 respectively);

---

[1] If the Treasury-bill rate and the average money rate tended always to move together, then the Bank of England's response to a lower Treasury-bill rate by making the discount houses borrow at Bank Rate could appear to have only a small influence upon the average money rate; but by stopping it from falling, borrowing at Bank Rate would be having a more important influence upon the Treasury-bill rate than would appear at first sight. The tendency for the Treasury-bill rate and the average money rate to move together was therefore tested by means of the partial correlation coefficients between them, given Bank Rate and borrowing at Bank Rate (for first differences) and given these and the dummy variable H (for levels). In both cases the partial correlation coefficients were negligibly small, showing no underlying tendency for the Treasury-bill rate and the average money rate to move together.

the coefficients of the independent variables in both equations were significant at better than the 1 per cent. level. (In all these equations, however, the Durbin–Watson figure was very poor.) Borrowing at Bank Rate was next introduced into both equations as an independent variable, giving equations 4 and 5:

4.
$$T = -1.028 - 0.095\,H + 1.110\,R - 0.0049\,B$$
$$4.803 \qquad t: -4.30 \qquad 79.3 \qquad -4.31$$
$$(0.123)$$
$$R^2 = 0.980 \qquad r^2_{14.23} = 0.117 \qquad d = 0.685$$

5.
$$T = -0.215 - 0.269\,H + 1.182\,A - 0.0075\,B$$
$$4.803 \qquad t: -11.4 \qquad 72.7 \qquad -6.03$$
$$(0.134)$$
$$R^2 = 0.976 \qquad r^2_{14.23} = 0.207 \qquad d = 0.731$$

In order to test for any cumulative effect of borrowing at Bank Rate upon the Treasury-bill rate, borrowing at Bank Rate over the preceding two and three weeks (B_2 and B_3 respectively) were successively substituted for B in equation 4, which is the equation with the best fit. The effect upon R^2 was very small, although the significance of the borrowing at Bank Rate variable was slightly improved, so that, in the form tested, the cumulative effect of borrowing at Bank Rate upon the Treasury-bill rate was hardly important. All of these results, however, have poor Durbin–Watson figures, so dropping the dummy variable H, equations 4 and 5 were then taken in first differences:

6.
$$\Delta T = -0.003 + 0.959\,\Delta R - 0.0010\,\Delta B$$
$$-0.0061 \qquad t: 28.7 \qquad -1.45$$
$$(0.087)$$
$$R^2 = 0.855 \qquad r^2_{13.2} = 0.015 \qquad d = 2.036$$

7.
$$\Delta T = -0.004 + 1.086\,\Delta A - 0.0021\,\Delta B$$
$$-0.0061 \qquad t: 25.6 \qquad -2.83$$
$$(0.095)$$
$$R^2 = 0.824 \qquad r^2_{13.2} = 0.054 \qquad d = 2.077$$

Both of these equations are satisfactory by the usual criteria; in each R^2 is quite high for an equation in first differences, and the Durbin–Watson figures are excellent. But the partial correlation coefficients are both very low, and in equation 6 the coefficient of borrowing at Bank Rate is not significant at the 5 per cent. level.

One feature of equations 4–7 is that borrowing at Bank Rate has a negative coefficient. In terms of market behaviour, the explanation seems clear. Given the level of Bank Rate, changes in market expectations are the chief source of exogenous changes in the Treasury-bill rate. The Bank of England might be expected to respond to changes which, in its view, make the Treasury-bill rate unduly low by making the discount houses borrow at Bank Rate. The partial correlation coefficients in equations 6 and 7 show only a very weak relationship of this kind (although if we permit ourselves to take any notice of them, equations 4 and 5 show a somewhat stronger one). But, if the market situation suggested above is anything like correct, and if we bear in mind that at different times the Bank of England may take different views upon the desirable level of the Treasury-bill rate relative to Bank Rate (and that it has ways of influencing the market other than by making the discount houses borrow at Bank Rate), it is not surprising that no useful relationship can be derived between the Treasury-bill rate and borrowing at Bank Rate on the basis of the simple single equation approach used here.[1]

The chief result of this study must be to raise doubts about the Bank of England's view that by making the discount houses borrow at Bank Rate it increases their average money rate, and so exerts an upward pressure on the rate at which they tender for Treasury bills. In our period, at least, the effect on the average money rate of borrowing at Bank Rate seems to have been too small to make this explanation convincing.[2] Further, in the cases tested, the average money rate was generally worse

[1] Tests were also carried out upon a series of equations in which borrowing at Bank Rate was the dependent variable to be explained by the margin between Bank Rate and the Treasury-bill rate, or the Treasury-bill rate and the average money rate. Some of these equations were in levels and some in first differences; in all cases the fit of the equations was extremely poor.

[2] There has, however, been an upward trend in the average amount borrowed by the discount houses on the days on which they do have to resort to the Bank of England, both during our period and since. See Appendix 3, Table 3.

at explaining the Treasury-bill rate than was Bank Rate. Attempts to go beyond these simple tests and to detect any direct influence of borrowing at Bank Rate upon the Treasury-bill rate were unsuccessful. This is, perhaps, not surprising, since we have used only very simple methods to look at one facet of a complex market situation in which expectations appear to play a very important role. All our results can only be tentative for this and other reasons—for example, several regression results were statistically unsatisfactory, and there are quite likely to be weaknesses in the data estimates used. Finally, it must be said that these results tell us nothing positive about the channels through which the Bank of England can influence the Treasury-bill rate, and give us no indication of how successful the Bank of England is in achieving the Treasury-bill rate it wishes to see in the market.

APPENDIX 1

ONE matter of some interest is the extent to which average money-rate experience varies between discount houses on any day—the patchiness of the market; our original daily first-difference data throw some light upon this. Using all 840 observations in each of the four discount house series, the mean daily change for each series was less than 0·001 percentage points in absolute magnitude, but the sign of the mean change varied between series. The standard deviations lay between 0·077 and 0·081 percentage points, and the correlation coefficient, r, between each pair of series lay between 0·904 and 0·955.

However, using all observations allows the nine large changes in the average money rate, occurring on the days when Bank Rate changed, to swamp the more normal day-to-day experience. Excluding these large changes, we have 831 observations in each of our four series; the mean of each series is positive and of the order of 0·001 percentage points or less, and the standard deviations lie between 0·016 and 0·032 percentage points. These standard deviations were inversely related to the size of the discount house, and to the eye the four points showed a considerable degree of linearity. The correlation coefficients between all pairs of these series lay between 0·358 and 0·547. This indicates a substantial degree of heterogeneity of day-to-day average money-rate experience between the four houses concerned.

As a simpler indication of this variety of experience, a sample of

100 days was chosen on which the average money rate of each house changed (this meant discarding about one day in four during the choosing of the sample, because at least one house had a zero change). Out of this sample, on 41 per cent. of days the changes in the average money rate of each house had the same sign; on 34 per cent. of days three houses had changes of one sign and one house had a change of the opposite sign, and on 25 per cent. of days two houses had changes of one sign and the other two had changes of the opposite sign.

APPENDIX 2

Observa- tion no.	Date (Thursday or Wednesday if marked *)	Average money rate % (A)	Bank Rate % (R)	Borrowing at Bank of England (£m) (B)	Treasury- bill max. tender rate % (T)
	1960				
0	31 Mar.	4·100	5·0	0·0	4·656
1	7 Apr.	4·033	5·0	0·0	4·690
2	13 Apr.*	4·033	5·0	0·0	4·690
3	21 Apr.	4·043	5·0	0·0	4·690
4	28 Apr.	3·989	5·0	0·0	4·690
5	5 May	4·027	5·0	3·5	4·724
6	12 May	4·048	5·0	15·5	4·589
7	19 May	4·040	5·0	20·5	4·589
8	26 May	4·107	5·0	10·5	4·589
9	2 June	4·053	5·0	6·0	4·589
10	9 June	4·106	5·0	10·5	4·656
11	16 June	4·082	5·0	7·5	4·724
12	23 June	4·987	6·0	6·0	5·740
13	30 June	4·946	6·0	0·5	5·723
14	7 July	4·921	6·0	0·0	5·723
15	14 July	4·872	6·0	0·5	5·553
16	21 July	4·909	6·0	0·0	5·536
17	28 July	4·922	6·0	0·0	5·621
18	4 Aug.	4·910	6·0	0·0	5·638
19	11 Aug.	4·913	6·0	0·0	5·638
20	18 Aug.	4·926	6·0	0·0	5·638
21	25 Aug.	4·930	6·0	0·0	5·638
22	1 Sept.	4·936	6·0	0·0	5·638
23	8 Sept.	4·945	6·0	0·0	5·553
24	15 Sept.	4·982	6·0	10·5	5·534
25	22 Sept.	4·992	6·0	7·5	5·536
26	29 Sept.	4·997	6·0	7·5	5·638
27	6 Oct.	4·995	6·0	3·0	5·621
28	13 Oct.	4·998	6·0	0·0	5·519
29	20 Oct.	4·979	6·0	0·0	5·367

Observa-tion no.	Date (Thursday or Wednesday if marked *)	Average money rate % (A)	Bank Rate % (R)	Borrowing at Bank of England (£m) (B)	Treasury-bill max. tender rate % (T)
	1960				
30	27 Oct.	4·505	5·5	0·5	5·147
31	3 Nov.	4·518	5·5	6·5	4·927
32	10 Nov.	4·512	5·5	17·5	4·808
33	17 Nov.	4·514	5·5	13·0	4·707
34	24 Nov.	4·458	5·5	10·5	4·673
35	1 Dec.	4·488	5·5	16·0	4·656
36	8 Dec.	4·024	5·0	0·0	4·521
37	15 Dec.	4·007	5·0	0·0	4·403
38	22 Dec.	4·054	5·0	20·0	4·386
39	29 Dec.	4·085	5·0	12·5	4·386
	1961				
40	5 Jan.	4·022	5·0	17·5	4·386
41	12 Jan.	4·003	5·0	10·5	4·335
42	19 Jan.	4·022	5·0	7·5	4·217
43	26 Jan.	4·024	5·0	15·5	4·200
44	2 Feb.	4·023	5·0	23·0	4·200
45	9 Feb.	4·014	5·0	20·0	4·386
46	16 Feb.	4·012	5·0	3·0	4·437
47	23 Feb.	4·005	5·0	0·0	4·437
48	2 Mar.	4·006	5·0	0·0	4·487
49	9 Mar.	4·019	5·0	7·5	4·521
50	16 Mar.	4·002	5·0	0·0	4·521
51	23 Mar.	4·010	5·0	0·0	4·521
52	29 Mar.*	3·984	5·0	0·0	4·521
53	6 Apr.	3·988	5·0	0·0	4·470
54	13 Apr.	3·956	5·0	0·0	4·538
55	20 Apr.	4·000	5·0	0·0	4·538
56	27 Apr.	4·030	5·0	3·0	4·437
57	4 May	4·027	5·0	10·5	4·437
58	11 May	4·024	5·0	12·5	4·352
59	18 May	4·012	5·0	20·0	4·470
60	25 May	3·978	5·0	0·0	4·470
61	1 June	4·028	5·0	0·0	4·470
62	8 June	4·035	5·0	0·0	4·504
63	15 June	4·042	5·0	0·0	4·538
64	22 June	4·046	5·0	0·0	4·572
65	29 June	4·038	5·0	0·0	4·572
66	6 July	4·096	5·0	33·0	4·572
67	13 July	4·059	5·0	0·0	4·606
68	20 July	4·028	5·0	0·0	4·656
69	27 July	5·720	7·0	10·5	6·809
70	3 Aug.	5·780	7·0	0·0	6·809
71	10 Aug.	5·822	7·0	0·0	6·809

Observa-tion no.	Date (Thursday or Wednesday if marked *)	Average money rate % (A)	Bank Rate % (R)	Borrowing at Bank of England (£m) (B)	Treasury-bill max. tender rate % (T)
	1961				
72	17 Aug.	5·838	7·0	6·0	6·775
73	24 Aug.	5·830	7·0	10·5	6·775
74	31 Aug.	5·918	7·0	15·5	6·775
75	7 Sept.	5·911	7·0	6·0	6·707
76	14 Sept.	5·952	7·0	12·5	6·656
77	21 Sept.	5·958	7·0	3·0	6·588
78	28 Sept.	5·930	7·0	0·0	6·639
79	5 Oct.	5·571	6·5	3·0	6·181
80	12 Oct.	5·578	6·5	18·0	6·062
81	19 Oct.	5·625	6·5	37·5	5·977
82	26 Oct.	5·584	6·5	13·5	5·774
83	2 Nov.	5·230	6·0	27·5	5·469
84	9 Nov.	5·238	6·0	47·5	5·469
85	16 Nov.	5·208	6·0	10·5	5·435
86	23 Nov.	5·228	6·0	18·0	5·435
87	30 Nov.	5·232	6·0	11·0	5·401
88	7 Dec.	5·237	6·0	15·5	5·367
89	14 Dec.	5·224	6·0	40·5	5·367
90	21 Dec.	5·205	6·0	12·5	5·418
91	28 Dec.	5·254	6·0	25·0	5·452
	1962				
92	4 Jan.	5·191	6·0	3·0	5·486
93	11 Jan.	5·114	6·0	3·0	5·486
94	18 Jan.	5·153	6·0	10·5	5·350
95	25 Jan.	5·110	6·0	15·5	5·282
96	1 Feb.	5·129	6·0	32·5	5·265
97	8 Feb.	5·139	6·0	20·5	5·486
98	15 Feb.	5·074	6·0	0·0	5·570
99	22 Feb.	5·077	6·0	0·0	5·604
100	1 Mar.	5·115	6·0	0·5	5·604
101	8 Mar.	4·710	5·5	3·0	5·062
102	15 Mar.	4·657	5·5	3·0	4·927
103	22 Mar.	4·195	5·0	0·0	4·487
104	29 Mar.	4·172	5·0	20·0	4·437
105	5 Apr.	4·189	5·0	15·5	4·403
106	12 Apr.	4·202	5·0	15·5	4·369
107	18 Apr.*	4·198	5·0	15·5	4·301
108	26 Apr.	3·691	4·5	0·0	4·149
109	3 May	3·688	4·5	0·0	4·183
110	10 May	3·696	4·5	12·5	4·014
111	17 May	3·693	4·5	10·5	3·879
112	24 May	3·677	4·5	25·0	3·846
113	31 May	3·676	4·5	15·5	3·812

Observation no.	Date (Thursday or Wednesday if marked *)	Average money rate % (A)	Bank Rate % (R)	Borrowing at Bank of England (£m) (B)	Treasury-bill max. tender rate % (T)
	1962				
114	7 June	3·674	4·5	15·0	3·778
115	14 June	3·677	4·5	7·5	3·744
116	21 June	3·688	4·5	20·0	3·896
117	28 June	3·702	4·5	7·5	3·964
118	5 July	3·703	4·5	20·0	3·930
119	12 July	3·681	4·5	3·0	3·930
120	19 July	3·638	4·5	0·0	3·997
121	26 July	3·674	4·5	3·0	3·913
122	2 Aug.	3·638	4·5	12·5	3·846
123	9 Aug.	3·678	4·5	20·0	3·812
124	16 Aug.	3·690	4·5	15·5	3·812
125	23 Aug.	3·688	4·5	7·5	3·795
126	30 Aug.	3·694	4·5	7·5	3·778
127	6 Sept.	3·702	4·5	12·5	3·744
128	13 Sept.	3·669	4·5	7·5	3·727
129	20 Sept.	3·702	4·5	17·5	3·727
130	27 Sept.	3·695	4·5	0·0	3·660
131	4 Oct.	3·689	4·5	25·0	3·643
132	11 Oct.	3·651	4·5	0·0	3·643
133	18 Oct.	3·656	4·5	17·5	3·778
134	25 Oct.	3·601	4·5	0·0	3·896
135	1 Nov.	3·639	4·5	0·0	3·879
136	8 Nov.	3·651	4·5	3·0	3·829
137	15 Nov.	3·700	4·5	15·5	3·829
138	22 Nov.	3·702	4·5	0·0	3·761
139	29 Nov.	3·719	4·5	7·5	3·727
140	6 Dec.	3·726	4·5	7·5	3·643
141	13 Dec.	3·708	4·5	20·0	3·643
142	20 Dec.	3·736	4·5	0·0	3·643
143	27 Dec.	3·756	4·5	3·0	3·778

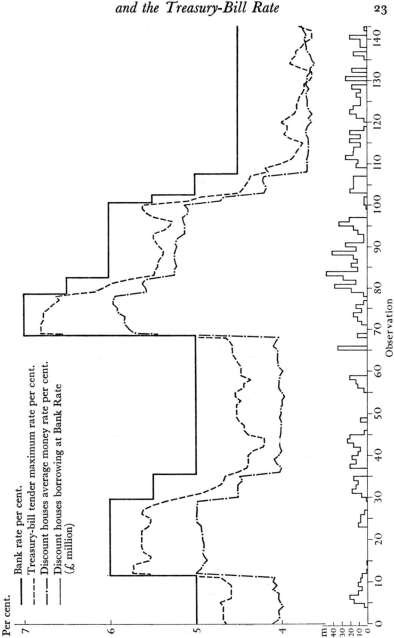

APPENDIX 3

Analysis of days on which discount houses borrowed at the Bank of England, 1960–2

By day of week   TABLE 1*a*

	1 Apr.– end 1960	1961	1962 to 27 Dec.	Total days 1 Apr. 1960– 27 Dec. 1962
Monday	8	15	12	35
Tuesday	10	23	31	64
Wednesday	11	16	11	38
Thursday	7	5	2	14
Friday	2	6	4	12
Saturday	1	..	1	2
Total days	39	65	61	165

TABLE 1*b*

By size of borrowing and number of houses[1]

1 Apr. 1960–27 Dec. 1962
(840 working days)

Amount of borrowing	Marginal /trifling	Very small	Small	Moderate	Fairly large	Large	Very large	
Estimated range ($\pounds$m)	Under 1	1–5	5–10	10–15	15–20	20–30	Over 30	
Number of houses								Total days
1	14	34	11	..	..	..	..	59
2	1	11	17	1	1	..	..	31
3	..	4	17	6	..	..	..	27
4	..	1	11	12	4	..	..	28
5	..	..	..	4	3	..	..	7
6	..	..	..	5	1	2	..	8
7	..	..	..	3	..	1	..	4
8	..	..	..	..	..	..	1	1
Total days	15	50	56	31	9	3	1	165

[1] In the daily money-market reports in the press, when the market borrows at the Bank, besides the adjective for the scale of the borrowing, the report always quotes the number of houses which borrowed as 'one or two', 'four or five', and so

TABLE 2

Borrowing at Bank Rate 1960–7

Year†	Days on which discount houses borrowed	Total borrowing (£m.)	Average borrowing (£m.)
1960	53	249	4·7
1961	66	485	7·35
1962	63	494	7·85
1963	50	399	8·0
1964	7	58	8·3
1965	49	562	11·5
1966*	18	218	12·1
1967* (to 18 Oct.)	35	623	17·8

† These are not calendar years, but are 'years' running between the London clearing banks' make-up days in December. This is one source of minor discrepancies between some figures in this Table and in Table 1*a*.

* Excluding overnight borrowing.

SOURCE: *Bank of England Quarterly Bulletin*, Statistical Annex.

on. It is certain that, on occasions, only one house borrows, and as the number quoted never falls below 'one or two' it seems reasonable to take the lower number quoted as the appropriate one. This has been done here.

ARTHUR I. BLOOMFIELD

Rules of the Game of International Adjustment ?

THERE is general agreement that one of the main requirements for strengthening the international monetary system
is to improve the process of correcting large and persistent
imbalances in international payments and to reduce the likeli-
hood or frequency of such imbalances in the future. The adjustment policies[1] pursued by the industrial countries after the
restoration of convertibility in the late 1950s tended too often
to be inefficient and uncoordinated among the individual
countries. At times, moreover, they were unduly delayed. There
is increasing recognition by the industrial nations of the desirability of closer consultations and mutually supporting policies,
with a view to ensuring a smoother functioning of the adjustment process in the light of national economic goals and the
common interests of the group as a whole. In particular, there
is growing awareness of the need for international discussions,
and, where possible, agreement as to the most suitable mix
and timing of adjustment measures, and sharing of adjustment
responsibilities in cases of important payments imbalances. This,
in turn, implies the need for a more explicit mutual understanding as to the general criteria, standards, or norms for
guiding individual or collective decisions and policies in preserving and re-establishing balance in international payments.

In the years following the restoration of convertibility the
industrial countries as a group found themselves groping for
some such set of 'rules of the game' of international adjustment
within the framework of the international monetary system as

---

[1] Throughout this paper the term 'adjustment policies' will be interpreted
broadly to include what have variously been called 'market' and 'non-market'
measures of adjustment (Haberler), 'genuine' and 'spurious' adjustment (Johnson),
and 'real adjustment' and 'correctives' (Machlup).

it evolved. A certain body of tradition as to what constitutes 'appropriate' behaviour by countries in payments imbalance tended to develop (if not always to be practised) on the basis of experience and mutual consultations. An official report in 1966 outlined some broad guide-lines as to appropriate adjustment policies in varying sets of circumstances; and it made other suggestions for collaborative efforts to improve the adjustment process.[1] But there remains considerable divergence of views as to the nature of the 'rules' called for. And, of course, many economists believe that the problem of adjustment cannot be adequately solved without a greater degree of exchange-rate flexibility than has prevailed in recent years.

The term 'rules of the game'—as far as I know, first used in connexion with adjustment policies by Keynes in the early 1920s—has long had a distasteful connotation. It evokes associations in many minds with the contractionist and expansionist monetary policies supposedly pursued before 1914 in the interests of international equilibrium, regardless of their domestic consequences. Except by a few extreme disciplinarians who romantically yearn for a return to the old gold standard, these are clearly not the kind of rules sought. No government would countenance any set of rules of adjustment policies that did not take full account of their compatibility with the domestic goals of low-level unemployment, reasonable price-level stability, and adequate rates of growth.

It is by no means clear, however, that even the old-fashioned rules of the game were observed under the pre-1914 gold standard, or contributed significantly to its maintenance over a long period of years without direct controls over trade and payments.[2] Certainly any such rules, if formulated at all, were never the subject of an explicit or, as far as I know, implicit understanding among the various central banks. Indeed, monetary authorities showed little or no overt awareness of a mutual responsibility for the smooth functioning of the international gold standard, or of the need for collaboration in any form. And whether or not rules of the game were in fact systematically

---

[1] *The Balance of Payments Adjustment Process* (Organization for Economic Cooperation and Development, Paris, Aug. 1966).

[2] Only a trifling number of countries were forced off the gold standard, once adopted, and devaluations of gold currencies were highly exceptional.

pursued depends upon how one chooses to define them in the light of the requirements of a gold-standard system.

If interpreted in the passive sense of the avoidance by central banks of *deliberate* 'offsetting' of gold drains or acquisitions in their effects on commercial bank reserves, the rules of the game might be said to have been followed. For there is no evidence, and much reason to doubt, that central banks systematically engaged in deliberate 'offsetting' policies, as they are known to have done during the period of the restored gold standard in the 1920s. If the rules are defined in terms of changes in discount rates, as the reserve holdings or reserve ratios of central banks changed, the evidence is less conclusive. In six of the eleven main central banks examined, discount-rate changes tended characteristically to move in opposite directions from changes in central bank reserve ratios (on the basis of annual averages of monthly data).[1] Admittedly, the maintenance of gold parity was the primary objective of monetary policy, and central banks invariably acted decisively, in one way or another, when the monetary standard was threatened by external (or internal) drains. But they were not insensitive to domestic considerations. In fact, in order to avoid changes in discount rates when these would have had undesired effects on domestic activity, central banks resorted with increasing frequency during the period to other techniques, such as (minor) manipulations of the gold points and operations in the spot and forward exchange markets, so as to influence international movements of short-term funds and gold in desired directions. These techniques seem often to have been sufficient for the purpose in hand. In certain cases where reserves were relatively substantial, notably in the case of the Bank of France, frequent changes in discount rates could be avoided. And some of the smaller central banks appear to have geared their discount rate changes primarily to rate movements elsewhere, rather than to the immediate state of their own balances of payments.

[1] A. I. Bloomfield, *Monetary Policy under the International Gold Standard: 1880–1914* (Federal Reserve Bank of New York, 1959), pp. 29 ff. At times, changes in the availability of central-bank credit undoubtedly reinforced or substituted for changes in discount rates. Open-market operations (or their equivalent) were used as deliberate instruments of credit control only by the Bank of England and the Reichsbank.

In his study of international currency experience during the inter-war period Ragnar Nurkse interpreted the rules of the gold-standard game to mean action by central banks to *reinforce* the effects of reserve movements on the domestic credit base. According to this view, central banks were supposed to change their holdings of domestic assets in the same direction as changes in their holdings of international assets (gold and foreign exchange). Examining the statistical data for twenty-six central banks from 1922 to 1938, Nurkse found that the year-to-year changes in the international and domestic assets of central banks were much more often in the opposite than in the same direction.

Using the identical technique for the pre-1914 gold-standard period, I obtained this same result in the case of each of the eleven main central banks examined.[1] On the basis of the Nurkse interpretation, then, the rules of the game would appear not to have been observed before 1914, but to have been 'violated'. I concluded, however, that the opposite movements in central banks' international and domestic assets before 1914 did *not* reflect deliberate 'offsetting' policies, but were probably attributable in large part to what Nurkse had called 'automatic neutralization',[2] which central banks did not counteract, or counteracted only in part.

Still another interpretation of the rules of the gold-standard game has been offered by Michael Michaely. All that the rules required or should have required, he argues, was an appropriate

---

[1] Ibid., pp. 48–51. A similar result was reached for thirty-three countries in the period 1950–9, although on the basis of broadening the Nurkse formula to include the foreign and domestic assets of the banking system as a whole (see P. Baffi and A. Occhiuto, 'La componente esterna della liquidità e le regole della condotta monetaria', *Giornale degli Economisti*, nov.–dec. 1960, pp. 715–33). Lack of the necessary data makes it impossible to apply this broadened formula to the pre-1914 period.

The series used in my original study were not adjusted for trend. When the trends were eliminated, the finding was unchanged. In fact, the percentage of opposite movements in the total observations actually rose from 60 to 67. It might be noted that the use of a year as the unit of observation was entirely arbitrary. But I venture to suggest that the results would not have been significantly altered had different (or varying) time units been chosen.

[2] By 'automatic neutralization' Nurkse referred to the tendency for an inflow of gold (or foreign exchange), by increasing liquidity on the domestic money market, to cause the market to repay debt to the central bank; and for an outflow, by reducing the funds available to the market, to cause it to increase its borrowing from the central bank. Inaction by the central bank would thus tend to result in its international and domestic assets' moving in opposite directions.

fall in the money supply in the reserve-losing countries and a rise in the reserve-gaining countries, with opposite movements in discount rates in the two sets of countries.[1] He points out, quite correctly, that such a pattern of changes in the money supply could have been consistent with *any* pattern of direction of movement as between central banks' foreign and domestic assets.[2] He implies, though does not explicitly assert, that central banks during the classical gold-standard period did in fact guide their monetary policies with a view to achieving degrees of change in the money supply which they regarded as 'appropriate' for the proper functioning of the price-specie-flow mechanism. Whether or not central bankers actually operated on the basis of such a criterion of policy is a moot question. In any case, this interpretation of the pre-1914 rules cannot be subjected to empirical testing.

However exactly the rules might be defined in operational terms, the success of the classical gold standard seems to have been attributable, in the opinion of most serious students of the period, primarily to a combination of unusually favourable institutional circumstances rather than adherence to any specific code of rules of central banking behaviour. Certainly, it is clear that, within the limits imposed by the need to maintain gold parity, there was room for a wide variety of patterns of central bank objectives and policies, and there is no evidence of any uniformity in these patterns as among the individual central banks or over time. In any case, we find little of the harsh deflationary effects often believed to be associated with the working of the system. To the extent that marked deflationary or inflationary periods did occur in individual gold-standard countries, they appear most commonly to have been the result of world-wide cyclical movements rather than of national monetary policies associated with the supposed observance of rules of the game.

During the 1920s, in contrast to the pre-1914 period, there was

---

[1] M. Michaely, *Balance-of-Payments Policies: Japan, Germany, and the Netherlands* National Bureau of Economic Research, New York, forthcoming.

[2] It might be noted that even the opposite movements exhibited before 1914 by changes in these two categories of assets were consistent with multiple changes in the money supply in the appropriate directions. For, as noted in my study (ibid., p. 50), the absolute changes in central banks' international assets tended most commonly to be larger than the (opposite) changes in their domestic assets.

considerable discussion by central bankers of the rules of the game. These were generally interpreted as the avoidance of 'offsetting' policies or as the reinforcement of the effects of movements in gold and foreign exchange reserves. Much lip service was in fact paid by central bankers to the need for gearing credit policies to the balance of payments if the restored gold standard was to work satisfactorily. In actual practice, however, priority was generally given to domestic economic goals when they conflicted with the requirements of external balance. To be sure, the period was marked by the emergence of close relations and consultations among the leading central banks, and by co-operation in the financing of payments imbalances; and at times notable efforts were made to co-ordinate discount-rate policies in the interests of international equilibrium. But these co-operative efforts served to palliate only to a limited degree the effects of the growing weight attached by central bankers to domestic objectives. They were in any case wholly inadequate to sustain the gold standard in the face of the underlying disequilibria and major institutional changes of the 1920s that were fundamentally responsible for its collapse.

The architects of the International Monetary Fund rejected the philosophy of the gold-standard rules as then understood. They clearly intended that in the post-war period member countries would not, as far as possible, be forced to pursue deflationary policies resulting in unemployment in order to defend exchange rates, or to acquiesce in persistent unemployment arising from, or coexisting with, payments deficits. While laying down the general principle of exchange-rate stability and, in the post-transitional period, convertibility on current account, the Fund Agreement provided that members could, in accord with given procedures, alter their parities in cases of 'fundamental disequilibrium'. The Fund was authorized to make its resources available to members to help them finance, or adjust to, less deep-rooted payments difficulties without resort to unnecessary deflation, devaluation, or restrictive trade and payments measures. Members were allowed to control capital movements, even in the post-transitional period, so as to ensure that autonomous monetary policies aimed at the achievement of domestic goals would not be frustrated by disturbing shifts of capital provoked by international interest-rate differentials, speculation, or other developments. Keynes, in fact, described the proposed international monetary arrangements as 'the exact opposite of the gold standard'.

The Fund Agreement, then, laid down obligations and a code of 'good behaviour' regarding exchange rates and exchange restrictions.[1] But the Agreement provided no rules or guide-lines as to appropriate policies for members to follow in conditions of payments imbalance other than 'fundamental disequilibrium', or in order to reduce the possibility of such disequilibrium. Moreover, the Fund could not compel a member to adjust its exchange rate, and the term 'fundamental disequilibrium' was left undefined. It so happened, as the Bretton Woods system evolved, that few if any countries displayed enthusiasm for altering their exchange rates to correct large or persistent payments imbalances. Except for the widespread devaluations of September 1949, changes in parities by the industrial countries were relatively infrequent, even when existing parities seemed clearly out of line with relative costs and prices; and in general such changes were not encouraged by the Fund. The 'adjustable-peg' system tended to harden into a system of *de facto* fixed exchange rates for these countries.

Since its establishment the Fund has made general pronouncements from time to time as to what it regards as suitable adjustment measures under varying circumstances—with reference mainly to deficit countries, and with special emphasis on the need for monetary-fiscal policies to control inflation. It has also recommended specific policies to individual members, and in many cases made Fund assistance conditional upon their adoption. But the Fund cannot be said to have formulated a detailed statement of the rules of adjustment behaviour it regards as appropriate for the international monetary system over which it presides.[2] Such rules, to the extent that they exist, have had to be developed by the members themselves on the basis of evolving experience, the exigencies of the balance of payments, and consultations with each other.

[1] Rules regarding the use of direct trade controls and other commercial policy devices were to be left to a proposed international trade organization, which never came into existence. Such rules are now administered by GATT.

[2] A brief statement of such rules appeared in the Fund's 1964 *Annual Report*, pp. 26–29.

In the particular circumstances of the 1950s it was possible for many deficit countries to shield their reserves by tightening or delaying liberalization of trade and payments restrictions, or by disinflationary policies which had only temporary and relatively mild adverse effects on output and employment. Many surplus countries were able to pursue expansionist domestic policies without running into strong inflationary pressures, and to dismantle gradually their import and exchange controls. The surplus countries welcomed the opportunity of replenishing, where possible, their depleted gold and exchange reserves; and the United States, the major deficit country, was content to let its ample gold reserves run down modestly and to accumulate growing short-term foreign liabilities without taking any corrective measures.

The underlying adjustment dilemmas of the present system, in which countries are reluctant or unwilling to alter their exchange rates or to depart significantly from the pursuit of their domestic economic goals because of balance-of-payments considerations, came strikingly to the fore in the first half of the 1960s, following the establishment by the industrial countries of convertibility on current account and a high degree of convertibility on capital account. Large payments deficits frequently coincided with unsatisfactory levels of domestic employment or rates of economic growth (notably the United States and the United Kingdom), and large payments surpluses with domestic inflationary pressures (notably the countries of continental Western Europe). Demand policies appropriate for a correction of these external imbalances were in conflict with those required for the achievement of domestic objectives, and vice versa. In addition, the freedom accorded to capital movements placed severe restraints on the effective use of monetary policy for domestic stabilization purposes. Ingenious mixes of policy were adopted in an effort to resolve these conflicts, particularly by the deficit countries on which the pressure to adjust mainly fell. Surplus countries co-operated to the extent of providing financing facilities in a variety of forms, prepaying external debt, and to some extent encouraging outward movements of private capital.

To an increasing degree, however, a number of the industrial countries had to resort to a wide variety of selective balance-of-payments measures, mainly restrictive in character. Restraints on capital movements, and the use of import surcharges, tied-aid provisions, and other such devices, involved a departure from liberal payments and trading arrangements, the promotion of which is supposed to be one of the primary purposes of a system of fixed exchange rates. To some extent, moreover, deficit countries were forced by balance-of-payments constraints to adjust their internal policies in ways not consistent with the achievement of their domestic targets—in contrast to the original hope of the Bretton Woods founders. And in actual practice surplus countries were often unable to counteract fully the undesired automatic expansionary effects on the level of domestic demand that were directly associated with their surpluses.

The difficulties of reconciling internal–external conflicts were at times exacerbated by mutually inconsistent policies and objectives among the leading deficit and surplus countries, and a failure to come to an understanding regarding their respective adjustment responsibilities. Too often, moreover, there was a reluctance to take remedial action in any form until imbalances had cumulated to an extent necessitating drastic measures that might have been avoided had more modest corrective measures been initiated earlier.

Considerations such as these have led to increased recognition by policy-makers in the industrial countries (the so-called Group of Ten) of the need to strengthen the adjustment process consistently with the pursuit of their individual domestic objectives and with the broad interests of the group as a whole. Countries must seek to improve further the means of reconciling their internal economic goals with the need for achieving and maintaining reasonable balance in their external accounts. They must seek such reconciliation in ways which exert the least adverse effects on the economies of other countries, and which, in fact, support as far as possible the efforts of other countries in the pursuit of their own goals. There is need for greater compatibility in the balance-of-payments policies and aims of the various countries. Large and persistent payments imbalances, as well as the kind and timing of the measures taken to correct or avoid them, are recognized as matters of common concern and often common responsibility.

There is need, at least in cases of imbalances of this kind, for closer consultations among the countries, and, where possible, agreement as to suitable, timely, and mutually supporting remedial actions. Criteria or rules are required to guide policy-makers in their decisions on such matters as the choice of corrective measures in particular circumstances of imbalance, the timing of such measures, and, perhaps of greatest importance, the distribution of adjustment responsibilities among the deficit and surplus countries.

Rules of adjustment behaviour appropriate to present international monetary arrangements, to the extent that they can be formulated and accepted, would clearly have to differ in kind from those supposedly observed under the old gold standard. This is because of the far greater relative weight attached today to the achievement of domestic economic objectives, the wider range of these objectives, the larger number of policy instruments available and of agencies handling them, and the vastly different institutional environment now prevailing. And such rules would be applied, along with other actions to improve the adjustment process, within a framework of international co-operation that was almost wholly lacking in the pre-1914 period. As indicated earlier, some broad criteria for appropriate adjustment policies under certain sets of circumstances have already come to be accepted in principle. In actual fact the acceptance often conceals differences in the interpretation of terms, or embraces counsels of perfection that many countries cannot be expected to follow in practice.

In official discussions of improving the adjustment process the continued existence of the adjustable-peg (but essentially fixed-exchange-rate) feature of the present international monetary system is usually taken for granted. There seems to be little official disposition among policy-makers in the Group of Ten countries to envisage more frequent resort than in the past to periodic exchange-rate adjustments, let alone adoption of other exchange-rate systems. Clearly, if there were a move towards greater exchange flexibility, as the majority of academic economists have advocated, the problem of payments adjustment would be greatly facilitated, and the need for rules of the game of adjustment behaviour correspondingly reduced. Or at least the nature of the rules would be altered.

Some of the industrial countries may, of course, be expected from time to time to find an exchange-rate adjustment unavoidable in the light of the costs of alternative measures. No easy generalizations can be laid down as to the circumstances under which the individual countries in 'fundamental disequilibrium' would or should make such a choice. To the extent that periodic changes in parities do take place, they cannot realistically be expected to be a subject for prior consultations with other members of the group, as other adjustment measures might be. Each country will have to make the decision independently in the light of its own particular situation and interests. Important countries will do so, it is to be hoped, giving due consideration to the impact of their action on other countries. But co-operative measures will continue to be needed to minimize the disturbing impact of changes in parities on foreign exchange markets and to counteract speculative movements in anticipation of such changes.

The quality and timing of adjustment measures and their distribution among deficit and surplus countries are of course closely related to the state of international liquidity. The smaller the volume and rate of growth of world reserves, the greater the possibility of deficit countries' being forced into quick and often harsh corrective measures, and of resulting world-wide deflationary tendencies and restrictive trade and payments practices. On the other hand, the greater the volume and rate of growth of reserves, the less the pressure on deficit countries to take remedial action, the greater the possibility of inflationary tendencies, and the greater the pressure on surplus countries to eliminate their surpluses.[1] Wide disagreement among the deficit and surplus countries of the Group of Ten as to the adequacy of existing levels of world reserves was a hallmark of the 1960s. So also were the questions of the urgency of new reserve-creating mechanisms and the form they should take. Yet the level, rate of growth, and form of world reserves have a major bearing on the possible extent and duration of payments imbalances, the nature of adjustment policies, and the distribution of the adjustment burden. The degree of effectiveness of international consultations and co-operation on

[1] Conversely, the kind of adjustment policies pursued influences the need for reserves.

adjustment problems, moreover, will depend on the rate and mechanics of reserve growth in the future.

There has been voluminous discussion by academic economists and officials of governments and international organizations regarding methods of correcting payments imbalances under a fixed exchange-rate system without sacrifice of major domestic objectives or resort to controls on trade and payments. Various kinds of imbalances have been distinguished and possible suitable combinations of policy tools in each case have been explored. The availability of policy instruments in relation to the variety of policy targets has been examined. And the possibility of improving the effectiveness of the instruments and enlarging their number has been discussed.

There would be general agreement, for example, that if a particular payments deficit is recognized as temporary or self-reversing in character, it should be financed—assuming adequate reserves or borrowing facilities are available for the purpose—and recourse to adjustment measures avoided. Of course, it may often not be possible to diagnose with sufficient certainty the probable duration or self-reversibility of a given imbalance. And differences of opinion will inevitably exist as to how long 'temporary' should be. International consultations may help to resolve uncertain cases. Where reasonable doubt exists, preference should be given to financing rather than adjustment. When adjustment is chosen, there is the problem of deciding whether the measures adopted should be of the slow-working or quick-working variety.

Reducing external imbalances without sacrifice of domestic goals need pose no major problems for countries where payments surpluses coincide with deficient domestic demand, or where payments deficits are the result of, or are associated with, excessive aggregate demand at home. In such cases the monetary-fiscal policies that appear appropriate from an internal point of view (demand expansion in the surplus countries and restraint in the deficit countries) would coincide with the policies needed to reduce the external imbalances. Deficit countries, however, could be left with a continuing payments disequilibrium, even after the inflation had been stopped, if wage rates had already moved up. Where pure 'demand inflation' exists, therefore, it is important that corrective action should be taken as soon as possible before the country's competitive position is further impaired.

The prescription of monetary-fiscal restraint would be clearly inappropriate for deficit countries when inflation is of the cost-push variety, unaccompanied by any excessive demand pressures. It would also be inappropriate where payments deficits, arising from whatever cause, coincide with unsatisfactory levels of domestic employment and growth. Policies of monetary-fiscal expansion would likewise be unsuitable where payments surpluses are accompanied by domestic inflationary pressures. In all such cases aggregate-demand policies of the indicated sort would help to eliminate the payments imbalances, but only at the cost of adding to unemployment or inflation, as the case might be.

For deficit countries an appropriate way out of situations such as these, especially where the deficits are associated with a weakened competitive position in world markets, would be the application of 'incomes policies' or wage-price guide-posts. If average money wage rates can be kept from rising as fast as average productivity, unit costs and prices can be brought down[1] and the balance of payments improved without causing or adding to unemployment. More promisingly, if the general trend of world prices is upward, the needed reduction in prices relative to those in competing countries can be achieved without an absolute fall in the price level by keeping the rise in wage rates roughly in line with that in productivity. Indeed, in such circumstances, it might be sufficient to prevent prices and costs from rising as fast as elsewhere. Incomes policies, however, would tend to be relatively slow-working in their effects on the balance of payments. They presuppose the existence of adequate reserves and borrowing facilities to tide the deficit countries over during the period when their current-account balances are strengthening. Where cost and price levels have already been pushed up too far, devaluation may be the only acceptable way out.

Much scepticism has been expressed regarding the practicability and effectiveness of incomes policies as a means of

---

[1] Assuming, of course, that the decline in wage costs per unit of output is not simply offset by an increase in profits, in which case the price level would not come down.

controlling the price level, at least under conditions of relatively high demand and low unemployment. Admittedly, the possibilities vary widely from country to country. A final judgement would seem premature, however, until such policies have had an adequate chance to develop and all the evidence is in. It is to be hoped that official efforts will be increasingly directed towards winning greater public acceptance of them. For effective incomes policies, when used in conjunction with other policy variables, could contribute significantly to the viability of a fixed exchange-rate system without sacrifice of domestic economic objectives or resort to restraints over the balance of payments.[1]

Appropriate combinations of monetary and fiscal policy are often recommended as a means of helping to reconcile internal–external conflicts under a system of fixed exchanges.[2] Because of the relatively greater impact of changes in monetary policy on the balance of payments (via the capital account) than that of changes in fiscal policy, a suitable combination of the two could in principle eliminate a payments imbalance without undesired domestic effects; it might at the same time move the level of aggregate demand in the desired direction. Monetary policy would be aimed at keeping foreign payments in balance, and fiscal policy at maintaining the desired level of domestic demand. Changes in fiscal policy could themselves be accompanied by an appropriate set of tax changes designed to influence investment as compared with consumption in order to offset any undesired effects upon economic growth that might be induced by the changes in monetary policy. And the authorities, while moving to monetary restraint or ease, could attempt to twist the yield curve on the assumption that short-term rates are relatively more significant for capital movements and long-term rates for the level of domestic activity and the rate of economic growth.

Reliance on mixes of these kinds would undoubtedly help to reconcile conflicts of external and internal objectives. To some

---

[1] The potential importance of incomes policies as an instrument for payments adjustment has been stressed in particular by Sir Roy Harrod, *Reforming the World's Money* (Macmillan, London, 1965), pp. 27–33, 36–42.

[2] See especially R. A. Mundell, 'The Appropriate Use of Monetary and Fiscal Policy for Internal and External Stability', *International Monetary Fund Staff Papers*, Mar. 1962, pp. 70–77.

extent they have in fact done so. They would seem particularly appropriate in cases where large capital outflows or inflows are contributing importantly to payments imbalances. Doubts may reasonably be raised, however, as to how effective or acceptable such mixes would be as a general prescription on a continuing basis. Among other things, fiscal policy is as yet insufficiently flexible in many or most industrial countries to carry the whole burden of stabilizing the domestic economy. Capital movements, while not insensitive to changes in interest rates and monetary conditions, may not respond to the extent needed for payments equilibrium, at least without continuing changes in interest rates. Most countries are not indifferent to the composition of their balances of payments as between current-account and capital-account transactions. In particular, few if any of the industrial countries would be willing to accept as a persisting state of affairs an over-all payments balance reflecting a current-account deficit matched by a capital-account surplus. Nor would such a pattern of capital flows be likely to be an efficient one from a world point of view. At best, monetary-fiscal policy mixes, however valuable, would seem to be only a temporary or partial solution for deep-seated payments disequilibria.[1] And even these shorter-run benefits would require for their effective realization close international co-operation among the industrial countries to ensure that national interest-rate policies were not incompatible. An understanding would also have to be reached, in the light of the demand conditions in the group as a whole, as to an appropriate average international level of interest rates around which the needed differentials would be allowed to form.

Official intervention in the forward exchange market, as Keynes recognized long ago, is an alternative to changes in interest rates as a means of influencing the flow of short-term funds. It could thus provide an opportunity to reduce payments imbalances by acting on short-term capital movements, while affording a measure of autonomy in national interest-rate policy. There is undoubtedly scope for more aggressive resort to official forward exchange operations in the future in order

---

[1] The question may also be raised as to whether the monetary-fiscal policy mix prescription represents 'adjustment', however broadly defined, or merely induced private external financing.

to influence the flow of covered interest arbitrage in desired directions in the ordinary course of events, as well as to meet speculative attacks on currencies. But few would disagree that forward rate policy can help only temporarily and to a limited degree to reconcile conflicts of internal and external objectives. As long as the range of fluctuation of spot exchange rates around fixed parities is narrowly limited, moreover, the extent to which forward rate policy can separate domestic from foreign short-term interest rates under normal exchange-market conditions is itself limited.

For surplus countries experiencing inflationary pressures unilateral tariff reductions could contribute to international balance in a highly desirable fashion, while simultaneously easing those pressures. Such action, however, is almost never taken in actual practice. Liberalization of restrictions on capital exports, where they exist, and tax incentives to promote such exports, could also assist in the same direction. Deficit countries could take measures to increase their exchange receipts by 'export drives', by tax incentives to attract long-term foreign investment, and by stimulation of foreign tourism. Such measures would, of course, tend to be slow-working in character.

There are circumstances in which countries find the imposition of restraints on various categories of private capital movements a necessary supplement or alternative to corrective measures of the kinds indicated above. High capital mobility under a régime of convertibility limits the scope for monetary policy as an instrument for domestic stabilization purposes. Some countries may thus choose—because of insufficiently flexible budgetary policies, the slow-working character of other remedies, or related considerations—to impose restraints on capital flows when domestic objectives and the balance of payments are in conflict. By so doing they can maintain a needed measure of autonomy in domestic monetary policy. Thus, a deficit country experiencing large capital outflows, at a time when the domestic situation does not call for a tightening of credit, may prefer to restrict those outflows if reserves and borrowing facilities are limited. Or a surplus country faced with large capital inflows may choose to restrict the movement if the effectiveness of an anti-inflationary monetary policy is thereby threatened. The alternative in both cases may be an undesired adjustment of the domestic economy and the current-account balance. In other instances the outflow of capital from deficit countries may be of such a volume or such a kind, even when monetary policy is tightened, that restraints in one form or another may be unavoidable. Some categories of capital movements simply do not respond readily to interest-rate treatment. There may at times be other valid economic reasons for choosing temporary restrictions on, or the creation of disincentives to, large-scale capital flows of a disturbing kind. Continuing restraints on capital movements, however, would raise larger questions of efficiency, enforceability, and effectiveness. They would point to the desirability of more fundamental remedial action on the balance of payments.

If the regulation of capital movements by restrictions and disincentives is in fact becoming an increasingly common instrument of balance-of-payments policies, there is need for agreement among the industrial countries as to the broad circumstances and conditions under which they might properly be imposed. There is also need for an understanding as to the most effective and least costly and discriminatory methods of restraint to be applied in individual cases, whether by tax disincentives, administrative regulation of the net foreign position of commercial banks, 'voluntary controls', or more formal restrictions. In many instances, moreover, the effectiveness of the controls would be enhanced by co-operative action on the part of the capital-exporting and capital-importing countries. In these areas, as in others relating to the adjustment process, there is need for close international consultations and collaboration.

Some of the industrial countries may in particular circumstances regard the temporary restriction of imports for balance-of-payments reasons, or direct action on other specific current-account transactions, as less costly or more effective than alternative remedial measures. Prior agreement, where not already existing, with regard to the application of many of these devices would be desirable in order to reduce the possibility of retaliatory action. International consultations would help to ensure that the devices chosen in individual cases would exert a minimum of disturbing and discriminatory effects on other countries and be as efficient as possible. There would be general agreement, however, that the suppression of payments imbalances by persisting restraints on current-account transactions (as on capital movements) would be undesirable, and indicate the need for measures to bring about a realignment of relative price levels at home and abroad.

On a broader front, close and continuous consultations among the industrial countries would be of value in diagnosing the nature of payments imbalances, in determining whether or not they are likely to be temporary or self-reversing, and, if not, in reaching a collective judgement as to how quickly or gradually they should be eliminated. Such consultations could also facilitate decisions as to the most suitable remedies to be applied by the individual countries. They could strengthen the possibility of co-operative and mutually supporting actions when needed to remove the imbalances, and of a more equitable sharing of the adjustment burden.

The most difficult problem will be to reach agreement on rules as to the apportionment of adjustment responsibilities among the deficit and surplus countries. Where the cause of the imbalances can be unambiguously attributed to inappropriate demand policies being currently pursued by individual countries, it might be argued, though not always validly, that the responsibility for adjustment must rest with those countries alone. But many if not most important imbalances cannot be so attributed. In such cases, at least, adjustment is a mutual responsibility of deficit and surplus countries alike. Two-sided measures would facilitate solution of the adjustment problem and be of benefit to all, in view of their common interest in the orderly elimination of payments disequilibria. On this there is general agreement in principle. But in actual practice both sides find difficulty in coming to an understanding regarding an equitable division of adjustment responsibilities. Each side is likely to accuse the other of not doing enough. In fact, the pressure to adjust falls mainly on the deficit countries.

There are few general criteria to guide decisions on an appropriate sharing of the adjustment burden, at least in cases where demand is not excessive in deficit countries or deficient in surplus countries. A reduction in restrictions on merchandise imports or capital exports by surplus countries is to be preferred on grounds of efficiency to the imposition of restrictions by deficit countries. If restraints on capital movements are regarded as necessary, there would be much to be said in favour of most of the action's being taken by the capital-importing countries. Surplus countries should consider increasing their official aid to the less developed countries, although it is recognized that the amount of such aid should be governed primarily by the broader criterion of aid-giving capacity rather than the state of the balance of payments alone. At the least, surplus countries should reduce or eliminate any tied-aid requirements. When significant sacrifices are called for, however, notably in terms of unemployment or inflation, each side is likely to resist action. Neither will want to use aggregate-demand policies to correct payments imbalances when not called for on strictly domestic grounds. There would seem in any case to be no way of measuring accurately the relative costs of (a little more) unemployment on one side against (a little more) inflation on the other, and thus of deciding upon an equitable basis for sharing adjustment burdens of this kind. Although rules regarding relative adjustment responsibilities are thus hard to come by, nevertheless, one of the probable benefits of closer consultations in this area would be to put greater pressure on the surplus countries to reduce their surpluses.

The problems of payments adjustment and allocation of adjustment obligations would be simplified to the extent that large and persisting disequilibria could be averted in the first place. Co-ordination and mutual adaptation of national monetary, fiscal, and wage policies, where possible, would assist in this direction. Fuller exchange of information might help to reduce mutual inconsistencies in national balance-of-payments targets and in the policies planned to achieve them. The 'early warning system' instituted by the Group of Ten could aid in the early detection of certain kinds of emerging imbalances with a view to initiating timely corrective measures at the source. But one should have no illusions as to the probable degree of success in these areas.

Closer international consultations and collaboration on adjustment problems and policies would undoubtedly contribute to a smoother functioning adjustment process. Improvements in budgetary and incomes policies and other instruments would enable countries to achieve a more efficient reconciliation of their domestic goals with the need for maintaining reasonable external balance. But it would be a quite different matter to conclude that effective international agreement can be reached on detailed rules of the game to guide adjustment policies and responsibilities. Admittedly, as indicated above, some broad guide-lines have come to be informally accepted in principle as to the appropriate kind of policies and choice of instruments countries should adopt in particular circumstances of imbalance; and others may yet come to be recognized. But it seems doubtful how much further rules of suitable adjustment behaviour can be carried.

Countries tend to attach different weights and priorities to the various objectives of economic policy. They also tend to have differing views as to the degree of desirability or undesirability of various kinds of adjustment policies and policy instruments. For these and other reasons there will at times be inevitable differences of opinion among the various countries as to the appropriate therapy or the sharing of adjustment responsibilities in particular cases of important imbalances. It is highly doubtful, moreover, that any set of rules of the game could encompass the wide variety of situations that might arise, or accommodate themselves to the differing sizes, institutional frameworks, economic structures, and importance in the world economy of even the limited group of industrial countries discussed in this paper. For example, a detailed set of rules could hardly be formulated that would be appropriate for, and acceptable to, both a reserve-currency country and world banker like the United States, on the one hand, and smaller industrial countries like Belgium and the Netherlands, on the other. To try to formulate rules for different kinds of countries would only increase the difficulty of reaching agreement.

International discussions should help to resolve differences of opinion and to reach an understanding on suitable adjustment measures to be taken in individual cases. But they can be expected to do so, if at all, primarily on the basis of negotiated compromises tailored to the particular situations, and not on that of mechanical reliance on detailed criteria and rules. Few countries have shown any willingness to bind themselves, however informally, to any prearranged set of rules of the game of international adjustment, unless of the most general and flexible kind. Still less would they be likely to be willing to delegate authority to an international organization to decide on the kinds of adjustment policies to be taken by deficit and surplus countries in cases of important imbalances.

This reluctance reflects, among other things, the high priority placed by national authorities on the achievement of national goals and the fear of its being compromised. And yet, in the end, countries may well have to choose between a somewhat lower priority for domestic objectives and reliance on greater exchange-rate flexibility—hopefully the latter. For the forbidding alternative may be to reconcile themselves to the proliferation of direct controls over the balance of payments.

LESTER V. CHANDLER

Some Issues in Federal Reserve
Discount Policy

A T the time of the Treasury–Federal Reserve Accord of March 1951 the Federal Reserve discount mechanism had lain largely unused for about seventeen years. From 1934 to 1942, thanks largely to huge gold inflows and some Treasury purchases of silver, member banks were flooded with excess reserves and had no need to borrow. During the nine years following March 1942 they had little need to borrow, because the Federal Reserve stood ready to purchase, passively and at relatively stable prices and yields, all United States government securities offered to it. Thus, at the time of the Accord many member banks had not borrowed for about seventeen years, and during the same period Federal Reserve officials had little experience in operating discount windows. In fact, there is little evidence that they had thought much about the future role of discount policy.

It was clear, however, that after the Accord, which relieved the Federal Reserve of the duty of pegging prices and yields on government securities, discounting and discount policy would again become of some importance. More banks would have to borrow more frequently to meet their liquidity needs. Yet there was not then agreement, nor is there now, as to what discount policy should be. What should be the relative roles of discounting, open market operations, and alteration of member-bank reserve requirements in supplying and regulating the reserves and liquidity position of the banking system ? On what conditions and terms should an individual bank be permitted to borrow? On what types of collateral ? To what extent should discounting be regulated by discount rates and to what extent by non-price methods? What should be the criteria and procedures for setting and changing discount rates ? These are only some of the questions concerning discount policy that continue to be debated both within and outside the System.

For several reasons it was almost inevitable that discounting and discount policies would become less important, relative to open-market policies as instruments for general monetary management, than they were in the 1920s and early 1930s. For one thing, there had been marked changes in national objectives and in concepts of the responsibilities of the Federal Reserve. In the earlier period, when there was no national commitment to maintain continuously high levels of employment, many Federal Reserve officials and some economists believed that the System should supply funds primarily through discounting. It should provide 'elasticity' by responding to 'the needs of trade', as these needs were evidenced by business demands for credit from the banks and by bank applications for discounts to enable them to meet these demands—though not necessarily in full or at constant interest rates. To such officials, and others, open market operations undertaken on the initiative of the Federal Reserve were 'unnatural', 'artificial', and likely to lead to later trouble. The Federal Reserve should supply funds in response to demands, not force funds on the market or make forcible withdrawals from it. Ideas and attitudes such as these, rather than lack of power, were largely responsible for the failure of the Federal Reserve to make large open-market purchases earlier in the 1930s.

Ideas and attitudes had changed markedly by 1951. The nation had adopted the Full Employment Act of 1946 and Federal Reserve officials acknowledged their responsibility to contribute to its objective of promoting 'maximum employment, production and purchasing power'. They believed that this required counter-cyclical actions taken on the Federal Reserve's own initiative and that open-market operations were more appropriate, powerful, and reliable than discount policy.

The elevation of open-market policy and relative decline of discount policy were also promoted by the increase of nearly $200 billion in the debt of the Federal Government during World War II. Early in 1951 the amount of Federal debt held outside the Treasury still amounted to nearly $218 billion. Of this, the Federal Reserve held about $21 billion and the commercial banks $62 billion; the remainder was widely

distributed among all the principal types of financial intermediaries, non-financial corporations, and individuals. Moreover, the market for government securities was highly active and
increasing in efficiency. These facts were relevant to Federal
Reserve policy in several ways. The Federal Reserve, with its
large holdings of governments, was in a position to absorb any
likely accretion of unwanted reserve funds, and it could easily
supply more funds by purchasing some of the large outstanding
stock of government securities. The commercial banks, holding
government securities equal to 47 per cent. of their total loans
and securities and 40 per cent. of their total deposits, were in a
highly liquid condition. Thus, it was reasonable to expect that
they would meet their liquidity needs largely within their own
resources, with little recourse to borrowing from the Federal
Reserve.

It was under such conditions that the Board of Governors in
1955 issued Regulation A, which stated the principles governing
member bank borrowing. This regulation stated that banks
should borrow only to meet needs that could not reasonably
be foreseen.

Federal Reserve credit is generally extended on a short-term basis
to a member bank in order to enable it to adjust its asset position
when necessary because of developments such as a sudden withdrawal of deposits or seasonal requirements for credit beyond those
which can reasonably be met by use of the bank's own resources.
Federal Reserve credit is also available for longer periods when
necessary in order to assist member banks in meeting unusual situations, such as may result from national, regional, or local difficulties
or from exceptional circumstances involving only particular member
banks. Under ordinary conditions, the continuous use of Federal
Reserve credit by a member bank over a considerable period of time
is not regarded as appropriate.

Though these principles applied to borrowings by individual
member banks, it was also clear that Federal Reserve officials
did not want any considerable part of total bank reserves to be
supplied by borrowing. In fact, during the entire period since
World War II, discounts have provided a much smaller part
of total bank reserves than in the 1920s. In the earlier period
member bank borrowings were often equal to 20 per cent., and
at times even 40 per cent., of total member bank reserves.

However, in the post-war period borrowings have rarely exceeded 6 per cent. of total bank reserves, and they have usually been much smaller. This is not to say that fluctuations of borrowings between virtually zero and $1·5 billion are insignificant.

Several critics, primarily academic economists, believe that the Federal Reserve has not gone far enough in suppressing discounting. Their most common complaint is that discounting constitutes a 'slippage' or 'escape hatch' in monetary management. This point of view has been stated most clearly by Milton Friedman. As is well known, be believes that the Federal Reserve's objective should be to increase the money supply at a uniform rate through time, and that for this purpose the System requires an accurate and precise control over the size of the reserve base. As he sees it, discounting weakens this control. Banks are tempted to borrow more in times of boom and to repay in times of recession, thus tending to make the money supply behave in a pro-cyclical manner. Moreover, the effects of Federal Reserve purchases and sales in the open market tend to be blunted by partially offsetting decreases and increases in bank borrowings. He therefore recommends that the Federal Reserve should abolish discounting altogether and levy fines on member banks if they fail to meet their reserve requirements. The fines would be set at such a high level as to make it unprofitable for banks to run reserve deficiencies.

This prescription has been criticized on at least two grounds. For one thing, it does not deal explicitly with discounting as a source of liquidity for individual banks. Friedman apparently believes that each bank should solve its liquidity problems by selling assets or borrowing from sources outside the Federal Reserve. His critics believe that these sources may at times be inadequate. This point will be discussed later. Some also deny that discounting, if properly regulated, is an undesirable 'slippage' in general monetary management. Rather, it can provide a useful safety-valve or buffer which gives the Federal Reserve time to react to events, whether these events are its own actions or external shocks.[1] It is significant that most of those taking this position reject Friedman's contention that the behaviour of the money supply is a reliable guide to policy, and contend

[1] I am indebted to James Tobin for interesting comments on these subjects, but he is not to be held responsible for my interpretations.

instead that the proper guide is the behaviour of interest rates, or more broadly the cost of capital, for it is through this channel that monetary policy influences aggregate demand. If discounting were abolished, interest rates might react rapidly and sharply to such events as increases or decreases in demands for credit and changes in the supply of reserves, whether because of open-market operations or for other reasons. Discounting serves as a shock-absorber which spreads the effects over time. It need not weaken control over interest rates or the money supply, for the Federal Reserve can achieve its desired results through appropriate open-market operations and changes in discount rates. It if fails to do so the fault is not of the discount mechanism but of policy.

Another controversial question is: To what extent should the Federal Reserve regulate the volume and allocation of discounts through changes in discount rates, and to what extent by non-price rationing? In fact, the Reserve Banks rarely change their rates more than three times a year, and usually less frequently. Since open-market rates change frequently if not continuously, one result is a fluctuating relationship between discount rates and open-market rates. Control through the discount rate is supplemented by such Federal Reserve devices as emphasizing that borrowing is a 'privilege and not a right', nurturing the 'tradition against borrowing', admonitions, bringing pressure to bear on banks to reduce borrowings, and outright refusals of loans. Rationing through these methods rather than by price has been criticized on several grounds. For one thing, it may promote undesired changes in total discounts, for banks are likely to want to borrow more in boom periods and less in recession. To regulate discounting by some 6,200 member banks through non-price methods is difficult administratively. But even if changes in total discounts are appropriately offset through open-market operations, non-price rationing may lead to arbitrary and inefficient allocations of reserves and lending power among the banks. Reserves may go to those banks that are least heedful of Federal Reserve admonitions rather than to those whose customers can use loans most productively. Some conclude that reliance on non-price rationing of discounts should be abolished, or at least sharply reduced, greater reliance being placed on a more vigorous discount-rate policy. This would call for more frequent, and perhaps wider, changes of rates.

This leads to still other controversial questions: How should the discount rate be set and changed? How high should it be? As indicated earlier, the Federal Reserve promulgates specific discount rates and changes them only infrequently. Each rate change has at least two kinds of effects—effects on the cost of discounts, and 'announcement' or 'expectational' effects. Perhaps partly because rate changes are so infrequent, they are viewed by many as important indicators of Federal Reserve intentions or expectations with respect to future credit conditions. Rate increases are viewed as harbingers of future rates at least as high as those current, while rate decreases suggest the opposite. In earlier periods such announcement effects were considered to be, on the whole, beneficial to the effectiveness of monetary policy. More recently many economists have become more critical, contending that announcement effects are erratic and undependable in their strength, and even in their direction, and may be perverse. One reason for this is that a discount change is an ambiguous signal as to Federal Reserve intentions. For example, a rate increase may indeed be a part of a Federal Reserve policy of raising interest rates, or it may be only a 'technical adjustment', an alignment of the discount rate with market rates, with no intention of allowing rates in general to rise. In the absence of any other announcement, the public may be misled. Rate changes, if they occur, may lead to undesirable effects on expectations, or the Federal Reserve, fearing such results, may be inhibited in changing rates.

A number of economists have proposed that the Federal Reserve should abandon the present system and adopt instead a 'floating rate system', in which the discount rate would always be kept at some margin above a selected market rate. For example, it might be provided that the discount rate during any week would be equal to the average yield on 90-day Treasury bills during the preceding week plus one quarter of one per cent. Two advantages over the present system are claimed. For one thing, this would virtually eliminate announcement effects, for rate changes would occur automatically every week and in accordance with a fixed formula. Also, by keeping the discount rate at a fixed height above the selected market rate, it would in a sense provide an unchanging penalty on borrowing. It would thus avoid the fluctuations in the size of the penalty which occur under the present system when the discount rate remains constant while market rates change.

Though a number of economists have come out in support of a floating rate system, others oppose it. Some of these favour more frequent changes in discount rates and less reliance on non-price rationing of discounts, but believe that for several reasons the Federal Reserve would be unwise to abandon discretionary control of discount rates. (1) The awkwardness and perversity of announcement effects have been exaggerated. Though discount-rate changes have at times been misinterpreted, the same is true of other policy actions, such as open-market operations. The lesson is not that the Federal Reserve should discard an instrument but that it should provide more specific information concerning its aims and intentions. (2) Announcement effects can be useful for domestic as well as international purposes. (3) A floating rate system, in which the discount rate would change automatically with every change in the selected market rate, would respond more radically to outside shocks—such as changes in demands for credit or in the supply of reserves—and would produce quicker and wider fluctuations of interest rates. On at least some occasions this might be undesirable; it might be preferable for the Federal Reserve to absorb some part of the shock by lending more or less at an unchanged discount rate; with discretionary control of discount rates, it retains freedom of choice. (4) Advocates of a floating rate system have not given sufficient attention to the difficulties involved in selecting one out of many market rates to which the discount rate would be tied and in determining the appropriate margin above that rate. They might well discover that they had selected the 'wrong' market rate or the 'wrong' margin, or that a fixed margin would yield fluctuating and unexpected results. This leads us into a whole series of unresolved questions concerning 'penalty rates'.

From the beginning there has been strong support within the system for the idea that the discount rate should be a 'penalty rate'—that in some sense it should penalize, not reward, borrowing. Yet the concept has never been clearly defined in operational terms by either Federal Reserve officials or economists.

An earlier concept has long since been abandoned—that the appropriate discount rate is a rate somewhat higher than the yield on the particular type of paper offered for discount. For one thing, it has long been recognized that there need be no relationship between the type of paper discounted and the type of use to which the borrowed funds will be put. Also, the borrowing bank still bears the risk of loss on the paper discounted or pledged as collateral for advances. Though this concept has been abandoned, no satisfactory substitute has been found.

In deciding whether and how much to borrow from, or remain in debt to, the Federal Reserve, a rational banker presumably compares the marginal cost of borrowing and the marginal benefits accruing to him. The marginal cost of borrowing at a given discount rate may not be an unambiguous concept, especially if borrowing entails some danger of Federal Reserve displeasure. But to identify and quantify the marginal benefits of borrowing presents much more difficult problems. The benefits of borrowing are presumably the avoidance of alternatives that would otherwise have to be chosen—the sacrifice of yields on loans or investments that would otherwise have to be sold, the cost of borrowing from other sources, or forgoing returns on new loans or investments. To permit rational comparisons with the discount rate and the marginal cost of borrowing, the benefits of avoiding these alternatives to borrowing would have to be valued and stated in terms of an interest rate or yield. At any point of time, what do bankers consider to be the leading alternatives to borrowing ? Is it to sell some of their earning assets ? If so, which ones—Treasury bills, longer-term governments, or customer paper ? Is the alternative to borrow outside the Federal Reserve ? If so, what rates are considered most relevant—the rate on Federal funds, rates on repurchase agreements on government securities, or rates on inter-bank loans ? Is the alternative to forgo acquiring new loans or investments ? If so, what types—government securities, mortgages, or customers' loans ? At any given time the explicit rates or yields represented by these alternatives differ widely, ranging all the way from the yield of the shortest term Treasury bills to rates on consumer instalment loans. This wide range of explicit yields would in itself make it difficult to define precisely a 'penalty' discount rate.

However, this is not the end of the difficulties, for it seems unlikely that bankers make decisions solely on the basis of comparisons of explicit market rates with the discount rate. For one thing, the rate expected by the banker may differ from the prevailing market rate. For example, the yield expected on a government security depends in part on expectations as to its price behaviour. And the yield expected on a loan to a customer may deviate significantly from the stated market rate because of such things as compensating balance requirements, the expected value to the bank of future business because the loan was made, and so on. Perhaps more important, other costs and benefits are also relevant to bankers' decisions. These include marginal transactions costs of acquiring, holding, and disposing of assets, effects on the liquidity and safety of the bank, and so on. We still have much to learn about how bankers value such things or how their valuations change through time.

It might be thought that the discount rate is a penalty rate if it is above the yield on the lowest-yielding earning asset in a bank's portfolio, for the bank could get money by selling this asset. Thus, it has at times been argued that a discount rate above the yield on 90-day Treasury bills is a penalty rate, because for a bank the leading alternative to borrowing is to sell such bills. This is of doutful general validity. It is clearly invalid for banks which do not hold such bills. Moreover, banks sometimes borrow at discount rates above yields on the Treasury bills that they continue to hold, and there are numerous instances in which banks sell longer term government securities with yields significantly above yields on the Treasury bills that they retain. Such behaviour may be quite rational, explicable by such things as marginal transactions costs, expectations relating to future prices and yields on assets, and effects on the liquidity and safety positions of banks.

The upshot of all this is that the concept of a 'penalty rate' will continue to be ambiguous until we know much more about decision making in banks. It suggests some of the difficulties of a floating rate system—difficulties of selecting the rate to which the discount rate would be tied, and difficulties of determining an appropriate margin. A given system might well turn out to encourage borrowings at some times and discourage them at others, and there is no assurance that the fluctuations of borrowings would be counter-cyclical. It also suggests that if the Federal Reserve should abandon non-price rationing and rely solely on rationing through changes in the discount rate, it would have to rely heavily on trial and error changes in the rate, rather than on some fixed formula for a penalty rate.

The preceding sections have concentrated largely on discount policy as an instrument of general monetary management—as a means of regulating the reserves and liquidity of the banking system as a whole. We turn now to discounting as an instrument for supplying liquidity to individual banks or groups of banks within the system. Though these functions are closely related, they are separable. For example, the Federal Reserve might consider its function of providing liquidity to individual banks to be so important that it would provide discount facilities even if this did constitute a 'slippage' in its general monetary management. The system might even look upon discounting not as an important instrument of general monetary management but as almost solely a device for allocating reserves among the banks and of meeting the liquidity needs of individual banks. It might rely upon open-market operations, and perhaps also changes in reserve requirements, to regulate the reserve and liquidity positions of the banking system as a whole but lend generously to those particular banks experiencing unusual deposit losses or unusually high demands for credit. In effect, it could secure funds by selling securities in the open market and reallocate these reserves by discounting. Few have argued that the Federal Reserve should do this on a large scale, but there remain wide differences of opinion concerning the responsibility of the system for meeting the liquidity needs of individual banks.

The American banking system is comprised of some 13,800 banks; a majority of these operate only a single office and virtually none operates branches outside its home state. This banking structure makes it possible and even probable that banks will experience widely differing behaviour of deposits and loan demands. Even when total deposits in the system are increasing, individual banks may suffer deposit drains, either temporary or more prolonged, this because of seasonal fluctuations in the receipts and expenditures of their depositors, local crop failures, depression of local industry, and so on; or most of the banks in a given region may suffer drains because of adverse changes in local industries. When this occurs there is a danger that legitimate local needs for credit will not be met. Banks may also experience widely differing behaviour of demands for loans, some facing large increases while demands in other areas remain low. There is no assurance that banks facing the largest demands will also experience the largest increases of deposits and lending power. There may also occur more prolonged credit shortages in regions where demands for credit are growing more rapidly than bank resources. This danger is alleviated to the extent that business in the area has access to distant banks or to the central capital and money markets, but regions in which small and medium sized businesses predominate may not have such access. It will be noted that in some of these cases a bank's need for liquidity is only temporary, but in other cases it is more prolonged.

Individual banks have, of course, many sources of liquidity other than recourse to borrowing from the Federal Reserve. For example, they can sell some of their Federal government securities in the highly organized and active market for these securities. There is also an organized, but less active, market for certain other bank assets, such as debt obligations of state and local governments and corporations. They can borrow in the Federal funds market, which has developed rapidly and in which increasing numbers of banks are participating, or from their correspondent banks, or even from non-financial corporations. In recent years many banks have also sought funds by bidding actively for time and savings deposits. Most spectacular has been the growth of negotiable time certificates of deposit. These have been most fruitful for the largest banks, though some smaller banks have also used them.

In the first part of the post-war period there was a widespread belief that such sources would by themselves be sufficient to provide adequate liquidity for individual banks and for adequate interregional flows of funds among banks, so that there would be little need for recourse to borrowings from the Federal Reserve. However, opinion has shifted somewhat in recent years. For this there appear to be several reasons. One is certainly the sharp decline of bank holdings of Federal government securities as a percentage of their total loans and

investments and as a percentage of their deposit liabilities. As
shown in Table 1, commercial bank holdings of Federal securities

TABLE I

*Commercial Bank Loans and Investments: Seasonally Adjusted
Amounts (in billions of dollars)*

June 30	Total loans and securities	Loans	U.S. government securities	Other securities	U.S. government securities as a percentage of total loans and investments
	$	$	$	$	
1951	126·5	55·0	58·8	12·7	46·4
1952	135·0	59·3	61·7	14·0	45·7
1953	138·5	64·9	59·4	14·2	42·8
1954	146·9	67·0	64·5	15·5	43·9
1955	155·6	74·3	64·5	16·8	41·4
1956	159·7	85·4	57·8	16·5	36·1
1957	164·6	91·1	56·8	16·8	34·5
1958	178·6	92·7	65·9	19·9	36·8
1959	184·6	101·7	62·3	20·6	33·7
1960	187·1	111·5	55·7	19·8	29·7
1961	201·3	115·8	63·4	22·0	31·4
1962	218·3	126·2	65·2	26·9	29·8
1963	237·2	141·0	63·9	32·3	26·9
1964	255·3	158·7	60·3	36·2	23·6
1965	281·7	181·4	58·2	42·1	20·6
1966	305·4	203·7	54·5	47·1	15·4

SOURCE: *Federal Reserve Bulletin*, July 1966, pp. 952–5.

in mid 1951 were equal to 46·4 per cent. of their total loans and
securities. During the next fifteen years their loans increased 270
per cent. and their holdings of other securities 271 per cent.,
while their holdings of Treasury securities actually declined
somewhat. The general pattern has been for banks to increase
their holdings of governments during periods of business recession and to decrease them during boom periods when credit
demands rose. However, during the fifteen years ending in
mid 1966 the percentage of bank holdings of governments to
their total loans and securities fell from 46·4 per cent. to 15·4
per cent. Member-bank holdings of governments as a percentage

of their total deposit liabilities fell from about 40 per cent. to 14·2 per cent. These statistics may overstate the extent and ease with which member banks could secure liquidity through their holdings of these securities. For one thing, some of these securities are pledged as collateral for government deposits, and thus are not available for sale or as collateral for borrowings at the Federal Reserve. Moreover, more than half of these securities have maturities in excess of a year, so that their sale, at times of unusually high interest rates, such as those reached in 1966, would entail book losses. There can be little doubt that the over-all liquidity of bank assets has diminished in recent years.

It also seems likely that in recent years banks have become subject to larger shifts of deposits, both shifts among banks and shifts between categories of deposits. This probably reflects both greater sensitivity of depositors to changes in relative yields on assets and also wider fluctuations in relative yields. The 'Corporate Treasurers' Revolution' has been widely noted. Never before have managers of the financial assets of large and medium sized non-financial corporations been so sophisticated and willing to shift their holdings in response to changes in relative yields on such things as demand deposits, various classes of time deposits, government securities, repurchase agreements, acceptances, Federal funds, commercial paper, and even Eurodollars. Households, with increasing holdings of liquid assets, also seem to have gained financial sophistication and readiness to shift in response to changes in relative yields.

There have also been large changes in relative yields. Federal laws still prohibit payment of interest on demand deposits, and rates on time and savings deposits have varied widely. Up to 1957 the highest rate permitted by the Federal Reserve and Federal Deposit Insurance Corporation ceilings was 2½ per cent., and the rates actually paid by many commercial banks were even lower. These were well below the rates at savings banks, savings and loan associations, and on some short-term direct securities. The result should have been predictable; time and savings deposits at commercial banks grew only slowly, while the public increased rapidly its holdings of higher yield assets. The situation has changed markedly since early 1957 and especially since early 1962. Ceiling rates have been raised in several steps, and banks in general have bid actively for these deposits, many paying the ceiling rates. The results have been several. One has been a very rapid growth of savings and time deposits, primarily the latter, at commercial banks, especially when their rates were high relative to rates at savings banks and savings and loan associations, and to yields on such open-market assets as short-term government securities. Another result is that many banks now have large amounts of deposit liabilities which they might lose quickly if their rates fell below competing rates. The potential dangers of this situation were widely discussed in 1965 and 1966 at times when yields on short-term government securities rose above the ceiling rates. Some even feared crises for banks heavily dependent on time deposits, especially those with large outstanding amounts of large denomination negotiable certificates of deposit. There was one obvious solution: to remove ceiling rates, or to raise them to such high levels that they would become ineffective and thus enable banks to compete freely for funds. However, the authorities were reluctant to do this, partly because of effects on competing institutions, especially savings and loan associations, and on supplies of funds for home-building. The danger of large shifts of deposits among banks, and from time to demand deposits, remains.

Such are some of the conditions which support the position that Federal Reserve discount policy should play a continuing, and perhaps increased, role in providing liquidity for individual banks or groups of banks: (1) The marked decline of bank holdings of Federal government securities in relation both to their total loans and securities and to their total deposit liabilities, and the decrease in the over-all liquidity of bank assets; and (2) the possibility of large shifts of deposits among banks and between the categories of demand and time deposits, a possibility which is enhanced if ceiling rates limit the freedom of banks to bid for funds as competing rates change. Many economists and others favour abolition of ceiling rates on time and savings deposits at commercial banks. However, it is doubtful that this view will prevail, or even that comparable ceilings will be imposed on rates paid by competing financial intermediaries.

Several proposals have been offered to change the discount

mechanism. One is to amend the Federal Reserve Act to permit the Reserve Banks to lend at their regular discount rates on a wider range of bank assets. As the law now stands, only two types of paper are 'eligible' as collateral for loans at the regular discount rate: Federal government securities and certain short-term private paper of the 'real bills' type. No one knows how many bank assets would meet these 'eligibility requirements', but it is clear that a large part of them would not. Any Federal Reserve loan on other bank assets must be at a rate at least ½ of 1 per cent. above the regular discount rate. In every year since 1962 the Board of Governors has recommended legislation which would permit member banks to borrow at the regular rate on any sound assets. This, it is believed, would both increase the ability of the Federal Reserve to provide liquidity and also encourage banks to meet the changing credit needs of the economy. Such a bill actually passed the Senate in August 1965, but the House took no action on it.

The Board of Governors has also recommended that insured non-member banks, as well as members, should be permitted to borrow from the Federal Reserve, but only if they are subjected to the same legal reserve requirements as those applicable to comparable member banks. One clear purpose of this two-part recommendation was to eliminate the discrimination against member banks in the form of legal reserve requirements more burdensome than those applying to most non-member banks. Federal Reserve officials complain that this is inequitable to member banks, that it has been a factor in accelerated withdrawals from membership of the System, and that withdrawals are 'fast reaching the point where System effectiveness in the implementation of monetary and credit policy may be impaired'.[1] Another purpose was to give the insured non-member banks, numbering about 7,300, direct access to the Federal Reserve discount window. Their lack of such access must on occasion impair their ability to serve their customers, and in time of crisis might weaken the entire banking system. The acid test of the 1930s showed that for many banks of these types their sources of liquidity outside the Federal Reserve were neither reliable nor adequate. The Congress has taken no action on this Board proposal, and history provides little basis for optimism.

[1] *Annual Report of the Board of Governors, 1965*, p. 236.

Such have been some of the recent events and issues relating to Federal Reserve discount policies. They do not suggest that discount policy will again achieve the high position it enjoyed in the early years of the System. They do indicate, however, that earlier forecasts of a demise of discount policy were a bit premature.

FRANK W. FETTER

The Transfer Problem: Formal Elegance or Historical Realism

THE transfer problem has a long and rich history. It has produced theoretical writing by many outstanding figures in economics; and it has been at the centre of hard-fought policy controversies that have figured prominently in domestic politics and international relations.

As the term is generally used, the transfer problem refers to unilateral international payments such as reparations, subsidies, gifts, making or repayment of foreign investments, and payments of interest and earnings on outstanding investment. In logic a distinction can be made between transfers like reparations and gifts, that, even when the whole time horizon is surveyed, are unilateral in that no return payment is ever made, and loans and returns on investment that, if a sufficiently long time period is considered, might be considered bilateral, in that they are payments for either past or future services. But as regards the immediate problem of short-run international adjustment it makes no difference whether the transfer is a gift, repayment for goods or services received ten years ago, or payment for which a return is expected ten years hence.

In strict analysis the problem of adjustment to a new set of balance of payments influences is the same, whether the disturbance is in bilateral transactions, such as changes in the prices of exports and imports, crop failure, or expansion or decline of a foreign market, or is a unilateral transaction. But sometimes in economic analysis, and even more in economic and political controversy, the transfer problem is treated as if it were a unique problem in international adjustment. This differentiation can be explained in part by the fact that 'imports' represented by unilateral transfers are not price-elastic in the way the commodities are, and hence may present a more intractable problem of adjustment than does a disturbance in the commodity trade. Furthermore, in some cases a new unilateral transaction represents a more abrupt and proportionately greater disturbance in an existing balance of payments than do changes in prices, or in quantities of goods and services exported and imported. And probably most important in explaining the frequent consideration of unilateral transfer as a special problem in international adjustment are the political issues associated with some of the great transfer controversies: British subsidies and foreign military expenditures during the Napoleonic Wars; remittances to absentee Irish landlords; the French indemnity to Prussia after the War of 1871; reparations and war debts following World War I.

Previous to the Napoleonic Wars the transfer problem played virtually no part in economic analysis, although the existence of such payments was recognized in the earliest discussions of international economic relations. Thomas Mun, writing in the 1630s in *England's Treasure by Forraign Trade*, made specific reference to, but gave no theoretical analysis of, unilateral transfers:

> Likewise if it happen that His Majesty doth make over any great sums of mony by Exchange to maintain a forraign war, where we do not feed and clothe the Souldiers, and Provide the armies, we must deduct all this charge out of our Exportations or add it to our Importations; for this expense doth either carry out or hinder the coming in of so much Treasure. And here we must remember the great collections of mony which are supposed to be made throughout the Realm yearly from our Recusants by Priests and Jesuits, who secretly convey the same unto their Colleges, Cloysters and Nunneries beyond the Seas, from whence it never returns to us again in any kind.[1]

Undoubtedly, transfers of this type continued throughout the seventeenth and eighteenth centuries, but there was practically no contemporary discussion of the theory of transfer. Interest in international adjustment from Mun to Adam Smith centred on criticizing the mercantilist idea that positive state action was necessary to ensure an adequate supply of the precious metals. David Hume's analysis of international adjustment stressed the relationship between a country's supply of

---

[1] Ashley edn. (Macmillan & Co., New York and London, 1895), p. 116.

the precious metals, prices, and the balance of trade, and also pointed out that a depreciation of the exchange, even though not sufficient to cause an export of specie, was a stimulus to commodity exports.[1] He by-passed the transfer problem, however, and gave no attention to disturbances arising out of changes in the supply of, and demand for, internationally traded goods, as distinguished from disturbances arising out of internal inflation. But an extension of Hume's analysis to a problem with which he was not immediately concerned provided a theory of unilateral transfers: when the demand for foreign exchange lowers the exchange rate there is a stimulus to exports in relation to imports that effects the transfer—first by a stimulus before the specie export point is reached, and then, when specie is exported, by a contraction in the money supply and a fall in prices. Hume's theory, adapted to this larger problem by Henry Thornton and John Stuart Mill, came to be known as the 'classical transfer theory', or the 'gold-flow, price-adjustment theory'.

In two areas, however, the transfer problem was discussed in the eighteenth century, but almost completely divorced from economic analysis of the mechanism of transfer. Following the English conquests in Ireland and the growth of a large body of landlords resident in England most of the year, transfers of rent to these absentees had been a source of festering discontent in Ireland. But the emphasis was not on transfer theory; it was on what the rent payments did to impoverish the people of Ireland, or on what the absentee system did to remove the 'natural leaders' from Ireland. Arthur Young, in his *Tour of Ireland* (London, 1780), devoted a chapter to absentees, listed absentee landlords receiving £732,000, and estimated that total transfers from Ireland to England from absentee rents, pensions, and interest were in the neighbourhood of £1,000,000. But neither he nor any other eighteenth-century writer gave any organized discussion of the mechanism of these transfers.

The other extensive unilateral transfers that figured in economic literature before 1797 were England's foreign war expenditures. These were discussed by Adam Smith, but in

---

[1] 'Of the Balance of Trade', in *Political Discourses* (Edinburgh, 1752), reprinted in *Early Economic Thought*, A. E. Monroe, ed. (Harvard University Press, Cambridge, 1930), pp. 323–38.

terms of economic and social philosophy rather than analysis of economic processes. His discussion, although one may read into it traces of an income-shift explanation of transfers, was in effect an appeal to history to support his view that if the forces of the market were allowed to operate, a country need not be concerned about its supply of precious metals, even if making large foreign payments.[1]

The enormous expence of the late [Seven Years] war, therefore, must have been chiefly defrayed, not by the exportation of gold and silver, but by that of British commodities of some kind or other. When the government, or those who acted under them, contracted with a merchant for a remittance to some foreign country, he would naturally endeavour to pay his foreign correspondent, upon whom he had granted a bill, by sending abroad rather commodities than gold and silver.

The flowering of transfer theory came in England with the large foreign payments during the Napoleonic Wars: the loan to Austria in 1794, subsidies to the countries at war with Napoleon, and the expenses of Wellington's army in the Peninsula. But the immediate occasion for the emergence of transfer theory was not concern as to how transfers were made; it was a by-product of the debate over the causes of the rise in the price of gold and silver, and of the depreciation of the British currency on the foreign exchanges. The suspension of payments by the Bank of England in February 1797 was, despite a widely held view, the result of a depletion of reserves due to an internal run rather than foreign transfers.[2] In August 1799 the Bank's specie holdings were about 75 per cent. greater than at the outbreak of war in February 1793, and exchange and the prices of gold and silver were virtually at par. Like the Irish payments to absentee landlords and the British overseas expenses of the Seven Years War, England's transfers for over six years of the Napoleonic Wars took place with little identifiable impact upon specie holdings, exchange rates, or the prices of gold and silver.

Late in 1799 the English pound went to a greater discount on the exchanges than would have been possible under the

---

[1] *Wealth of Nations*, Cannan edn. (Methuen & Co., London, 1904), p. 409.
[2] In my book, *The Development of British Monetary Orthodoxy, 1797–1875* (Harvard University Press, Cambridge, Mass., 1965), pp. 16–21, I give in more detail my reasons for this view.

specie payments, and the price of gold and silver rose. In the debate that followed, Henry Thornton, in his *Paper Credit of Great Britain* (1802), developed a price-adjustment transfer theory by extending Hume's analysis of disturbances arising out of internal monetary expansion to disturbances arising from crop failures and from unilateral transfers. He pointed out that unilateral transfers 'contribute, exactly like the circumstance of a bad harvest, to render the balance of trade unfavourable; they tend, that is to say, in the same manner, to bring Great Britain into debt to foreign countries, and to promote the exportation of our bullion'.[1] Thornton then described how, in the face of such a development, the Bank of England could, by credit restriction, encourage the export of commodities (p. 151).

This was the essence of the price-adjustment theory of unilateral transfers, as later developed by J. S. Mill and Taussig. On two important points, however, Thornton's analysis differed from the later textbook version of the price-adjustment theory of transfer. He assumed that income changes also had an impact on the balance of payments:

> There is in the mass of the people, of all countries, a disposition to adapt their individual expenditure to their income. . . . If, therefore, through any unfortunate circumstances, if through war, scarcity, or any other extensive calamity, the value of the annual income of the inhabitants of a country is diminished, either new economy on the one hand, or new exertions of individual industry on the other, fail not, after a certain time, in some measure, to restore the balance. And this equality between private expenditures and private incomes tends ultimately to produce equality between the commercial exports and imports (pp. 142-3).

Secondly, Thornton recognized limits to the deflation that should be attempted, and suggested that in some circumstances it would be wise for the Bank of England, when faced with pressure on the exchanges, to permit gold to flow out, and even to expand credit (p. 152).

From contemporaries of Thornton, notably John Leslie Foster and Lord King, writing with reference to the remittances to absentee landlords of Ireland, came an explanation of transfer as effected primarily by a shift in demand resulting from the

[1] Hayek edn. (George Allen & Unwin, London, 1939), pp. 144-5.

increased purchasing power of residents of England and decreased purchasing power of residents of Ireland. John Wheatley in 1803 and 1807, and later David Ricardo, also challenged parts of Thornton's explanation of transfer as resulting from an export of specie and consequent price changes. Some passages in both Wheatley and Ricardo are consistent with a demand-shift explanation of transfer, but they did not elaborate this idea. Wheatley stressed that a 'due compression' of the currency in the remitting country would so reduce prices as to bring about transfer without any loss of specie, or even pressure on the exchanges. Ricardo made the same point, and also argued that the export of specie would be obviated by the inducement to export commodities that would result from exchange variations within the specie points, or by capital movements in the opposite direction by merchants who felt that the pressure for specie export would be only temporary.

After Waterloo, with the end of the heavy overseas expenditures, and the resumption of specie payments by the Bank of England in 1821, the transfer problem for nearly a century was hardly more than a footnote in economic theory. Yet this was a century of great international investments by Britain, and of intensified controversy over the absentee ownership of Irish land. It saw the French war indemnity of 5 billion francs to Germany, involving a payment in two years of a sum substantially greater, both in gold and in real terms, than the total unilateral payments of England during more than twenty years of war against France. Yet these developments added little to the theory of transfer beyond a few suggestions, arising out of the controversy over Irish absenteeism, that transfers *may* have had an unfavourable effect on Ireland's terms of trade.[1]

The controversy over Irish absenteeism after the Napoleonic period was primarily political.[2] But the Irish experience, apart from the suggestion of a possible deterioration of the Irish terms of trade, raised two points relative to transfer theory. The Irish transfers apparently were proportionately much larger in relation to the country's exports than were many transfers which

[1] Jacob Viner discusses this point in *Studies in the Theory of International Trade* (Harper, New York [1937]), pp. 320–2.

[2] R. D. Collison Black, in *Economic Thought and the Irish Question, 1817–1870* (Cambridge University Press, Cambridge, 1960), reviews the controversy in Ch. iv, 'The Absentee Landlords'.

in the last half-century have been subjected to theoretical analysis and statistical study. However, transfer developed gradually, was in effect built into the foreign trade structure in the same way that any imports would be, and hence no more disturbed the balance of payments nor called for adjustments in prices and exchange rates than would a long established pattern of imports of wheat or any other commodity.

A second point is the possible bearing of the Irish situation upon the persistence of a demand-shift explanation of the transfer mechanism. Emphasis in the political discussion of Irish absenteeism was principally on the inequality of land ownership that transferred income from a miserably poor Irish peasantry to a small group of already wealthy landlords. The Irish animosity to, and the political controversy over, land ownings in Ireland would have existed even had all landlords been residents. This situation, particularly in the absence of any substantial evidence that transfers had caused price disturbances, fitted in nicely with an income-shift as contrasted with a price-adjustment theory of transfer. I would suggest that it was no accident that throughout the nineteenth century the income-shift theory of transfer had its most articulate expression from economists with Irish associations, or concerned with the Irish land problem: John Leslie Foster, Lord King, Sir Henry Parnell, Nassau W. Senior, Mountifort Longfield, J. E. Cairnes, and, later in the century, C. F. Bastable and J. S. Nicholson.[1]

J. S. Mill in his *Principles of Political Economy* gave an analysis, along the lines of Hume and Thornton, of adjustment to unilateral transfers on the basis of price changes accompanied by a shift in the terms of trade against the paying country.[2] Mill made no attempt to test this theory against experience, but his

---

[1] See Will E. Mason, 'Some Neglected Contributions to the Theory of International Transfers', *Journal of Political Economy*, lxiii, Dec. 1955, pp. 529–35, and his unpublished Princeton Ph.D. thesis (1952), 'The Classical Theory of Adjustments to Unilateral Capital Transfers'; Jacob Viner, op. cit. 297–304. In a footnote to his discussion of 'Relative Changes in Demand as an Equilibrating Force' Viner says: 'It may be significant, as indicating possible indebtedness, that of these writers Longfield, Cairnes and Bastable, had all been associated with Trinity College, Dublin, as students or professors, or both, and Nicholson had received help from Bastable' (p. 303). Viner does not, however, push his suggestion as I have that this similarity of approach may have had its roots in the special economic and political situation in Ireland.

[2] Book III, Ch. xxi, section 4.

lucid presentation became in large part what late nineteenth-
and twentieth-century economists thought of as classical, and
even Ricardian, transfer theory. The great international lending of the nineteenth and early twentieth century took place
so smoothly that the process of transfer went virtually unnoticed.
In so far as one can speak of a 'transfer problem' in the three-
quarters of a century before 1914, it was largely associated with
the effects of transfers on short-term interest rates and their
influence in causing an offsetting inflow of short-term capital.
Nor did repayments present the problem, so much discussed in
the 1920s and 1930s, of a supposed distinction between debtors' ability to pay internally and their ability to pay in foreign
exchange. To men of the Hundred Years Peace such a distinction was meaningless, because even to the most casual
observer it was evident that in the more publicized cases where
no transfer was made it was because there was nothing to transfer. British investors who were not paid on the bonds of Latin
American countries, of American states before the Civil War,
of the Confederate States, of the Carpetbag governments of
Southern States were not concerned with any subtleties of
transfer—the debtors had simply defaulted. The same was true
of European investors in railroads in the United States: investors knew that their difficulties sprang, not from the breakdown
of any transfer mechanism, but from unfavourable business
conditions, or from the excesses of financial promoters. The
French war indemnity did not, in the aggregate, involve any
appreciable international transfer on current account by
France at the time the indemnity was paid. The French Government delivered to the German Government foreign assets
already owned by French nationals, or borrowed abroad.[1]

After World War I, German reparations and the Inter-
Allied debts rekindled analytic interest in unilateral transfers,
and produced an extensive literature. Much of this controversy
was marked by three weaknesses: (1) failure to understand the
nature of nineteenth-century transfer theory, and a general

---

[1] The principal discussions in English of the payment of this indemnity are:
A. E. Monroe, 'The French Indemnity of 1871 and its Effects', *Review of Economic
Statistics*, i, Oct. 1919, pp. 269–81; Harold G. Moulton and Constantine E.
McGuire, *Germany's Capacity to Pay* (McGraw-Hill, New York, 1923), Ch. vii,
'How France Met the Indemnity of 1871'; F. W. Taussig, *International Trade*
(Macmillan, New York, 1927). Ch. 22, 'Franco-German Indemnity of 1871'.

belief that the price-adjustment mechanism, as summarized by J. S. Mill, represented the consensus of the nineteenth-century economists and was an accurate description of the process by which unilateral transfers had been effected; (2) overlooking, in large part, of the institutional settings and political attitudes that had made possible these great transfers with so little economic disturbance; and (3) entangling of economic analysis with policy attitudes that were basically those of international relations or domestic politics.

In the United States, theoretical discussion and statistical investigations of pre-1914 transfers owe much to the article in 1917 by F. W. Taussig, 'International Trade under Inconvertible Paper'.[1] Taussig outlined what was basically the Thornton–Mill theory of price adjustment, and his article was the stimulus to four Ph.D. theses by men who went on to make their mark in economics:

> John Henry Williams, *Argentine International Trade under Inconvertible Paper Money, 1880–1900*.[2]
> Frank D. Graham, 'International Trade Under Depreciated Paper: The United States, 1862–1879'.[3]
> Jacob Viner, *Canada's Balance of International Indebtedness, 1900–1913*.[4]
> Harry D. White, *The French International Accounts, 1880–1913*.[5]

These studies did much to sharpen analysis of the mechanism of transfer. The statistical findings showed that transfer took place largely through adjustments in commodity trade. Although the end result that traditional gold-flow price-adjustment theory had predicated was fully confirmed, the intermediate steps in economic causation between the unilateral financial transfer and the adjustment in the commodity trade balance were largely lacking. The adjustment just took place. Even in the Canadian case where there was a price adjustment consistent with the Thornton–Mill–Taussig price analysis, more than one economist has suggested that the movement of

---

[1] *Quarterly Journal of Economics*, xxi, May 1917, 380–413.
[2] Harvard University Press, Cambridge, 1920.
[3] *Quarterly Journal of Economics*, xxxvi, May 1922, 220–73.
[4] Harvard University Press, Cambridge, 1924.
[5] Harvard University Press, Cambridge, 1933.

Canadian prices could be equally well explained by economic forces that did not arise out of the transfer mechanism.

Professor Taussig was baffled by the results of these pre-1914 transfers that showed but minor traces of the intermediate adjustments called for by traditional price-adjustment theory. He wrote, in the honest perplexity of a great teacher:[1]

> Yet the recorded transactions between countries show surprisingly little transfer of the only 'money' that moves from one to the other —gold. It is the goods that move, and they seem to move at once; almost as if there were an automatic connection between these financial operations and the commodity exports or imports. That the flow of goods should ensue in time, perhaps even at an early date, is of course to be expected; it is a commonplace in the theoretical reasoning that this must be the ultimate outcome. What is puzzling is the rapidity, almost simultaneity, of the commodity movements. The presumable intermediate stage of gold flow and price changes is hard to discern, and certainly is extremely short.
>   I find it impossible to see how there can be a complete skipping of the intermediate stage—anything in the nature of an automatic connection.

These studies of great unilateral transfers before 1914 suggested that such transfers could be made without appreciable gold flows, and with no serious disturbance to exchange rates and prices. Yet in 1931 the Hoover moratorium for all practical purposes wiped out the great volume of unilateral transfers called for by the financial settlements of World War I. In addition, by 1933 there had been wholesale defaults on bonds of foreign corporations and governments, particularly in Latin America, Germany, and Eastern Europe. The events of the years 1931–3 seemed to confirm the most pessimistic predictions of some economists—notably J. M. Keynes and Harold G. Moulton—in the 1920s that it would be impossible to make the unilateral transfers of war debts and reparations; and doubts were held, by layman and economist alike, as to whether it was possible to make large unilateral transfers of any kind.

The explanation of the contrast between experience before 1914 and after 1930 must come in large part not from the formal elegance of theory but from an examination of the economic setting in which transfers are attempted and of

[1] *International Trade*, pp. 260–1.

the political attitudes of the articulate public in the countries involved. Before 1931 many individual transfers, at least in the
short run, were offset by other individual transfers in the opposite direction. A notable example was Germany in the middle
and late 1920s. Although economists, after resumption of foreign
loans to Germany in 1924, talked of the German transfer problem, this was a problem of the future. For the late 1920s the
theoretical problem was to explain how the rest of the world
was able to make such a large net transfer to Germany. Yet
economists and the public gave and have given practically no
attention to that transfer. Like so many of the great capital
transfers of the century before 1914, it just took place, and left
no theoretical debate in its wake. The same could be said about
some of the payments of war debts to the United States being
offset in whole or in part by loans from the United States.
Given world political and economic situations after 1930, the
possibility of unilateral transfers' continuing to be handled
temporarily by such reverse movements of capital was practically nil.

In other cases, less publicized or on a more modest scale, the
'transfer' on which public attention was focused had been
taken care of by a transfer in the opposite direction. With the
British transfers during the Napoleonic Wars the problem, in
part, was not that of increasing the commodity export surplus
but that of persuading foreigners to make loans to the British.
Ricardo, in an imperfectly analysed and cryptic statement, suggested that short-term credits might ease the impact of transfer.[1]
From others came the suggestion that over a longer period the
transfers were made by borrowing abroad. John Hill indicated
that 'international transfers of capital' were an alternative to
adjustment of commodity trade as a means of taking care of the
foreign expenditure of government.[2] Even more specific was
the statement of John Charles Herries, Commissary General of
the army, who had the responsibility for the remittances to support British military operations in the Peninsula, that probably
'with respect to our drafts from abroad at this time—we are

---

[1] Appendix to *The High Price of Bullion*, in Ricardo, *Works*, ed. Piero Sraffa,
(Cambridge University Press, London, 1951), iii, p. 103.
[2] *An Inquiry into the Causes of the Present High Price of Gold Bullion in England*
(London, 1811), pp. 8–9, 35.

borrowing money to carry on our foreign expenditures, at a high rate of interest'.[1]

In the short run such a reverse transfer was a common feature of large-scale international lending throughout the nineteenth and early twentieth centuries. Not only did borrowers often leave part of the loan proceeds on deposit in the lending country for months, or even years, but if the transfers put pressure on the exchanges or tightened the money market, a temporary inflow of short-term funds often followed. From the long-run point of view this may have done little to reduce the total transfer, but it meant that the impact on exchange rates and prices, instead of being concentrated within a few weeks, was spread out over time. This undoubtedly provides one of the reasons for Professor Taussig's bafflement at the smoothness of so many great international capital transfers.

More basic in explaining the apparent smoothness of transfer before 1914 were economic conditions, in both the lending and the borrowing country, at the time of transfer. There is no perfect correlation between a large supply of savings, seeking investment abroad, and industrial leadership that makes the lending country a favourable market in which to buy capital goods and services, but historically there has frequently been such an association. In the receiving country a desire to borrow abroad is likely to be associated with a tariff policy that places few obstacles in the way of goods needed for economic development, and with an increased demand for such goods. The history of English, German, and French foreign investment before 1914, and of the investment that came to the United States, Canada, Australia, Argentina, and the Scandinavian countries, would seem to support these generalizations. Dennis H. Robertson was one of the first economists to sharpen this point, when he wrote in 1930 that in using a purely theoretical analysis 'the analogy between reparations and capital export is apt to be most treacherous'.[2]

For in the nineteenth century at least (apart from the definite stipulations about the mode of expenditure of foreign loans which

[1] *A Review of the Controversy Respecting the High Price of Bullion* (London, 1811), pp. 43–44. The pamphlet appeared anonymously.

[2] 'The Transfer Problem', in A. C. Pigou and Dennis H. Robertson, *Economic Essays and Addresses* (P. S. King, London, 1931), pp. 178–9.

in some countries were common) it seems to have been something like a law of nature that the countries whose investors were rich enough to want to lend abroad were also the countries whose industrialists were ingenious enough to need, and enterprising enough to find, an expanding market for the products of large-scale industry; while the countries which were poor enough to want to borrow were also the countries which were sufficiently simple in economic structure to have a high demand for the specialised products of factory industry. Thus the needs of exporters, of importers, and of borrowers and lenders walked for the most part hand in hand in apparently pre-ordained harmony. It would be rash to make the same assertion about the post-war 'reconstruction' borrowing of European countries; and it would be rasher still to make it about the payment of reparations. Where reparations are concerned, such compensatory movements of real demand are not indeed impossible; but they require more deliberate organisation, about which in practice many difficulties may arise. Further, there may well be a counter-influence working in the opposite direction—namely, an organised distaste in the reparation-receiving country for buying the goods of the defeated enemy.

To a large degree, formal transfer theory has assumed that the countries involved had their balance of payments disturbed by a unilateral transfer. But many of the great international capital movements before 1914 were a response to a development already under way within the borrowing country and were not the origin of that development. Foreign investment in such a situation, instead of being a disturbance of an existing equilibrium, was in effect a means of correcting a disequilibrium arising out of the new international supply and demand conditions created by the country's internal development. In the case of the two greatest recipients of foreign capital, the United States and Canada, recent studies buttress the idea that it was the 'historical environment of growth' that provided the setting for the smooth working of the transfer mechanism.[1]

In a less striking way, this built-in transfer mechanism goes

---

[1] C. M. Meier, 'Economic Development and the Transfer Mechanism: Canada, 1895–1913', *The Canadian Journal of Economics and Political Science*, xix, Feb. 1953, pp. 1–19; Jeffrey G. Williamson, 'International Trade and United States Economic Development: 1827–1843', *The Journal of Economic History*, xxii, Sept. 1961, pp. 372–83; and 'Real Growth, Monetary Disturbances and the Transfer Process: The United States, 1879–1900', *Southern Economic Journal*, xxix, Jan. 1963, pp. 167–80.

far to explain the smooth functioning of a number of cases of repayments on foreign investment before 1914: the United States in a number of years after the middle 1890s, Australia in the early years of this century, Italy from the 1890s until about 1910, Sweden from 1909 to 1913, and Japan for a few years before 1914. These were largely voluntary actions, where conditions in the debtor country made corporate or government debtors, or individual investors, choose to repatriate securities. In some cases, the existence of these net transfers was barely recognized until decades later, when they were picked up in the statistical drag-net of national accounts. The problem presented by war debts, reparations, and service after the late 1920s on private international investment may have been symmetrical in formal theory with the great transfers before 1914, but it was completely different in its institutional setting. The pre-1914 transfers were in large part voluntary. Those responsible for them decided when they wished to make them, and they were not under a treaty or contractual obligation to continue to make them when economic conditions were not favourable. The transfers to be made after the late 1920s were in large part involuntary. There was no 'historical environment of growth', no built-in transfer mechanism. The transfers were not related to the dominant economic desires in either the transferring or the receiving country, or to economic conditions in the countries.

Closely associated with the compulsory and long-term nature of this new transfer problem was the attitude of taxpayers toward internal raising of the sums to be transferred. Even had the necessary sums been available for the purchase of foreign exchange, the creation of a current-account surplus without severe pressure on prices and foreign exchange rates posed difficulties that had not been present in the 'historical environment of growth'. But in much of the discussion of the transfer problem after World War I, whether up to the late 1920s in analysing what might happen, or in the early 1930s in analysing what was happening, the difficulty of transfer was magnified out of all proportion to its relevance. *Sub silencio*, the question whether government could raise taxes from its people, or whether corporations would have sufficient earnings to pay interest on their bonds, was assimilated with, and in some cases even substituted for, the question of international transfer. These were important economic questions, and, in the setting, they were more significant than the transfer problem, but they were no more the international transfer problem than is the question today as to how the New Haven Railroad can pay interest on its bonds held in Canada or Europe.

Even more subtle was an issue of international ethics and high-level diplomacy that in the 1920s and early 1930s sometimes intruded itself into what pretended to be a theory of transfer: whether it was right to expect Germans to pay reparations founded on a 'war guilt' thesis, or moral to ask England and France to repay loans made to support a common war effort, or reasonable to expect Latin American countries in economic distress to make payments on loans part of whose proceeds had not been used for productive purposes. And apart from morality, was it in the long-run political interests of the creditors to exact such payments, even if they could be obtained?

This view, and not any analysis of the transfer mechanism, was the principal basis of the opposition in the 1920s of policy-oriented economists toward reparations and Inter-Allied debts. J. M. Keynes's trenchant criticism in *The Economic Consequences of the Peace* (1919) and *A Revision of the Treaty* (1922) was virtually devoid of transfer theory. His thesis was that it was beyond the realm of the possible for the German economy to produce the internal surplus necessary to make the payments, and even if the payments could be made, the moral and political consequences would be disastrous. Keynes neither agreed nor disagreed with the transfer theories of Thornton, Ricardo, Mill, or Taussig; his argument was simply not concerned with transfer theory. His attitude and his analysis are epitomized in the statement: 'The policy of reducing Germany to servitude for a generation, of degrading the lives of millions of human beings, and of depriving a whole nation of happiness should be abhorrent and detestable,—abhorrent and detestable, even if it were possible, even if it enriched ourselves, even if it did not sow the decay of the whole civilized life of Europe.'[1] And the same unconcern with transfer mechanism is shown in his judgement on the whole structure of reparations and war debts: 'In short, I do not believe that any of these tributes will continue

[1] *Economic Consequences of the Peace*, p. 225.

to be paid, at the best, for more than a very few years. They do not square with human nature or agree with the spirit of the age.'[1]

In one of Keynes's few discussions before 1929 of the economics of transfer, as distinguished from its politics or morality, he appeared to argue along conventional lines that transfer could be made if the countries involved so desired. But he held that it would be economically wasteful, even for receiving countries, to go through the pains of readjustment in their export industries if the process was to be reversed when politics forced the abandonment of transfers:

> America will not carry through to a conclusion the collection of Allied debt, any more than the Allies will carry through the collection of their present Reparations demands. Neither, in the long run, is serious politics. . . . If this is so, it is not good business for America to embitter her relations with Europe, and to disorder her export industries for two years, in pursuance of a policy which she is certain to abandon before it has profited her.[2]

In the United States the most vigorous and most publicized statement of an economist to the effect that Germany could not make large reparations payments came from Harold G. Moulton in his book, *Germany's Capacity to Pay* (1923), with Constantine E. McGuire as co-author. The book had virtually no international transfer theory, beyond an implied rejection of any idea that income shifts affected the balance of commodity trade. Moulton drew a distinction between payment within Germany and payment by Germany abroad. But so strongly did he make the argument that any attempt by Germany to raise the necessary taxes would depress German living standards to an unbearably low level and that transfer of reparations would disrupt the economies of the receiving countries, that his case against large reparations would have been little changed whether he had accepted a theory of frictionless international transfer or argued that transfer was impossible.

Large reparations payments can be made only provided the German standard of living is held down to the minimum of subsistence, or at least to the minimum below which social revolt

---

[1] *Economic Consequences of the Peace*, p. 282.
[2] *A Revision of the Treaty*, pp. 176–7.

becomes inevitable. . . . Implied in this is a driving down of wages and production costs below the level of the world at large, in order that Germany may persistently undersell competitors in world markets. This is the only possible way whereby any substantial exportable surplus can be procured. Whether it is a way that would please and prove profitable to the rest of the world constitutes another story.[1]

In 1929 Keynes discussed reparations in terms of transfer theory in an article that provoked an historic interchange with Bertil Ohlin.[2] But what Keynes had to say added nothing to transfer theory, and completely ignored the historical record of transfer in the preceding century. It was pure Mill price-adjustment theory, joined to the suggestion that the price elasticities of foreign demand for German goods were so low that reduced prices would, at best, impose an unbearable burden on the German standard of living, and at worst lead to a reduction of German foreign exchange earnings. In the controversy Ohlin, drawing largely upon a demand-shift theory of transfer, had the better of the argument.

With the ending of reparations and war debts and wholesale defaults on foreign bonds, the transfer problem as a policy issue virtually disappeared from the economic stage for nearly a quarter of a century. However, several brilliant contributions were made to the pure theory of transfer, notably Lloyd Metzler's 'The Transfer Problem Reconsidered',[3] Paul Samuelson's 'The Transfer Problem and Transfer Costs',[4] and Harry G. Johnson's 'The Transfer Problem and Exchange Stability'.[5]

[1] Ibid., p. 245.

[2] Keynes's original article, 'The German Transfer Problem', was in the *Economic Journal*, xxxix, Mar. 1929, pp. 1–7, and Ohlin's reply, 'Transfer Difficulties Real and Imagined', in June 1929, pp. 172–8. Keynes's rejoinder was in the same issue, pp. 179–82; Ohlin's rejoinder and Keynes's closing comment were in Sept. 1929, pp. 400–4 and pp. 404–8. The two original articles, but not the rejoinders, are reprinted in *Readings in the Theory of International Trade* (Blakiston, Philadelphia, 1949). The current reprint of the volume is published by Richard D. Irwin, Homewood, Illinois.

[3] *Journal of Political Economy*, l, June 1942, pp. 397–414, and reprinted in *Readings in the Theory of International Trade*, pp. 179–97.

[4] *Economic Journal*, lxii, June 1952, pp. 278–304; and lxiv, June 1954, pp. 264–389.

[5] *Journal of Political Economy*, lxiv, June 1956, pp. 212–25, and reprinted, with some expansion, in Harry G. Johnson, *International Trade and Economic Growth* (London, George Allen & Unwin, 1958), Ch. vii.

But these articles, although they developed subtle and previously neglected aspects of transfer theory, did not provide an answer to the historical question, 'Why did some transfers take place so smoothly, and other attempts at transfer collapse?' And they threw only limited light on the policy question, 'Under what conditions may we expect a projected transfer to be accomplished smoothly, and under what conditions is it likely to break down, or to lead to politically unbearable economic strains?'

Beginning in 1940, the unilateral transfers of the United States under Lend Lease, the British loan of 1946, UNRRA, the Marshall plan, economic and military assistance, and governmental and private long-term investment far exceeded any transfer that the world had known hitherto. For 1940–5 net unilateral payments were over $40 billion, and in 1946–9 approximately $25 billion. Yet these massive transfers did not appear to present any transfer problem. Gold holdings of the United States increased by over $7 billion in those ten years. The transfers were in large part an attempt by the American Government to correct a great disequilibrium in the trade position of the countries to which the transfers were made. The basic problem was: What are the minimum unilateral transfers by the United States necessary to prevent the collapse of the economies of the Grand Alliance against the Axis, and after 1945 of the economies of the non-Communist world? Statistically these were the largest unilateral transfers in history, yet they were not of the type that traditional theory had sought to explain.

Large unilateral transfers by the United States continued after 1949, and their net amount up to 1966—after making allowance for foreign investment in the United States and earnings on United States investment abroad—was in the neighbourhood of $50 billion.[1] But there is a striking difference between the over-all picture for these years and that for the years 1940–9. The unilateral transfers beginning in 1950 were no longer fully taken care of by an excess of earnings on goods

---

[1] This is less by some $40 billion than the figure frequently given for the net unilateral transfers by the United States in these years. The explanation is that the larger figure makes no allowance for the net unilateral transfers to the United States from investments abroad, because of the common statistical practice of including such unilateral transfers under the category of exports and imports of goods and services.

and services, and were accompanied by a net loss of about $8 billion gold, and an increase in the short-term liabilities to foreign countries of nearly $25 billion. Over 75 per cent. of this gold loss and increase in short-term liabilities came in 1958–66.

The contrast between the balance-of-payments changes associated with the great American unilateral transfers in 1940–9 and in 1950–66 presents some puzzling problems in transfer theory. Yet until the last years of the later period it produced little in the way of explanation of transfer, either by testing the statistical record against older transfer theory or by offering a new interpretation. Up to 1950 the fairly close relation between American unilateral transfers and the surplus on commodity trade and services was thoroughly consistent with a demand-shift theory. But with other pressing economic problems calling for solution, no one spent much time on the mechanism of a transfer that went so smoothly. Until the early 1950s—and to a considerable degree up to 1958, even though the situation had changed greatly after 1949—much discussion by economists, both in the United States and England, was nothing but floundering in the morass of an endemic 'dollar shortage' myth, with the result that generalities about the superior productive power of the United States inhibited tough analysis of what had happened.

In the last decade a number of statements have been made about the United States' having priced itself out of world markets, or to the effect that the world no longer has the urgent demand for American goods of the 1940s, but the few attempts made to give specific content to these generalizations have failed to provide any clear conclusions. The Brookings Institution study (1963), *The United States Balance of Payments in 1968*, made use of both price and income analysis, but more to project the future of the American balance of payments than to interpret recent history. Its general statement, 'The available price statistics leave much to be desired, but they indicate that the price competitiveness of the United States has indeed declined in the past decade. How much this decline has affected the balance of payments is a question to which no conclusive answer can possibly be given' (p. 70), is undoubtedly true, but the study provided no answer to the basic problem of post-war transfer by the United States—why it took place so easily in some years and caused such problems in other years. A number of passages in the Brookings study suggest—although the statement is not made specifically—that the answer is to be found not so much either in over-all changes in price levels or aggregate income as in changes in the productive conditions of individual products, or in the structure of demand both within the United States and elsewhere. American trade figures support such an idea, and Professor Egon Sohmen of the University of the Saar has argued persuasively that high prices in the American iron and steel industry have been a major factor contributing to the American balance-of-payments problem.[1]

Professor Charles F. Kindleberger has suggested that the increase of foreign short-term assets in the United States is not a breakdown of transfer, but rather a new way of effecting transfer in a changed world situation.[2] The idea that the immediate response to long-term unilateral transfers can be the creation of short-term claims against the country making the transfer is an old one, and has already been discussed. What distinguishes the more recent development is the size of these short-term balances and their long continuance. If the piling up of short-term claims against her was simply an act of goodwill toward the United States by foreigners not attracted to buy goods and services there, though they held their dollars on deposit so as not to embarrass a world banker who had overextended himself, this would be a breakdown of transfer and a cause of alarm to the United States. On the other hand, if the reverse capital flow of some $25 billion is the result of decisions made by businesses, commercial and central banks, and governments, that they would prefer dollar liquidity to American goods and services, or to liquidity in their own currencies, then what has happened is no more a breakdown of transfer than would be the decision of foreign dollar holders to use dollars for travel

---

[1] 'Competition and Growth: the Lesson of the United States Balance of Payments', in *Trade, Growth, and the Balance of Payments: Essays in Honor of Gottfried Haberler* (Rand McNally & Company, Chicago, 1965), pp. 249–63.

[2] *Balance of Payments Deficits and the International Market for Liquidity*, Essays in International Finance, No. 46 (International Finance Section, Princeton, 1965); *International Monetary Arrangements* (Brisbane, University of Queensland Press, 1966); and as co-author with Emile Despres and Walter S. Salant, 'The Dollar and World Liquidity: a Minority View', *The Economist*, 5 Feb. 1966, reprinted as a pamphlet (The Brookings Institution, Washington, 1966).

in the United States rather than for the purchase of automobiles.

In any case the real issue raised by Kindleberger is one of degree rather than of categorical difference. Some increase in the short-term debtor position of the United States was to be expected, once Europe and Japan were in a position to afford such liquidity. Whether an increase of $25 billion is to be considered normal is another matter, and one could accept much of Kindleberger's analysis and still argue that with a different price situation in the United States, or a different demand structure, the increase would be considerably less than $25 billion.

It is doubtful whether anyone can answer this question with numerical precision and find that the transfer mechanism had broken down to the extent of, say, $8 billion, but not of $18 billion. Kindleberger's thesis, no matter how applicable it may be to the present situation of the United States, would have much more limited application in the case of subsidies to a wartime ally, capital exports to under-developed countries, or a unilateral transfer in the form of net repayments to the United States or any other international creditor.

There is no simple explanation of the apparent paradoxes of international transfer, whether the contrast be between the almost frictionless transfers in the century before 1914 and the collapse of transfers in the Great Depression, or between American experience in 1940–9 and in 1950–66. But either to interpret the past or to judge the future calls for more than formal models, whether of the two-commodity or the multi-commodity type. These can be useful, but they do not encompass the difference between (i) economically motivated transfers like most British capital exports before 1914; (ii) politically motivated transfers, whether of capital flight or foreign aid, for which export potential is less likely to grow alongside the desire, either of private parties or government, to make unilateral transfers; (iii) reparation and war debts payments that must be extracted from reluctant or hostile taxpayers; and (iv) long-term capital transfers to countries that have a high demand for short-term liquidity in the currency of the transferring country.

All unilateral transfers have one thing in common: the transferring to someone abroad of a claim on resources without the requirement of immediate payment. There is danger, however, that this common feature may conceal the great differences between the problems involved in specific cases of unilateral transfer. Any realistic approach to unilateral transfers, whether with the hindsight of history or the foresight of prediction, must temper the rigours of the theorist's analysis with the judgements of the historian, the political scientist, and the student of public opinion.

LAURENCE HARRIS[1]

Regularities and Irregularities
in Monetary Economics

Note. Numbers in square brackets refer to items in the appended Bibliography.

A. INTRODUCTION

IN 1917 Pigou wrote that 'competent writers of all schools are . . . really in substantial agreement' regarding the influences on the demand for and supply of money [37]. Subsequent developments destroyed any such agreement, but more recently a similarly strong statement has been made by Milton Friedman: 'One of the chief reproaches directed at economics as an allegedly empirical science is that it can offer so few . . . fundamental regularities. The field of money is the chief example one can offer in rebuttal . . .' [16]. With respect to empirical work, this 'field of money' has been ploughed and reploughed many times in the past two decades. In this paper some major examples of this work are surveyed in an attempt to discover which 'fundamental regularities' have been unearthed and to evaluate their implications.[2]

In classifying various studies and clarifying some of the disputes in this field, it is useful to consider the questions: What is the general aim of empirical work in monetary economics? What questions are researchers trying to answer? A plausible

---

[1] Lecturer at the London School of Economics. This paper was written in 1967 when the author was Visiting Assistant Professor at the University of California, Berkeley. Responsibility for it is the author's, but his concern for such subjects owes much to Richard Sayers, Alan Day, Roger Alford, Vicky Chick, John Grant, and Stan Fischer.

[2] The main categories of studies in this area not covered in this survey are those that do not use United States data, are not based on time-series data, and are primarily concerned with the supply of money. These omissions are partly due to lack of space, and partly to the fact that the most lively and complicated controversies in empirical monetary economics are based on the studies considered here.

answer is that researchers are ultimately concerned with improving economic policy and with estimating the connexions between a policy instrument (e.g. bank reserves) and a variable which it is desired to influence (e.g. GNP or aggregate prices). In the remainder of this Introduction some points relevant to that aim are discussed.

Consider the following simple model of a goods market and money market:

Goods market
equilibrium
$$\Upsilon = C + I$$
$$= k + a\Upsilon + bM + cr + \mu_1 \qquad (1)$$

Demand function
for money
$$M^D = d\Upsilon + er + \mu_2 \qquad (2)$$

Supply function
for money
$$M^S = f\Upsilon + gr + hR + \mu_3 \qquad (3)$$

Money market
equilibrium
$$M^D = M^S = M \qquad (4)$$

The only unusual symbol is R, which represents the exogenously determined volume of bank reserves. The other symbols have their usual meanings and (except for r) are in real terms. The variables μ_1, μ_2, μ_3 are random disturbance terms. The only substantial differences between this and a textbook Keynesian model are that planned expenditure is a function of real balances (eq. (1)), and the money supply is endogenously determined (eq. (3))—the banking system adjusting its desired levels of assets and liabilities in response to variations in Υ, r, and R. The implication of the preceding paragraph is that research is concerned with such questions as: If open market operations change R, how much will Υ change?

There are two ways of answering such questions. This can be seen when one has noted that eqs. (1) to (4) may be combined to obtain a *reduced-form* equation in which Υ is expressed as a linear function of the only exogenous variable, R.[1] The first

---

[1] The reduced form of eqs. (1) to (4) expressing an equilibrium relationship between Υ and R can be derived as follows. We may solve eqs. (2), (3), and (4) for the equilibrium money stock:

$$M = \left(\frac{gd - fe}{g - e}\right)\Upsilon - \left(\frac{he}{g - e}\right)R + \left(\frac{g}{g - e}\right)\mu_2 - \left(\frac{e}{g - e}\right)\mu_3. \qquad (5)$$

way to answer is to estimate the parameters *a* to *k* by estimating each of the *structural equations* (1) to (4) of the model. Using these estimates of *a* to *k*, the parameters (*l, m*) of the reduced-form eq. (7) can then be calculated from the definitions of *l* and *m* in footnote 1, p. 86, and an estimate of the effect of *R* on *Y* is thereby obtained. Secondly, one could estimate *l* and *m*, the parameters of the reduced form, directly by regressing eq. (7) on data of *Y* and *R*.

Most empirical work in monetary economics has attempted to estimate structural equations. In particular, aggregate demand functions for money like eq. (2) have received much attention. More recently, however, a significant debate has centred on attempts to estimate reduced forms.

B. THE DEMAND FOR MONEY: THREE HYPOTHESES

In estimating the structural equations of the above model, one is not only estimating the values of their parameters (*a* to *k*) in order to quantify a relationship between *Y* and *R* (eq. (7)). In addition, such estimates are designed to test the empirical validity of the theories of behaviour represented by these equations. Empirical studies of the demand for money are a succession of attempts to evaluate competing theories'

We may also solve eqs. (2), (3), and (4) for the money market equilibrium relationship between *r* and *Y*:

$$r = \left(\frac{d-f}{g-e}\right)Y - \left(\frac{h}{g-e}\right)R + \left(\frac{1}{g-e}\right)\mu_2 - \left(\frac{1}{g-e}\right)\mu_3. \tag{6}$$

Substituting these expressions for *M* and *r* into eq. (1), we have an expression for *Y* in terms of the exogenous variables, which holds if the money and goods markets are in equilibrium. Carrying out this substitution and rearranging terms, we obtain:

$$Y = l + mR + v \tag{7}$$

where:

$$l = \left[\frac{e-g}{(1-a)(e-g)+d(bg+c)-f(be+c)}\right]k$$

$$m = \left[\frac{h(be+c)}{(1-a)(e-g)+d(bg+c)-f(be+c)}\right]$$

$$v = \left[\frac{(e-g)\mu_1 - (bg+c)\mu_2 + (be+c)\mu_3}{(1-a)(e-g)+d(bg+c)-f(be+c)}\right].$$

Alternatively, eq. (7) can be derived by the application of Cramer's Rule to eqs. (1) to (4).

correspondence to data. Each different theory will imply a different form for eq. (2). They differ either by postulating different explanatory variables, or else by postulating different values for the parameters (d, e). Most theoretical controversy has concentrated on which explanatory variables are most appropriate, rather than on the value of the parameters. The competing theories may be classified into three broad groups: 'Keynesian' liquidity-preference models; 'wealth' models; and 'permanent- (or expected-) income' models of the demand for money.

Chronologically, the *Keynesian* studies have priority. The earliest of these attempted to test very faithful versions of the Keynesian theory by estimating a relationship between 'idle balances' and interest rates [26] [42]. Since 'idle balances' are not observable, these writers adopted assumptions by which they could construct data on idle balances. The studies are successful in finding an empirical liquidity-preference relationship much like that postulated by Keynes, but are of doubtful importance, since the assumptions on which the data are based are of doubtful validity.[1] More significant, and more in line with modern liquidity-preference theory (see [24], p. 345), are those studies, such as C. F. Christ's [9] and H. A. Latané's [30] [31], which are concerned with the hypothesis that total money balances rather than 'idle' balances are interest-elastic. These studies estimate functions relating velocity of circulation (rather than demand for money) to interest rates, and have obtained results which give strong support to the liquidity-preference hypothesis.[2] However, apart from some generally

[1] Keynes's hypothesis was $pM^D = pM^{active} + pM^{idle} = pk'\Upsilon + L_2(r)$. (Since p is the absolute price level, pM^D, etc., is the demand for nominal balances, etc.). The method of estimating pM^{idle} is to assume that $pM^D = pM$ (i.e. the money market is in equilibrium) and to calculate historical data on $\dfrac{\Upsilon}{M}$. It is then assumed that, in that year when $\dfrac{\Upsilon}{M}$ is at its maximum, $pM = pM^{active}$: i.e. $pM^{idle} = 0$.

Thus, it is assumed that $\left(\dfrac{\Upsilon}{M}\right)_{max} = \dfrac{1}{k'}$ in that year, and it is further assumed that k' is the same in all subsequent years. On the basis of these assumptions, pM^{idle} is calculated from data on M, Υ, p, and the equation $pM^{idle} = pM - pk'\Upsilon$. Apart from the arbitrariness of the assumption that $pM^{idle} = 0$ when $\left(\dfrac{\Upsilon}{M}\right)_{max}$ is reached, the assumption that k' is constant conflicts with the hypothesis of W. Baumol [2] and J. Tobin [43] that pM^{active} increases less than proportionately in response to a rise in Υ.   [2] See Appendix, lines 1, 2, 3.

applicable criticisms, these studies, because the dependent variable is M/Y or Y/M, have the special weakness of constraining the income-elasticity of demand for money to be unity (see [41], p. 54). This renders the models different from Keynes's hypothesis (and different from W. Baumol's and J. Tobin's hypotheses of transactions- or active-balances [2], [43], which are the theoretical basis of a relationship between *total* balances and interest rates).

Several studies have estimated equations which are more sophisticated developments of Keynes's hypothesis.[1] A major post-Keynesian *theoretical* development of liquidity-preference was to recognize that wealth should be an argument of the demand function (see [24], p. 346, [44], [46]). Money is an asset. A utility-maximizing individual's optimum money holdings will depend on the price of money relative to other assets (determined by the rate of interest in liquidity-preference theory) and upon the budget constraint. Since money is an asset, the appropriate budget constraint is the volume of wealth—the size of the individual's asset portfolio.[2] A study of a Keynesian liquidity-preference equation extended to include a wealth variable is published by M. Bronfenbrenner and T. Mayer [4]. Their results, however, do not support any strong conclusions. When total balances are the dependent variable in their equation, the wealth variable is found to have a negative effect on desired cash balances (contrary to the implications of most theories), and this effect is not significantly different from zero; when 'idle balances' are the dependent variable, the wealth effect is positive, but the data on 'idle-balances' are subject to the same important objections as in footnote 1, p. 88, and so this result throws little light on 'true' behaviour relations.[3]

---

[1] Two particularly advanced studies are A. M. Khusro, 'Investigation of Liquidity Preference', *Yorkshire Bulletin of Economic and Social Research*, Jan. 1952, and R. J. Ball, 'Some Econometric Analysis of the Long-Term Rate of Interest in the United Kingdom, 1921–61', *The Manchester School of Economic and Social Studies*, Jan. 1965.

[2] Of course, the volume of wealth need not be treated as an exogenously determined constraint. It may be determined by saving decisions taken simultaneously with the decision on optimum money balances.

[3] A discussion of some controversial aspects of Bronfenbrenner and Mayer's study is found in [14], [5], and [33]. Their main results are presented in Appendix, lines 4, 5.

More significant contributions to our knowledge of the role of *wealth* in the demand for money have been made by K. Brunner and A. Meltzer. Meltzer's major contribution [32] obtains results which strongly support the following hypothesis: in choosing their desired level of cash balances, wealth owners are constrained by the volume of their wealth and take account of the yields available from assets other than money. That is, he finds that nearly all the observed variance in the money stock (using several definitions) is accounted for (using annual data 1900–58) by two explanatory variables—a financial market interest rate and a measure of wealth.[1] The strength of this result is increased by Meltzer's publication of the results of regressing equations representing alternative theories (in particular, theories like Keynes's, which postulate that income rather than wealth is, with interest rates, an explanatory variable). It is seen that, by common criteria (coefficient of determination, *t*-test for significance of regression coefficients, etc.), these theories fit the data less well than Meltzer's 'portfolio' theory of the demand for money. Meltzer's result is supported by a different test published by Brunner and Meltzer [6]. In [6] theoretical explanations of *velocity* rather than *money balances* are tested. The criterion by which the theories were evaluated was not how well the regression equation fitted past data, but how well the regression equation with parameters estimated from past data predicted future velocity. It was found than an equation with an interest rate, a ratio of income to wealth, and a measure of 'transitory' income[2] gave better predictions of velocity than did Keynesian or other models without a wealth variable.

The measure of wealth which is found by Brunner and Meltzer to be so successful is a measure of private-sector, non-human wealth. Theory suggests, however, that several alternative measures of wealth may be important influences in the demand for money (see [32]). Of major importance in recent monetary controversies have been Milton Friedman's arguments (see [16]) in favour of including human wealth[3] as an influence on

---

[1] See Appendix, line 6.
[2] See below, p. 91, n. 1, for an explanation of 'transitory' income.
[3] The capitalized value of the expected yield from the application of human skills.

the demand for money. The hypothesis that human wealth is an important component of the portfolio whose size influences the demand for money is difficult to test against existing data. An approximation of this theory, however, has been the subject of much empirical work. This approximation uses the concept of *permanent income*, which is a theoretical measure of the expected yield of all assets (including human wealth). Permanent income is itself a non-observable variable, but empirical studies in this field use a series of data which represents permanent income if permanent income at any one time is a weighted sum of past observed incomes (the weights declining exponentially as the observations decrease in recency).[1] The basic empirical study of the hypothesis that the demand for money (or velocity) is a function of permanent income is Friedman's in 1959 [18]. The demand function for money has as independent variables 'permanent income', population, and 'permanent prices' (a weighted sum of past observed prices), and a velocity equation, with similar arguments, is derived. From annual data (1869–1957) the parameters of these equations are estimated,[2] and by using these parameter estimates the ability of the equation to predict velocity is evaluated. It is found that when the observed values of the independent variables (constructed values in the case of 'permanent' variables) are used in the equation to generate a computed series of velocity data, the computed series on velocity closely approximates the series of

---

[1] See [17] and [18]. In any period actual income, as measured in the national income accounts, is the sum of permanent income and transitory income. It is postulated that these two components are uncorrelated. The 'permanent-income' data are constructed on the hypothesis that permanent income is based on individuals' expectations and these expectations are adjusted in response to differences between previous expectations and the actual outcome:

$$Y_t^e = Y_{t-1}^e + \lambda(Y_t - Y_{t-1}^e) \quad (0 < \lambda < 1), \tag{8}$$

where Y^e is the constructed measure of permanent income. (The theoretical concept of permanent income will be denoted by Y^P, whilst the empirical measure, 'permanent income', is denoted by Y^e.) Eq. (8) can be expanded to:

$$Y_t^e = \lambda[Y_t + (1-\lambda)Y_{t-1} + (1-\lambda)^2 Y_{t-2} + \ldots + (1-\lambda)^n Y_{t-n} + \ldots] \tag{9}$$

by substituting into eq. (8) the formulae $Y_{t-1}^e = Y_{t-2}^e + \lambda(Y_{t-1} - Y_{t-2}^e)$, etc. As can be seen from eq. (9), Y^e is a weighted average of past incomes, the weights declining exponentially. Actually, eqs. (8) and (9) are not exactly the same as Friedman's formulation. In particular, they neglect Friedman's allowance for growth. See [17], pp. 142–5.

[2] See Appendix, line 7.

actual historical velocity data. In particular, Friedman finds that his equation can account for the alleged historical phenomenon of a positive correlation between velocity and income during business cycles and a negative correlation in secular data.[1] He finds, moreover, that there is no 'very sensitive adjustment of cash balances to interest rates'.

The finding of a relationship between money balances and 'permanent-income' data has been corroborated by other studies. Meltzer [32] finds that Friedman's equation fits 1900 to 1958 data well, but he finds that the wealth hypothesis fits the data even better, and, discovering that the explanatory power of Friedman's equation is improved by including interest rates as an independent variable, he rejects Friedman's finding on the unimportance of interest rates. Similarly, Brunner and Meltzer [6] find that the inclusion of interest rates in the demand function for money improves the power of Friedman's theory in predicting velocity, but find that Friedman's theory is in any case better able to predict velocity than is a Keynesian theory or a 'naive' model (although, again, the wealth hypothesis gives more satisfactory predictions). Laidler [28] finds, by comparing regression results on four basic hypotheses, that 'permanent income' is a better explanatory variable for the demand of money than is either measured income (NNP) or non-human wealth (again, the permanent-income equation that Laidler tests includes an interest rate as an independent variable). Chow [8] obtains similar results: in an equation to explain the equilibrium money stock, 'permanent income' is a better explanatory variable than either non-human wealth or net national product.[2]

C. THE DEMAND FOR MONEY: COMPARING THE RESULTS

The studies surveyed in Section B give support to three different hypotheses, which are usually considered to be rivals. If different studies support different hypotheses, how can we choose between the hypotheses? In particular, what, in the light

[1] The existence of this phenomenon has been questioned. See, for example, Tobin [45].

[2] See Appendix, line 6 for Meltzer's results; line 10 for Laidler's results; and lines 8, 9 for Chow's results.

of empirical results, are the answers to the following questions: (*a*) Is there a relationship between the demand for money and some financial interest rate? (*b*) Is the more stable relationship between the demand for money and a measure of non-human wealth, or between the demand for money and Friedman's 'permanent-income' series? In this section these questions are examined by a more detailed comparison of the relevant studies.

On the question of whether or not there is a relationship between an interest rate and the demand for money the overwhelming finding of empirical studies is that there is. This is a matter of controversy only because Friedman's fundamental study [18] leads him to the strong conclusion that interest rates are not an important explanatory variable for secular or cyclical changes in the demand for money when 'permanent income' is an explanatory variable.[1] There are several possible reasons for the difference in findings. One of these concerns the definition of money. In Friedman's studies money is defined to include time deposits (and is often written as M_2), whereas Latané [30], [31], Bronfenbrenner, Mayer [4], and other writers who have estimated a significant relationship with interest rates define money as currency outside banks plus demand deposits adjusted (M_1).[2] This difference in the definition of money may account for the different findings on the interest-elasticity of the demand for money. Since time deposits in commercial banks bear interest at rates related to market rates of interest, a change in market rates may lead to a substantial desire to switch wealth out of M_1 balances and into time deposits, but a lesser movement out of M_2 balances into other assets. Hence, the volume of M_1 will fluctuate more sensitively in response to interest-rate changes than M_2. Johnson ([24], p. 355) suggests that this difference in the definition of money balances is the major source of difference between Friedman and Latané, and C. Christ [9] provides empirical support for that proposition.[3]

[1] He supports this finding elsewhere (see [21]). Other writers, however, do find a significant role for r in an equation with Y^e; see [6], [8], [28], and [32].

[2] $M_2 = M_1 +$ time deposits.

[3] By finding that (*a*) the behaviour of velocity can be well explained by a long-term rate of interest when defined as Y/M_1, but not when defined as Y/M_2, and (*b*) that there is significant substitution between demand deposits and time deposits in response to changes in the yield of time deposits. Meltzer [32] also finds support for the proposition that the use of M_2 partly obscures the full effects of r, and so does Tobin [45].

The difference in the definition of money balances, however, cannot be the only reason for Friedman's unusual results. For Meltzer ([32], p. 237) finds that, even when the money stock is defined as M_2, a long-term rate of interest enters significantly into a demand function with permanent income. This result is supported by Brunner and Meltzer ([6], p. 339), and by Laidler ([28], p. 62) and others. Another means of reconciling Friedman's results with those of other studies is to note the difference in statistical techniques. Friedman, instead of estimating a regression equation with permanent income and interest rates as explanatory variables (as do other researchers), estimates an equation with permanent income but not interest rates as an argument, and then regresses interest rates against the residuals from the permanent income equation. As has been suggested by Meltzer ([32], p. 235) and Teigen ([40], p. 56), this technique biases the results against the interest rate if there is any correlation between the 'permanent income' series and interest rates. This suggested explanation of Friedman's results has been given strong empirical support by Laidler [29]. If, as seems to be the case, Friedman's finding that interest rates are unimportant arises from this inferior estimation technique, then we must accept the findings of other studies that an interest rate is an important variable in the demand function for money.

Apart from the question of the importance of interest rates in the demand function, controversy exists over the relative merits of non-human wealth and 'permanent income' in an aggregate demand function for money. Although Friedman [18] demonstrates that a large percentage of the variations in velocity over a long period can be accounted for by a relationship with his data on permanent income, Meltzer [32] finds that the equation representing his (non-human) wealth hypothesis invariably fits the data better than does Friedman's permanent-income equation. Similarly, Brunner and Meltzer [6] find that an equation with wealth as an explanatory variable predicts velocity better than one with 'permanent income' as an explanatory variable (at least when money is defined as M_1). In addition, F. de-Leeuw's analysis of quarterly data since World War II [11] supports a measure of non-human wealth as an explanatory variable in the demand function for demand deposits, but finds that a quarterly reconstruction of Friedman's 'permanent income' data is a better explanatory variable for currency holdings, and it is difficult to choose between the variables as affecting time deposits. Chow [8] finds that 'permanent income' is a better explanatory variable than non-human wealth (using data on money defined as M_1); and Laidler [28] finds that, whereas non-human wealth performs better than 'permanent income' when the dependent variable is time deposits $(M_2 - M_1)$, 'permanent income' in general accounts for more of the variance in M_1 or M_2 than does non-human wealth.

The existence of these different results can be explained by differences in data, time periods, and the exact formulations of the models. One difference in data concerns the measures of wealth. Meltzer [32] uses a measure of wealth at the end of each year, whereas Chow [8] uses the mean of beginning-of-year wealth and end-of-year wealth. Since their data on money refers to the money stock at the middle of each year, Chow's measure of wealth may be more appropriate than Meltzer's (but the appropriateness of Chow's measure depends on the smoothness of changes in wealth during the year). One of deLeeuw's data [11] is a quarterly interpolation of end-of-year wealth figures and is used against quarterly averages of the money variable. DeLeeuw's data also differ from Meltzer's and Chow's by excluding from wealth the liabilities of state and local governments, instead of excluding only Federal debt. As a measure of the consolidated net wealth of the money-holding sector, deLeeuw's data are, therefore, better than those of Chow or Meltzer, since state and local governments' money balances (but not Federal balances) are included in the measures of the money stock.[1]

---

[1] This, however, raises two problems. Firstly, is the appropriate measure of wealth the consolidated net wealth of the sector whose demand for money is being studied, or (on the hypothesis that individuals view liabilities differently from assets, and their demand for money depends on their gross wealth) is a sector's unconsolidated gross wealth more appropriate (see Meltzer [32])? Secondly, it is plausible that local governments have objectives which are different from those of individuals and firms, and their demand for money is a function of different variables. Their inclusion in aggregate studies complicates the interpretation of results. More generally, it may be found fruitful to study disaggregated data, since the behaviour of firms and households may differ substantially. The studies surveyed here concentrate almost exclusively on aggregate data. Two recent studies of demand for money by households are [22] and [34].

Laidler's results on the relative merits of a wealth hypothesis cannot be traced to errors in the measurement of wealth, for he tests the hypothesis indirectly and without using data on wealth. In fact, his equation is based on two hypotheses— (*a*) Friedman's permanent-income theory of saving and consumption, and (*b*) the theory that the demand for money is a function of non-human wealth. Only if hypothesis (*a*) were 'true' would the analysis be a test of the wealth hypothesis.[1] In a different form, this problem of formulating equations so that they unambiguously test a single hypothesis is of major importance in choosing between the wealth hypothesis and the permanent income hypothesis of the demand for money. For the 'permanent-income' data are based on the hypothesis that permanent income is a function of past income, and an equation in which these data are used as a variable therefore comprises two hypotheses: the hypothesis that the demand for money is a function of permanent income, and the hypothesis on which the 'permanent-income' data are constructed. Some of the difficulties posed by this are further discussed in the following section.

The interpretation of the results on 'wealth versus permanent income' are further complicated by differences in the use of 'permanent-income' data and differences in the money-stock data. One important difference is that Chow deflates 'permanent income' by current prices rather than by following other writers and deflating by 'permanent prices'. There is apparently no theoretical justification for doing so. Another difference is that Laidler uses annual averages of Friedman's and Schwartz's quarterly money-stock series, whereas Meltzer and Chow use data on the money stock at mid year, but a comparison of

---

[1] Laidler's form of the wealth theory could be written as:

$$M_t^D = \phi\left[\sum_{i=-\infty}^{t}(1-\gamma)\,\Upsilon_i^P, \sum_{i=-\infty}^{t}(\Upsilon_i^T-C_i^T),\,r_t\right].$$

The first two terms within [   ], when added together, equal the current level of wealth (i.e. the sum of all past saving) if $\Upsilon^P + \Upsilon^T = net$ national product. The first term represents permanent saving (the difference between permanent consumption and permanent income), if permanent consumption is, as postulated, a constant proportion γ of Υ^P. The second term represents transitory saving (the difference between Υ^T and C^T, the non-permanent components of measured NNP). Assuming ϕ [   ] to be of the form: $\alpha_0 + \alpha_1 \sum (\quad)\Upsilon_i^P + \alpha_2 \sum (\quad) + \alpha_3 r_t$, Laidler obtains the equation for $M^D - M_{t-1}^D$ and, after making a further restrictive assumption, tests this equation.

Chow's results with results he obtained using the quarterly series indicates that this is not an important difference.

D. LAGGED VARIABLES, EXPECTATIONS, AND ADJUSTMENT HYPOTHESES

Most general theories of the demand for money postulate a relationship between desired (or portfolio-equilibrium) money holdings and a set of independent variables. Friedman's theory, for example, considers the relationship between permanent income and the money stock individuals desire to hold when their portfolios are in equilibrium. Those studies described in the last section which find a relationship between the money stock and, say, permanent income (or wealth and interest rates) interpret these findings as supporting the permanent-income hypothesis (or wealth hypothesis). Ignoring other difficulties for the time being, it should be noted that such an interpretation is valid only if the observed money stock is actually being held by wealth owners whose portfolios are in equilibrium at the time of observation. Clearly, in general, this cannot be assumed to be the case. Unless, after a change in the independent variable, money holdings are instantaneously adjusted to their desired level, there will generally be a discrepancy between the actual observed money stock and the desired, portfolio-equilibrium, money stock. That is, money holdings would respond with a lag to changes in the independent variable, and the actual observed money stock at any date would depend partly upon past values of the independent variable.

If it is the case that the demand for money is adjusted with a lag, then the evidence discussed above as supporting the permanent-income hypothesis is ambiguous. For the data on 'permanent income' are, in fact, a weighted average of past measured incomes (see p. 91, n. 1). A relationship between the money stock and this weighted average is consistent with the permanent-income hypothesis (if this average is a good approximation to permanent income), but it is also consistent with the hypothesis that desired money holdings depend upon current measured income and are adjusted with a lag.[1]

[1] Let M^* be equilibrium or 'long-run' desired money holdings. Suppose the demand function for money is such that

$$M_t^* = \beta Y_t. \tag{10}$$

H

Several studies, however, do estimate models based on the hypothesis that money holders adjust their holdings with a lag. In one part of his article Chow [8] tests some 'short-run' adjustment hypotheses. His basic 'long-run' hypothesis is that equilibrium-desired money holdings are a function of non-human wealth or permanent income. In the 'short-run', however, the actual money stock does not equal this desired stock. One theory is that it equals instead last period's actual money holdings plus a proportion of the difference between the equilibrium stock currently desired and the actual stock held last period.[1] Estimating the equations derived from this hypothesis, it is found that a high proportion of the variance of M_1 is accounted for. Moreover, the variance of M_1 is best explained by the hypothesis that A_t equals permanent income rather than non-human wealth. A second 'short-run' hypothesis postulates that,

At the beginning of any period, actual balances (M_{t-1}) may not equal balances desired for that period (M_t^*), and it is postulated that only a proportion (π) of $M_t^* - M_{t-1}$ is made up in any period:

$$M_t = M_{t-1} + \pi(M_t^* - M_{t-1}) \quad (0 < \pi < 1). \tag{11}$$

Expanding eq. (11):

$$M_t = \pi[M_t^* + (1-\pi)M_{t-1}^* + (1-\pi)^2 M_{t-2}^* + \ldots + (1-\pi)^n M_{t-n}^* + \ldots] \tag{12}$$

and substituting from eq. (10) into eq. (12):

$$M_t = \pi\beta[Y_t + (1-\pi)Y_{t-1} + (1-\pi)^2 Y_{t-2} + \ldots + (1-\pi)^n Y_{t-n} \ldots).] \tag{13}$$

Clearly, if $\lambda = \pi$, eq. (13) is the same as eq. (9), except that $\pi\beta \neq \lambda$. If the permanent-income hypothesis is $M_t = M^* = \beta Y_t^e$, then in combination with eq. (9) we obtain:

$$M_t = \lambda\beta[Y_t + (1-\lambda)Y_{t-1} + (1-\lambda)^2 Y_{t-2} + \ldots + (1-\lambda)^n Y_{t-n} + \ldots], \tag{13'}$$

which is indistinguishable from eq. (13). Support for this version of the permanent-income hypothesis, therefore, may equally well be interpreted as support for the simpler hypothesis from which eq. (13) was derived. Note that this criticism cannot be applied directly to published studies of the permanent-income hypothesis, for, in general, more complicated versions of the theory are regressed. For example, as seen above, it has been found that equations with both permanent income and (unlagged) interest rates perform well. If this were really because of a lagged relationship between money, current income, and interest rates, then the interest-rate variable should be lagged. But such equations still do not unambiguously support the permanent-income hypothesis, for they are generally not compared with equations which include lagged interest rates and which may be found to give better results.

[1] The first short-run hypothesis Chow tests is
'Long-run demand for money'

$$M_t^* = \alpha_0 + \alpha_1 A_t + \alpha_2 r_t \qquad A_t = Y^P \text{ or non-human wealth)} \tag{14}$$

'Short-run adjustment mechanism'

$$M_t = M_{t-1} + \pi(M_t^* - M_{t-1}) \tag{15}$$

in addition to the adjustment mechanism of the first hypothesis, money holdings in any period also depend upon saving in that period, and that saving is a function of current permanent income or current wealth. In the form in which this hypothesis is estimated, current income enters as an independent variable.[1] Chow estimates the equations of this hypothesis and finds that Y_t is a much more significant explanatory variable than A_t (as either 'permanent income' or wealth). This result is in accordance with his (second) short-run hypothesis, and he interprets it as supporting his hypotheses that permanent income is the best explanatory variable for long-run equilibrium money holdings, whilst, through saving's positive effect on disequilibrium balances (and the postulated negative effect of permanent income on saving), the effect of permanent income on disequilibrium balances is weakened.

This interpretation is, of course, open to the criticism that (as in the case of Laidler's conclusion on the role of wealth) the estimated equation incorporates the hypothesis that consumption depends upon permanent income as well as incorporating the demand-for-money hypothesis. Chow's conclusion would have been strengthened by estimating an equation in which saving enters directly as an independent variable. It should also be noted that the results of Chow's estimation of this equation are strongly consistent with the simple hypothesis that desired equilibrium money holdings depend upon current measured income and interest rates, and that there is a lag in the adjustment of money holdings to changes in these variables.[2] Hence

---

[1] The second short-run hypothesis is:

$$M_t^* = \alpha_0 + \alpha_1 A_t + \alpha_2 r_t \tag{14}$$

$$M_t = M_{t-1} + \pi(M_t^* - M_{t-1}) + \theta(Y_t - \gamma Y_t^P). \tag{16}$$

If γ is the ratio of consumption to permanent income, $(Y_t - \gamma Y_t^P)$ equals saving.

[2] Postulating that $A_t = Y_t^P$, eqs. (16) and (14) imply:

$$M_t = \pi\alpha_0 + \theta Y_t + (\pi\alpha_1 - \theta\gamma) Y_t^P + (1 - \pi)M_{t-1} + \pi\alpha_2 r_t. \tag{17}$$

Estimating eq. (17), Chow finds that $(\pi\alpha_1 - \theta\gamma)$ is not significantly different from zero, whereas all the other regression coefficients are significant. Thus, the data support the existence of an equation of the form:

$$M_t = \delta_0 + \delta_1 Y_t + \delta_2 M_{t-1} + \delta_3 r_t, \tag{18}$$

but this is the same as one version of the 'lagged-income hypothesis' of eqs. (10) and (11). Instead of eq. (10), let the hypothesis be:

$$M_t^* = \beta_0 + \beta_1 Y_t + \beta_2 r_t. \tag{10'}$$

Chow's result, contrary to his own interpretation, may be interpreted as supporting the view that a relationship between money holdings and 'permanent-income' data really represents a lagged relationship between the demand for money and current income.

DeLeeuw's paper [11] is concerned with the hypotheses that the demand for money is a lagged function of an interest rate and non-human wealth, or 'permanent income', or 'transitory income'. The results concerning the choice of explanatory variables are outlined above. In addition to those results, de-Leeuw finds convincing evidence that there are very long lags in the adjustment of money balances to their desired equilibrium levels.[1]

A particularly interesting study of lags in the demand function for money is that by Feige [15]. Its main advantage over the study of deLeeuw and others who test lagged or unlagged versions of the permanent-income hypothesis is that it does not use a constructed series of 'permanent-income' data as an explanatory variable. It was noted above that the existing series of 'permanent-income' data is constructed on the theory that permanent income is a weighted average of past incomes— the weights depending on λ, and, in all studies so far discussed, being based upon estimates of these weights made by Friedman in his work on the consumption function. Feige, instead, estimates a model which allows him to identify simultaneously the expectation coefficient (λ) and the adjustment coefficient (π). More specifically, Feige postulates that the following model describes aggregate demand for money:

$$M_t^* = \beta_0 + \beta_1 \Upsilon_t^e + \beta_2 r_t^e \qquad (19)$$

$$\Upsilon_t^e = \Upsilon_{t-1}^e + \lambda(\Upsilon_t - \Upsilon_{t-1}^e) \qquad (8)$$

Substituting from (10′) into (11) we obtain:

$$M_t = \pi\beta_0 + \pi\beta_1 \Upsilon_t + (1-\pi)M_{t-1} + \pi\beta_2 r_t, \qquad (13′)$$

which is empirically indistinguishable from eq. (18). Thus, Chow's finding of support for eq. (18) may be interpreted as supporting the theory represented by eqs. (10′) and (11), rather than eqs. (14) and (16).

[1] DeLeeuw finds that the most satisfactory estimate of $(1-\pi)$ ($= k$ in his notation) is approximately 0·9. This implies that only 0·1 of the difference between desired balances and actual beginning-of-quarter balances is adjusted within the quarter. This conclusion is roughly the same irrespective of the definition of money or the explanatory variables.

$$r_t^e = r_{t-1}^e + \rho(r_t - r_{t-1}^e) \tag{20}$$

$$M_t = M_{t-1} + \pi(M_t^* - M_{t-1}). \tag{11}$$

That is, desired equilibrium balances are a function of 'expected' income and 'expected' interest rates, these variables being based on hypotheses similar to the theoretical basis of Friedman's 'permanent income' data. Actual money balances are a lagged function of these variables. The reduced-form equation of a system which includes eqs. (19), (8), (20), (11) is then estimated in such a way as to identify the estimated values of λ, ρ, and π.

Since his estimate of π does not differ significantly from unity, Feige concludes that money holdings are adjusted to their long-run desired levels without a lag. Moreover, the estimated values of λ and ρ indicate whether expected income and expected interest rates, rather than current (measured) income and interest, are the relevant determinants of equilibrium money holdings.[1] Since ρ is found to be not significantly different from unity, but λ is, it is concluded that the demand for money is a function of current interest rates and expected income.

These conclusions strongly contradict the hypothesis, mentioned above, that successful tests of the permanent-income hypothesis using 'permanent-income' data may merely indicate a lagged relationship between current income and the demand for money. However, as Feige notes, the results do not give unqualified support to Friedman's permanent-income hypothesis either, for they are fully consistent with an alternative hypothesis and they are not consistent with one interpretation of Friedman's model. That is, Friedman's theory [16] is that the demand for money is a function of human and non-human wealth and the expected yields on assets alternative to money. A proxy for total wealth may be permanent income discounted at some rate. This discount rate may be the *expected* or 'permanent' (rather than current) yield on some marketable assets,[2] but, even if this is not the appropriate discount rate, expected yields should enter the demand function for money as an

---

[1] For if, say, $\lambda = 1$, then it can be seen from eq. (8) that $Y_t^e = Y_t$ (and similarly for r_t^e), and it may be concluded that Y_t is the relevant variable in the demand function for money.

[2] This is suggested by Meltzer [32], p. 234 footnote.

explanatory variable to account for the possibility of substituting between money and other assets.[1] Since Feige finds that expected interest rates do not enter the demand function for money, such a version of Friedman's hypothesis is not supported. However, an alternative theory, more Keynesian in nature, is consistent with Feige's results. The expected income generated by eq. (8) may be interpreted as being expectations of income in the period immediately following the calculation rather than as permanent income.[2] On this interpretation, Feige's results suggest that money is held for transactions purposes, and the demand for money is a function of the income expected next period (as an indicator of next period's transactions requirements) and of the current rate of interest (which 'reflects the relevant substitution possibilities confronting the holder of cash balances' [15]).[3]

A matter of some concern in the interpretation of these results is the difference between Feige's results (no lag in adjustment of balances, a significant role for expected income which is a function of past income) and deLeeuw's results (a long lag in adjustment of balances, plus some role for 'permanent income' which is functionally related to past income in the same way as Feige's income variable). One possible reason for the difference might be that Feige's estimates of λ in the expected income equations are different from those used by Friedman, from which deLeeuw calculates his 'permanent-income' series. That explanation, however, is untenable, for Feige's estimates of λ are remarkably similar to the value estimated by Friedman in his consumption function study and used

---

[1] According to Friedman's hypothesis in [16].

[2] Muth [35] has demonstrated that Y_t^e from eq. (8) is an optimal prediction of Y_{t+1} if the time series of Y_t has certain properties. He also examines the hypothesis that $Y_t^e = Y_t^p$.

[3] A study which has the same advantage as Feige's inasmuch as it does not use Friedman's estimates of Y^e, but instead uses Y data and a version of eq. (8), is Brillinger's and Hatanaka's [3]. Their study uses spectral analysis rather than the conventional methods of analysing time-series data. From the permanent income hypothesis they derive some of its implications for the behaviour of different spectra of the relevant variables' time series, and compare these with the behaviour of the spectra of the actual series. Their single-equation approach does not enable them to estimate the expectations and adjustment coefficients, λ, π, as does Feige. However, their results support some implications of a hypothesis based on our eqs. (8) and (11), and they also find a significant role for interest rates within the qermanent-income hypothesis.

by subsequent researchers in the monetary field.[1] A second possible reason for the difference is that the two authors do not use a common definition of money in their estimates. A third possible reason for the difference is that deLeeuw's or Feige's estimates of the coefficients of their equations may be biased.

The possibility of bias in the estimates is important. In deLeeuw's case the possibility is likely, since simultaneous-equation bias probably arises from the fact that deLeeuw does not specify a supply function as well as a demand function, and so does not use any two-stage computation method to estimate his equation. This omission may lead to biased estimates of the coefficients, for it is probably the case that, if the true complete model were known, some of the variables which deLeeuw treats as exogenous would be seen to be in fact endogenous (e.g. rate of interest). In Feige's case, although a supply function is specified, this supply function is undoubtedly an inaccurate representation of the world, and, since it does not allow that the supply of money may be dependent upon interest rates and expected income, specification error, similar to that of de-Leeuw's model, is introduced. Similar problems arising from the simultaneity of economic relations are important in the interpretation of the results of all the studies so far outlined. In the next section, these problems and some studies which attempt to solve them are discussed.

E. DEMAND AND SUPPLY FUNCTIONS

In testing hypotheses of the demand for money there are two different aspects of estimated equations which are important. Firstly, a theory may be supported merely by finding that a particular explanatory variable has a regression coefficient significantly different from zero. For example, the basic form of Brunner and Meltzer's wealth hypothesis would be supported merely by finding that an equation which accounts for a high proportion of the variance in M (i.e. has a high $\bar{R}^2$) has a significantly positive regression coefficient on wealth. Secondly, some theories can be supported only if the regression coefficient of an explanatory variable is estimated to be significantly within

[1] A possible source of difference is that deLeeuw uses a quarterly interpolation of Friedman's weights.

a certain range of values. For example, Friedman's hypothesis that money is a 'luxury' is only supported if the income elasticity of demand for money (the regression coefficient on income when logarithmic data are used in the estimates) is significantly greater than unity.[1] In monetary economics there are several cases where the value of a coefficient is important (as in models which involve the measurement of lags), and in such cases it is particularly important that the regression coefficients should be unbiased[2] estimates of the true behavioural coefficients.

Unfortunately, there are several possible sources of bias in the estimated equations of most of the studies of demand functions for money. One of the most important is simultaneous-equation bias. This results from estimating a demand function by the techniques of ordinary least-squares regression (OLS), for the coefficients estimated by OLS are unbiased only if the explanatory variables are uncorrelated with the random disturbance term. In general, this condition is not satisfied by the demand function for money. Explanatory variables are correlated with the random disturbance term because the explanatory variables are not truly exogenous but are themselves influenced by M^D.[3] One way to overcome this source of bias is to specify all the relationships and interdependencies of variables which one thinks affect the demand function, and to use an indirect method of estimating the demand function. In general, this involves specifying a supply function as well as a demand function for money, and estimating both the equations simultaneously by a method such as two-stage least squares (TSLS). An important

[1] So that a change in income leads to a more than proportional change in demand for money.

[2] For the strict definition of bias and unbiasedness see [27], pp. 50–52.

[3] The reason why the condition is not satisfied is that there is a two-way interaction between the dependent and independent variables. Consider eqs. (2), (3), and (4). An estimate of eq. (2) will be biased because M^D (and hence μ_2, which determines M^D) influences r and Y as well as vice versa. From eqs. (2), (3), and (4), we know that μ_2 influences *either r or Y* or both, for a change in μ_2 causes a shift in the demand curve, and the new equilibrium which is reached must involve either a change in Y (which would return the demand curve to its original position) or a change in r, or both. Conventional monetary theory postulates that the direct adjustment to the new equilibrium comes via a change in r, in which case there is clearly a relation between changes in μ_2 and changes in r. In addition, in our model there is an indirect effect from μ_2 to Y, for the change in r caused by the change in μ_2 leads, via eq. (1), to a change in Y. Thus, both r and Y are related to μ_2 and the estimates of the coefficients of eq. (2) will be biased.

study which uses this method is that by R. L. Teigen [40]. In his study the demand function is Keynesian, with current income and a current interest rate as arguments. The supply function is based on the hypothesis that the supply of money depends on bank reserves created by the Federal Reserve and the banks' desire for excess reserves, which, in turn, depends on the difference between the short-term interest rate and the authorities' discount rate. Using TSLS to estimate the model comprising these two equations (and an explanatory equation for income), Teigen is taking account of the simultaneous, inter-dependent relationship between r, M^D, and M^S, and eliminates this one source of simultaneous-equation bias.[1] His results indicate that his equations account for a high proportion of the variance in the stock of money. Moreover, the regression co-efficients, when compared with those obtained using OLS, suggest that some downward bias is involved in the use of OLS to estimate single equations. In Teigen's study it is important to have unbiased estimates of the regression coefficients, be-cause his demand hypothesis[2] is not merely that $M^D = eY + fr$, but also that the values of e and f fall within a certain range.

Brunner and Meltzer, too, have published TSLS estimates of a model which includes a demand function and a supply function for money [7]. The results support the findings of their earlier published studies. In particular, the coefficients esti-mated by this superior method confirm the earlier finding that the use of M_2 rather than M_1 obscures the full effects of interest-rate changes.[3] In addition, deLeeuw has published the results of simultaneous estimations of demand and supply equations as part of a uniquely extensive model of financial markets, which, in turn, is part of an aggregative econometric model of the U.S. economy [12]. The use of TSLS appears to have made little difference to the estimates of the regression coefficients. De-Leeuw is not really concerned with comparing the results for

[1] From prior knowledge, however, the model appears to be not fully specified, and unacknowledged interdependencies remain to cause bias. TSLS and related techniques are described in [25].

[2] Being based on the Baumol–Tobin theory of transactions balances [2] and [43].

[3] The study also includes OLS estimates and the authors conclude that the OLS and TSLS estimates of demand elasticities 'practically coincide' (implying, contrary to Teigen, that bias is unimportant). Nevertheless, comparative inspection of their OLS and TSLS estimates partially supports Teigen's finding that OLS estimates are lower than TSLS.

different hypotheses. The demand function he estimates is based on the theory that M^* is a function of r and Y^e, and that there is a short-run adjustment function (which is like eq. (11), except that π is not constant but depends upon a factor like gross income that acts as a short-run constraint on portfolio adjustments). In principle, the importance for this study of obtaining unbiased estimates of the coefficients arises because the model is directly oriented toward the making of policy.

Simultaneous-equation bias is not the only technical problem that arises in empirical work in monetary economics. Equally important is the identification problem. Those studies which estimate demand functions, of course, use data on *actual* money balances for the dependent variable. If we assume that actual money balances at any time represent a point of equilibrium between supply and demand, then it is clear that a change in money balances only represents a move along a demand curve if the change is caused solely by a shift in the supply curve. If we cannot assume that the changes are caused in that way, then we cannot assume that the estimated equation represents a demand curve.[1] This problem can be overcome only if we know the supply function; those studies which estimate a demand equation without specifying a supply function cannot claim to identify the resulting equation as a demand function,

---

[1] If the observations are, in fact, generated by shifts in the supply *and* demand curves, the observed relationship between money and the explanatory variables will not represent the true demand function. In the diagram the estimated demand function will be XX rather than any one of the true demand curves (D_1D_1, D_2D_2, D_3D_3).

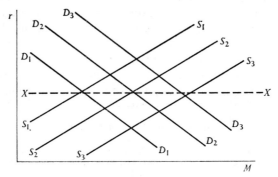

for the true supply function may be of a form which prevents identification.[1]

F. TESTED KNOWLEDGE OF MONETARY BEHAVIOUR

The preceding sections indicate that Friedman's assertion on the state of monetary economics and his claim that monetary behaviour demonstrates many regularities are rather controversial.[2] The only regularity on which there is substantial agreement is the existence of some relationship between the demand for money and some rate of interest. Even here, however, it should be noted that there is not complete agreement. Friedman denies the significance of such a relationship and, amongst those who strongly support the existence of such a relationship, there is disagreement as to *which* interest rate is the most important. Meltzer, Brunner and Meltzer, and Chow use a long rate of interest, whilst Bronfenbrenner and Mayer,

---

[1] Suppose that the true demand and supply functions are:

$$M^D = tY + ur + vW + \epsilon_1 \tag{21}$$

$$M^S = wY + xr + \epsilon_2. \tag{22}$$

We can multiply the demand equation and supply equation by the arbitrary constants θ_1, θ_2 respectively, and, assuming we are observing equilibrium positions ($M^D = M^S$), we may substitute M^D for M^S in eq. (22). Having carried out these operations, we may add the two equations to obtain:

$$M^D = \left(\frac{\theta_1 t + \theta_2 w}{\theta_1 + \theta_2}\right)Y + \left(\frac{\theta_1 u + \theta_2 x}{\theta_1 + \theta_2}\right)r + \left(\frac{\theta_1 v}{\theta_1 + \theta_2}\right)w + \left(\frac{\theta_1 \epsilon_1 + \theta_2 \epsilon_2}{\theta_1 + \theta_2}\right) \tag{23}$$

Now suppose that an econometric study finds that a linear relationship between M^D, Y, r, and W exists. There is no way of determining whether the regression coefficients of that linear relationship are the coefficients of the true demand equation (eq. (21)), or of the mongrel equation (eq. (23)). Of course, if the estimated equation had a zero regression coefficient on W, it could be interpreted as an estimate of eq. (22), for no mongrel equation can be formed which does not include W. Thus, whether a demand equation or a supply equation can be identified from an estimated equation depends on which variables enter the true demand and supply functions (and other factors), and, without specifying the supply function, we cannot know whether an estimated equation represents a demand function or a mongrel equation (see [25], Ch. 9 and [27], Ch. 3). An additional technical problem, not discussed in the text, is the problem of autocorrelation. The existence of autocorrelation causes two difficulties. First, it leads to overestimates of the significance of regression coefficients (for an example of this difficulty see [10]). Second, where an attempt is made to estimate adjustment lags, the length of lag is likely to be wrongly estimated (see [11]).

[2] Actually, the only example of a regularity which Friedman offers is a relationship between the money stock and the price level.

Laidler [28], and Teigen use a short rate. In an attempt to settle this issue, Laidler [29] finds some evidence to support the theory that the demand for money is better related to short than to long interest rates.

The finding of a regular relationship between an interest rate and the demand for money is in accordance with the implications of all portfolio theories of the demand for money. Another implication of such theories is that the demand for money depends on (is constrained by) the size of the portfolio. Several studies find evidence to support such an implication, inasmuch as a measure of wealth enters significantly into the estimated demand function. However, the question of whether the most significant constraint is a measure of non-human wealth, or is wealth defined to include human wealth (and approximated by 'permanent income'), is far from settled, despite the amount of energy recently devoted to this question. Some of the doubt is caused by the difficulty of interpreting the 'permanent-income' variable as equivalent to the theoretical concept of permanent income and, hence, as a proxy for wealth rather than a proxy for transactions needs.

It is clear, then, that we cannot be sure of the exact form of eq. (2). Thus, it is impossible to evaluate from the structural equations the reduced-form relationship between monetary policy and objective variables. This problem is even more intractable because so little is known about the supply function of money (eq. (3)) or about the parameter b in eq. (1).[1] To overcome such problems one could estimate a reduced form such as eq. (7) directly. A pioneering study taking this direction is that of Friedman and Meiselman [19], who, taking consumption as the endogenous variable to be explained, found a very stable relationship between this variable and the money stock. The study is important but has several weaknesses. In particular, it is illegitimate to draw from the results conclusions about the relative merits of Keynesian and other systems, as do Friedman and Meiselman, and the results themselves seem to depend upon the particular (controversial) definitions of the variables which Friedman and Meiselman employ. The significance of the study is more fully discussed in [1], [13], [20], and [23].

---

[1] The little that is known about b suggests that the real balance effect is very weak. (See [36], Note M; [38]; and [39].)

The claim that this survey has attempted to evaluate—that monetary behaviour demonstrates many regularities—is closely related to the proposition that 'money matters'. For, if it were found that there were no systematic relationship between other variables and the demand for or supply of money, then monetary policy would be a very weak instrument indeed.

The question Does monetary policy matter? has recently been a subject of considerable debate. This survey suggests that (at least when we look at U.S.A. data) the answer is Yes, for the empirical studies surveyed here all lead us to think that there are important systematic relationships between money and other economic variables. However, there is no such agreement on the question of *how* monetary policy affects the economy. Is it through a relationship between money and interest rates (and, if so, which rate)? a relationship between money and non-human wealth? or one between money and permanent income? The resolution of these questions is a necessary prerequisite for the maximum use of econometric results in the formulation of monetary policy.

BIBLIOGRAPHY

[1] A. ANDO and F. MODIGLIANI, 'The Relative Stability of Monetary Velocity and the Investment Multiplier', *American Economic Review*, Sept. 1965.

[2] W. J. BAUMOL, 'The Transactions Demand for Cash: An Inventory Theoretic Approach', *Quarterly Journal of Economics*, Nov. 1952.

[3] D. R. BRILLINGER and M. HATANAKA, 'A Permanent Income Hypothesis Relating to the Aggregate Demand for Money (An Application of Spectral and Moving Spectral Analysis)'; forthcoming.

[4] M. BRONFENBRENNER and T. MAYER, 'Liquidity Functions in the American Economy', *Econometrica*, Oct. 1960.

[5] —— ——, 'Rejoinder to Professor Eisner', *Econometrica*, July 1963.

[6] K. BRUNNER and A. H. MELTZER, 'Predicting Velocity: Implications for Theory and Policy', *Journal of Finance*, May 1963.

[7] —— ——, 'Some Further Investigations of Demand and Supply Functions for Money', *Journal of Finance*, May 1964.

[8] G. C. CHOW, 'On the Long-Run and Short-Run Demand for Money', *Journal of Political Economy*, Apr. 1966.

[9] C. F. CHRIST, 'Interest Rates and "Portfolio Selection" Among Liquid Assets in the U.S.', in C. F. Christ and others, *Measurement in Economics: studies . . . in memory of Yehuda Grunfeld*. Palo Alto, 1963.

[10] T. J. COURCHENE and H. T. SHAPIRO, 'The Demand for Money: A Note from the Time Series', *Jour. of Pol. Econ.*, Oct. 1964.

[11] F. deLeeuw, 'The Demand for Money—Speed of Adjustment, Interest Rates and Wealth', *Staff Economic Reports*, Board of Governors of the Federal Reserve System. Washington, 1965.

[12] —— 'A Model of Financial Behaviour', in J. S. Duesenberry, G. Fromm, L. R. Klein, and E. Kuh (eds.), *The Brookings Quarterly Econometric Model of the United States*. Chicago, 1965.

[13] M. DePrano and T. Mayer, 'Tests of the Relative Importance of Autonomous Expenditures and Money', *Am. Econ. Rev.*, Sept. 1965.

[14] R. Eisner, 'Another Look at Liquidity Preference', *Econometrica*, July 1963.

[15] E. L. Feige, 'Expectations and Adjustments in the Monetary Sector', paper delivered at the meetings of the American Economic Association, San Francisco, Dec. 1966.

[16] M. Friedman, 'The Quantity Theory of Money—A Restatement', in M. Friedman (ed.), *Studies in the Quantity Theory of Money*. Chicago, 1956.

[17] —— *A Theory of the Consumption Function*. Princeton, 1957.

[18] —— 'The Demand for Money: Some Theoretical and Empirical Results', *Jour. of Pol. Econ.*, Aug. 1959.

[19] —— and D. Meiselman, 'The Relative Stability of Monetary Velocity and the Investment Multiplier in the United States, 1897–1958', in Commission on Money and Credit: *Stabilization Policies*. Englewood Cliffs, N. J., 1963.

[20] —— —— 'Reply to Ando and Modigliani and to DePrano and Mayer', *Amer. Econ. Rev.*, Sept. 1965.

[21] —— A. J. Schwartz, *A Monetary History of the United States, 1867–1960*. Princeton, 1963.

[22] M. J. Hamburger, 'The Demand for Money by Households, Money Substitutes and Monetary Policy', *Jour. of Pol. Econ.*, Dec. 1966.

[23] D. Hester, 'Keynes and the Quantity Theory: Comment on Friedman and Meiselman CMC Paper', *Rev. of Economics and Statistics*, Nov. 1964.

[24] H. G. Johnson, 'Monetary Theory and Policy', *Amer. Econ. Rev.*, June 1962.

[25] J. Johnston, *Econometric Methods*. New York, 1963.

[26] A. Kisselgoff, 'Liquidity Preference of Large Manufacturing Corporations', *Econometrica*, Oct. 1945.

[27] L. R. Klein, *A Textbook of Econometrics*. Evanston, 1953.

[28] D. Laidler, 'Some Evidence on the Demand for Money', *Jour. of Pol. Econ.*, Feb. 1966.

[29] —— 'The Rate of Interest and the Demand for Money—Some Empirical Evidence', *Jour. of Pol. Econ.*, Dec. 1966.

[30] H. A. LATANÉ, 'Cash Balances and the Interest Rate—A Pragmatic Approach', *Rev. of Econ. and Stat.*, Nov. 1954.

[31] H. A. LATANÉ, 'Income Velocity and Interest Rates: A Pragmatic Approach', *Rev. of Econ. and Stat.*, Nov. 1960.

[32] A. H. MELTZER, 'The Demand for Money: The Evidence from the Time Series', *Jour. of Pol. Econ.*, June 1963.

[33] —— 'Yet Another Look at the Low Level Liquidity Trap', *Econometrica*, July 1963.

[34] B. MOTLEY, 'A Demand-For-Money Function for the Household Sector—Some Preliminary Findings', *Journal of Finance*, Sept. 1967.

[35] J. F. MUTH, 'Optimal Properties of Exponentially Weighted Forecasts', *Jour. of American Statistical Association*, June 1960.

[36] D. PATINKIN, *Money, Interest, and Prices*, 2nd edn. New York, 1965.

[37] A. C. PIGOU, 'The Value of Money', *Quart. Jour. of Econ.*, 1917.

[38] C. SCHOTTA, Jr., 'The Real Balance Effect in the United States, 1947–1963', *Jour. of Finance*, Dec. 1964.

[39] —— 'The Real Balance Effect in the U.S.: Some Further Empirical Evidence', paper delivered at the meeting of the American Statistical Association, Los Angeles, Aug. 1966.

[40] R. L. TEIGEN, 'Demand and Supply Functions for Money in the United States: Some Structural Estimates', *Econometrica*, Oct. 1964.

[41] —— 'The Demand for and Supply of Money', in W. L. Smith and R. L. Teigen, *Readings in Money, National Income, and Stabilization Policy*. Homewood, Ill., 1965.

[42] J. TOBIN, 'Liquidity Preference and Monetary Policy', *Rev. of Econ. and Stat.*, Feb. 1947.

[43] —— 'The Interest-Elasticity of Transactions Demand for Cash', *Rev. Econ. and Stat.*, Aug. 1956.

[44] —— 'Liquidity Preference as Behavior Toward Risk', *Rev. Econ. Stud.*, Feb. 1958.

[45] —— 'The Monetary Interpretation of History', *Am. Econ. Rev.*, June 1965.

[46] R. TURVEY, *Interest Rates and Asset Prices*. London, 1960.

APPENDIX

Line	Study	Regression equation	R^2	Notes
1	Latané [30]	$\dfrac{M_1}{Y} = 0\cdot8\,\dfrac{1}{r_L}+0\cdot1$	0·76	Annual data 1919–52.
2	Latané [31]	$\dfrac{Y}{M_1} = 0\cdot77r_L+0\cdot38$	Not available	Annual data 1909–58.
3	Christ [9]	$\dfrac{M_1}{Y} = \dfrac{0\cdot72}{(0\cdot05)}\,\dfrac{1}{r_L}+0\cdot13$	0·76	Annual data 1892–1959.

APPENDIX (*cont.*)

Line	Study	Regression equation	R^2	Notes
4	Bronfenbrenner and Mayer [4]	$M_1^{\text{idle}} = -4{\cdot}21 - 0{\cdot}53 r_S$ $\quad (0{\cdot}048)\ (0{\cdot}203)$ $\quad + 1{\cdot}68 W + 0{\cdot}54 M_1^{\text{idle}}(t-1)$ $\quad (0{\cdot}891)\ (0{\cdot}132)$	$0{\cdot}81$	Annual data 1919–56. M^{idle} calculations described in n. 1, p. 88. $W =$ real national wealth (including government-owned wealth). All variables in logarithms.
5	Bronfenbrenner and Mayer [4]	$M_1 = 0{\cdot}11 - 0{\cdot}093 r_S$ $\quad (0{\cdot}003)\ (0{\cdot}013)$ $\quad - 0{\cdot}115 W + 0{\cdot}722 M_1(t-1)$ $\quad (0{\cdot}088)\ (0{\cdot}058)$ $\quad + 0{\cdot}344\ Y'$ $\quad (0{\cdot}086)$	$0{\cdot}99$	Notes from line 4 applicable. $Y' =$ real private-sector GNP.
6	Meltzer [32]	$M_1 = -1{\cdot}48 - 0{\cdot}949 r_L$ $\quad \{21{\cdot}8\}$ $\quad + 1{\cdot}11 W$ $\quad \{42{\cdot}0\}$	$0{\cdot}98$	Annual data 1900–58. $W =$ real private-sector wealth ($= W$ as used in line 4, minus government assets, plus private holdings of government liabilities). All variables in logarithms.
7	Friedman [18]	$M_2 = 0{\cdot}003 \left(\dfrac{y^P}{N} \right)^{1{\cdot}81} N P^P$	Not available	Annual data 1869–1957. $P^P =$ permanent prices. $y^P = \dfrac{Y^P}{P^P}$. $N =$ Population. Data on Y^P is the constructed series Y^e (constructed from data on Y with weights from [17]).
8	Chow [8]	$M_1 = -0{\cdot}139 + 1{\cdot}055 Y^P$ $\quad (0{\cdot}010)$ $\quad - 0{\cdot}745 r_L$ $\quad (0{\cdot}045)$	$0{\cdot}996$	Annual data 1897–1958 (excluding 1917–19; 1941–5). This equation is Chow's 'long-run hypothesis'. All variables in logarithms.
9	Chow [8]	$M_1 = 0{\cdot}307 + 0{\cdot}062 Y^P$ $\quad (0{\cdot}143)$ $\quad + 0{\cdot}327 Y - 0{\cdot}333 r_L$ $\quad (0{\cdot}094)\ (0{\cdot}060)$ $\quad + 0{\cdot}588\ \text{M}\ (t-1)$ $\quad (0{\cdot}067)$	$0{\cdot}999$	Annual data 1897–1958 (excluding 1917–19; 1941–5). This equation is Chow's 'short-run hypothesis'. All variables in logarithms.
10	Laidler [28]	$M_2(t) - M_2(t-1) =$ $0{\cdot}622\ (Y^P(t) - Y^P(t-1)$ $\quad (0{\cdot}097)$ $\quad - 7{\cdot}197\ (r_S(t) - r_S(t-1))$ $\quad (1{\cdot}946)$	Not available	Annual data 1892–1960 (excluding 1917–18; 1941–5).

NOTES:

$r_L =$ long-term interest rate.
$r_S =$ short-term interest rate.
$M_1 =$ currency + demand deposits adjusted.
$M_2 = M_1 +$ time deposits.
( ) underneath regression coefficient = standard error.
{ } underneath regression coefficient = t ratio.

HARRY G. JOHNSON

Problems of Balance-of-Payments Adjustment in the Modern World[1]

T HE subject of this paper is problems of adjustment of imbalances of international payments so as to restore equilibrium within the present international monetary system. In the United Kingdom such problems appear as the problem of overcoming chronic balance-of-payments deficits, in order to permit pursuit of full employment, economic growth, and social justice objectives—a problem shared for the past nine years by the United States, where, however, the task appears as remedying a chronic deficit to permit fuller pursuit of both domestic objectives—full employment, growth, and the Great Society—and foreign economic-policy objectives—defence of the Western world, a liberal world-trade and payments system, and economic assistance to the less developed countries. This, however, is to see the problem from the point of view of a particular deficit country, assigned that role by circumstances, in an international system in which others have surpluses. From the point of view of the international system, balance-of-payments adjustments concern both deficit and surplus countries; and from the point of view of anyone interested in the system —as we shall be in this paper—the problem is what mechanisms, if any, exist for adjustment of balance-of-payments disequilibria, how automatic and effective they are, and how efficient.

The present international monetary system is the product in part of careful planning for post-war reconstruction of the international monetary system. That planning was carried on primarily by expert economists and officials of the United States and the United Kingdom, and was based on a desire to construct a system free of the defects of the gold exchange standard that

---

[1] Being the substance of a public lecture delivered at the University of Kent on 10 Feb. 1967.

grew up during the later nineteenth century and especially after World War I, and that broke down so disastrously in the great liquidity crisis and scramble for gold of the 1930s. In larger part, however, the present system is the outcome of certain failures in the planners' analysis, together with post-war trends they probably could not have predicted, which have directed the evolution of the system into something far different from the one intended.

The planned system, embodied in the International Monetary Fund, was designed to secure the benefits of the old gold-standard system as a framework for a liberal world trading order, by re-establishing a régime of fixed exchange rates. The planners sought, however, to guard against the major problem of the inter-war gold standard—shortage of the basic international reserve, gold, the supply of which is determined by the profitability of production rather than by international needs —by providing additional international liquidity in the form of drawing rights—international credit money—and establishing a residual power to increase the world price of gold in all currencies by international agreement. At the same time, the new system was designed to meet a major problem of the gold standard, as revealed in the 1930s, viz. the probability that countries would be unable to maintain a fixed exchange rate by making adequately substantial and rapid adjustments to the domestic economy consistent with maintaining domestic policy objectives; this was done by providing for changes in exchange rates, in an internationally agreed and orderly fashion, whenever there arose a situation of fundamental disequilibrium. (The experience of the 1930s had shown that if countries sought to use their sovereign right to change the exchange rate, guided only by national self-interest, exercise of freedom by each would frustrate the achievement of adjustment.) Two other provisions were also aimed at preventing recurrence of the problems of the 1930s: national freedom to control short-term capital movements (to prevent the recurrence of the hot money movements of the 1930s); and provisions to discriminate collectively against 'scarce currency' countries—i.e. countries with such persistent surpluses that their currencies became scarce in the International Monetary Fund and could no longer be drawn therefrom (these provisions derived from the view that chronic U.S.

surpluses had aggravated the gold shortage in the inter-war period, especially in the 1930s).

In summary, the plan was designed to provide additional liquidity to supplement gold; an agreed adjustment mechanism through exchange-rate change in case of fundamental disequilibrium; protection against losses of reserves occasioned by short-term capital movements prompted by the loss of confidence in a currency; and a means of disciplining surplus countries that failed to play an adequate part in the process of international adjustment.

In the light of these objectives and the careful work that went into designing the international monetary system, it is ironic in the extreme that a group of thirty-two international monetary experts, meeting at Princeton and Bellagio successively in 1964, could agree on describing the three major problems of the present international monetary system as the liquidity problem, the adjustment problem, and the confidence problem—the three major problems of the inter-war system.[1] The only difference between the problems of the 1930s, which the designers of the IMF thought they had solved, and the problems facing the system today is that, whereas a fourth problem of the 1930s appeared to be to discipline the surplus countries, the fourth major problem at present appears to many experts to be to discipline the deficit countries—specifically the United States, and, to a lesser extent, Great Britain.

What went wrong with post-war planning? From the point of view of fundamental principle—as was, indeed, pointed out at the time, in criticism of the IMF Charter, by the great American expert, John H. Williams, of Harvard University and the Federal Reserve Bank of New York—the experts made the politically imperative but economically erroneous assumption that all national currencies could be treated as equal. They disregarded the 'key currency principle'—the principle that in fact only one or a few currencies will be useful enough in international commerce and finance to play an active international role, the others being useful domestically but not serving as an international means of payment, such payments being effected

---

[1] F. Machlup and B. Malkiel, *International Monetary Arrangements: the Problem of Choice. Report on the Deliberations of an International Study Group of 32 Economists.* International Finance Section, Princeton University, 1964.

instead by conversion of the domestic currency into a key currency. In consequence of this principle, it did not make sense to create an international credit supplement to gold by pooling all national currencies. This point has been recognized *de facto* in the development of the General Arrangements to Borrow as a supplement to the IMF; these arrangements provide for special loans to the IMF from the ten major industrial countries, the most important countries in world trade and payments.

In view of subsequent developments, the planners failed—only in part for explicable reasons—to foresee the effects on the evolution of the international monetary system of the failure to fund the sterling balances, and, much more important, of the prolonged dollar shortage and the emergence of the cold war. The failure to fund the sterling balances left an important part of the world relying on holdings of a chronically weak currency —the pound sterling—as its prime international reserve. The prolonged period of dollar shortage, and the dominance in the Western world economy of the United States as the supplier of industrial goods and capital for European economic reconstruction and world economic development, led—without any conscious planning or forethought—to growing use of the dollar as an international reserve money in substitution both for gold —the supply of which increasingly fell short of the growth of demand for international reserves—and for expansion of the IMF quotas. Thus, the international monetary system of the 1920s—a gold exchange standard system in which a national currency (in the modern system, two national currencies) served the function of an international reserve money—re-emerged, and with it the problems of liquidity and confidence.

To be more specific, the problem of providing for international liquidity arises because the country whose currency serves as international reserve money provides supplementary liquidity to the rest of the world by running a deficit, financed partly by gold losses and partly by increased holdings of its currency in the reserves of other countries; this involves a weakening of its own international liquidity position, because its liabilities rise while its gold reserves fall; the weakening of its international liquidity position undermines confidence in the reliability of its currency as a reserve money, and sets limits to the extent to which the use of its currency as an international reserve money can be allowed to expand. Hence some more reliable, internationally guaranteed and acceptable, credit substitute must eventually be found. This is the point at which the international monetary system arrived some years back.

The problem of confidence arises because a loss of confidence in a reserve currency could prompt the central banks that hold it to demand conversion of their holdings into non-existent gold, thereby wiping out international liquidity and precipitating a liquidity crisis, as happened in the 1930s. It is important to observe that such a crisis could be precipitated only by the actions of national central banks, *not* by the actions of private speculators in generating international short-term capital movements, since only central banks are allowed to convert the reserve currencies (pounds and dollars) into gold at the central banks of the reserve currency countries. This is important because both financial journalists and academic economists frequently write as if the private speculators dominate the system, and display much righteous—but quite irrelevant—indignation in fulminating against 'the gnomes of Zurich'. However, central banks are unfortunately too often prone to be the mental slaves of private financial opinion, and their reserve-holding choices may be swayed by the sentiments prompting private capital flights; in this connexion it is relevant to observe that, contrary to the assumptions of the planners of the IMF, it has proved impossible to develop controls over private short-term capital movements, even with exchange controls, because such movements may be effected through the leads and lags of trade credit, as well as in other unpoliceable ways.

There is, however, one way in which private speculators could precipitate an international liquidity crisis, a way whose potential seriousness became evident in 1966–7. This is through substitution, not of one currency for another, but of gold for national currencies, by purchase of gold in the London gold market for private hoarding by citizens whose governments allow them to hold gold. Since 1960 an agreement by central banks to stabilize the price of gold in the London market has provided such private hoarders an indirect means of access to the gold reserves of the United States and the other participating countries. Until 1966 the stabilization operations resulted in net acquisitions of monetary gold by the participants; but in that year an increase in private hoarding demand combined with the cessation of Russian gold sales to produce a small decrease in monetary gold reserves.[1] A massive loss of private confidence in paper money and flight into gold could precipitate a liquidity crisis either by forcing the central banks to disgorge massive amounts of gold in the stabilization operations, or by causing them to lose their nerve and discontinue the stabilization arrangements, allowing the price of gold in London to rise as it did in 1960. Here again, however, a crisis could only occur if the central banks themselves joined in the scramble for gold; their existing gold stocks are more than ample to stave off any likely private flight into gold if they determine to do so.

Our concern here, however, is with the adjustment problem. In this connexion, the trend of post-war international monetary developments has steadily eroded the major new instrument of adjustment imposed by the planners of the IMF on the old gold exchange standard system, the possibility of changing a country's exchange rate in the case of 'fundamental disequilibrium'. The reserve currency countries naturally—though not necessarily rightly—take the view that their obligations to their creditors make it morally inconceivable for them to devalue. (This view is not necessarily right, because these countries are paying their creditors interest for the privilege of holding barren gold on their behalf, and these interest payments might be held to be fair compensation against the devaluation risk; and further, it is not beyond the wit of man to devise a compensation scheme for creditors losing by devaluation.) The major non-reserve-currency countries have become equally attached to the maintenance of their exchange rates, or at least averse to appreciating their currencies; this attitude springs in part from remembered resentment of the immediate post-war lecturing of the European countries by the United States on the need for devaluation, and more directly from the belief that the deficit reserve-currency countries and not they should bear the burden of adjustment of the deficit–surplus position. In addition to these exchange rate rigidities, the power to discriminate against chronic-surplus countries under the scarce-currency clause of

---

[1] The liberalization of gold-holding by private citizens effected by France early in 1967 can be interpreted as a policy change designed to expose the United States gold reserves to attack by private French gold hoarders.

the IMF has atrophied through disuse: no one was prepared to invoke that clause against the United States in the immediate post-war period, when the alternative was for the United States to provide loans and grants for reconstruction. As a result of the growth of the dollar as an international reserve currency, the boot is now on the other foot: for the acceptance of a country's currency as an international reserve currency means that it can rely on automatic financing of any deficits it chooses to incur, initially because its currency will be automatically accepted, and eventually because other countries will realize that they cannot afford to precipitate a world liquidity crisis by attempting to cash it for gold. In these circumstances the problem of exercising discipline in the international monetary system to force adjustment of deficit–surplus situations may be formulated thus: How can the non-reserve-currency countries exercise their ability to demand gold instead of reserve currency, and bring the threat of using this ability to bear, so as to make the reserve-currency country behave responsibly and run deficits no larger than those required to finance stable expansion of the world economy without actually risking precipitating the collapse of the system? Obviously, it becomes necessary to resort to psychological warfare; such warfare began with the chronic United States deficit in 1958, and became especially intense as domestic expansion and the escalation of the war in Vietnam worsened the United States deficit after 1965.

The international monetary system has therefore become *de facto* a gold exchange standard, a system of fixed rates of currency exchange supported by reserves in the form of gold, dollars, and sterling, and borrowing rights at the International Monetary Fund—not to speak of a host of supplementary *ad hoc* unconditional and conditional borrowing arrangements among the major nations. The fact that it is a gold exchange and not a pure gold standard underlies the problems of liquidity and confidence, and is responsible for the felt need for a new international reserve asset to be created by an international credit operation. Our concern, however, is with the adjustment mechanisms available for the preservation or restoration of international equilibrium in the present system of fixed international rates of exchange.

Under the classical gold-standard system of maintaining

fixed exchange rates on the basis of gold reserve holdings, the mechanism of adjustment to balance-of-payments disequilibria —at least in principle—worked automatically. A country in deficit would lose gold reserves. In consequence, either automatically as a result of a decrease in the supply of money, or deliberately as a result of the central bank's efforts to protect its reserves, interest rates would rise. In the short run the rise in interest rates would attract a short-term capital inflow or reduce the short-term capital outflow, while in the longer run it would deflate income and employment and ultimately the level of wages and prices, so enabling the country eventually to balance its balance of payments consistently with full employment. Conversely, the surplus country would gain reserves, interest rates would fall, in the short run capital would flow out (or flow in less rapidly), and in the long run an inflation of wages and prices would restore equilibrium.

This mechanism of adjustment relies on an intervening stage of deflation-induced unemployment in the deficit country and of wage–price inflation in the surplus country. In contemporary circumstances, however, deficit countries are reluctant to accept unemployment on the requisite scale, in view of the obligations their governments have adopted to maintain full employment and promote economic growth. Equally, surplus countries are averse to accepting wage and price inflation, in view of the policy obligation to maintain price stability and avoid inflation. As it happens, the chronic-deficit countries—the United States and the United Kingdom—had an inter-war economic history that renders their present governments particularly sensitive to the problem of unemployment, while the chronic-surplus countries of the past decade—the Continental European countries, and especially Germany—had an inter-war experience, specifically a post-World War I experience, of the disruptive effects of inflation that has left their policy-makers hypersensitive to this problem.

This does not mean that the classical gold-standard mechanism of adjustment has not been at work in the present international monetary system. The persistent stagnation of the U.S. economy from 1958 to 1964 and the recurrent stop phases of Britain's stop-go policies, on the one hand, and the substantial wage and price inflation that has taken place on the Continent, on the other hand, are evidence to the contrary. The important point, however, is that these equilibrating adjustments have occurred contrary to the announced policy objectives of the countries concerned; in the case of the deficit countries because their balance-of-payments situations, together with the moral pressure of the surplus countries, have forced them to adopt domestically distasteful policies, and in the case of the surplus countries because they have been unable to contain by policy the monetary inflationary pressures impinging on them through their balances of payments. Because it works through the reluctance or inability of national economic policies to achieve fully their stated domestic policy objectives, the contemporary adjustment mechanism may appropriately be described as 'the mechanism of reluctant adjustment'. This characteristic of the adjustment mechanism has important implications, the discussion of which is deferred to a later stage in this paper.

Abstracting from the fact that some elements of a mechanism of adjustment are at work, however reluctantly on the part of the governments concerned, and assuming as a first approximation that governments are successful in maintaining full employment and restraining price inflation, what alternative methods of adjustment are available?

At this point it is necessary to distinguish sharply between two quite different types of policy, which are generally confused in the official literature and pronouncements on the problem, either because the officials themselves are confused or because they hope to confuse the public into not realizing what is going on. The two policies distinguished may be termed real adjustment policies, and balance-of-payments financing policies. Real adjustment policies comprehend all policies that are self-liquidating, in the sense that they will gradually restore a relationship between domestic and foreign wage–price levels that will permit balance-of-payments equilibrium to be achieved consistently with the termination of the policy. Financing policies, a term which is used more broadly here than by some writers on the subject, include all policies of operating on items in the balance of payments by government actions to ensure that the country's international transactions will balance without loss of reserves (or, more loosely, policies which seek to reduce the loss of reserves by this means). Such policies are effective only so long as they are maintained, and are a means of disguising international disequilibria rather than adjusting them. To put the point more positively, they are a way of preserving disequilibrium by suppressing the consequences of disequilibrium for the country's international reserve position. Resort to such policies, on the assumption that they will be required only temporarily, obviously implies that the disequilibrium will resolve itself in a given time. This, in turn, implies that there is an adjustment mechanism at work behind the scenes; but, as has already been argued, the available mechanism is one of reluctant adjustment, so that the use of financing policies assumes that this mechanism, in spite of itself, will work reasonably expeditiously.

It is immediately apparent—almost, but not quite, as a tautology—that the balance-of-payments policies to which governments in both deficit and surplus countries have resorted in the face of international disequilibria in the past decade or so have been financing policies, even though they have usually been described as balance-of-payments adjustment policies. Such financing policies include a tremendous variety of balance-of-payments measures, ranging from direct international lending and borrowing of reserves through more indirect borrowing, like the issue of Roosa bonds, and the negotiation of the prepayment for defence-equipment deliveries to Germany resorted to by the United States in 1961–2, to such matters as the tying of foreign aid and defence spending, special subsidies to exports and tariff surcharges on imports, financial and fiscal devices to encourage capital inflows or discourage capital outflows, such as 'operation twist', the interest-equalization tax, the 'voluntary' restraint programmes on portfolio and direct foreign investment in the United States, and changes in corporate taxation in the United Kingdom designed to discourage overseas investment.

Three general comments can be made about measures of this kind, beyond the observation that they are financing policies and not adjustment policies. First, even as financing policies some of them are of very doubtful real value, though they may nevertheless create considerable nuisance, for the reason that they can be avoided by adroit substitution. Consider the homely example of the tourist allowance: one of the main consequences of cutting it has been a splurge of advertisement offering package holidays designed to maximize holiday per tourist pound by exploiting the possibility of classifying part of the cost as domestic expenditure. The possibility of avoiding controls is particularly great where the attempt is to regulate foreign spending through control of particular types of financing of expenditure, as with aid-tying and overseas investment financing. Second, and a related point, the use of control methods of these kinds inevitably entails considerable economic inefficiency, because the degrees of restriction applied to different kinds of purchases from abroad, and of encouragement given to different kinds of sales abroad, will inevitably differ widely from one kind of transaction to another. Thus, to take the same homely example of the tourist allowance, one can stay in England and drink all the French wine and eat all the French cheese one can stomach, but one is not allowed to go to France and do the same thing. Again, consider the wide differences between the rate of exchange for ordinary transactions, the rate for buying dollars to invest in dollar securities, and the rate for buying foreign exchange to invest in Mediterranean real estate, created by current control policy. It is possible, however, to distinguish between more and less desirable types of control: for example, if a country already has substantial restrictions on imports, it would be better advised to subsidize exports than to impose still further import restrictions.

The third, and most fundamental point, concerns the purpose of it all. The argument for a fixed-rate system, particularly as contrasted with the alternative of a floating-rate or even an adjustable-peg system of the kind the IMF was intended to provide, must be that it promotes a liberal international economic system, in which goods and capital—if not labour—can move around freely in search of maximum profits, with a minimum of discrimination according to national origin or destination. Once the principle is accepted that interferences with the flows of goods and capital are justified by the need to maintain the existing fixed exchange rates, means have been exchanged for ends, and ends turned into means, with the result that the system has lost its purpose.

Financing policies have been exemplified in the foregoing argument by various kinds of government intervention in international trade and payments. But the same description applies to a policy method of reconciling domestic full employment with balance in the international accounts that has been analysed in detail by international monetary theorists; it has been to a significant extent the basis of U.S. balance-of-payments policy in recent years, and it superficially appears to be thoroughly consistent with the principles of a liberal international economic system. This is the method of the so-called 'fiscal-monetary policy mix'.

In the traditional theory of international monetary adjustment, as refined into a theory of international economic policy in the immediate post-war period, a country with the two policy objectives of domestic full employment and equilibrium in its balance of payments needs two policy instruments to be able to achieve them—(1) macro-economic policy, fiscal and/or monetary policy, to control the over-all level of effective demand and keep it at full-employment level; and (2) control of the exchange rate or the domestic price level, so that the country's price level relative to those of other countries can be so fixed as to balance the balance of payments at a full-employment level of output. With exchange-rate adjustment ruled out by the conventions of the present international monetary system, and adjustment of the domestic price level level ruled out by the desire to maintain full employment, it appears that a country committed to the present international monetary system is short of one of the two policy instruments it needs to achieve its objectives.

This apparent dilemma, however, has been resolved by recognition, first, that capital is internationally mobile in response to interest-rate differentials between national capital markets, and second, that expansion (or contraction) of the level of aggregate demand by monetary policy and by fiscal policy respectively have contrasting effects on the prevailing level of interest rates, and therefore on capital movements and on the capital account and over-all balance of the balance of payments. Specifically, a country facing domestic unemployment and a payments deficit can remedy both by combining fiscal expansion with (in normal cases) monetary contraction. The expansion of aggregate demand by itself, while raising employment, will tend to worsen the balance of payments by increasing imports and possibly diverting exports to the home market. But the tightening effect on domestic interest rates of increased government expenditures or reduced taxes, financed by sales of government debt, reinforced to the extent necessary by monetary contraction, can be made to attract sufficient capital inflow, or deter sufficient capital outflow, to over-compensate these effects and balance the over-all international accounts.

It thus appears that by choosing a proper fiscal-monetary policy mix a country can secure the two objectives of internal and external balance, and do so by relying entirely on accepted general methods of control over aggregate demand, without the need for resorting to questionable methods of direct intervention in international trade and payments.

The appearance of orthodoxy, however, is illusory—perhaps, more accurately, it should be said that the use of orthodox tools in this manner does not ensure that the results will be more satisfactory from the point of view of economic welfare analysis than would the results of controls, say, on international capital movements. Rather, the reverse can be demonstrated. The reason is that, under the fiscal-monetary-mix policy, the levels of domestic investment and saving (and therefore the rate of economic growth) are adjusted by the mix policy to what is consistent with the level of the domestic interest rate required to match the country's capital outflow or inflow to the current-account surplus or deficit determined beforehand by its international competitiveness or lack of it. Any excess of domestic saving over domestic investment in excess of the predetermined capital outflow has to be absorbed by the budget deficit financed by the issue of public debt, and conversely. Thus, the economy is forced to save more (or less) and invest less (or more) than it would do in the absence of the balance-of-payments constraint. If, on the contrary, controls were used to confine capital movements to what the current account would allow, the ratio of domestic investment and saving could be allowed to attain a natural equilibrium at an unconstrained interest rate, without the need to frustrate private investment, saving, or consumption decisions by forcing them into conformity with a balance-of-payments-determined interest rate.

It must be pointed out, however, that the superiority of controls over orthodox methods of regulating capital movements in this case is a result of the acceptance of the current-account position at the given exchange rate as the determinant of the amount of capital inflow or outflow the country can safely afford. There is, of course, no reason why the pattern of international capital movements so determined should be optimal from the world economy's point of view; that is, there is no reason to assume that a deficit country will make more productive use of the capital brought in by its deficit than the surplus country from which the capital comes would have made of it.

Apart from these considerations of economic welfare and efficiency, the important point to note is that the aim of the fiscal-monetary-mix policy is precisely to tailor the size of the capital inflow or outflow to the predetermined size of the current-account deficit or surplus so that there is no reserve loss. In other words, its purpose is to finance the deficit, not to adjust the price level of the economy relative to those of other economies so as to remove the deficit.

Moreover, in the context of an international system rather than of a single country in such a system, the fiscal-monetary-mix solution may encounter the difficulty of inconsistencies between the policies of the various countries, and of controversy over which country, if any, shall control the one degree of policy freedom that the system affords. The points here are, first, that the analysis just presented assumes that other countries keep their monetary and fiscal policies constant while the country considered alters its fiscal-monetary mix. But the others are not bound to maintain their own policies unaltered, and unless they wish to co-operate they may make it impossible for the first country to achieve international balance (e.g. they may raise their interest rates to offset any increase in its interest rate). Second, since when all countries but one have achieved international balance the remaining one must also be in balance, there is one degree of freedom in the system. One country, and one alone, can determine its fiscal or its monetary policy by extraneous criteria. Naturally, all countries will want to claim the degree of freedom for themselves, or, alternatively, will have their own ideas of how it should be used for international objectives.

This has been a rather lengthy discussion of financing policies. Are there any real adjustment policies available to a deficit country, on a fixed exchange rate, that is unwilling to deflate demand and employment enough to deflate domestic prices (and possibly wages) according to the classical principles of balance-of-payments adjustment? There are, indeed, plenty of spurious candidates for the task, spurious in the sense that they will not work unless something is added to them that their advocates generally fail to specify, and probably would reject if they recognized the necessity of adding it. Thus, for example, the unthinking tendency to recommend measures to increase productivity overlooks the fact that increased productivity tends to be absorbed in higher incomes, so that this remedy for international uncompetitiveness requires supplementation by deflation or by an effective policy of wage stops and forced reduction of prices. Again, the popular recommendation in the United States to cut foreign aid, and in this country to cut overseas defence expenditures, could bring only temporary balance-of-payments relief, unless—as is never explicitly argued—the resources thus freed were left unemployed as a means of exerting deflationary pressure on wages and prices.

The only course of action to which the governments of the deficit countries—the United Kingdom and the United States —have resorted that ranks as a real adjustment policy is incomes policy, which in the United States has taken the much milder form of wage–price guidelines policy. If one accepts the usual assumption that the best that such a policy can do is to maintain price stability on the average—and it is doubtful that it can do much better than that, since a complete wage freeze cannot be maintained for long without destroying collective bargaining and generating serious inequities—it is obvious that even if successful it can serve as an adjustment mechanism only in certain special circumstances. Specifically, it can only work to adjust the relative prices of the deficit country's products downwards in relation to other countries' prices if prices elsewhere are rising. This implies, incidentally, that the world as a whole will be typically undergoing an inflation of prices, on the average. Moreover, the speed of international adjustment, given a successful incomes policy in the deficit country (which most probably will require the maintenance of a margin of unemployment), will be determined by the rate of inflation that occurs or is allowed to occur in the surplus countries. In practice, it is likely that incomes policy will be variably successful and that adjustment by this means will be interrupted by outbursts of price increases in the deficit country. Finally, it should be remarked that incomes policy is by nature an adjustment policy that can be applied only in deficit countries, and thus is asymmetrical: it is extremely difficult to imagine a surplus country setting out deliberately to increase its rate of inflation in order to promote adjustment to international equilibrium.

In conclusion, let us return to the main theme, that international adjustment in the present international monetary system is a process of reluctant adjustment, dependent, on the one hand, on the failure of the surplus countries to prevent the monetary implications of their surpluses from leading to wage and price inflation; and, on the other hand, on the failure of the deficit countries to maintain as full employment as they would like, and possibly on their success in implementing an incomes policy. An adjustment process dependent on these policy imponderables is certain to be both uncertain and slow. One can, in fact, discern a long cycle in the process of international adjustment since World War II, consisting first of the prolonged period of dollar shortage, from 1945 to 1957, and then of a prolonged period of dollar glut, from 1958 until the present, with the end not yet clearly in sight. One is led to hypothesize that the adjustment process works so slowly that it necessarily imparts a relatively inflationary character to the economies of the surplus countries and a relatively deflationary character to the economies of the deficit countries, through socio-economic processes which are difficult to reverse; and that consequently the adjustment of international disequilibrium is bound to overshoot the mark, necessarily giving rise to an oscillatory process of adjustment characterized by long phases of chronic surplus or deficit.

The length of these phases constitutes a serious problem for intelligent balance-of-payments policy-making, for two reasons. First, it is substantially longer than the lives of most elected governments, and still longer than the six months to two years horizon that dependence on popular election imposes on political party leaders. Thus there is a mismatching of the time-dimension of the problem with the time-perspective of those responsible for policy decisions, which inevitably creates strong incentives to adopt expedients and palliatives. This tendency has been particularly marked in the formation of policies to deal with the chronic U.S. deficit. Second, the cumulated total of surpluses and deficits over such a long period requires an amount of financing far in excess of what reserve-holding central banking on traditional lines is equipped to manage. Central banks are by institutional nature equipped to cope with short-run imbalances expected to be relatively speedily reversed, not to provide for massive long-term international borrowing and lending. Hence, when international imbalances are serious and sustained long enough to require such massive long-term financing, as they have been and are likely to continue to be under the present international monetary system, the policy-makers are driven by force of circumstances to relieve the impossible pressure on their central banks by resorting to other forms of balance-of-payments financing. The result of these two factors together, as previously noted, is the cumulation of interferences with the free international flow of goods and capital, which cumulation raises the fundamental question of the ultimate purpose of maintaining the system of fixed exchange rates. If the system is to be retained—which appears indubitable—it is highly desirable that the time-dimension of the adjustment problem should be appreciated by politicians and public opinion, and that some technique should be developed for providing massive long-term balance-of-payments lending from surplus to deficit countries.

Postscript

This paper went to press before the devaluation of sterling on 18 November 1967. It is too early yet to pass judgement on the question of whether world financial opinion will interpret the circumstances of that devaluation as confirming the necessity of strict adherence to exchange rate rigidity on the lines analysed above, or will instead interpret it as demonstrating the possibility of orderly correction of fundamental disequilibria by appropriate exchange rate changes implemented by international co-operation, as envisaged by the planners of Bretton Woods. It is greatly to be hoped that the latter view will in time prevail.

E. P. NEUFELD

The Relative Growth of Commercial Banks

THE decline in the size of commercial banking systems relative to other financial intermediaries has attracted considerable attention among monetary economists, perhaps more than any other single institutional change. Emphasis on the similarities between financial claims issued by banks and those issued by non-bank financial intermediaries has influenced discussion on the theory of the demand for money, which in turn has raised the matter of the effectiveness of economic stabilization techniques oriented toward controlling the supply of money. However, we wish to direct attention mainly to explaining the relative decline of commercial banks over long periods of time, excluding changes over the business cycle. We intend to do this by confining our discussion to the experience of the Canadian banking system, that is, the Canadian 'chartered' banks. But since the experience of the Canadian chartered banks, as we shall presently show, has been very similar to that of the commercial banks of the United States, it is quite probable that similar fundamental forces have been at work in the two countries, and other countries as well. For this reason some of the findings outlined in this paper may have general relevance.

A word of caution. The statistics used are deficient in many ways and much desirable statistical data simply are not available. We have tried to avoid depending on statistical analysis more than the quality of the data seemed to justify, and all the numbers used should be regarded as approximations. We are interested primarily in dominant trends.

What lies behind the growth of financial intermediaries? The principal function of any capital market is to accumulate the funds of surplus spending units, to distribute those funds, and to facilitate the change in ownership of the financial claims that the process inevitably creates.[1] The transfer of funds to deficit spending units can be effected in two ways. It can be effected directly, as when ultimate lenders purchase the financial claims or liability instruments of ultimate borrowers (primary securities), in which case the role of the capital market institution is essentially that of a broker; and it can be effected indirectly, as when ultimate lenders purchase the financial claims of financial intermediaries (indirect debt or claims), who in turn purchase the direct claims of ultimate borrowers and also the indirect claims of other financial intermediaries. The growth of financial intermediaries will depend on the extent to which indirect financing can be substituted for direct financing.

Why should such substitution take place? It seems that there are really only two important reasons for it, economies of scale and product differentiation. Economies of scale undoubtedly appear on both the accumulation and distribution sides of the intermediation process. For many individual savers it would be exceedingly expensive in terms of time, and perhaps even in direct outlay of funds, to invest their savings only in primary securities. For the ultimate borrowers there are undoubtedly cost advantages in selling a large block of securities to a few financial intermediaries rather than to many small individual savers. Financial intermediation, therefore, is one route by which productivity increases may be realized in the transfer of funds.

So a certain degree of financial intermediation, that is, the existence of some financial intermediaries, can be explained simply by economies of scale. But an additional degree of intermediation can be explained by product differentiation in the form of the new range of indirect financial claims that intermediation introduces—claims varying in risk, net monetary yield, associated non-monetary services, denomination, transferability, ease of acquisition and storage, and in the division of income from them between capital gains and interest. Intermediation probably also makes possible the introduction of new direct claims, for financial intermediaries may be prepared and

[1] We follow the terminology used in J. G. Gurley and E. S. Shaw, *Money in a Theory of Finance*, The Brookings Institution, Jan. 1960.

in a position to buy direct claims that direct lenders are not prepared to buy.

So it seems sensible to view the secular growth of financial intermediaries in general and of particular financial intermediaries as depending on their success in (a) exploiting their economies-of-scale advantages over direct financing, (b) innovating in the creation of new indirect financial claims, (c) innovating in the provision of new forms of credit (i.e. in being prepared to accept new direct financial claims from ultimate borrowers), and (d) innovating in administrative procedures associated with transferring funds from lenders to borrowers. If a particular financial intermediary grows less quickly or more quickly than others, we should expect to find the reasons for this among the aforementioned factors—reasons rooted in legislative restrictions, institutional practices, and entrepreneurial innovation.

From the point of view of financial intermediation, commercial banks fulfil the same general function as other financial intermediaries—they transfer funds from surplus spenders to deficit spenders. As such, they are in a position to exploit economies-of-scale advantages over direct financing. If they were thought to suffer from externally imposed disadvantages in this activity it would have to be because of legal constraints on such things as branch banking. Also, if they were thought to suffer from external disadvantages in the provision of new financial claims to the public or new forms of credit to borrowers, it would have to be because of legal restrictions on their borrowing and lending activities, such as interest-rate ceilings.

But what is the significance for the growth of the commercial banks of their liability instrument—the bank deposit—being accepted generally as a medium of exchange? To the extent that commercial bank deposits provide the major part of the nation's medium of exchange, the banks are able to finance the purchase of revenue-earning assets by issuing deposits sufficient for satisfying the transactions demand for money. If the banks issued instruments held only for media-of-exchange purposes, if they retained their share of the total 'market' for media of exchange, and if the ratio of media of exchange to output did not change over time, then, obviously, satisfying the demand for media of exchange would permit them to grow at the same rate as Gross National Product. Further, because they issue financial claims that are readily accepted as media of exchange, they must endure external controls that limit the long-term growth of such media of exchange to—in the above instance—the rate of growth of GNP. If the objective of the external controllers is price stability, the relevant rate would be growth of real GNP. The question that needs to be answered is whether the banks' long-term growth rate suffers because monetary controls must be imposed on them. The answer seems to be 'no', for controls on the rate of growth of media of exchange do not necessarily imply restriction of the rate of growth of financial claims held for other than media-of-exchange purposes. To be specific, if banks increased the attractiveness of their deposits as an asset to hold through, say, appropriate interest rate, insurance, and non-monetary service incentives, thereby inducing a shift of deposits from transactions to savings balances, it would be necessary for the central banking authorities to increase cash reserves at an increased rate—assuming they retained their original price-level objectives. So quantitative monetary controls by themselves should not inhibit the long-term growth of commercial banks. The introduction of competing forms of media of exchange would of course do so.

If the above analysis is correct, then it should also be the case that a sudden expansion of bank cash, without any change in the character (i.e. relative attractiveness) of bank deposits, will not lead to a permanent increase in the size of commercial banks relative to other financial intermediaries. One would expect a sudden expansion of bank cash to be followed by a sudden expansion of bank loans, investments, and deposits, as banks individually seek to maximize profits (since each bank has to assume that it has no control over market interest rates) and by a decline in interest rates of all kinds, including bank-loan and savings-deposit rates. The public's holdings of bank deposits for non-transactions purposes will now be excessive. They will tend to restore equilibrium (which may take some time) through purchases of current output and real and financial assets, with possible further (although temporary) declines in interest rates and increases in prices and money incomes, thus accelerating the growth of non-bank financial intermediaries.

As long as bank deposits continue to retain public confidence as media of exchange, this process will not drain cash from the banks (apart from the *normal* increase in note circulation) and so will not reverse the earlier expansion in bank assets. When the process is complete, there is no obvious reason to believe that the ratio of bank to non-bank financing will have changed. This is principally because there seems to be no reason why the structure of interest rates, and specifically the position of bank deposit and loan rates within that structure, would have changed; and because we assume that the public has retained confidence in bank deposits as media of exchange; and finally, because we assume there has been no other change in the character of bank deposits.

The experience of the Canadian banking system in the periods influenced by First and Second World War financing support these conclusions concerning the long-term impact on the relative size of the banks of a large expansion of cash reserves. In both periods the relative size of the banking system increased noticeably during war-time monetary expansion, and in both instances this relative increase proved to be transitory, for it was followed by an increase in the size of non-bank financial intermediaries, with the result that the banks soon resumed their long-term decline in relative size (see Figure 1).

We may now examine the extent of the long-term decline in the relative size of the chartered banks, and the reasons for it. The ratio of commercial bank assets to total financial intermediary assets for Canada and the United States in selected years over approximately one century is shown in Table 1. The similarity between the two banking systems with respect to both their relative size and their relative decline is striking. In 1880, for example, Canadian chartered bank assets amounted to 56 per cent. of total Canadian financial intermediary assets, while United States commercial bank assets amounted to 59 per cent. of total United States financial intermediary assets. The two systems were still virtually identical in relative size eighty-three years later, both having undergone about the same relative decline in size. Thus, in 1963, after both banking systems had been subjected to a great variety of, and not always identical, external influences (economic and political or legal), the Canadian

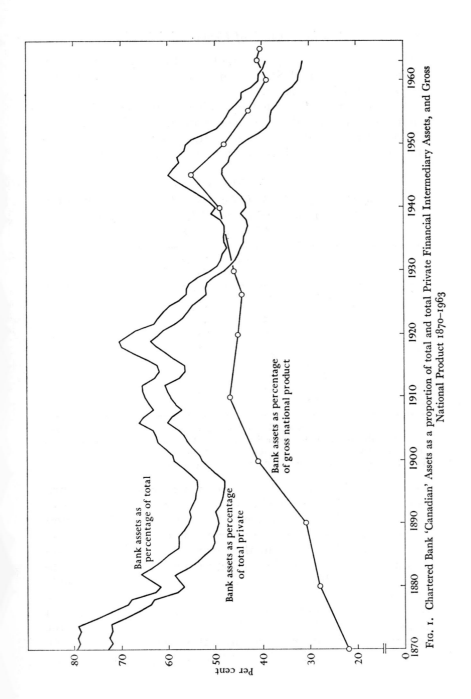

Bank assets as
percentage of total

Bank assets as percentage
of total private

Bank assets as percentage
of gross national product

FIG. 1. Chartered Bank 'Canadian' Assets as a proportion of total and total Private Financial Intermediary Assets, and Gross National Product 1870–1963

sytem accounted for 31 per cent. of total financial intermediary assets and the United States commercial banking system for 32 per cent. of such assets.

A further point indicated by Table 1 (and for Canada by Figure 1 as well) is that the decline in the relative size of the Canadian and United States banking systems was not an uninterrupted process. There was a period that began before the

TABLE I

Assets of Commercial Banks in Canada and the United States as a Proportion of Total Financial Intermediary Assets Selected Years: 1860–1963

	Canada %	United States %
1860	N/A	67
1870	73	N/A
1880	56	59
1900	53	63
1912	60	64
1929	51	50
1939	45	40
1948	47	41
1960	32	33
1963	31	32

SOURCES: Statistics relating to United States financial intermediary assets were made available to me by Professor Raymond W. Goldsmith, for which I am most grateful. Canadian data were compiled by the author from a variety of sources. The details of these estimates have not yet been published.

First World War when both increased in relative size; then both systems declined again in relative size until the 1930s——the United States system more than the Canadian, almost certainly because of the complete absence of bankruptcies among Canadian banks in the 1930s; then both systems increased in relative size, beginning in the late 1930s and continuing on into the years of the Second World War; and finally both systems entered into their most recent period of relative decline at the end of the Second World War. Obviously, it is not sufficient to consider only the long-term relative decline of the banking system; one must consider also the reasons for the long swings in their relative size, and this we propose to do later.

In examining possible reasons for the long-term decline of the Canadian chartered banks, we shall discuss the possible impact of legislative restraints, changes in the demand for money, and the nature of the non-bank financial intermediaries that accounted for the relative decline of the banks. We begin with legislative restraints.

The view has frequently been expressed that legislative restraints imposed on banks but not on their near competitors are partially responsible for the decline in the relative size of commercial banking systems. In the case of the Canadian chartered banks, the restrictions that might be thought to have had this effect are the interest-rate ceiling on bank loans, the cash reserve ratio, restrictions on the issue of bank notes and long-term debt, and prohibition against lending on the security of real estate. Until 1858 most lenders in British North America were subjected to the 6 per cent. interest-rate ceiling of the usury laws. In that year in the Province of Canada the usury laws were abolished for non-bank lenders, and the ceiling for the banks was raised to 7 per cent.[1] However, in 1866[2] those banks were relieved of all penalties for usury, and were merely denied legal processes for collecting interest in excess of 7 per cent. Not until 1934[3] were penalties for lending in excess of 7 per cent. reintroduced, so from 1866 to that year the banks in effect faced no effective interest-rate restrictions. In 1944 the ceiling was reduced to 6 per cent.,[4] but until the early 1950s interest rates generally were so low that this ceiling imposed no handicap on the banks. Indeed, when the banks first began to make government-guaranteed National Housing Act mortgage loans in 1954 they soon bid the rate down to 5 per cent. It seems highly probable, therefore, that over the long period from 1866 to 1955, when chartered bank assets as a proportion of total financial intermediary assets declined from about 75 per cent. to 39 per cent., interest-rate restrictions did not impede the growth of the banks. Even after that the restriction was less severe than might appear, because of the banks' effective rate of about 11 per cent. or 12 per cent. on their growing consumer

---

[1] *Statutes of Province of Canada*, 1858, c. 85. For a useful review of the interest-rate restrictions on the banks see Royal Bank of Canada, *Economic Trends and Topics*, June 1966.

[2] *Statutes of Province of Canada*, 1866, c. 10.

[3] *Statutes of Canada*, 1934, c. 24.   [4] Ibid., 1944, c. 30.

instalment loans and the apparent tendency of the banks to request compensating balances from loan customers.

The chartered banks' cash-reserve ratio requirements also cannot explain the long-term decline in their relative size. Until 1934 the chartered banks were not required to maintain any specific cash ratio. The matter itself arose as early as 1870, but the banks successfully opposed introduction of such a ratio. The only requirement was that, until 1880, of any cash they did hold, at least one-third should be in the form of Dominion notes. This was changed to 40 per cent. in 1880. A 5 per cent. legal cash ratio was introduced in 1934, which was hardly a deterrent to growth, since the banks voluntarily held about 10 per cent. In 1954 the legal cash ratio was raised to 8 per cent. and the banks brought their actual ratios *down* to that figure, where it has remained. The only further question is whether the banks were unjustifiably discriminated against because they were required to hold non-interest-earning cash reserves while other institutions were not. It seems that they were not. In the absence of cash ratio requirements, the banks would probably continue to hold the same cash (i.e. Bank of Canada notes and deposits with the Bank of Canada). When the legal ratio was 5 per cent., they held additional cash in that form. It appears, therefore, that their opportunity cost in the matter is zero.

There were statutory restrictions on the note issue of the chartered banks, and beginning in 1866 there was a competing government note issue. But as things worked out, these restrictions mattered little as far as the banks were concerned. The Provincial Notes Act of 1866 in effect became the Dominion Notes Act of 1870, thereby permanently ending the chartered banks' monopoly of the note issue. However, the way the Dominion Notes Act was utilized left the banks with about 85 per cent. of the public's demand for notes from 1870 to 1934,[1] and what they lost was essentially the demand for notes of under $5, a part of the note issue that was expensive to service and troublesome in time of financial crisis.

As for legal restrictions on the banks' ability to issue notes, these too were not important until 1934. The new Dominion banking legislation of 1870 and 1871 continued the already

[1] Estimated by the writer, using statistics in C. A. Curtis, *Statistical Contributions to Canadian Economic History*, Macmillan, Toronto, 1931.

familiar requirement that a bank's note circulation must not exceed its paid-up capital. But the legislation provided that a bank's capital could be increased by a mere vote of share-holders, government approval no longer being necessary. In addition to that, until 1900 the actual ratio of notes to paid-up capital of the banks seldom exceeded 65 per cent. during the seasonal peak of note circulation (October).[1] When the ratio did begin to cause worry in 1908, it having begun to exceed 90 per cent. in spite of rapid increases in bank capital, the Bank Act was changed to permit additional seasonal note circulation. By the Finance Act of 1914 and the Finance Act of 1923 the chartered banks acquired easy access to Dominion notes, which in turn could be deposited as backing for further chartered bank note circulation during the crop-moving season. However, after 1934 the chartered banks were deprived of their note issuing privileges. The extent to which this affected the growth of the banks will be considered later.

Finally, there is the matter of the statutory restrictions on the issue of long-term debt and the making of mortgage loans by the banks. Actually, the Bank Act over the years did not mention such borrowing, either to allow it or disallow it, but to this writer's knowledge the banks did not attempt to develop that field, even during the years when no legal cash ratio require-ment existed. As for mortgage lending, the banks had been prohibited from engaging in it since the granting of the first bank charters in the 1820s.[2] This prohibition, however, reflected the views of the bankers themselves. Minor exceptions to the prohibition began to appear after the 1930s, but even in 1954 the chartered banks opposed the Bank Act amendment giving them the power to make government-guaranteed National Housing Act mortgage loans. We shall see later that the failure of the banks to issue debentures and to enter the mortgage lending field probably impeded their growth to some extent, but at the moment it is sufficient merely to note that since they did not want such powers, the impediment can hardly be regarded as a legal one.

In general, when these legislative restrictions are examined

[1] Estimated, using statistics in Curtis, op. cit.
[2] Cf. E. P. Neufeld (ed.), *Money and Banking in Canada*, McClelland and Stewart, Toronto, 1964, p. 60.

within their institutional context it is difficult to see how they could have been responsible for the decline in the relative size of the chartered banks up to the 1930s. After that, loss of the note circulation had a small effect on them, as we shall see, but the interest-rate restriction was probably not felt until after 1955.

We must now consider the demand for money. Why did chartered bank assets grow much more quickly than GNP until 1910, and why, generally speaking, did they not do so thereafter (see Figure 1)? The chartered banks have been the principal suppliers of Canada's media of exchange since they began to issue notes in the 1820s. They enjoyed a legal monopoly of the note issue for some years prior to 1866, and, as we have seen, an effective one until 1934; and ever since the 1850s, when bank deposits seem to have begun to be used increasingly as media of exchange, they have been in a strategic position to supply this form of money. Therefore any change in the nation's demand for media of exchange is likely to affect the growth rate of the chartered banks.

Table 2 shows the ratios of Canadian money supply (two definitions) and of bank assets to Gross National Product. All three ratios rose steadily until about the time of the First World War; all three ratios remained approximately steady until 1930; and, ignoring the high ratios created by the depressed GNP of the 1930s, the ratios reached their peaks in 1945, and declined steadily thereafter. By 1960 the money supply ratios were little different from what they had been in the 1910–30 period (perhaps two percentage points lower), and the bank asset ratio was running about five percentage points lower than it had in that period—of which about three percentage points are explained by the banks' loss of their note circulation. So from 1910 to 1965, taken as a whole, bank assets did not grow more quickly than did GNP, and this was probably because the demand for money increased no faster than did GNP.[1]

But what caused the pronounced increase in the demand for money and therefore the rapid growth of bank assets up to

---

[1] This conclusion is not altered if we include non-bank deposits in money supply. We estimate that if the deposits of the Quebec Savings Banks, mortgage loan companies, trust companies, credit unions and *caisses populaires*, and government institutions are added to our broad definition of money supply, the money supply to GNP ratio in 1910 was 49 per cent. and in 1963 was 48 per cent.

TABLE 2

Canadian Money Supply and Chartered Bank Assets as
a Proportion of Gross National Product
Selected Years: 1870–1965

| | GNP Current (1) dollars ($ millions) | Money supply | | Chartered Bank 'Canadian' assets |
		Narrow definition (2)	Broad definition (3)	
		%	%	%
1870	459	10	17	22
1880	581	13	21	28
1890	803	13	23	31
1900	1057	17	35	41
1910	2235	18	43	47
1920	5529	17	41	45
1926	5152	16	44	44
1930	5728	15	41	46
1935	4315	20	55	62
1940	6743	21	47	49
1945	11835	27	59	55
1950	18006	23	50	48
1955	27132	20	45	43
1960	36287	17	40	39
1963	43424	17	42	41
1965	51996	15	40	40

SOURCES: Computed by the writer, using statistics found in Curtis, op. cit.; Bank of Canada, *Statistical Summary*, Annual Supplements; M. C. Urquhart (ed.), *Historical Statistics of Canada*, Macmillan, Toronto, 1965.

(1) For limitations of this series see Urquhart, ibid., pp. 113–29.

(2) Includes total subsidiary coinage, total chartered bank notes in circulation, Dominion and Bank of Canada notes held by the general public, and chartered bank public demand deposits. Rough coinage estimates for 1870–1900.

(3) Includes chartered bank savings deposits and Federal and provincial deposits as well as items included in Note 2 above. All money-supply and asset series are based on year-end figures, to make them consistent with other series in this paper for which only year-end data are available. If monthly average money supply figures had been used, the money supply to GNP ratio would have been one to two percentage points lower.

1910? Trends after 1910 cast doubt on the ability of income and wealth effects to explain it. A more plausible explanation may be found in financial innovation and changes in the financial structure of the nation. It seems that it was in the 1850s that the chartered banks' deposits began to increase faster than their note circulation, which may therefore mark the beginning of increasing acceptance of bank deposits as media of exchange; and it was in the late 1860s that the banks began explicitly to develop their savings deposit business. In 1870 therefore the bank deposit, both as medium of exchange and asset to hold, may in important respects still have been a relatively 'unabsorbed' financial innovation. Then came the rapid increase in the density of the banking system through the expansion of branches. This provided the means by which the innovation of the bank deposit was made available to the general public.

But it could not be done quickly. Table 3 shows the ratio of population to bank branches for selected years from 1868 to 1963. In spite of the limitations of the statistics, it can be said with a certain confidence that up to 1910 the banking system expanded so as to approximate its long-term 'normal' ratio of population to branches, the same period during which the money supply to GNP ratio and the bank assets to GNP ratio reached approximately their long-term plateau levels. That is, it took branch banking many decades to be developed so as to enable the economy to absorb the financial innovation of the bank deposit, and until it was absorbed the asset holding of the population was in a state of long-term disequilibrium. Also, until it was absorbed, money supply and total bank assets grew faster than did Gross National Product (see Table 2), while after that they did not.

The development of the bank chequing and saving deposits and their increasing accessibility through branch banking probably increased the nation's demand for indirect financial claims relative to direct claims and real property, that is, it increased the relative attractiveness of indirect financing; it probably reduced the relative attractiveness of barter transactions; and it probably replaced less efficient forms of media of exchange. The first two of these influences for which we have no Canadian quantitative evidence would have the effect of increasing the demand for money in general (at least if we use the broad definition), and the third would have the effect of increasing the demand for those financial claims that we have defined as money and reducing it for those that are not included in that definition. One striking example of the latter influence at work is the virtual disappearance of the local, non-note-issuing private banker in the period up to the end of the First

World War. We estimate that there were approximately 200 such local operators, many of them taking deposits, at a time when there were less than 500 bank branches. By the early 1920s most of them had disappeared, being replaced by bank branches.

TABLE 3

Chartered Bank Branch Density
Selected Years: 1868–1963

	Population per branch (thousands)
1868	29·0
1879	14·4
1890	11·3
1900	7·6
1910	3·0
1920	1·8
1930	2·5
1940	3·4
1950	3·7
1960	3·5
1963	3·5

SOURCES: M. C. Urquhart (ed.), *Historical Statistics of Canada*, Macmillan, Toronto, 1965, pp. 14, 246; and Dominion Bureau of Statistics, *Canada Year Book, 1965*, Queen's Printer, Ottawa, 1965, pp. 188, 1042.

Figures for 1920 and after include sub-agencies. If sub-agencies for 1963 were excluded, the figure in the Table would be 4·0 instead of 3·5.

It is interesting that the ratio of chartered bank notes to GNP, contrary to chartered bank demand and savings deposits, did not increase in the period 1870 to 1910. This, however, is not surprising, since notes were by no means a new and 'unabsorbed' instrument in 1870, and their use in contrast to the bank deposit did not depend so much on the density of branches. The greatest thrust of the banks' growth was the growth of their savings deposits. In the 1873–5 period (year-end averages) they accounted for 17½ per cent. of total chartered bank liabilities, while in the 1896–1900 period the figure was 46½ per cent.— after which the ratio changed little.[1] The decision to cultivate the savings deposit was one of the most important the banks

[1] Computed from statistics in Curtis, op. cit. Limitation of space prevents us from including detailed Tables.

ever made. Demand deposits grew less quickly up to 1910 than total liabilities, as did chartered bank notes. It should also be noted that the absence of legal restrictions on the size of bank deposit liabilities to bank equity permitted the 'leverage' in the banks' capital structure to rise freely and so adjust quickly to reduced risks of banking brought about by the development of branch banking, improved internal controls and procedures, and government inspection.

There seem not to have been major innovations on the lending side of the banks' operations up to 1910, apart from the minor ones of engaging in railroad financing through purchasing railroad securities, and increasing their call-loan business with the growth of the securities markets. After 1910, and as a consequence of World War I financing, the banks permanently increased their holdings of government securities. But further new changes in their asset structure (ignoring the effects of World War II financing) did not occur until the 1950s.

To conclude this section, the apparent increase in the relative demand for money up to 1910 may possibly be explained by the replacement of inferior (and unrecorded) media of exchange for superior (and recorded) ones in the form of bank deposits; by a relative shift to indirect financing from direct financing, because of the increasing availability of a superior indirect financial claim, the bank deposit; and by a relative decline in barter transactions—all of which was made possible by the increasing density of the system of bank branches, the physical means through which the innovations of the chequing and savings bank deposits were finally absorbed by the economy. Until they were absorbed, the banks could grow faster than GNP and so soften somewhat their decline in relative size, but in the absence of further innovation they could not do so thereafter.

We must turn our attention now to the nature of the non-bank financial intermediaries that caused the decline in the relative size of the chartered banks over the period 1870–1963. It can be seen from Table 4 that over this period the relative size of chartered bank assets declined from 73 per cent. to 31 per cent., or 42 percentage points. If we classify Canadian financial intermediaries, somewhat arbitrarily to be sure, into 'near competitors' of the banks and 'distant competitors' as shown in Table 4, a rather interesting point emerges. The near competitors of the banks as a group showed almost no change in relative size from 1870 to 1963, almost the whole of the relative decline of the banks being accounted for by the growth of the distant competitors—the insurance, pension, and equity investment institutions, both private and public.

It is true, of course, that the relative decline of the banks might have been less than it was if they had been able, through effective competition, to cause a decline in the relative size of their near competitors after 1870. What happened was that the relative decline of the mortgage loan companies, Quebec Savings Banks, and Post Office and Government Savings Banks was offset by the appearance of trust companies (after 1880), credit unions and *caisses populaires* (after 1900), and finance companies (after 1916). To have competed more effectively than they did the banks would have had to begin issuing debentures and making mortgage loans to compete with mortgage loan and trust companies, to issue short-term notes and enter aggressively and early into instalment financing[1] to compete with finance companies, and presumably to change their public image to compete more effectively with the credit unions and *caisses populaires*.

Also it is possible that had the banks been more aggressive they might have reduced the drift of deposits to the trust companies and credit unions and *caisses populaires*. The loss of their note circulation after 1934, however, was forced on them by legislation. The note circulation they lost was equivalent, in 1963, to about 3 per cent. of the assets of all financial intermediaries, the deposits of trust companies about 1 per cent., and the deposits of credit unions and *caisses populaires* about 2 per cent.—or roughly 6 per cent. in total.[2] We have already

---

[1] This they did in the later 1950s with astonishing success. Whereas the chartered banks provided 15 per cent. of total consumer credit in 1956 and the sales finance companies 26 per cent., by 1964 the chartered banks were providing 29 per cent. and the sales finance companies 17 per cent. See E. P. Neufeld, 'The Economic Significance of Consumer Credit', in J. S. Ziegel and R. E. Olley (eds.), *Consumer Credit in Canada*, Proceedings of a Conference on Consumer Credit, pub. University of Saskatchewan, Saskatoon, 1966. The sales finance companies have now entered into their own period of relative decline in size.

[2] We assume that in the absence of legislation abolishing the chartered-bank note issue, the banks would have retained their historical share of about 85 per cent. of the market for bank notes. For statistics of bank-note circulation and deposits see Bank of Canada, *Statistical Summary*, Annual Supplements.

noted that from 1870 to 1963 bank assets declined 42 percentage points.

So taking the period 1870–1963 as a whole a number of impressions and conclusions emerge. First, almost all of the relative

TABLE 4

Change in Relative Size of Assets of Canadian
Financial Intermediaries
1870 to 1963

	Percentage point change 1870–1963
I. Chartered Banks	−42
II. Near Competitors of the Banks	
Quebec Savings Banks	−3
Mortgage Loan Companies	−8
Trust Companies	+4
Credit Unions and *Caisses populaires*	+3
Finance Companies	+6
Dominion Note Issue and Bank of Canada	+1
Post Office and Government Savings Banks	−2
Provincial Savings Banks	..
TOTAL	+1
III. Distant Competitors of the Banks	
Life Insurance Companies	+15
Fraternal Benefit Societies	+1
Fire Insurance Companies	..
Investment Companies	+3
Trusteed Pension Funds	+9
Federal Annuity, Insurance and Pension Account	+9
Industrial Development Bank	..
Farm Credit Corporation	..
Central Mortgage and Housing Corporation	+4
TOTAL	+41

SOURCE: See note to Table 1.

decline of the chartered banks is explained by their inability to issue financial claims with insurance and pension benefits or features attractive to investors interested in capital gains, and almost none by any increase in the relative size of 'near' competitors. Second, the banks failed to introduce competition of a kind that might have resulted in a relative decline of their 'near' competitors, and this largely because of their failure or inability to develop the debenture and to enter the mortgage loan business, and by their long delay in competing in the short-term market for funds and in entering the instalment loan business. Third, their loss of the note issue had only a small effect on their relative size, as had the drift of deposit business to competing institutions. Fourth, legislative restrictions as such probably did not slow down the growth rate of the chartered banks, and so did not speed their relative decline, until after 1955. Fifth, it does not seem that there was any decline in the demand for money of a kind that retarded the growth of the chartered banks. Sixth, until about 1910 the banks were able to grow at an historically high rate (faster than GNP) and so reduce their relative decline from what it would otherwise have been, because of their success in expanding the branch system to exploit the growing demand for their relatively new savings and chequing deposits; but by 1910 that demand had been fully exploited, and since the banks then introduced no essentially new or unique financial claims or important new types of credit, they were doomed to grow at about the rate of Gross National Product, in contrast to some other new intermediaries with new claims and new credit to offer.

We noted earlier that the decline in the relative size of the commercial banks has not been uninterrupted, and Figure 1 shows the long swings in the banks' relative size that have occurred. We may define the phases of those swings as follows:

Downswing	1870–96
Upswing	1896–1919
Downswing	1919–34*
Upswing	1934*–45
Downswing	1945–63

* The year 1937 might also have been chosen.

Table 5 shows the extent to which the various non-bank financial intermediaries accounted for the change in the relative size of the banks over each one of those phases.

Space limitations prevent us from discussing adequately developments in each one of those periods, and we must restrict ourselves to a few generalizations. From 1870 to 1896

TABLE 5

Ratio of Assets of Specific Financial Intermediaries to Total Financial Intermediary Assets over Long Cycles in the Relative Size of Chartered Bank Assets

	1870 %	1896 %	Change	Peak 1919 %	Change	Trough 1934 %	Change	Peak 1945 %	Change	1963 %	Change	1870 to 1963 Change
I. Chartered Banks	73	48	−25	64	16	44	−20	48	4	31	−17	−42
II. Private non-bank	19	41	22	27	−14	49	22	32	−17	49	17	30
(a) Quebec Savings Banks	4	3	−1	2	−1	1	−1	1	..	1	..	−3
(b) Life Insurance Coys.	2	13	11	12	−1	31	19	21	−10	17	−4	15
(c) Fraternal Benefit Soc.	..	1	1	2	1	2	..	1	−1	1	1	1
(d) Fire Insurance Coys.	3	3	..	3	..	4	1	2	−2	3	1	..
(e) Mortgage Loan Coys.	10	22	12	7	−15	5	−2	2	−3	2	..	−8
(f) Trust Coys.	..	..	..	2	2	4	..	2	−2	4	2	4
(g) Credit Unions and Caisses populaires	..	..	..	..	..	..	..	1	1	3	2	3
(h) Finance Coys.	..	..	..	..	..	1	1	1	..	6	5	6
(i) Investment Coys.	..	..	..	..	..	1	1	1	..	3	2	3
(j) Trusteed Pension Funds	..	..	..	..	..	..	..	..	..	9	9	9
III. Government	8	11	3	10	−1	7	−3	19	12	20	1	12
(a) Dominion Note Issue Bank of Canada	5	3	−2	8	5	4	−4	15	11	6	−9	1
(b) Federal Annuity Ins., Pension A/C	..	..	..	..	..	2	2	3	1	9	6	9
(c) Post Office and Government Savings Banks	2	7	5	1	−6	..	−1	..	..	..	..	−2
(d) Provincial Savings Banks	..	..	..	..	..	..	..	..	..	..	..	..
(e) Industrial Dev. Bank	..	..	..	..	..	..	..	..	..	..	..	..
(f) Farm Credit Corp.	..	..	..	..	..	..	..	..	..	1	..	..
(g) Central Mortgage Housing Corp.	..	..	..	..	..	..	..	..	..	4	4	4

Source: See note to Table 1. Because of rounding, totals do not always balance.

the relative size of chartered bank assets declined by 25 percentage points, while mortgage loan companies, which introduced their sterling and Canadian dollar debentures, and life insurance companies, which were bringing their unique financial claims to more and more people, increased in relative size. Both catered to the demand for mortgage credit, a field not open to the banks.

The increase in the relative size of the banks from 1896 to 1919 is explained largely by the decrease in the growth rate of the mortgage loan companies; and by an increase in the growth rate of the banks as a result of the continuing growth of their savings deposit business, together with the effects of war finance and an acceleration in the demand for bank credit. From 1919 to 1934 the banks grew at an historically low rate, while the life insurance companies were in their last stage of rapid growth, which, of course, had the effect of reducing the relative size of the banks. War finance largely explains the small increase in relative size of the banks from 1934 to 1945.

In 1945 bank assets accounted for 48 per cent. of financial intermediary assets. By 1951 they had declined to their 1934 level and in 1963 stood at 31 per cent., a decline of 17 percentage points. As a proportion of GNP, bank assets were lower than in the 1910–30 period, but, as noted earlier, this is largely accounted for by their loss of the note issue. Of the 'distant' competitors, it was the trusteed pension funds, the Federal government's annuity, insurance, and pension account, the investment companies, and the Federal government's Central Mortgage and Housing Corporation that grew most rapidly, the total of such competitors increasing their share of total financial intermediary assets by 17 percentage points. The 'near' competitors as a group did not increase their share of financial intermediary assets, although within that group the finance companies, trust companies, credit union and *caisses populaires* did. The advantage enjoyed by the sales finance companies was that they moved early and aggressively into instalment financing and into the short-term money market for funds, whereas the banks did not. This mistake the banks began to correct in the late 1950s. The trust and mortgage loan companies were in a position to offer debentures (called guaranteed investment certificates in the case of the former), as well as savings and demand deposits to savers; they expanded their branches and offered better hours of service; and they were in the mortgage loan business. Not very different from this were the credit unions and *caisses populaires*, which, however, also had the apparent advantage of a unique non-commercial image. None of the aforementioned institutions faced an interest-rate ceiling on their loans, whereas the banks did, which may have begun to place the banks at a disadvantage after 1955.

Recent legislation has given the chartered banks limited debenture-issuing powers, a lower minimum cash ratio, as well as the right to make conventional mortgage loans, and it also makes provision for the removal of the interest-rate ceiling on bank loans.[1] If to these changes is added a certain aggressiveness on the part of the banks, it is conceivable that their decline in relative size will decelerate in future and that that of 'near' competitors will accelerate.

[1] See Canada, Parliament, Bill C-222, *An Act Respecting Banks and Banking*, 1966, as passed by the House of Commons, 21 March 1967.

W. T. NEWLYN

An African Monetary Perspective

INTRODUCTION

I N view of the character of this volume a genealogical introduction to this essay is appropriate. It was Richard Sayers
who first awakened my interest in 'colonial' monetary
matters by asking me to contribute a chapter on that subject to
Banking in the British Commonwealth.[1] This had further issue in
1951, in my study of money and finance in East Africa (Kenya,
Uganda, and Tanganyika) and Central Africa (the Rhodesias
and Nyasaland). It was Sayers's interest and encouragement
that resulted in the marriage of my research to that by David
Rowan of West Africa (Nigeria and Gold Coast), from which
union there issued in 1954 our joint study *Money and Banking
in British Colonial Africa.*[2]

Ten years later I conceived the idea of a third generation of
studies to replace the Newlyn and Rowan volume with four
detailed case studies of developments in English-speaking Africa
since 1951. This conception has recently borne fruit in three
theses for doctorates of the University of Leeds—on the Federation of Rhodesia, on East Africa, and on Ghana respectively,
and it is hoped that all three may be published.[3] Independently
of this project, a study of Nigeria had been initiated earlier
by Dr. C. V. Brown, which has since been published.[4] Although
not in the direct line of descent, Brown's study is of the same

[1] R. S. Sayers (ed.), *Banking in the British Commonwealth*, O.U.P., Oxford,
1952.
[2] W. T. Newlyn and D. C. Rowan, *Money and Banking in British Colonial Africa*,
O.U.P., Oxford, 1954.
[3] R. A. Sowelem, *Towards Financial Independence in a Developing Economy*, Allen
& Unwin, London, 1968; J. Loxley, 'The Development of the Monetary and
Financial System of the East African Currency Area, 1950 to 1964', Ph.D. thesis,
University of Leeds; A. Appiah, 'The Development of the Monetary and Financial
System of Ghana, 1950 to 1964', Ph.D. thesis, University of Leeds.
[4] C. V. Brown, *The Nigerian Banking System*, Allen & Unwin, London, 1966.

generation and bears a strong family likeness to the legitimate progeny in taking Newlyn and Rowan as its starting-point; moreover, I can claim some distant relationship through having examined the thesis on which it is based.

Apart from tracing Sayers's part in opening up the field, this sequence is significant in indicating the growth of the subject and the present state of knowledge. In 1949 one chapter covered the whole colonial empire; in 1954 one volume served for English-speaking Africa; now a separate volume is required for each of the four monetary areas covered in that volume. This process will continue both in territorial and in institutional specialization.

The termination of the Rhodesian Federation in 1963 gave rise to the separate monetary systems of Rhodesia, Zambia, and Malawi, each with its own central bank; similarly, the break-up of the East African Currency Union in 1966 has led to the introduction of separate monetary systems in Kenya, Uganda, and Tanzania, each with its own central bank. Moreover, detailed studies of particular institutions and aspects of monetary policy are now in progress in these countries. Of these, my own study, and those which I was directing in the East African Institute of Social Research, should be included in the third generation of progeny; indeed, the fourth generation recently started with a study of the Nairobi Stock Exchange, which is being supervised at Makerere by Dr. Loxley, the author of the East African study.

The present essay is an attempt at a synthesis of one aspect of monetary and financial development as revealed in the Nigerian, Rhodesian, East African, and Ghanaian studies. It is proposed to concentrate on the expansion of credit by the banking system. Moreover, it is proposed to generalize as much as possible—the studies themselves must be consulted for the variations and qualifications. In all cases, except Rhodesia, there are ambiguities in the currency statistics due to changes in the geographical coverage of the currency boards during the period. The necessary adjustments to the official figures which have been made are not such as to distort the over-all trends. All values are in pounds sterling, the local monetary units having remained at parity with the pound sterling in all cases.

COMMERCIAL BANK EXPANSION

The starting-point is 1950: the Newlyn and Rowan bench-mark. At that time all of these sterling-exchange monetary areas were served by currency boards operating on the standard pattern of the British colonial system, under which the responsibility of the currency board (the only monetary authority) was confined to issuing local currency against sterling and redeeming local currency in sterling. Until 1955 all the boards were prohibited from holding securities of participating governments as part of the currency reserve, with the result that the system implied 100 per cent. external reserves against the currency liability.

A long-standing fallacy (still not completely dead) interpreted this system as making the money supply uniquely determined by the balance of payments. This would only be true if the money supply consisted entirely of currency, and could not be true in a system in which there are banks able to create debts that act as a medium of exchange. Nor, in that situation, is it true of the currency element alone, for the existence of banks allows the public to determine at will the extent to which it holds money in currency or deposits. True, in Nigeria in 1950, with the level of bank deposits half that of currency in circulation and the banks acting in a passive manner, the balance of payments dominated; but this was not a necessary result of the currency board system. The money supply under the currency board system was determined by (i) the balance of payments, (ii) the policy of the commercial banks, and (iii) the propensity of the public to hold currency; it was just as in any other system, except for the absence of a monetary authority able, within limits, to manipulate these basic determinants according to policy objectives.

The other major characteristic of the system was the automatic interchange of local currency and sterling; it is convenient to think of the sterling balances of the banking system and local currency as indistinguishable and together comprising the *primary money* of the system into which bank deposits (*secondary money*) was convertible. The term 'money supply' is used to mean currency held by the public plus *total* commercial bank deposits, and thus corresponds with the liabilities of the clearly identifiable banking system, including the monetary authority.

By 1950 the commercial banks operating in these countries (mainly the large expatriate British banks based on London) had more or less eliminated the excess liquidity directly resulting from war-time restrictions on imports, and had returned, roughly speaking, to the point of expansion which had been characteristic in the inter-war period. In all four monetary

TABLE I

Banks' Local Earning Assets Ratio

	E.A.	Rhodesia	Ghana	Nigeria
1950	0·34	0·40	0·33	0·22
1955	0·77	0·55	0·33	0·48
1960	0·99	0·82	0·67	0·84
1965	1·01	(0·92)*	1·06	0·99

NOTE: The ratio is calculated on total *operational* assets defined as local earning assets plus cash plus net external balances, so that the banks' reserve ratio is equal to one minus the local assets ratio.

* 1963 (Federation dissolved).

areas the banks were employing less than half their funds locally —the larger part being invested in London. The extent to which the banks as a whole were employing funds locally differed according to the stage of development of the respective economies. This is shown in the first line of Table 1, which sets out the local earning asset ratio (LEA ratio), i.e. the proportion of earning assets in the local economy to the total *operational assets* comprising local earning assets, cash (currency and balances with the monetary authority), and net external balances. The banks' reserve ratio is defined as the proportion between cash plus external balances, and total operational assets. We thus have the useful identity that the LEA ratio is equal to one minus the reserve ratio; the two ratios being alternative expressions of the degree of expansion of bank credit locally.

The reasons for this unexpanded banking situation have been much discussed in the literature, and they boil down to: (i) lack of demand for bank finance, except in connexion with the financing of export crop movements and of imports; (ii) the inadequate branch coverage; (iii) conventional security requirements, which excluded lending for the main economic activity of agricultural production; and (iv) the non-availability of liquid assets to satisfy the traditional banking asset structure. Such funds as were employed locally were employed by making advances and, although the low ratios for Nigeria, Ghana, and East Africa were clear evidence of slack to be taken up, the Rhodesian ratio was not so obviously abnormal for an *advances* ratio. The writer recalls the mild consternation with which his calculation of the potential increase in bank credit implicit in the current reserve ratio was greeted at a public lecture in Salisbury in 1951.

Theoretically, subsequent events might have resulted in alternative types of banking behaviour that have been classified as (i) *responsive*, where the marginal reserve ratio remains constant (in other words an elasticity of bank deposits with respect to reserves of unity); (ii) *passive* (elasticity less than unity); (iii) *active* (elasticity greater than unity); and two limiting cases of *absolutely passive* behaviour (no response to increase in reserves) and *autonomous* behaviour (expansion independently of changes in reserves). Looking back, I now think that the Newlyn and Rowan treatment of these possibilities failed to bring out the significance of the autonomous element in the development of any banking system.

Putting it in its simplest terms, any banking system must start with the ratio of currency to total money supply (currency plus bank deposits) at unity. By the time it has expanded to the maximum (the banks and the public having reduced their propensity to hold cash relative to deposits to a minimum) the coefficient of expansion of money with respect to cash will have a value of between three and four, depending on how deposits are defined. Thus, we should expect the development phase of banking to exhibit a threefold or fourfold increase in the money supply at constant prices on an unchanged primary money base, solely as a result of the reduction in the propensity of the banks and public to hold cash relative to deposits.

With the rapid rise in income and the expansion of the money economy which (except for a period of sharply falling export prices between 1955 and 1960) have characterized these economies in the post-war period, the demand for bank credit expanded rapidly. By greatly increasing their branch coverage, by adopting rather less restrictive credit criteria, and by the introduction of risk-avoiding devices (such as lending through co-operatives), the commercial banks exploited their opportunities in a remarkable way. This is indicated in Table 1, which shows the LEA ratio increasing to over 0·9 in all cases by 1965 (1963 in the case of Rhodesia, that being the date at which the Federal monetary area ceased to exist). Only in the case of Ghana does this represent a significant increase in government debt, and in the other three areas the local assets still consisted mainly of loans and advances to the private sector in 1965.

This huge expansion of domestic assets more than doubled bank deposits in East Africa and Rhodesia, and in Nigeria and Ghana (both from a much lower 1950 level) increased deposits by nearly eightfold and tenfold respectively. The pattern of this expansion for each area is shown in Figure 1, which plots the relationship between the banks' external reserves and bank deposits. The graphs are all on the same scale and are thus directly comparable as to absolute changes over the period.

The remarkable common characteristic is the autonomous behaviour shown in the persistence of expansion in the face of sustained losses of external reserves over most of the period, resulting in all cases in an overdrawn external position. The premature occurrence of this situation in East Africa and Rhodesia in 1960 was due to capital flight induced by political events. The fact that this over-commitment could happen (as it certainly could not in a self-contained banking system) is due to the supra-territorial character of the expatriate banks operating in these areas.

A representative of one of the banks concerned, giving evidence to the Radcliffe Committee,[1] stated that his bank would certainly not be happy to see a continually overdrawn position in any monetary area, but that one of the advantages of their supra-territorial operation was that it allowed considerable seasonal flexibility. On the other hand, it can be argued that a permanent overdraft can be regarded as that part of the bank's total capital which is associated with the business carried on in

[1] Committee on the Working of the Monetary System (*Radcliffe Report*), Cmnd. 827, H.M.S.O., London, 1959. Minutes of Evidence, Questions 4367/76.

any particular area. It is simply because these banks are not incorporated in the countries in which they operate that no capital item appears in the balance sheet relating to their operations in these countries.

Whether or not a seasonal or small permanent overdrawn position persists in future, it is clear that the banks can reduce no further their propensity to hold reserves relative to deposits. No doubt there will remain some element of flexibility (if it is not prevented by the authorities) in the net credit/debit position,

TABLE 2

Ratio of Public's Cash to Deposits

	E.A.		Rhodesia		Ghana		Nigeria	
	1950	1965	1950	1965	1950	1965	1950	1965
Cash £m.	21·3	54·7	9·0	25·1	22·9	62·0	28·4	87·6
Deposits £m.	63·7	152·7	52·9	103·6	10·9	99·9	16·4	132·5
Ratio	0·34	0·36	0·17	0·24	2·1	0·62	1·6	0·66

but the expansion described above must be regarded as a unique event similar to that which took place in England in the nineteenth century. In that case, the banks were in the process of transition from being purveyors of credit to being its creators; in the present case, the banks have been in transition from being exporters of credit to being its creators in the domestic economy. This process can go no further, and, with the completion of this transition, the banks can expand their lending only to the extent that they can get increased reserves. One of the sources of increased bank reserves is a reduction in the public's propensity to hold cash, but rapid credit expansion associated with economy in cash-use is confined to the development phase of banking, though opportunities for secular economies may continue slowly to reduce the public's cash/deposit ratio even in advanced economies. As Table 2 shows, the contribution this factor has made to the credit expansion under examination has been significant only in West Africa; indeed, in Rhodesia the ratio of cash to deposits has actually risen. This is probably due to the expansion of African cash-crop production relative to low cash-using capital-intensive economic activity, which had been responsible for the initially high level of deposits in Rhodesia. In East Africa the ratio has not changed significantly (having regard to the margin of error in the statistics), while in Ghana and Nigeria the ratio has been dramatically changed by the large relative increase in deposits. This convergence towards the stable East African ratio of about one-third suggests that there is still scope for economies in cash-use in West Africa,

TABLE 3

Sources of Increase in Deposits
1950–65 £m

	E.A.	Rhodesia	Ghana	Nigeria
Change in LEA	+125·8	+78·2	+95·3	+125·9
Change in Reserves	−36·8	−27·4	−7·6	−9·8
Net increase	+89·0	+50·8	+87·7	+116·1

but that any reduction below one-third is unlikely in the near future, having regard to the fact that the ratio in the United Kingdom is one-fifth.

It must be stressed that this massive monetary expansion, taken as a whole, owed nothing to the balance of payments; indeed, in all cases reserves were lower at the end of the period than at the start; had reserves not fallen, the level of deposits would have been that much higher. This is shown in Table 3, which prompts the question: to what extent did this increase in bank credit *cause* the fall in reserves? There is no difficulty in formulating an expression for the reserve loss resulting from a given amount of additional credit (or rise in the rate of credit creation); writing C for the additional credit; e for the proportion of the credit spent directly on imports; m, s, and t respectively for the propensities to import, save, and be taxed; and X for any export-generating (or import-saving) effect of the expenditure; the loss of reserves will be:

$$eC - X + m\left(\frac{C(1-e) + X}{m+s+t}\right)$$

All of the parameters are capable of reasonable estimation, except X, which would be specific to the particular expenditure.

Putting X equal to zero, the expression works out at $0.61C$, using East African values of the remaining parameters as typical. It is clear from the expression that, even if X is zero, the loss of reserves must be less than C unless s and t are both zero or are both ineffective. The latter may well be the case in the economies with which we are dealing (with the probable exception of Rhodesia).

The marginal propensity to pay tax must, of course, be positive; but it is highly unrealistic to credit these governments with undesigned hoarding. It is more realistic to assume that extra tax receipts will be matched, without significant time-lag, by extra expenditure. Furthermore, the Keynesian marginal propensity to save and the concept of a savings 'leak' are appropriate only to the extent that savings decisions are divorced from investment decisions by differences in time and person. In the economies with which we are dealing (with the exception of Rhodesia) private capital formation is, mostly, either financed from current profits (being on a small scale) or it is financed from external sources, particularly by direct investment of expatriate companies. In other words, there is relatively little indirect financing through financial intermediaries, and capital markets play a relatively small role. Hence, domestic savings and investment financed from domestic sources are virtually in neutral equilibrium. In the absence of both the traditional domestic leaks the external leak, determined by the marginal propensity to import, plays the role attributed to savings in the simple Keynesian model, and the leak through imports must eventually aggregate to an amount equal to any monetary injection into the economy.

In this situation, and leaving aside any favourable effect of the expenditure on the balance of payments, the ratio of loss of reserves to any given credit injection would approach unity as a limit. Investigation of this relationship for a large number of countries by J. J. Polak[1] suggests that, with a high marginal propensity to import, the reserve loss approaches very near to this limit within three years. However, this loss is reduced to

[1] J. J. Polak, 'Monetary Analysis of Income Formation and Payments Problems', *I.M.F. Staff Papers*, vol. 6, 1957–8; and (with L. Boissozult) 'Monetary Analysis of Income and Imports and its Statistical Application', *I.M.F. Staff Papers*, vol. 7, 1960.

the extent that money balances increase; hence credit creation minus net increase in deposits measures the effect on reserves of the credit expansion which has taken place in these economies. To go further into this relationship would require detailed study in each case,[1] but it is clearly one which is of importance to the monetary authorities of these countries; to their contribution to the expansion of credit we must now turn.

THE MONETARY AUTHORITIES

At the end of 1965 East Africa was the only one of the four monetary areas (and, indeed, the only major politically independent area in the world) not to have a central bank. The attainment of political independence has provided a strong impetus in favour of monetary and financial independence in Africa, and in Nigeria's case the manifestation of this in the establishment of a central bank took place under colonial rule; in Ghana it took place at the same time as independence; and in the Federation of Rhodesia and Nyasaland the establishment of the Reserve Bank of Rhodesia immediately followed the creation of the 'independent' Federation.

The reason for the delay in the case of East Africa was that it was not a single political entity but three separate political units sharing a common market, a common monetary system, and important common services. Towards the end of the colonial régime there was general agreement that the time had come to replace the East African Currency Board (EACB) by introducing central banking, but it was argued by Uganda and Tanzania that an East African central bank would be located in Nairobi (rapidly developing as the financial centre) and would be dominated by Kenyan interests. On the other hand, there was reluctance on the part of the colonial administrators to break up the monetary union by setting up separate monetary systems and central banks. Many compromise proposals were made and rejected, and the discussions continued through the attainment of independence by Tanzania, Uganda, and Kenya in succession. Eventually, in a context of inter-country dispute over the distribution of gains from the common market, the decision to set up separate central banks was announced in

[1] The writer is engaged on such a study in respect of Uganda.

June 1965; but the EACB was still the monetary authority at the end of our period. It was, however, a very different institution[1] from what it had been at the beginning.

In West Africa the earlier established central banks operated at first rather like the old currency boards (indeed, until revised in 1962, the constitution of the Central Bank of Nigeria obliged it to do so). The EACB, on the other hand, has been more and more acting like a central bank, in spite of its constitution. Not only has it taken advantage of successive relaxations of the rule against fiduciary issues (first allowed generally under the colonial régime in 1955) but it has also provided seasonal elasticity by using a part of its fiduciary issuing powers to lend to the banks at the seasonal peaks.

The limits on the credit-creating capacity of the four monetary authorities in terms of asset maxima and/or external reserve minima are summarized in Table 4.

Against this background we now examine the behaviour of these monetary authorities solely with regard to credit creation. In 1955 all the currency boards were still operating 100 per cent. sterling-backed currency, so that in Table 5, which gives the local asset ratio, 1955 is zero in all cases; five years later the EACB was leading the field, in spite of the general presumption that the establishment of central banks tends to quicken the pace of credit creation. At the end of our period the EACB was still not far behind the Central Bank of Nigeria, which can be considered the leader—Ghana having, by then, clearly entered a different kind of race.

These ratios do not reveal either the relative magnitude of the changes in external assets and domestic assets or the absolute magnitude of the expansion. These aspects are brought out in Table 6, which shows the changes in the assets of the monetary authorities in millions of pounds. The only monetary authority that expanded its domestic assets by less than the change in external assets over the whole period was the Reserve Bank of Rhodesia. Of the increase of £38m. in total assets, however, only £14m. found its way into the credit base, £24m. going to increase government balances. This figure reflects external reserves previously held outside the banking system

---

[1] Due largely to the enterprise of Mr. J. B. de Loynes, C.M.G. (of the Bank of England), the Board's technical member.

TABLE 4

Legal Limits on Credit Creation by Monetary Authorities

| | Maximum lending | | Minimum external reserve |
	To Government	To private sector	
E.A.	1956: £10 m. 1959: £20 m. 1963: £25 m. 1964: £35 m.	Seasonal Loans to Banks 1963: £5 m. 1964: £10 m.	1956: C—£10 m. 1959: C—£20 m. 1963: C—£30 m. 1964: C—£45 m.
Rhodesia	NS	NS	25% of DL (1)
Ghana	1957 Advances 10% of RR Securities £12 m. 1963 Advances 10% of RR (2) Securities 40% of C (3)	NS	NS
Nigeria	1958 Advances 12% of RR Securities 20% of DL 1962 Advances 12% of RR Securities 33⅓% of DL	NS	1958 60% of C+35% of other DL for first 5 years then 40% of DL 1962 40% of DL

NS None specified.
RR Recurrent revenue.
DL Demand liabilities.
C Currency in circulation.
(1) Minister may suspend for 60 days at a time, up to a maximum of 6 months.
(2) 60% if Minister so requests.
(3) 15% if President so requests.

and taken over by the Reserve Bank. It also illustrates the
financial strength of the Federal Government, which had no
difficulty in raising loans from the public and was opposed in
principle to borrowing from the Central Bank. When the
Federation broke up in 1963, the reserve ratio was 85 per cent.,
and the new central banks of Malawi and Zambia were able to
start off with very comfortable external reserves, but both
countries imposed a minimum reserve requirement of 50 per
cent.

The EACB assets available to be distributed between the central banks of Kenya, Tanzania, and Uganda consist of 78 per cent. sterling and 22 per cent. securities of the participating governments, but, because of greater borrowing from the EACB in the past, Uganda's share of sterling will be in a considerably

TABLE 5

*Monetary Authorities
Local Asset Ratio*

	E.A.	Rhodesia	Ghana	Nigeria
1955	0	0	0	0
1960	0·17	0·14	0·15	0·03
1965	0·22	0·15	0·86	0·26

lower ratio to currency liabilities than that of the other two countries. All three countries have legislated for a level of external reserves that will certainly inspire confidence in the new currencies but leave rather little scope for credit creation with external deficits in prospect.

TABLE 6

Changes in Assets of Monetary Authority £m.

	E.A.		Rhodesia		Ghana		Nigeria	
	External	Domestic	External	Domestic	External	Domestic	External	Domestic
1955–60	−5·8	+10·9	+17·7	+6·1	+16·8	+9·7	+23·9	+3·4
1960–65	−5·7	+7·7	+11·2	+2·9*	−53·5	+49·5	+5·0	+29·7
Total	−11·5	+18·6	+28·9	+9·0*	−36·7	+59·2	+28·9	+33·1

NOTE: Excludes capital, physical assets, and contra items.
* To 1963.

Nigeria, following a year of credit control and import restrictions in an effort to check a sharp fall in reserves, finished 1965 with external reserves comfortably above the prescribed minimum of 40 per cent. of demand liabilities, but with holdings of government securities at 25 per cent. of demand liabilities, approaching the maximum of one-third.

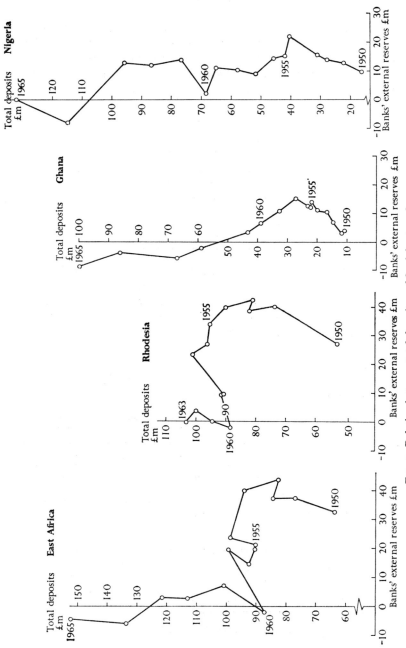

FIG. 1. Relation between total deposits and banks' external reserves

The 1963 revision of the Bank of Ghana's constitution imposed no minimum external reserve but limited lending to government, by way of securities held as currency cover, to 40 per cent. of currency outstanding. There was, however, provision for the maximum to be raised to 60 per cent. (if the Minister so requested) by legislative instrument. The higher of these two limits was reached at the end of 1964, and the fall in external assets conforms to our hypothesis regarding the effect of rapid credit expansion on the external balance in these open economies.

An over-all measure of the combined effects of the behaviour of the commercial banks and monetary authorities is provided by the change in the ratio of total money supply to total monetary reserves. The increase in this ratio was lowest in Rhodesia, from 1·62 in 1950 to 2·44 in 1963. Nigeria's ratio rose between 1950 and 1965 from 1·1 to 2·65, and East Africa's from 1·38 to 4·5. Ghana's rose from 1·8, about the same low level as Nigeria's, to a ratio of $\frac{162}{-8·6}$, which has no meaning; perhaps this is appropriate for a monetary system which had got out of control.

CONCLUSION

The massive post-war expansion of credit which has taken place in the countries of English-speaking Africa is a unique process associated with the development phase of banking, in which the ratio of secondary money to primary money has expanded to a maximum, subject only to secular change. The present monetary situation is that which obtains in most countries in the world having fully extended banking systems, that is to say commercial bank credit now depends on the volume of primary money forming the monetary base. This can be expanded only by a balance-of-payments surplus or an increase in lending by the monetary authority. The distinguishing feature of these economies, which they exhibit in different degrees, is that excessive monetary demand manifests itself more in inflated imports than in inflated prices. With reserves (for all except Rhodesia) at, or not far off, the minimum, and ambitious development plans exerting pressure for increasing government expenditure, the general prospect is one of tight money combined with chronic balance-of-payments constraints.

APPENDIX

Orders of Magnitude

	Population (Million 1965)	G.D.P. £ Million
EAST AFRICA	27·2	751 (1964)
FEDERATION OF RHODESIA AND NYASALAND	10·5	592 (1963)
GHANA	7·7	542 (1962)*
NIGERIA	56·4 (?)	1,148 (1962)*

* These figures are subject to varying margins of error but serve to indicate orders of magnitude. The use of 1962 G.D.P. figures for Ghana and Nigeria is designed to avoid the distortion due to the recent decline in the value of the local money.

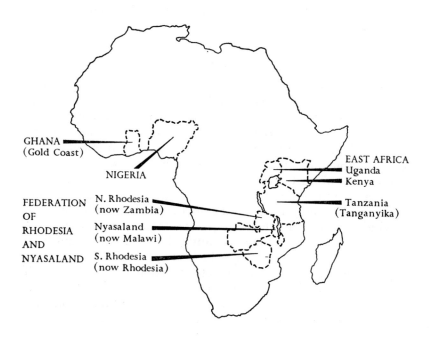

GHANA (Gold Coast)

NIGERIA

FEDERATION OF RHODESIA AND NYASALAND

N. Rhodesia (now Zambia)

Nyasaland (now Malawi)

S. Rhodesia (now Rhodesia)

EAST AFRICA
Uganda
Kenya
Tanzania (Tanganyika)

L. S. PRESSNELL

Gold Reserves, Banking Reserves, and the Baring Crisis of 1890[1]

I

THE financial crisis of 1890, immediately and ever since known as 'the Baring crisis', helped to crystallize the modern British monetary system. So much is familiar in

[1] I wish to thank the Bank of England for its courtesy and hospitality in allowing me to use its records, without which it would have been impossible to make this study. I am also grateful to the present Marquess of Salisbury for permission to consult the papers of the third Marquess and to Dr. J. F. A. Mason of Christ Church, Oxford, for help in using them; to the Midland Bank for allowing me to use the private letter book of George Rae; and to Mr. S. W. Shelton for supplying information about the participation of the West End private banks in the Baring guarantee of 1890. Footnote references have not been given to Bank of England sources.

The following abbreviations are used:

BPP   British Parliamentary Papers.
BPP 1875   Report from the Select Committee on Banks of Issue, BPP, 1875, ix.
Clapham   Sir John Clapham, *The Bank of England*, 2 vols. (C.U.P., Cambridge, 1944), ii.
Elliot   The Hon. Arthur D. Elliot, *The Life of George Joachim Goschen, first Viscount Goschen, 1831–1907*, 2 vols. (Longmans, Green & Co., London, 1911), ii.
Fetter   F. W. Fetter, *Development of British Monetary Orthodoxy, 1797–1875* (Harvard University Press, Cambridge, Mass., U.S.A., 1965).
Fulford   Roger Fulford, *Glyn's 1753–1953* (Macmillan, London, 1953).
Gibbs I   Correspondence between H. H. Gibbs, Esq., and Professor Bonamy Price on the Reserve of the Bank of England, appendix to B. Price, *Chapters on Practical Political Economy*, first edition (Kegan Paul & Co., London, 1878).
Gibbs II   H. H. Gibbs (Baron Aldenham), and B. Price, *Further Correspondence* . . . (privately printed, ?1879). Copy in the Goldsmiths' Library, University of London; paginated for second edition of Price's *Chapters*, but apparently not published with it.
HD   Diaries of E. W. (Sir Edward) Hamilton in British Museum; those consulted are 48645 to 48662.
HP   Hamilton Papers, Brit. Mus. Add. MS. 48614.
PD   Parliamentary Debates.
Rae   'Mr Rae's private letters on Banking questions', Midland Bank.

the existing literature,[1] but should it be? Earlier developments to which in many respects the crisis formed a climax, and the blind alleys into which it tempted monetary policy and controversy, are less well known. The crisis accelerated the amalgamation and strengthening of banks and it encouraged the keeping of higher and more stable cash ratios; it emphasized indisputably the primacy of the Bank of England, and encouraged grudging bankers to recognize their own and the national interest in co-operation with the Bank. This was no smooth or even obvious evolution; many contemporaries envisaged higher bank reserves less as an aid to Bank control than as a means of eliminating it. The banking atmosphere right up to 1914 was full of suspicions of centralized monetary management; it was fogged by a growing national neurosis, not just over the maintenance of substantial gold reserves in preference to discretionary prevention or treatment of panics, but also over the accumulation of a national gold hoard against war emergencies. If England none the less developed central banking, truly she did so absent-mindedly.[2]

II

The monetary arrangements of 1844 had failed to end anxiety about sterling's reserves. Domestically the growth of deposit banking circumvented the restraint on the creation of banking liabilities intended by the restriction of their note issues and those of the Bank of England, and it appeared also to diminish the influence of the Bank in the money market. Externally, London's evolution as an international financial centre was to magnify sterling's reserve currency functions. This situation posed continuing problems of the status and power of the Bank; it produced tensions between the commercial banks and the government and between the banks and the Bank; by no means least, it sustained anxiety about the country's inter-

SP   Papers of the third Marquess of Salisbury, Christ Church, Oxford.
Welby   Welby Papers, vols. 7 and 8, in the British Library of Political and Economic Science: papers of Sir Reginald Welby.
    [1] e.g. R. S. Sayers, 'Twentieth Century English Banking', *Transactions of the Manchester Statistical Society*, 1953–4.
    [2] R. S. Sayers, *Central Banking after Bagehot* (Clarendon Press, Oxford, 1957), p. 18.

national reserves. From the 1870s to the 1890s the bimetallic debate enmeshed the reserves question in alarm over the alleged shortage of international liquidity; it then became increasingly entangled with uneasiness over the adequacy of the cash reserves of commercial banks. The possibility of substantial reform emerged during the late 1880s, when the monetary authorities had a team of rare ability anxious to deal with accumulating monetary problems. At the Bank William Lidderdale was Deputy-Governor from 1887 to 1889 and then Governor for three instead of the normal two years, to cover the periodical renegotiation of Bank-Treasury arrangements. Expert in foreign exchange,[1] 'a model of a calm shrewd bold Scotch man of business',[2] he was above all a great central banker, with the remarkably appropriate family motto 'Foresight is all'.[3] Treasury memories ranked him second only to Cotton,[4] whom Sir Robert Peel in 1844 had been willing to make permanent Governor;[5] City people rated him (for a time) the best Governor ever.[6] At the Exchequer from 1887 to 1892 G. J. Goschen was a Chancellor of unusual competence; 'the fortunate youth' of merchant banking a generation earlier,[7] author of an influential monetary classic,[8] he remains the only ex-Bank Director to have become Chancellor. At the Treasury, much better staffed than in mid century, were Sir Reginald Welby and E. W. (later Sir Edward) Hamilton: outstanding civil servants moving freely in the influential inner circles of the clubs and country-houses, of leading politicians (largely Gladstonian), and of the Press (that is, *The Times*), they planned and patiently pressed for a strengthened monetary system.[9]

The Baring crisis disrupted Goschen's and Lidderdale's perhaps too leisurely progress towards more centralized control of the monetary system. The narrowly averted threat of an

[1] See Sheila Marriner, *Rathbones of Liverpool, 1845-73* (Liverpool University Press, Liverpool, 1961), *passim*.
[2] Welby to Gladstone, 16 Dec. 1891, Welby 7.
[3] 'Presentation to Mr Lidderdale' (6 May 1891), *Bankers' Magazine*, li (June 1891), 1005.
[4] Welby to Gladstone, 16 Dec. 1891, Welby 7.
[5] R. S. Sayers, ed. *Economic Writings of James Pennington* (The London School of Economics and Political Science, London, 1963), p. xxxix, n. 2.
[6] HD, 9 Aug. 1890.   [7] Elliot, i. 46.
[8] G. J. Goschen, *The Theory of the Foreign Exchanges*, first ed. (Effingham Wilson, London, 1861).   [9] HD and Welby MSS. *passim.*

unparalleled run on sterling seemed to confirm long sustained fears and precipitated official attempts at reforms. The opportunity was lost, dissipated, destroyed, by a miserable conjuncture of confusion over the problems involved, uncertain handling of the proposals, poor co-operation between bankers and the Bank of England, and political tensions.

Earlier discussions had viewed the choice of the means to protect sterling as lying between larger gold reserves at the Bank and a reduction of the strains that the domestic banking system appeared to place upon them. Opinion, including Goschen's but not the Treasury's, had repeatedly rejected a third way, that of allowing the Bank more discretion through 'elasticity' in the fiduciary issue.[1] It was not easy to isolate any of these approaches; the repeated attempts to do so landed plans and kept the monetary system in a series of impasses. There was a fourth possibility in bimetallism, but even in the deflating 1880s majority adherence to the gold standard never really wavered. British delegates attended international conferences, but mainly to protest their faith in gold. There was much virtue in silver and silver standards, Goschen would argue (below, p. 178), primarily—as was to be said of the gold-exchange standard in the 1920s—to facilitate the smooth operation of the superior gold standard. British governments might make qualified offers to use more silver, but as subsidiary coinage and perhaps in the Issue Department's reserves, up to the one to four ratio to gold permitted by the 1844 Act.[2]

The 1844 prescription for minimum monetary stability had been the maintenance of a gold-based currency, with limited and eventually centralized note issue. Monetary regulation concerned 'currency' questions; 'banking' operations other than note issue involved primarily minimum standards of management for a special category of business enterprise.[3] Discretionary

[1] See, e.g., Fetter, pp. 214–16, 219, 276; Goschen to Gladstone, Oct. 1865 in Gladstone Papers, Brit. Mus. Add. MS. 44161, fols. 141–2; Viscount Goschen, 'Seven Per Cent', reprinted from the *Edinburgh Review* of Jan. 1865 in his *Essays and Addresses* (Edward Arnold, London, 1905), pp. 10–47; PD, 23 Mar. 1873, cols. 112 ff.

[2] See, e.g., 'Mr Goschen on £1 Notes and the Gold Reserve', speech to the London Chamber of Commerce, 2 Dec. 1891 in *Bankers' Mag.* liii (Jan. 1892), 92–93.

[3] e.g. Gladstone, PD 23 Feb. 1865, cols. 617–18; and see Fetter, chap. viii.

control by the Bank was rejected in 1844[1] and subsequently on currency grounds and because of the political and economic dangers of monetary monopoly. Admittedly, lender-of-last resort action was accepted after the great mid-century crises, but Parliament's refusal to specify the conditions for the relaxation of the 1844 Act registered the formal limits of the Bank's power. The creation of legal tender money remained the State's prerogative.[2] This was the rationale of the allocation of the Issue Department's profits to the Exchequer. The accompanying tendency to view government finance as non-monetary, together with Whitehall's frequently stiff attitude to Threadneedle Street, reflected less a 'complete disregard for' or 'complete ignorance of their incidental retardation of central bank control of the market'[3] than the reverse. Gladstone, the principal moulder after Peel of monetary orthodoxy and architect of 'the Treasury view' of public finance, regarded the Bank's power as an insupportable anachronism, deriving from the low state of government credit in the seventeenth century. 'Hence a position of subserviency [for the State] which . . . it became the interest of the Bank and City to prolong . . . I was reluctant to acquiesce, and I began to fight against it'.[4] Symbolically, Gladstone's London statue in Chancellor's robes on the western edge of the City stands with its back to the square mile. Under cover of helping the working man he had founded the Post Office Savings Banks in 1861, but 'Behind all this', he wrote, he had aimed successfully to provide 'the minister of finance with a strong financial arm, and to secure his independence of the City by giving him a large and certain command of money'.[5] Even when the Bank and Treasury during Goschen's chancellorship sought improved co-operation, they strove for harmony in their separate operations rather than for co-ordination; the one had principally in mind improved control of the money market, the other the easing of its borrowing and funding problems.

It followed that attempts to strengthen sterling would concentrate on apparently technical problems of ensuring a good currency backed by adequate gold reserves, and that they risked

[1] Clapham, pp. 179, 182.
[2] Fetter, pp. 158–9.   [3] Sayers, *Central Banking*, p. 11.
[4] John Morley (Lord Morley), *The Life of William Ewart Gladstone*, 3 vols. (Macmillan, London, 1903), i. 650–1.   [5] Ibid. ii. 52.

foundering on any dilution of the 1844 prescription. It proved impossible, however, to sustain the paper barriers between currency and banking, between Bank and Treasury. This dilemma exercised successive governments which hoped to deal with the increasingly urgent, and superficially technical, question of restoring and maintaining the country's gold coinage.

III

By the 1880s, some forty years after the last substantial recoinage of 1842–5, estimates that half or more of the gold circulation was below the legal minimum weight were common.[1] Half-sovereigns were particularly troublesome, wearing almost twice as much in relation to their value as sovereigns.[2] This was wasteful; it was a degradation of the standard; it encouraged melting, export, and hoarding; and it involved loss to those (principally bankers) who paid light gold into the Bank or to public departments.[3]

Gladstonian considerations taught that public funds should not bear recoinage costs. These would have been equivalent to about one per cent. of total government income in the 1870s and, more to the point perhaps, to about half of the average budget surplus in that decade and considerably more than the average that seemed likely in the early eighties.[4] International pressures on gold supplies dictated care to avoid a gold scramble, W. S. Jevons warned the Royal Mint.[5] Imperially there was pressure to aid India by supporting silver, the depreciating basis of her currency.

Gold economy proposals for a token gold half-sovereign came from second-rank chancellors in 1872[6] and 1884[7] but were non-

---

[1] S. Montagu, PD, 1 Mar. 1886, cols. 1517–18; Sir John Lubbock, PD, 21 Apr. 1887, col. 1523; and see W. S. Jevons, *Money and the Mechanism of Exchange*, 25th ed., 1923 (Kegan Paul, Trench, Trubner & Co., London), p. 112, estimates for 1869, since when further deterioration had occurred, of $31\frac{1}{2}$ per cent. of sovereigns and nearly 50 per cent. of half-sovereigns below legal weight.

[2] Goschen, PD, 16 Aug. 1889, col. 1477.   [3] Jevons, op. cit., p. 112.

[4] Statistics from B. R. Mitchell and Phyllis Deane, *Abstract of British Historical Statistics* (C.U.P., Cambridge, 1962).

[5] Jevons to C. W. Fremantle of the Royal Mint, 1 Apr. 1882, Welby 7.

[6] Robert Lowe: Clapham, p. 290.

[7] H. C. E. Childers: Lt.-Col. Spencer Childers, *The Life and Correspondence of the Rt. Hon. Hugh C. E. Childers 1827–1896*, 2 vols. (John Murray, London, 1901), ii. 160–1.

starters. More ambitious schemes had evolved by 1885 and 1886, with a Cabinet memorandum in December 1886 by Lord Randolph Churchill, fleetingly at the Exchequer. This advocated a recoinage financed by a fiduciary issue of one-pound notes, although Churchill had previously declared that the State should bear the cost.[1] Noting India's claim 'to serious consideration', it recalled the recommendation of the International Monetary Conference of 1881 that Britain should use more silver in the Bank's reserve and should extend its legal tender from 40s. to £5. A draft parliamentary bill for 1887 proposed the establishment of a Coinage Fund and the issue of up to £6 million in one-pound notes against securities.[2]

In the discussions preceding these proposals, the Treasury had argued for a fiduciary issue of one-pound notes both to diminish the gold in circulation and to finance recoinage costs. It argued that to extend the fiduciary issue, one-third of the extra notes only being backed by gold, would not transgress the spirit of Peel's Act; and it argued that a greater use of silver would in fact diminish the replacement of sovereigns by notes.[3] As the potential issuer, the Bank was unenthusiastic about small notes; it feared forgery and reckoned the cost to be higher and the profits to be less than supposed. Considerable controversy would almost have certainly arisen around these proposals, but Churchill abruptly froze them when his clumsy and vain challenge of resignation and his classic lapse of memory[4] brought his replacement by Goschen at the beginning of 1887.

Goschen saw Churchill's memorandum but wanted and took time before himself proposing action. Neither the government's political position nor his own was strong; he was not head of the government nor, for party reasons, did he have his rightful place as Leader of the House of Commons.[5] Thus, the man who appeared to be technically the best fitted since Peel to attempt major monetary reforms, though he had an ultimately fatal irresoluteness, lacked the commanding political position which had assured Peel of the strength to drive through his great reform. These considerations apart, the massive conversion of

[1] Welby 7 and Churchill in PD, 9 Sept. 1886, col. 1725.
[2] Copy in Welby 7.
[3] Memorandum by Welby of the Treasury and Fremantle of the Mint on Currency Reform, Welby 7.
[4] Elliot, p. 113: 'I had forgotten Goschen'.   [5] Elliot, pp. 112, 186.

Consols was enough to occupy him until well into 1888, and the appointment in 1887 of the Royal Commission on Gold and Silver justified a pause.

By 1889 the Queen's Speech could promise a measure to restore the gold coinage, but Goschen temporized on details.[1] It coupled the long overdue abolition of private notes with the issue of one-pound notes, to economize on the gold circulation and to finance recoinage. Centralization of notes would belatedly fulfil the intentions of the 1844 Act and give the state the profits of issue. It was also proposed to end a curious and irritating anomaly of the Act. Out of its own resources, the Bank was obliged to pay composition to those 'Scheduled Banks' which had voluntarily suspended their issues before the 1844 Act against privileged arrangements with the Bank; subsequent surrenders of issue by banks otherwise eligible to continue them attracted a composition payable by the Bank but deductible from the Issue Department's profits, and therefore effectively paid by the public. Political considerations having inhibited outright suppression of private note issues, the Act compromised by envisaging for them a further life of up to twelve years, during which the composition might induce voluntary forfeiture or Parliament might move to outright suppression.[2] In 1856, however, rights to issue were quietly and indefinitely prolonged;[3] subsequent efforts to alter them were to fail. The Bank increasingly resented these payments;[4] perhaps the Treasury's own saving might have eased its perennial penny-pinching of the Old Lady. Pressure mounted in the late 1880s, from the Treasury, from parliamentary counsel examining legislative implications, and from the Bank.[5] By early 1888 a bill was in draft to suppress private issues.[6] On at least three counts it is understandable that it never became law and that Goschen

[1] PD, 21 Feb. 1889, cols. 4, 535–6, 566, 584; 21 May 1889, col. 649; 28 June 1889, col. 1003.

[2] Clauses xxiii–xxv and Schedule (C) of 7 and 8 Vict. c. 32.

[3] 19 and 20 Vict. c. 20. By a pardonable misreading of a further Act in 1875 (38 and 39 Vict. c. 66), Professor Fetter has erroneously deduced that the provisions for composition were abolished: Fetter, 198.

[4] Lidderdale to Welby, 28 Feb. 1890 and 31 Mar. 1891, Welby 8.

[5] Hamilton to M. W. Collet, Governor of the Bank, 16 Jan. 1888, Welby 8; Parliamentary Counsel's office to Welby, 7 Feb. 1888, Welby 7; memorandum by Collet, Feb. 1888, Welby 8.

[6] Copy in Welby 8.

spoke so circumspectly about it. First, tension already existed between commercial banks and the government as well as between banks and the Bank. Second, the Bank and bankers were lukewarm towards one-pound notes. Third, silver unexpectedly rescued Goschen and the bankers.

Banks in general feared and prepared to fight government pressures. The growth of savings banks and the possible extension of their facilities menaced their deposits,[1] and debt conversion their profits. They had largely frustrated one debt conversion scheme in 1884, through apprehension of diminished liquidity from poorly marketable securities as much as from loss of income, but they were beaten, being more cunningly tempted, by Goschen's Conversion of 1888.[2] For issuing bankers, the threat to their distinctive privilege was a resistance point which they had manned before parliamentary committees in 1858 and 1875. There some vocal bankers had affected to believe, contrary to the historical record and to others' reading of the 1844 Act, that the status of private issues had then been settled finally, and that Peel had not intended a short life for them.[3] Thus fortified, they urged the right to compensation for suppression: a claim supported by Bagehot, wearing his country banker's hat,[4] and by a senior ex-Governor. The government's draft bill in 1888 acknowledged these claims by providing for compensation for a ten-year period.

George Rae, leader and educator of bankers, saw further and doubtless representative objections to the ending of private issues. The government could finance recoinage from interest saved by conversion or from the profit of circulating more silver. Outright suppression, he declared in 1889, would 'and must result in the permanent withdrawal of [several millions of] existing advances, mainly in the agricultural districts' which were already distressed.[5] Country bankers, including Bagehot, had already urged in 1875 the continuance of issues and their

---

[1] Numerous letters in Rae, especially 10 Nov. 1880, 30 Nov. 1881, 3 Feb. 1882, 18 Apr. 1884, 3 Dec. 1890, 25 Apr. 1893.

[2] Childers, *Life*, ii. 163–4; Elliot, p. 146; Rae, 19 Aug. 1884 (6 letters to leading bankers), 22 Aug. 1884, 22 May 1888.

[3] BPP, 1857–8, V, Report from the Select Committee on the Bank Acts, QQ. 1276–7; BPP, 1875, QQ. 4607–13, 4705, 5541, 5577–87, 5590–1.

[4] BPP, 1875, QQ. 4617, 4636–41 and 7998 (Bagehot).

[5] Rae, 1 Feb. and 19 Feb. 1889.

extension to all willing to give appropriate security,[1] and these views were again pressed in the late 1880s.[2] A further bankers' objection to abolition was that they would find difficulty in maintaining adequate till money, part of which consisted of their own notes; issuers pressed for a cheap supply of cash through the Bank.[3]

Against one-pound notes Rae rehearsed arguments already well known and to be heard again in the 1890s. They were likely to lower interest rates and drive out gold; they would therefore further reduce reserves already deemed too slender; they could not pay if an adequate gold reserve were to be kept; and a mixed circulation of gold and paper would be troublesome in the pocket and to bank clerks having to sort them. He registered the tension in contemporary monetary arrangements in writing (in 1888) of 'the iron regime of Mr Goschen', of fears that disunited bankers might be 'as a rope of sand' in his hands, and (in 1889) that 'any offer of compensation [for suppression of issues] likely to be suggested by Mr Goschen would not be worth consideration'.[4]

One-pound notes had not been issued by the Bank or by commercial banks in England and Wales since the 1820s, although Scottish and Irish issues continued. Pressures for small notes characterized deflationary times,[5] and caused the scars of forgery, costly in lives and imprisonment, to throb painfully; the Bank did not like them.[6] Such reactions may have underrated the outpacing of counterfeiters by improvements in security printing but there was also concern at the alleged inability of ordinary people to distinguish forgeries; an unpleasing objection was the preference of rural folk for the notes of the local bank they knew over those of 'the Bank of Elegance'.[7] On the crucial question of gold-economy, would not the greater

---

[1] BPP, 1875, 6258–61, 6312–16, 6318–20, 6484–7 (John Dun) and 7980–8015, 8037–40, 8061–6 (Bagehot).

[2] Rae, 17 Nov. 1886, 10 May and 30 May and 7 Dec. 1888; and R. H. I. Palgrave to Milner (Goschen's private secretary), 29 Apr. 1889, Welby 8.

[3] Rae, 14 May, 30 May, 12 Nov. 1888 and 29 Apr. 1889; R. H. I. Palgrave to Milner 16 Mar. 1888 and 2 May 1889, Welby 8.

[4] Rae, 11 Jan. 1887, 26 Feb. 1886, 1 Feb. 1889, 30 May 1888, 7 Feb. 1888.

[5] Clapham, pp. 314–15 for some discussion on small notes.

[6] Clapham, p. 314; Memorandum by Collet (Governor) to Treasury, Feb. 1888, Welby 8.

[7] G. Rae, *The Country Banker* (John Murray, London, 1885), p. 158.

use of one-pound notes, compared with those of larger de-
nominations and their greater liability to be presented in
panics—being held by less educated people—require larger
gold reserves?[1] Weighty voices emphasized that sovereigns
exchanged for one-pound notes would go to the Issue Department's reserve, and would therefore be unavailable in need
except by suspension of the Bank Charter Act.[2] In any case, the
popularity of the Post Office's recently introduced postal order
system was supplying low denomination means of payment. In
the setting of the comparatively recent, slow, and controversial
return of the United States to gold convertibility, of the cries
of bimetallists, and of the discouraging experiences of other
countries with 'forced circulation' of notes, these cautionary
attitudes cannot be summarily dismissed.[3]

Despite its headshaking, the Bank co-operated dutifully and
with thoroughness. It gathered information, admittedly in the
hope that it would provide ammunition against 'a popular cry
from the Radical party or the theorists for paper money'.
Inquiries were made in 1888 of note-issuing methods and problems in France, Belgium, Spain, Ireland, and, through the
New York branch of Governor Collet's merchant bank, in the
U.S.A. On this basis and on its own experience, the Bank made
its adverse representations. It feared that an extended fiduciary
issue would drive gold from the country; it was scarcely possible
to prevent this by raising the Banking Department reserve for
this would unacceptably reduce the Bank's income, which
increased fiduciary issues—the profits going to the government
—would in any case erode. None the less, the Bank had come to
resign itself to increased issues by 1889; and the indispensable
agreement of Gladstone, Opposition leader, and the nation's
financial conscience having been secured,[4] drastic reform seemed
inevitable.

All this time Goschen had been characteristically hesitant.
He undoubtedly needed to be. His already complicated proposals accumulated complications from various directions and
threatened the jigsaw of English monetary arrangements. Not

---

[1] Clapham, pp. 314–15.   [2] Collet, Welby 8.
[3] H. P. Willis, *A History of the Latin Monetary Union* (University of Chicago,
Chicago, 1901), chaps. vii, xv, xvii.
[4] HD, 11 Dec. 1889.

least, the one-pound note was readily linked with the inflationary threats to the gold standard from clamant bimetallism, the
strength of which appeared in the report of the Royal Commission on Gold and Silver in 1888. There was unanimity on the
broad case for a fiduciary issue of one-pound notes, and opinion
was divided equally on issues of one-pound and ten-shilling
notes against silver.[1] If the gap between the orthodox and the
rest was now narrow it was a gap none the less, and all the more
dangerous to one in Goschen's position. As Hamilton saw, the
commission's report made bimetallism 'a question of expediency', and he felt that it would improve the chances of the
small notes against silver for which he had been urging the
Chancellor to legislate.[2] Goschen now found a middle course.
He always claimed allegiance to the 1844 Act, but he was not
an uncompromising monometallist.[3] In this he displayed that
fair-mindedness, so hazardous in public affairs, which invites
complete misunderstanding or accusations of equivocation—or,
even deadlier politically for one who had already crossed the
floor of the House of Commons, the taint of heterodoxy. On
silver he had in public speaking given Hamilton and Gladstone
the false impression that he was a bimetallist,[4] whereas his
view was essentially that the deposition of silver from equality
with gold need not mean its complete exile.[5] In his procrastina-
tion over the proposed reforms in 1889, Goschen managed to
find a neat solution: one that would nod to the bimetallists,
restore and economize on the gold circulation, and avoid
tampering with the 1844 settlement.

During 1889, despite a somewhat unsatisfactory issue of large
silver coins ostensibly in celebration of the 1887 Golden Jubilee,[6]
Goschen was encouraging the greater use of silver. Early in the
year he had urged the manufacturing departments of govern-

---

[1] BPP, 1888, XLV, *Final Report of the Royal Commission appointed to inquire into the recent changes in the relative values of the Precious Metals*, part i, para. 174, part ii, para. 137.

[2] HD, 8 Nov. 1888.

[3] Goschen, speech of 2 Dec. 1891, *Bankers' Mag.*, Jan. 1892, p. 86; but, on gold and silver, 'I belong to . . . the broad church in these matters. I do not consider myself a thoroughly high church, orthodox monometallist'—'Mr Goschen on Finance', 30 Apr. 1890, *Bankers' Mag.* l (June 1890), 965.

[4] HD, 21 Nov. 1887, 31 May 1889.

[5] Goschen, speech, *Bankers' Mag.*, Jan. 1892, pp. 92–93.

[6] Clapham, p. 315.

ment, with considerable success, to pay wages in silver as far as possible.[1] He asked the Bank to discourage demand for the half-sovereign—'this most expensive coin'—and discovered that the Bank's charge of $\frac{1}{4}$ per cent. commission for delivery had kept down the demand for silver. He therefore agreed that the government should meet this charge, and, helped by increased wages, silver flowed out abundantly.[2] This produced profits more than sufficient in the financial year 1889–90 to finance the gold recoinage, and therefore eliminated the original cause of the intended banking legislation, the abandonment of which Goschen announced in the 1890 Budget debate.[3] For the moment, however, he was to stop short (until 1891) of extending the recoinage beyond the 1889 Act concerning pre-Victorian gold, so that the possibility of a link with the introduction of one-pound notes survived and was shortly to be revived.

IV

The fundamental problems underlying concern about the reserves were the control of bank deposits and the ability of the Bank to protect its reserve by influencing money market rates of interest; linking them were bankers' balances at the Bank.

Deposit banking had been stimulated not simply by restrictions on note issue but also by the replacement in 1853 of the hitherto regressive stamp duties with a uniform duty of one penny on each cheque.[4] In the following year the clearing house oligopoly took two momentous steps, by at last admitting the joint-stock banks and by replacing settlement in notes and coin with settlement in Bank of England balances. Four years later in 1858 the country bankers were admitted to clearing, and in 1864 the Bank of England came in for payments due to itself.[5] As joint-stock banks in particular popularized bank accounts as substitutes for coin and notes, the hopes of the 1844 legislators

[1] Welby 7.
[2] HD, 20 June 1889; PD, 17 Apr. 1890, cols. 700–1.
[3] PD, 17 Apr. 1890, col. 775.
[4] J. Milnes Holden, *History of Negotiable Instruments in English Law* (The Athlone Press, London, 1955), p. 221.
[5] R. M. Holland, 'The London Bankers Clearing House' in *The English Banking System* (National Monetary Commission, Government Printing Office, Washington, 1910), pp. 277–82.

of controlling automatically the entire money supply receded;
pressure grew for larger banking reserves to ease the strain upon
the Bank and for larger reserves at the Bank itself, from which
banks' liquidity needs had ultimately to be met. In this context
Professor Fetter's suggestion that pre-1914 orthodoxy practically
excluded control of bank deposits may need modification.[1]

Although this growth of cheque-clearing payments offered
a potential weapon for control, it was easier to favour an
opposite interpretation. Within the confines of deplorably bad
statistics,[2] it may be hazarded that, from 1844 to the mid
1870s, the ratio of bank deposits to a money income that had
increased by about 20 per cent. probably rose from 1 : 6 to 1 : 2·5.
From being close to nine times the Bank's non-bank private
deposits, and about twelve times its government deposits, they
had risen to thirty-three times and seventy times respectively.
Bankers' balances at the Bank were frequently close to the
Banking Department's reserve of notes and specie, although
these items were widely misunderstood. Overall, the private
sector's share of the national income continued to rise and that
of the public sector to shrink, whilst economy-minded governments reduced the national debt after the Crimean War. Private
sector assets therefore predominated increasingly in the monetary system. The Bank's automatic involvement in money
markets on behalf of its chief customer, the government,
diminished; its active intervention implied relatively greater
dealing in private sector assets and what was bound to look like
competition in ordinary bill business. Not surprisingly, resentment persisted between Bank and bankers.

This situation complicated the protection of sterling. Banks
focused broadly upon a spectrum of liquid assets with low cash
holdings (till money and balances with other banks and with
the Bank). Their often aggressive competition created potential
pressures upon the Bank reserve through the drain of cash into
circulation; the impact upon the balance of payments brought
external drains or a reduction of net inflows. Further, increased
lending directly against bills or indirectly through call loans

---

[1] Fetter, esp. pp. 224, 249–50, 283.

[2] Estimates based on Mitchell and Deane, *British Historical Statistics*; John Dun,
British Banking Statistics (Stanford, London, 1876); Rondo Cameron, ed., *Banking
in the Early Stages of Industrialisation* (O.U.P., New York, 1967), pp. 42, 45–46.

drove down market rates of interest, thereby diminishing the attractiveness to foreigners of holding and raising that of borrowing sterling. Internally lower London rates reduced or reversed the movement of country funds into London assets, possibly impairing country banks' earning power, or tempting them into risky business, and in any case making their lives more difficult. These circumstances threatened erosion of the Bank's reserve and of Bank Rate's efficacy in protecting it, until the banks' need for cash drove up rates, reducing liquidity and perhaps their willingness to lend. Bank Rate would then be likely to rise, to draw gold from home and abroad, a jolt being given meanwhile to business.

In sum, to seek control of bank liabilities through their cash was inadequate; control through interest rates offered more hope. Symptomatic of this realization was the concern evident after the 1847 crisis for larger banking and Bank reserves[1] and the apparent adoption around 1860 of the Bank Rate policy advocated by Goschen: substantial rises and smaller reductions in order to influence the demand for London bills and thereby the inflow of gold.[2] Within a few years, however, concern over reserves degenerated into near obsessional fears of panics beyond the Bank's control. If from one angle this obscured the alternatives of Bank Rate policy and of larger reserves, from another it separated them into two problems, with an increasingly urgent stress on the second: that of routine Bank policy and that of reserves against catastrophe.

Sterling's increasing international role seemed to expose the reserves to unpredictable confidence runs, of which the 1866 crisis gave a taste. The temporary eclipse of the Paris money market during and after the Franco-Prussian war of 1870–1 further concentrated international liquidity upon London; and then experience with payments through London of France's war indemnity to Germany stimulated fears of sudden withdrawals of foreign deposits—of 'hot money'—beyond the slow influence of Bank Rate.[3] Internally, public men detected patterns of monetary disaster in the banking system. Even before the 1857

---

[1] Fetter, pp. 259–63.

[2] Goschen, *Foreign Exchanges*, chap. 6.

[3] W. Bagehot, *Lombard Street* (John Murray, London, 1873, 14th edition 1915, reprinted 1931), pp. 291–9.

crisis, which had illuminated the risks of the money market's over-competitive monetization of doubtful private debt, the Bank Governor had given advance support to the later warnings of Bagehot and Goschen. He asserted that the low cash reserves of London joint-stock banks constituted 'a new and hitherto little considered source of danger to the credit of the country'; and that the implications of a failure deserved more attention than possible amendment of existing banking legislation.[1] The 1866 crisis provoked comparable warnings from *The Times* and *The Economist*[2] and an echo from a senior Bank Director:[3] financial institutions and business firms generally needed higher reserves (i.e. liquidity) to avoid or to minimize panics, and to enable them to protect themselves better should panic come.

Undoubtedly unit banks of uneven sizes and of differing assets involved the risk of dangerously sharp fluctuations in deposits and liquidity. Moreover banks had to fortify their own resources against a local or general run on banks. Thus, George Rae was to illustrate the case for high bank liquidity by recalling the drain on one bank of as much as 26 per cent. of its deposits in 1878.[4] Wider considerations were that the collapse of weaker banks might provoke a sterling crisis; or intensify an existing one; or, particularly as gold circulated domestically, might result from and worsen internal panic following an external drain. Many identified these frightening possibilities with uncertain dependence upon the Bank as ultimate supplier of legal tender. Mistrust of the Bank's willingness or ability to sustain credit and hence to operate safely with fractional reserves led to a view of its reserve not as part of a credit manager's portfolio but as essentially a hoard of surplus gold. These feelings were understandable. Whilst recognizing a duty to operate as an efficient bank, the Bank was reluctant to acknowledge wider responsibility. Consequently there were fears that Bank and Government might allow bankruptcies to mount dangerously before undertaking support backed by suspension of the 1844 Act.

[1] BPP, 1857, X, part ii, 3–4, *Report from the Select Committee on the Bank Acts.*

[2] *The Times*, 15 May 1866, and *The Economist*, 19 May 1866, in T. E. Gregory, ed., *Select Statutes, Documents and Reports relating to British Banking, 1832–1928*, 2 vols. (O.U.P., London, 1929), ii. 150–1, 172–3.

[3] Thomson Hankey, *The Principles of Banking* (Effingham Wilson, London, 1867), pp. 36–37.   [4] Rae, *Country Banker*, p. 212.

There was evident anxiety for reassurance about elasticity in the supply of gold and notes: the one for external panics, the other or both for internal panics. The willingness of many bankers to give security for unlimited rights of note issue, thus reversing their traditional attitude and also undoing part of the 1844 settlement, was based on the assertion that country issues were more stable than the Bank's, and that their security would both ensure banks' strength and reduce their strain upon the Bank reserve.[1] Some yearned for free banking with multiple reserves or for reserves somehow freed from connexion with the Bank. As early as 1860 Sir John Lubbock, an influential London private banker, had urged the withdrawal of bankers' balances from the Bank,[2] a drastic step to be frequently urged but never taken; bankers recognized the impossibility of independence of the Bank or baulked at the cost of it. They were reluctant, moreover, to follow the notable banker John Dun in accepting that this meant forgoing profit to provide excess reserves (his particular proposal was to transform the Issue Department into a state body which would hold, in effect as a hoard, bankers' reserves).[3]

The popular view among bankers, blurring the concepts of liquidity and excess reserves, was that they could call upon their balances at the Bank at any time; hence they saw the Bank, not themselves, as needing to accumulate more reserves. The most notable exponent of this crudely alarmist view was R. H. Inglis Palgrave, country banker and briefly editor of *The Economist*.[4] Noting but then neglecting the clearing functions of these balances, he gravely deducted their amount from both sides of the Banking Department's return, in order to calculate the 'net' reserve supposedly available to meet the Bank's non-bank deposits after paying in full those of the bankers.[5] This produced disquieting ratios of reserve to liabilities ranging from 2 per cent. to 57 per cent. between 1844 and 1872. (The equally or possibly more justified assumption that balances were entirely for

---

[1] BPP, 1875, John Dun, QQ. 6458–62.   [2] Fetter, p. 269.

[3] Dun, *British Banking Statistics*, pp. 169–84 and BPP, 1875, QQ. 6456–62.

[4] On Palgrave, see Lewis Edwards, 'A Remarkable Family: the Palgraves' in J. M. Shaftesley ed., *Remember the Days*, Essays in Jewish History, presented to Cecil Roth (Jewish Hist. Soc. of England, London, 1967), pp. 302–22.

[5] R. H. I. Palgrave, *An Analysis of the Transactions of the Bank of England* (Stanford, London, 1874), pp. 15–21, 29–40.

clearing and unlikely to be withdrawn would have yielded the
more impressive range of 38·4 per cent. to 81 per cent.) With
such grossly misleading types of calculation went the accusation
that instead of earmarking reserves pound for pound the Bank
was lending out bankers' balances in competition with the bankers
themselves. This was not just neglect of clearing functions, nor
was it simply a muddling of the genesis of the Bank's deposits
by assuming that they arose wholly against primary deposits of
cash and against no other asset. It was above all a reaction of
unease over what a contemporary banker[1] styled the Bank's
'duplex' role: as a shareholding bank unable to neglect profit
it might keep dangerously low reserves, thereby contributing to
monetary pressure, and then as bankers' bank might exploit the
conditions it had helped to create by bailing out hard-pressed
bankers at highly profitable discount rates.

The alternative to excess reserves, inside or outside the Bank,
was by no means widely acceptable. This was due not solely to
mistrust of currency elasticity or of the Bank; more fundamentally there was mistrust of the efficacy of the differing treatments
for external and internal drains: a high Bank Rate might not
check and reverse the former and liberal lending might fail to
assuage the latter. The great crises did indeed evoke support for
adding to the 1844 Act expansive powers for emergencies,
notably after the 1866 crisis from Bagehot in *The Economist*[2] and
before a parliamentary committee,[3] though, over-cautiously,
not in his much more widely read *Lombard Street*; and, surprisingly, from Gladstone. The arch-Peelite's Chancellor, Robert
Lowe, proposed in 1873 to legislate for the suspension of the
1844 limits on the Bank's note issues under stringent conditions.
These were, however, self-defeating by ignoring the drawing
power of a high Bank Rate; relaxation was to be conditional on
a 12 per cent. Bank Rate *and* favourable foreign exchanges, as
though the former might not induce the latter. Parliament disliked the proposal.[4] Lowe dropped it and the government soon
dropped him from the Exchequer. In underlining the Bank's
need to operate within the 1844 constraints, this rejection of

---

[1] S. S. Lloyd to J. Dun in BPP, 1875, QQ. 6227, 6239.
[2] *The Economist*, 19 May 1866, cit. Gregory, *Select Statutes*, ii. 170.
[3] BPP, 1875, QQ. 8203, 8207–9.
[4] Fetter, pp. 221, 282; PD, 25 Mar. 1873.

flexibility scarcely dissipated fears that a gold hoard was necessary to face internal as well as external drains. Nor did it facilitate the realization that the external protection of sterling
required international means of payment, the internal problem
being soluble (as in the great panics) by the assurance of adequate supplies of legal tender. Indeed, the equivalence of their
apparent solutions explains the characteristic pre-1914 tangling
of the two distinct problems of international and cash reserves.

Goschen himself illustrated this strikingly in 1875 when cross-
examining Bagehot: he displayed the arguments and blind spots
that were to bedevil bankers, the public, and himself after the
Baring crisis. Deploring the allegedly low liquidity of business
and its dependence upon the Bank, he showed limited confidence in central banking; he implied that the Bank might be
prudent to restrict its lending in a panic to the amount of its
reserve.[1] Bagehot himself was alarmist, though more construc-
tively. By 1873, in full cry about banks' reserves in *Lombard
Street*, he underplayed the clearing aspect of bankers' balances
to stress their instability as channels for their foreign liabilities
to drain from the Bank—he damned them as 'a singularly
treacherous liability'.[2] Two years later he gave more placid
witness, much less widely read, alas, than the endlessly reprinted
and more sombre *Lombard Street*. He now admitted to anxiety
but jibbed at suggestions of alarm over the reserves. He specifically rejected the crudity of calculating the Bank's available
reserve by deducting liabilities from the nominal figure—'I
call the reserve the actual amount of cash held'.[3] No longer
hinting at the bogy of banks' withdrawal of their balances, he
implicitly removed the props that *The Economist*[4] and *Lombard
Street*[5] had previously provided to such fears: they were the safest
of the Bank's deposits. For all Bagehot's immense contribution
it should not be overlooked that its basis in practical expediency
rather than in economic theory, though doubtless helpful in
commending his views to practical men, helped to sustain contemporary confusions. His constant regrets for his unconcealed
first love of free banking and multiple reserves, his imputation

---

[1] BPP, 1875, QQ. 8098–135.   [2] Bagehot, *Lombard Street*, p. 290.
[3] BPP, 1875, QQ. 8116, 8211–12, 8217–20.
[4] *The Economist*, 19 May 1866, in Gregory, *Statutes*, ii. 172–3.
[5] *The Times*, 15 May 1866, in Gregory, ii. 150–1.

of modest limits to the Bank's protection of sterling, and his persistent advocacy of substantial reserves—a former Bank Governor was to describe him as one of 'the great Reserve men'[1]—left open the blind alley of maximum reserves and minimum central banking.

V

Even as Bagehot was writing and speaking the Bank was evolving a policy somewhat more discerning than the readers of *Lombard Street* might expect, though it reflected an unquantifiable debt to his ceaseless education of the City. With its restrictive '1858 Rule' the Bank had sought to protect its reserve by accelerating, after the 1857 crisis, the retreat from the money market that it had commenced after that of 1847.[2] This deprived it of a close 'feel' of the market, but at just this point the allegedly dangerous growth of deposit banking and of bankers' balances was offering fresh opportunities for influence. In this context the Bank's assertions that these balances had no greater and no less status than other deposits, that it ran the Banking Department just like any other bank, and that it saw no obligation to sustain general liquidity, deserve more attention than criticisms of its failure to earmark reserves against bankers' balances, or to vary its liabilities directly with its reserve, or to maintain some given reserve ratio. It is arguable that the Bank's assertions flowed inevitably from the political nature of a decision to suspend the 1844 Act to permit lender-of-last-resort action; and that the more moderate affirmations that its behaviour did not differ from that of any other bank strictly meant no more than the maintenance, like any other properly run bank, of adequate liquidity to meet its liabilities at any time. It is, indeed, only by regarding it as a bank, certainly with unique liabilities and assets but still a bank, that it is possible to glimpse more rationale in the Bank's activity than some of its heavier critics allowed.

By the mid 1870s the Bank had evolved a policy towards bankers' balances and its reserves that resembled Bagehot's

[1] Gibbs II, 565.
[2] Clapham, pp. 237–8. The 1858 Rule limited assistance to the money market to advances at the quarterly strains, or in exceptional circumstances.

recommendations within a banker's framework. Credit for it should probably go, Bagehot apart, to Benjamin Buck Greene, Governor 1873–5, and to Henry Hucks Gibbs, his Deputy-Governor who was subsequently Governor 1875–7. Half a century later one of Gibbs's sons was to recall,[1] evidently from conversations with his father, how the Bank under Greene behaved in 1873–4: 'the Bank, though they lent money as freely as before, simultaneously raised the Bank Rate with the result that as money was paid out gold flowed in from abroad and the plague was stayed.' H. H. Gibbs himself explained the policy in correspondence during 1877–9 with Bonamy Price, professor of Political Economy at Oxford.[2] He vigorously denied that bankers' balances were inherently dangerous to the Bank and that there was a simple connexion between movements in the Banking Department reserve and of Bank Rate.[3] If anything, bankers' balances worried the Bank less than other accounts, being larger and more broadly representative of economic trends than smaller individual accounts. It was the bankers themselves who nursed fears—fears of the Clearing House.[4] Aggregate bankers' balances were in fact, next to government balances, '. . . the most certain and the most intelligible of the Bank's accounts'.[5] They gave it 'the most perfect and accurate measure of how far the public can at all act independently of us'.[6] The Bank knew the minimum balances, x, that bankers needed; only y, the sum in excess, could be regarded as free balances. The Bank could hold earning assets against x; only y 'which must remain untouched and uninvested' required a corresponding amount in the Bank's reserve—and he added that bankers managed their own liabilities and assets on exactly such broad principles. With low balances, bankers could not withdraw cash from the Bank unless the Bank itself first lent the money (not necessarily to the bank concerned).[7] The Bank could operate this control in reverse by market sales of securities, making it 'the real arbiter'.[8] The use of more or less continuous open market operations from 1873 suggests an endeavour to operate such a policy.[9]

[1] Lord Hunsdon (H. C. Gibbs), PD, 7 June 1928, col. 335.
[2] 'Gibbs I' and 'Gibbs II' respectively.   [3] Gibbs I, 511.
[4] Gibbs I, 533.   [5] Gibbs II, 497–8.   [6] Gibbs I, 498.
[7] Gibbs I, 495.   [8] Ibid.   [9] Clapham, p. 297.

Gibbs defined the Bank's duty simply as the ability to meet its liabilities,[1] although he admitted that 'we do set our hearts on keeping a higher Reserve than our Accounts themselves would make necessary. But the Law compels us to publish, and we must take into account the ignorance and self-deception of those who read them.'[2] Bagehot, he averred, was wrong, was dreaming, in his assertion that the Bank should maintain some arbitrary minimum reserve; the necessary amount depended upon the nature of its liabilities.[3] In case of actual or potential weakness in the reserve, the Bank could fulfil its duty in good time by open market sales or by raising Bank Rate;[4] seasonal fluctuations were peripheral to the question.[5] Panics involving export of gold and domestic hoarding of notes could obviously destroy the reserve,[6] but though unpredictable the probability of their occurrence could be lessened by correct handling of a crisis: lending freely at an appropriately high rate. Gibbs emphasized that the 1866 crisis had badly frightened the Bank and was a sore point; it was its only real blunder in his experience[7] (he had been elected Director in 1853). The then Governor had erred in lending at too low a rate before the crisis turned into panic;[8] the Bank deserved blame for exposing the Banking Department to real danger.[9] Gibbs did not, however, blame the Governor, asserting confidently that 'the matter was not as well understood as it is now'.[10] Since then, the Bank had managed an equally severe crisis in 1873 by promptly and determinedly raising its rate.[11]

Might not publication of these problems and policies have avoided misunderstanding and incidentally have conformed to the nineteenth century's favourite prescription for sound business, namely publicity? To Gibbs, publication of anything but Issue Department accounts was 'a folly';[12] from 1877 the Bank ceased publication of bankers' balances until 1928. Intermittent pressure to resume publication brought the reply that such details were private between Bank and customer; suggestions that it might be keeping inadequate reserves against them brought the riposte that the Bank's reserve bore a far higher

---

[1] Gibbs I, 519.   [2] Gibbs II, 565–6.   [3] Gibbs I, 530.
[4] Gibbs I, 519.   [5] Gibbs I, 501–2.   [6] Gibbs I, 501.
[7] Gibbs I, 548–9; II, 561, 566.   [8] Gibbs I, 502.
[9] Gibbs II, 564, 566.   [10] Gibbs I, 502.   [11] Gibbs I, 502, 513.
[12] Gibbs I, 501.

ratio to its liabilities than the balances themselves bore to the banks' own liabilities to the public.

Despite the Greene–Gibbs policy, market relationships did not noticeably improve. With Bank Rate above and in poor contact with market rates, bankers resented making little or no profit: deposit rates were linked with the former and their earnings in money market assets were tied to the latter. Further, bankers disliked frequent fluctuations in Bank Rate. Palgrave's criticisms of the Bank for not weathering the regular autumnal pressures without raising Bank Rate seem, however, to be misplaced.[1] The Bank had certainly shown its awareness of seasonal fluctuations, and in 1875 Greene had prepared a detailed analysis of them for use within the Bank. The real trouble was that bankers drove down market rates in search of business and kept virtually no excess reserves.

The Bank's decision in 1878 to discount for its customers at market rate, thereby making its published rate a penalty rate, provoked bankers into anxious but abortive discussions about making rates and reserves independent of the Bank.[2] The massive collapse of the City of Glasgow Bank a few months later abruptly banished this delusion; the ensuing strain led the Bank to contemplate suspension of the 1844 Act.[3] High civil servants examined the adequacy of 'the banking reserve' and the state of Scottish banking, and favoured fuller publication of bank accounts to improve standards;[4] but the government kept to the favourite specifics of strengthening banks' capital position and of more publicity by the 'reserved liability' act of 1879. Fears that expected legislation to deal with Scotttish banking might extend to them kept English bankers tense.[5]

The persisting unease over reserves continued to reflect both genuine weakness in the monetary system and perplexity over its working. Significantly this emerges in the comments of even so wise and influential a banker as George Rae. Discerning an

---

[1] R. H. I. Palgrave, *Bank Rate and the Money Market* (John Murray, London, 1903), esp. chap. xiv.
[2] 'The Abolition of a minimum Rate by the Bank of England', *Bankers' Mag.* xxxviii (July 1878), 569–74.
[3] '. . . when panic was imminent in 1878 Rothschild went to Sir Stafford Northcote [Chancellor of the Exchequer] and asked him if, on going out of town for Christmas, he would leave a signed letter suspending the Act to be used on the moment if necessity arose'—Welby to Gladstone, 16 Dec. 1891, Welby 7.
[4] Welby 7.　　　　　　　　　　　　　　　[5] Rae, 11 Apr. 1881.

apparent dilemma in that, by having balances at the Bank the bankers 'fabricate a stick to break their own pates withal', he suggested in 1880 their partial withdrawal to provide a hoard and to reduce the Bank's power to lend in the market, thus bringing Bank and market rates closer together.[1] Rae here seems to repeat the popular misconception of bankers' balances as arising exclusively from primary deposits, and to beg the crucial question of excess reserves. If banks had excess reserves, the Bank-market rate gap would have been narrower; otherwise a partial withdrawal would have necessitated realization of market assets, this being in its turn dependent on an increase of the Bank's unpopular lending to the market, unless it was willing to risk bankrupting it and precipitating a crisis. Eventually, though convinced that a cash hoard would allow London banks to take the shock of a panic, he came to recognize that this was a dream while balances were normally not in excess of working needs, and that bankers must avoid action hostile to the Bank, to ensure its help in a crisis.[2]

With bankers at their Institute[3] and in the Association of Country Bankers[4] debating means of acquiring greater strength in the late 1880s, Rae, the Association's driving force, summed up grimly:[5] thoughtless competition—from London bankers and brokers he later asserted—depressed rates and threatened the reserves. This was 'financial suicide' inviting 'financial catastrophe'. Later, in 1889, he added a wider theme that was to haunt Goschen and others: the danger of war.[6]

Goschen was alive to war considerations. He was a former First Lord of the Admiralty and his appointment to the Exchequer had followed Lord Randolph Churchill's failure to secure cuts in defence expenditure.[7] In his Budget speech of 1890, some months *before* the Baring crisis, he had followed a proud report on the strengthened army and navy with disquieting reflections on the economy's dependence on credit in case of panic; and

---

[1] Rae, 10 Nov. 1880.

[2] Rae, 24 Nov. 1880, 14 Sept. 1881, 29 Aug. 1881.

[3] HD, 11 Dec. 1889.

[4] R. S. Sayers, *Lloyds Bank in the History of English Banking* (Clarendon Press, Oxford, 1957), pp. 174–5.

[5] Rae, 11 Jan. 1887.   [6] Rae, 1 Feb. 1889.

[7] Elliot, pp. 112–45; SP, D/VII, p. 245, Salisbury to Earl of Cranbrook, 25 Dec. 1886.

he solemnly associated the allegation that 'our bankers and merchants trade with too little reserve' with doubts about the adequacy of commodity stocks.[1] This elaboration of his 1875 fears appeared again two weeks later when he equated the government's responsibilities for defence to those of the commercial world to be prepared. Had manufacturers sufficient raw materials? Had railway companies enough coal? As for bankers, he suspected that competitive pressures led them to depend too much upon the Bank of England.[2]

At the Bank, which had some able Governors in the 1880s, the Greene–Gibbs policy had been continued, but the old difficulties remained despite modification of the 1858 rule. For these difficulties Governor Lidderdale, who scorned the bankers—'a less public-spirited class . . . I do not know'—blamed the inadequacy of bankers' balances. In September 1890 he summarized for Welby at the Treasury the problem with which this faced the Bank, in terms which he was to use many times after the Baring crisis:

I don't think any one who has not sat for 2 years in the Governor's chair during the last decade can realise fully—the dependence of the English Banking system upon the Bank—the difficulty that this dependence creates in our management. Banking liabilities have enormously increased, not so Bankers' reserves, & this makes our burden much heavier than before & leads to fluctuations in rates quite out of proportion to actual movement of currency.

To strengthen Bank control, Lidderdale worked along at least four channels; presumably he also tried to influence bankers directly. First, from the new county councils he secured deposits that commercial banks, who had held the older local authorities' accounts, would otherwise have obtained.[3] Second, by managing the India Council's substantial balances he regulated their impact upon the market. Third, he sought to harmonize Bank and Treasury actions in markets, although the Treasury managed the national debt and dealt with the national debt commissioners, who had considerable funds. As events in 1890 were to demonstrate, however, the Treasury's proneness to view its accounts through housekeeping spectacles hampered effec-

---

[1] PD, 17 Apr. 1890, col. 717.
[2] *Bankers' Mag.* June 1890, pp. 966–7.   [3] Clapham, p. 346.

tive control. Moreover, for all its public-spiritedness, the Bank had to watch its liquidity and could not neglect its obligation to operate with commercial efficiency; it could not accumulate indefinitely low or negative yielding assets (certain government debt and gold respectively) or expensive liabilities (interest-bearing deposits). Fourth, and by no means least, the Bank sought more influence in the money market in two ways. The less controversial was the abandonment of the remnants of the 1858 Rule in June 1890 when the Bank readmitted the money market to regular borrowing and rediscount facilities.[1] The other was more hazardous, reflecting Lidderdale's stern attitude to bankers and consciously risking their hostility. In 1889, having dispatched a Bank official to Liverpool to explore local conditions, he explained his wish to build up business with local bankers with the minimum 'liability to claims on us in times of stringency', if possible by persuading banks to put more business through it. Alternatively or additionally, with the aim of maintaining more contact by obtaining more business, the Bank was prepared to compete for it, even though it might tread on banking toes here and there. Should the bankers not respond the Bank might be less ready to help in stringencies, although Lidderdale stressed with underlining that 'bankers ought to welcome the changes we have tried to make'.

By 1890 there was clearly no comforting prospect of an easy passage should the long-feared sterling crisis threaten: not the old-style commercial crisis, but a financial crisis which Lidderdale had perceived in 1866 to be the new danger;[2] against which Bagehot had warned the country to prepare;[3] which London's expansion in international finance made more possible; and which percipient observers saw the events of the late 1880s as likely to produce.[4]

VI

The Baring crisis of November 1890 makes a good story,[5] but discussion of it here must keep within strict limits: its origins,

[1] Clapham, p. 357.   [2] Marriner, *Rathbones*, p. 141.
[3] Bagehot, *Lombard Street, passim.*
[4] Rae, 1 Feb. 1889: '. . . especially since the much vaunted Conversion scheme, all sorts and conditions of men have been running wildly into Companies of all descriptions, and if we are not sowing the seeds of another 1847, there is no truth in history.'   [5] Sayers, *Lloyds Bank*, p. 155, n. 26.

especially Argentinian; the involvement there of Baring Brothers; Bank and Treasury actions; the evolution of the crisis; and its impact upon subsequent monetary arrangements. The boom of 1888–9 was comparable in intensity with that of the early seventies.[1] Investment abroad rose strongly, especially in Argentina, whose poor credit rating had steadily improved since the 1860s.[2] As leaders in merchant banking, particularly for Latin America, Baring Brothers were closely concerned. In 1866 they had marketed Argentina's first public loan since 1825;[3] a decade later, when financial whirlwinds devastated much South American credit, they helped Argentina to consolidate hers.[4] By the eighties, strong government, a brief prospect of a stable currency, and the vista of rich pampas to which railway construction would give access, attracted substantial immigration of men and capital.[5] Low interest rates in Europe encouraged capital outflow, particularly from Britain, where speculation was already apparent in 1888 when Goschen accomplished his massive conversion of 3 per cent. Consols towards an eventual 2½ per cent.; then and subsequently concern was expressed at this possible further stimulus to speculation from even cheaper money.[6] Between 1885 and 1890 Argentina borrowed at least £142 million of which Britain supplied over two-fifths in new issues alone, about one-seventh at least of her total new issues on overseas account in a heady half-decade.[7]

With strong local colouring, a familiar pattern unrolled. Capital inflow rushed to a peak in 1888, to drop fairly symmetrically to 1890. Heavy investment promised and eventually yielded satisfying rewards, but initially it generated rising incomes and imports.[8] Much borrowing was at fixed interest, denominated in gold or sterling, and payable or guaranteed by

---

[1] Statistics conveniently assembled in W. Ashworth, *An Economic History of England: 1870–1939* (Methuen, London, 1960), pp. 186–9.

[2] A. G. Ford, *The Gold Standard 1880–1914: Britain and Argentina* (Clarendon Press, Oxford, 1962), chap. v, and H. S. Ferns, *Britain and Argentina in the Nineteenth Century* (Clarendon Press, Oxford, 1960), chap. xi.   [3] Ford, p. 86.

[4] W. H. Bishop, 'The Argentine Crisis', *Ec. Journ.* i (Sept. 1891), 533–4.

[5] Ford, *Gold Standard*, p. 87, and 'Argentina and the Baring Crisis of 1890' (*Oxford Economic Papers*, N.S. viii, 1956), p. 133; Ferns, chaps. xi–xiii.

[6] 'The Financial Crisis of November, 1890' (*Journal of the Institute of Bankers*, xii, part i, Jan. 1891, p. 1.   [7] Ford, 'Argentina', pp. 134–8.

[8] Ibid., pp. 139–40; Ferns, *Britain and Argentina*, pp. 443–8.

public authorities.[1] Weak, corrupt financial administration had by 1886 facilitated serious domestic inflation, which free—irresponsible—banking so accelerated as to alarm investors by late 1888.[2] Bad crops in 1889 foreshadowed difficulty in servicing debts; with London smelling its bills more carefully, Argentina approached financial disintegration.[3] Finally, social and political tensions erupted, to culminate in a coup in July-August 1890. Although the new government hoped to reassure investors, it needed time, but the slide had gone too far; temporary default and continuing gold losses, however explicable, could scarcely halt it.[4]

In inevitably overlapping fashion, Barings had both promoted investment and supported Argentine finances. As early as 1885–6 they appeared to be bolstering foreign exchange and security markets.[5] Caution was indicated; one merchant bank, Morgans, reacted appropriately by requiring special security.[6] About now, however, Barings began to act oppositely. They did not stumble publicly until 1888, when the instrument of their ultimate illiquidity, an issue of Buenos Ayres Water Supply and Drainage Company stock, which they had underwritten and the proceeds of which they were to make available by instalments through the contractors, fell flat.[7] Although their marketing methods were later to bring sharp comments,[8] superficially this set-back simply reflected the characteristic misjudgement by investors in Latin America of the pace rather than the direction of investment.[9] The Buenos Aires manager of a rock-solid British bank might see Barings at risk in 1889, but his bank had helped underwrite the wretched waterworks issue; his chairman was a director of the company, the chairman of which was a director and former Governor of the Bank of England.[10] Moreover, struggling to steady the market, Bar-

[1] Ford, 'Argentina', p. 135; Ferns, p. 439.
[2] Ford, *Gold Standard*, p. 87; David Joslin, *A Century of Banking in Latin America* (O.U.P., London, 1963), p. 122; Ford, 'Argentina', p. 134.
[3] Ferns, p. 449; Joslin, p. 124.   [4] Ferns, pp. 455–7.
[5] Joslin, p. 121.   [6] Bishop, 'Argentine Crisis', p. 534.
[7] Ferns, p. 458; Joslin, p. 122; Ford, 'Argentina', p. 134. Each of these writers gives a different figure in connexion with the capital issue, and all three inaccurately refer to it as a loan. The nominal capital was £10 million (Joslin's figure), of which £3·5 million (Ford's figure) was offered in 1888, consisting of £3 million in preference shares and £500,000 in ordinary shares: *Burdett's Official Intelligence for 1891*.
[8] *The Economist*, 22 Nov. 1890, p. 1465, cit. Gregory, *Statutes*, etc., ii. 196.
[9] Joslin, p. 101.   [10] Joslin, p. 123; Ferns, p. 449.

ings were probably too heavily involved to be able, had they wished, to follow less committed bankers from Germany and France in early retreat.[1] Other factors were at work, however. In 1891, when he knew more than anybody else outside the firm about its recent past, Lidderdale declared that even without its Argentine involvements the house would have struck trouble 'because the business was being entirely managed by [Lord] Revelstoke and he did not seem the least to know how he stood: it was hap-hazard management, certain to bring any firm to grief'.[2]

A partner's visit to Argentina in March 1890 suggested anxiety,[3] a further marketing of water stock failed in mid year,[4] and then political upheaval left uncertain only the date of disaster.[5] During later summer and autumn, falling prices and high contango rates on the London Stock Exchange squeezed in particular speculators in South American securities in the successive fortnightly accounts.[6] The shadow over these securities spread to Barings' acceptances, but their prestige prevented panic.[7] They had, however, been borrowing heavily from their bankers, Martins, at the end of September and desperately through Glyn, Mills, Currie & Co. in October;[8] this, of course, was not publicly known. By late October, indeed, *The Economist* felt the completion of liquidation of speculative positions on the stock exchange was in view; and the arrival of an Argentine emissary to negotiate about the waterworks and other debts strengthened Argentine security prices.[9] Within a few days, however, on Friday, 7 November, Bank Rate unexpectedly moved up to 6 per cent. (from 5) and attention soon focused on a single house and on the Bank of England.

VII[10]

The Bank had struggled for a year to forestall a crisis, and throughout 1888 and 1889 to protect its reserve against the

---

[1] Ferns, p. 449.   [2] HD, 8 Jan. 1891.
[3] Ferns, pp. 451–2.   [4] Joslin, p. 126.   [5] Ferns, pp. 454–7.
[6] *The Economist*, 22 Nov. 1890, p. 1467.   [7] *Journ. Inst. Bankers*, Jan. 1891, 2.
[8] G. Chandler, *Four Centuries of Banking* (Batsford, London, 1964), p. 330; Fulford, p. 209.
[9] *The Economist*, 25 Oct. 1890, p. 1351, and 8 Nov. 1890, p. 1422.
[10] I am indebted to a research student, Mr. S. Nishimura of Hosei University, Japan, for allowing me to consult his assembly of financial statistics in writing this section.

dribble of gold abroad, especially to South America, and against an internal drain which had fed 'a huge internal circulation' by mid 1890.[1] Bank Rate rose steeply from $2\frac{1}{2}$ per cent. in mid 1889 to 6 per cent. at year-end, when the Bank's reserve had penetrated Bagehot's 'apprehension minimum' of £10 million, and bankers' balances had dipped below the Bank's own 'apprehension minimum' (a similar figure) for this key indicator. High rates operated slowly; gold eventually came, more than half from domestic sources, much of it in response to the limited recoinage measure of 1889 (p. 179). Rates eased in February 1890, although Lidderdale forecast that 'it will not be a year of cheap money at any time & we shall have to keep a firm grip of our Reserve, but as we see the difficulties I have no doubt that we shall ... pull through all right'. The confidence presumably explains his courteous rejection of a New Year offer from the Bank of France, through Rothschilds, of £2 million in gold 'for a period of three, possibly six months, without any charges except for cost of transmission & return on repayment'.[2]

Lidderdale certainly knew that gold would be scarce in 1890 and advised the Chancellor in March that, having coasted Bank Rate down to 4 per cent., he would resist further reductions unless things improved. If notwithstanding Bank Rate soon dropped further and stayed at 3 per cent. from mid April to late June, this indicated less a revised diagnosis than tauter control and the Bank's habitual aversion to high rates whenever gold could be retained without them: by midsummer narrowing margins between Bank and market rates suggest that Lidderdale had strengthened direct control over the market, while he continued to expect trouble. 'Please be very careful with your advances', he warned the Bank's Birmingham Agent, 'there is a very fair prospect of a good squeeze during the period beginning Oct[r] and ending April—it may begin rather earlier if we lose gold.' Bank Rate was now about to rise again, to stay high until the New Year, apart from a briefly held cut in late summer following an abnormal and unexpectedly high gold inflow ahead of the usual autumn drain. This was associated with a characteristic reaction of cornered speculators: English holders of good U.S. securities were said to have unloaded

---

[1] Joslin, p. 121; HD, 14 Dec. 1888.   [2] HD, 1 Jan. 1890.

them in order to nurse depressed South American stocks.[1] If Lidderdale noted only American silver legislation as a cause of the inflow, and if he welcomed it as lifting the threat of a tight squeeze, he recognized the persisting fragility of markets: 'It remains to be seen whether it [gold] can be retained or whether the Bankers will send rates down rapidly & drive it away', he wrote.

In addition to routine risks from bankers, the Bank's policy of market strength grappled with Treasury economy-mindedness. Goschen skimped with miserably low Exchequer balances.[2] Further, to the usual Treasury distaste for high borrowing rates he added sensitive, almost reluctant, and sulky unwillingness to see his 2¾ per cent. 'Goschens' of 1888 below par.[3] Probably with borrowings of surpluses from the National Debt Commissioners and the Local Government Board,[4] he strove to strengthen the Consols market and was impatient to fund by switching Exchequer market borrowing from Treasury bills into Consols, thereby threatening those high rates which Lidderdale saw in August 1890 as 'all that stand between us & danger'. Earlier, at the end of 1889, Goschen had shared the Governor's anxiety about markets and had indeed endeavoured to help, but he stopped short of sustaining rates by renewal of Treasury bills when the Exchequer was in funds and at keeping cash unemployed.[5] For its part, the Bank felt unable to meet the Treasury's and National Debt Commissioners' wishes to exchange spare funds for particular securities, upon its limited supply of which it relied to control the market; nor, following tradition, would it take the Treasury's spare cash at interest. Thus, the formal institutional frontier between Treasury and Bank split the essential unity of the public sector's monetary operations; the year 1890 opened, Hamilton noted, in tense market conditions and with 'the interests of the Bank & Government in direct conflict'.[6] Foreseeing 'a hard fight to keep the outside

---

[1] O. M. W. Sprague, *History of Crises under the National Banking System* (National Monetary Commission, Government Printing Office, Washington, 1910), p. 131.
[2] Goschen to Hamilton, 26 Dec. 1889, HP; and see statistics of government balances in F. W. Hirst and R. H. I. Palgrave, *Statistics for Great Britain, Germany and France*. National Monetary Commission (Government Printing Office, Washington, 1910). [3] HD, 1 Oct. 1890.
[4] Goschen to Hamilton, 26 Dec. 1889, HP; see below, 198, 199.
[5] Goschen to Hamilton, 26 Dec. 1889, HP. [6] HD, 1 Jan. 1890.

market up to us' the Bank stressed that it hated working apart but saw no alternative. It did have 'various ways of counteracting' any Treasury easing of money; it could punish low Exchequer balances with hard terms on temporary advances; it could also continue to educate the Treasury.

There is only one market, Lidderdale had lectured Hamilton in August 1889 when the Treasury had dreamt of possibly cheaper borrowing outside the Bank. A year later, when they wriggled under high rates, he lectured 'you gentlemen of the Treasury' on elementary debt management. Despite this tutoring, the Treasury was to contribute to the ultimate market tensions which drove the hard-pressed Barings to seek Bank help; less than forty-eight hours previously, Lidderdale was coldly explaining that its mismanagement of local authority funds was falsely buoying up a weak market's hopes of relief, and that this might hamper the Bank's protection of the reserve.[1]

VIII

Summer's end found the City extremely uneasy.[2] Discriminating ears reported help to firms locked into South American securities from 'two of the great houses', probably Barings and another specialist in South American finance, Murrieta & Co.; they thereby worsened their own position, but though alarm intensified, Barings was *not* the most discussed name.[3] This was so even at the Bank within twenty-four hours of the crisis. When Hamilton arrived on Friday, 7 November, for Treasury bill tenders, he found, unusually for a Friday, an increase in Bank Rate. The Governor, saying that rumours about some big firms were 'not wholly groundless' confided that 'he was frightened about one house': it was Murrieta's.[4] Next day, however, Lidderdale heard of the Barings' troubles and the crisis had really begun.

---

[1] See 'The Dealings of the Treasury with Local Funds', a severely critical article in *The Economist*, 15 Nov. 1890, p. 1441.

[2] HD, 8 Oct. 1890—'N. Rothschild . . . confessed to being very uneasy about the present state of things in the City'; *The Economist*, 4 Oct., p. 1258, and 11 Oct. 1890, p. 1287.

[3] 'The Crisis of 1890', *Ec. Journ.* i (Mar. 1890), 194; *The Economist*, 4 Oct. 1890, p. 1258.

[4] HD, 6 Nov. 1890.

Action specifically about Barings had to await fuller accounts and their verification, which meant waiting until the following Thursday or Friday (13–14 November). Meanwhile it became clear that whether Barings were supported or not the standard crisis prescription might work too slowly. 'Unless you can stop the foreign export', Bagehot had warned, 'you cannot allay the domestic alarm.'[1] Lidderdale had already experienced earlier in 1890 the slowness of Bank Rate to draw gold but an effective Bank Rate now, he wrote to the Governor of the Bank of France on 12 November, would have a widespread impact beyond England;[2] and he was later to explain to Goschen that 'It would have taken a very high rate indeed to bring gold over in quantity, as Spain, Portugal, Germany and the United States were all under financial pressure'. In particular, France, which Professor Elmer Wood has strikingly suggested may have largely provided the reserves while England provided the management of the international gold standard,[3] almost traditionally disliked fluctuating rates, and was currently anxious to avoid disturbance to substantial loan operations in Paris.[4] Doubtless recalling the earlier offer, Lidderdale requested Goschen, who spent some hours in the City on Monday, 10 November, to ask Rothschilds to secure gold from France.[5] First £2 million and then a further £1 million were obtained, all of it crossing the Channel.[6] (The procuring of Treasury bills as security incidentally involved transactions between Bank, Treasury, and National Debt Commissioners which underlined the Treasury's excessively miserly management.)[7] The Bank itself purchased some £1½ million in German gold coin from Russia, which offered more; the Bank refused, but Russia indirectly further fortified the reserves before the week was out by undertaking not to carry

---

[1] Bagehot, *Lombard Street*, p. 56.   [2] Clapham, p. 330.

[3] See K. Bopp, 'Bank of France Policy', *American Journal of Economics and Sociology*, xi (1951–2), 244, n.

[4] A. Neymarck, *Finances Contemporaines*, 7 vols. (Alcan, Paris, 1911), vi, *L'Epargne française et les Valeurs mobilières, 1872–1910*, i. 322–4.

[5] Clapham, p. 339; HD, 10 Nov. 1890.

[6] Bopp, op. cit., p. 243, mistakenly suggests that the French gold never left France, but has relied on the extremely poor study prepared for the U.S. National Monetary Commission, M. Patron, *The Bank of France in its Relation to National and International Credit* (Government Printing Office, Washington, 1910), p. 143. *The Times* reported the completion of the shipment back: 18 Feb. 1891, p. 9, col. 6.

[7] Clapham, p. 330.

out its intention to withdraw substantial deposits from Barings.[1] Lidderdale himself was to assure the Russian ambassador, through Alfred Rothschild, of the safety of these deposits.[2]

The outstanding and ultimately most significant departure from precedent and from crisis routine was the collective City guarantee to forestall the domestic panic that seemed otherwise to be the inevitable consequence of public knowledge of Barings' situation. Some £15 million of their bills 'were scattered over the commercial world'. It was Nathan Rothschild's opinion that once it was realized that a syndicate was trying to support these 'there would be a general *sauve qui peut*' which 'would put an end to the commercial habit of transacting all the business of the world by bills on London'.[3] The collapse of the shares Barings had underwritten or would have had to unload would undoubtedly have spread to other securities. Goschen was far from exaggeration when he later declared that the catastrophe would have made the 1866 crisis look like 'child's play'.[4]

Some obscurity, which fresh information helps to dispel, characterizes the record both of the events leading to the guarantee and of the guarantee itself. Documents and interpretation apart, discontinuity exists because half-way through the drama the Old Lady's male lead, so to speak, had to leave the cast.

On the Monday (10 November) Goschen urged the Bank to support Barings in concert with the leading banking houses. Lidderdale in return pressed for government aid as essential to any guarantee.[5] Next morning Goschen again visited the Bank and Lidderdale repeated his request; subsequent consultation with W. H. Smith, First Lord of the Treasury and Leader of the House of Commons, and probably with the Prime Minister, Lord Salisbury, confirmed Goschen's instinctive rejection of direct government aid.[6] The Governor called on the Chancellor that afternoon. Goschen, with Smith, once more rejected Lidderdale's plea; they offered a suspension of the Bank Charter

[1] Clapham, p. 334.
[2] Smith to Salisbury, 16 Nov. 1890, quoting a letter from Lidderdale of 15 Nov., in SP.
[3] Salisbury to Smith, 12 Nov. 1890, SP.
[4] G. J. Goschen, *The Insufficiency of Our Cash Reserves and of Our Central Stock of Gold* (Leeds Speech of 28 Jan. 1891) (Effingham Wilson, London, 1891), p. 7.
[5] Elliot, pp. 171–2,   [6] Elliot, pp. 172–3.

Act, which Lidderdale rejected; and they urged a collective rescue operation by bankers, of the possibility of which Lidderdale was evidently doubtful. Goschen reported to Salisbury, warning him that 'tremendous pressure' would continue for government help, that Rothschilds were 'sure to put the screw on', but that 'direct intervention . . . would be impossible under any circumstances'.[1] Next day (Wednesday, 12 November), probably after consultation with Smith, Goschen appears to have eased to the extent of offering long-stop support: the government would help the Bank with the difference between what it could raise and what it needed to save Barings.[2] This, of course, required preliminary action by the Bank and an attempt to organize a guarantee which, if one emerged, might prove abortive. Later that day Nathan Rothschild, who appears to have been the person most active in the crisis outside the Bank and government, went to Lord Salisbury to explain two serious obstacles to this course; Lidderdale 'preferred not seeing the Government himself'.[3]

One difficulty was that Rothschild was quite sure that Barings could not be saved, and was accordingly certain that a guarantee was out of the question. Secondly, the Bank felt that its Charter debarred it from lending against even the good Argentine securities of the Barings. As Goschen had forecast, he pressed for direct intervention, which Salisbury refused, reiterating his readiness to authorize suspension of the Bank Charter Act. Salisbury agreed in principle, however, to two other proposals from Rothschild. To overcome the problem of the Bank's lending on Argentine securities he was agreeable to a Bill of Indemnity for such action by the Bank; this was conditional on the previous approval of Gladstone, leader of the Opposition, which Rothschild felt would be forthcoming.[4] The other proposition, which seems to have originated with Lidderdale on the Monday (10 November) was for arrangements to supervise the Argentine debts; subsequently an 'Argentine Committee' was formed for this purpose.[5] No mention appears to have been made of Goschen's offer of residual help.

[1] Ibid., p. 173.   [2] Smith to Salisbury, 16 Nov. 1890, SP.
[3] HD, 12 Nov. 1890.
[4] Salisbury to Goschen, and to Smith, 12 Nov. 1890, SP.
[5] Clapham, p. 329.

Disappointed at his failure to secure direct aid, Rothschild left in a pessimistic mood; he had eventually confessed to Salisbury, who had detected some oddity in his conversation, 'that the accounts of his house, when made up at the end of the year would not be pleasant reading: and that he should have to live more quietly'.[1] Rothschild none the less, or perhaps in consequence, gave Hamilton the impression that evening of being 'tolerably confident' that a guarantee could be organized to save Barings.[2] At this stage, however, there still seemed to be breathing-space: Salisbury understood that Lord Revelstoke, head of Barings, had some money available and that there would be 'no crisis for two or three weeks, if only he can be prevailed upon to hold his tongue'.[3]

The City was in fact gathering rumours; to avoid feeding them, Goschen felt that he must now travel to Scotland to keep a speaking appointment,[4] so that continuity on the government side was broken. Lidderdale, however, was still treading water pending verification of the Barings' accounts which he received that day. To help in this he asked Bertram Currie of Glyn, Mills, Currie & Co., a leading London private bank.[5] Currie was a natural choice, 'than whose judgement there is no better', Hamilton had once noted;[6] an oracle even for the formidable Gladstone;[7] and a friend of the Barings who already, through his bank, knew their troubles. He asked to work with Benjamin Buck Greene, a senior Bank Director.[8] Currie's brief comment upon Greene as being 83 years old,[9] apart from ageing him by a year, may mislead about a man younger than Gladstone was to be on forming his last government; who retained evident skill and alertness; who ranks high among Bank Governors; and whom Welby reckoned (a year later) to be 'the second best man at the Bank'.[10]

Currie and Greene presented a necessarily cursory report 'on Thursday p.m.'. It indicated solvency with eventually 'a substantial surplus'.[11] That and the extra French gold made the

---

[1] Salisbury to Smith, 12 Nov. 1890, SP.   [2] HD, 12 Nov. 1890.

[3] Salisbury to Smith, 12 Nov. 1890, SP.

[4] Elliot, p. 173.   [5] Fulford, p. 209.   [6] HD, 4 Jan. 1889.

[7] Lidderdale reported Gladstone saying that 'until he had talked to Currie he was "like Mahomet's coffin in suspense" ', HD, 1 Feb. 1891.

[8] Fulford, p. 210.   [9] Ibid.

[10] Welby to Gladstone, 16 Dec. 1891, Welby 7.   [11] Clapham, p. 331.

situation look 'somewhat more hopeful' to Lidderdale.[1] Next day (Friday, 14 November), however, before a decision on salvage could be reached, 'it began to ooze out that something was up' and the Bank had to take in Barings' bills rather than prematurely destroy credit they might wish to protect.[2] By lunch-time closer scrutiny had convinced Greene of the necessity for a cash advance of £8–9 million—to him an impossible amount; but Lidderdale instantly said: 'They must be carried on—provided sufficient guarantee was immediately forthcoming.'[3] Clearly the crisis was rushing to boiling-point and Lidderdale went to the government, able to argue if need be that the Bank had put itself at risk already and therefore merited at least temporary government aid. He saw Smith, who had realized the need for bold action; when Salisbury arrived the two ministers again offered and Lidderdale again refused a Chancellor's letter; and they repeated Goschen's 'long-stop' offer of two days previously.[4] Lidderdale wanted immediate help. After threatening to throw out the Barings' bills and to ride out the crisis alone,[5] he finally came away convinced that he had secured two undertakings: that the government would raise its balances to cover the Bank's possible payments on behalf of Barings up to £9 million; and that it would meet one-half of any loss incurred by the Bank in discounting Barings' bills during the twenty-four hours from 2 p.m. that day, during which the Bank would endeavour to organize a guarantee fund.[6]

In formal correspondence[7] some days later, Lidderdale asked Goschen in general terms to confirm to the Bank 'the undertaking as to financial support verbally given to me on the 14th instant, without which they would not have been justified in assuming so enormous a responsibility'. In similarly vague terms Goschen's reply confirmed that the government had undertaken to support the Bank 'in case of necessity by such measures of financial assistance as might be required to put the necessary amount of additional resources at the disposal of the Bank . . .'.

[1] HD, 14 Nov. 1890—Lidderdale had written to Hamilton.
[2] Clapham, pp. 330–1.   [3] Clapham, p. 332.
[4] Smith to Salisbury, 16 Nov. 1890, SP.
[5] Clapham, p. 332.   [6] Ibid.   [7] Clapham, p. 335.

When Hamilton, whose illness in the last days of the crisis, like Goschen's Scottish journey, deprives us of valuable testimony, first heard from Lidderdale nearly two months later of the alleged offer to raise government balances, he felt 'sure that either the Governor misunderstood Lord Salisbury & M͟r Smith or else they misunderstood him'. Goschen, when Hamilton put it to him, 'was certain that M͟r Smith had never committed him to any very abnormal increase of Exchequer balances' and noted in his diary: 'How could I have undertaken to find — millions without breaking Bank Charter Act at least?'[1] Lidderdale's 'long fight' with Salisbury and Smith had been over the nature of the temporary umbrella that the government eventually agreed to hold over the Bank while it organized a guarantee fund.[2] It would therefore seem that the offer over balances had in fact remained in its original conditional, residual form. If, however, supposition be stretched to speculation that the restricted interpretation of the government's commitment would have deterred Lidderdale from organizing the guarantee fund, and that he would have opted to face an open crisis, he would almost certainly have been driven to seek the despised Treasury letter which he had the comfort of knowing at least trebly was his for the asking. It is true that, as he was repeatedly to reiterate subsequently, he had been adamant against suspension—reliance on it had been 'the cause of a great deal of bad banking in England'[3]—but any Governor was bound to resist instinctively the virtual branding of failure to operate the venerated 1844 Act; no Governor involved in the three previous suspensions had precisely admitted to requests for a Chancellor's letter,[4] and Lidderdale had in any case disbelieved in the possibility either of survival without a guarantee or of a guarantee without government help. Fortunately the guarantee was to lift the government's immediate commitment, although Smith regarded it as remaining a contingent one.[5]

The guarantee was quickly organized. The participants agreed to make good, proportionately to their contributions, any

---

[1] HD, 8 and 9 Jan. 1891; Elliot, p. 178; Clapham, p. 335, n.
[2] Clapham, p. 332.   [3] Ibid.   [4] Fetter, pp. 277–81.
[5] Smith to Salisbury, 16 Nov. 1890, SP: 'The Government is still bound to take such steps as may be necessary to find money for the Bank if the advances required are in excess of the resources available . . . I do not myself expect the necessity will arise.'

loss sustained by the Bank in liquidating the Barings' liabilities over a period not exceeding three years.[1] First, eleven merchant and private commercial banks and the Bank itself subscribed a total of £3,250,000 on the Friday evening. Rothschilds held back, presumably for reasons which obviously could not be disclosed (above, p. 202), and provoked unfavourable comparisons with their earlier initiative in the crisis; not until the Governor insisted on immediate agreement or omission from the list did they join.[2] The same evening, a similar sum was virtually assured from five leading joint-stock banks. Next day Lidderdale sent a message to Smith's secretary to be telegraphed to Salisbury, Smith, and Goschen that 'the great affair is practically settled. Guarantees already to £7,000,000, and coming in fast'.[3] By the afternoon the total had reached almost £10,000,000. Many other financial institutions in the City and provinces joined in, to bring the eventual total to £17,105,000: not far short of twice Greene's pessimistic estimate and almost £10 million above the maximum advance the Bank was to make.

IX

Too much has been made of the admittedly unusual device of a collective guarantee and of the credit supposedly due to this or that individual. It is rarely remembered that France had had a Baring-style crisis in 1889, when the Bank of France collaborated with leading finance houses to check the threat of crisis in the Paris market by supporting the Comptoir d'Escompte, which was bogged down in overseas investment and from financing an attempted copper corner.[4] As a French historian has put it, France helped England in two ways in 1890: with gold and by her example.[5]

Unquestionably City, Bank, and Treasury had watched the French crisis and its resolution by collective guarantee,[6] so

[1] Details in Gregory, *Statutes*, etc., ii. 199–200.
[2] Fulford, p. 211, and HD, 15 and 23 Nov. 1890.
[3] Copy in SP, thus amending Clapham, p. 334, and Elliot, p. 173.
[4] Neymarck, *Finances Contemporaines*, vi. 297–311, and André Liesse, *Evolution of Credit and Banks in France* (Government Printing Office, Washington, 1909), pp. 179–85.
[5] Neymarck, vi. 328.
[6] *The Economist*, 9 Mar., p. 306, and 16 Mar. 1890, p. 335; HD, 12 Mar. 1889.

that Lidderdale, much praised as originator of the Baring guarantee, no doubt recollected accurately that the idea 'was present to all our minds at a very early date'.[1] If indeed priority can be accorded to one person, that should probably be Goschen. He had already suspected trouble at Barings before the meeting (Monday, 10 November) at which Lidderdale informed him of it, and he recalled to the Governor the French episode and the necessity for a similar guarantee.[2] In the organization of the guarantee, Nathan Rothschild, who had been initially in the forefront and whose house alone was to be subsequently thanked by name in public by Lidderdale,[3] may have sounded out possible subscribers. Certainly several people were involved in building up the fund. One Bank Director approached the West End banks[4] and Lidderdale himself chided three Scottish banks for their meanness. Bertram Currie's role seems to have been overstated, less by his own dispassionate written account than by somewhat extravagant claims attributed to him some months later.[5] Greene was later to assert that he had played a minor role; once they had checked Barings' accounts and some of the books, Currie 'took no further part' beyond providing a phrase ('a substantial surplus') in their joint report which Greene had prepared, 'working pretty late at night without any clerical assistance'. Currie could scarcely have helped about the guarantee before being called in and informed of the Barings' troubles by the Governor on Tuesday, 11 November, by which time the guarantee was already in the official wind; nor could he have done much if busy inspecting the Barings' accounts. His own narrative simply recorded his help, not to be underestimated in view of his prestige, in bringing two of his three fellow private bankers to the initial list, and in rallying Rothschild;[6] any further participation by Currie remains supposition.[7] If in fact it was anybody's crisis, it was Lidderdale's. He alone of the principal figures was present throughout and was obviously in charge; from his 'Governor's rise' in Bank Rate the Friday before Barings' troubles were

---

[1] Clapham, p. 332. [2] Elliot, pp. 170–1.
[3] *Bankers' Mag.*, June 1891, p. 1006. [4] Records of Child's Bank.
[5] Wilfred Scawen Blunt, *My Diaries. Being a Personal Narrative of Events 1888–1914. Part One. 1888–1900* (Martin Secker, London, 1919) entry for 6 Aug. 1891; see Fulford, p. 212.
[6] Fulford, pp. 211–12. [7] Fulford, p. 212, and Clapham, p. 333, n.

known to him, he played events very much by his own ear, even in the Bank, even towards his Deputy-Governor.

X

The news of the guarantee allowed knowledge of Barings' troubles to spread beyond the inner circles without causing panic; indeed, anxiety lifted. Praise abounded for sterling's saviours. A Stock Exchange delegation went to the Bank with an address of thanks.[1] The Lord Mayor entertained the Directors to dinner, presenting the Governor with the freedom of the City. The usual casket was in 18-carat gold, with enamels and precious stones, the over-all design being 'suggested by some of the leading architectural features of the Bank of England'.[2] The government gave Lidderdale an honour: not the routine baronetcy, which he despised, but a more coveted Privy Councillorship.

All this was splendid but it was not central banking. It did, however, mark a conjuncture uniquely favourable to long-pondered monetary reforms. The loss—the squandering—of so rare an opportunity may, it will be argued, owe much to early and strong misgivings about the management of the crisis. Were this a political study, much might also be made of personal factors. Goschen's characteristic defects were to have a prolonged run. Hamilton noted that 'His critical powers make him a very improving man with whom to work; but he is an unsatisfactory man in other respects to serve, by reason of his inability to make up his mind and come to decisions . . .'.[3] He wanted to carry public opinion with him and to avoid the reproaches made against Peel in 1844 of inadequate consultation, particularly with bankers.[4] He did not avoid reproaches, took thirteen months instead of Peel's three months or so, and lost where Peel won. For more than a year he was to preach monetary reform but never prescribed it with Peel's precision. As his parliamentary tormentor was to taunt him, he proposed monetary reform at public dinners but never moved a resolution on it in the House of Commons.[5] He was notoriously sensitive

[1] *Journ. Inst. Bankers*, Jan. 1891, pp. 9–10.
[2] *Bankers' Mag.*, June 1891, pp. 961–7.   [3] HD, 13 Feb. 1888.
[4] A. J. Balfour, PD, 9 Feb. 1892, col. 74.
[5] Sir William Harcourt, PD, 16 Feb. 1891, col. 671, and 9 Feb. 1892, col. 62.

—'Poor Goschen! He is too sensitive for this world', wrote Lord Salisbury,[1] and Lidderdale deplored 'his extreme sensitiveness & at times want of courage'.[2] Not unconnected with all this he could scarcely have drawn encouragement in autumn 1891, during his final preparations for monetary reform, from being passed over for the leadership of the House of Commons —he had joined the Conservatives but not yet the Carlton Club.[3]

Before the crisis had been resolved, Hamilton at the Treasury had foreseen that reform of the 1844 Act would become an issue, and other voices and rumours were soon to be heard on this theme.[4] Goschen now took the two months he had once deemed necessary to consider detailed reforms,[5] meanwhile prevaricating about his gestating plans. His own thoughts centred around three points: flexibility of note issues in emergencies, upon the German model of taxing the excess; the issue of small notes backed by silver; and a fiduciary issue of one-pound notes which he disliked, but accepted as a means of acquiring gold.[6] The Treasury particularly urged one-pound notes, pressing for them to be linked with the overdue completion of recoinage.[7] Lidderdale broadly accepted Goschen's points, but stressed his long-standing concern (which Goschen shared) that the overriding need to strengthen the country's gold reserves required the joint-stock banks to maintain larger cash balances, which regular publication of accounts might persuade them to do.[8]

Detailed discussions between Bank and Treasury, some at Goschen's country home,[9] preceded what was intended to be a campaign in three phases: kite-flying of reform ideas; public discussion and private consultations; finally, a firm plan to be followed by amendment of the 1844 Act. By late January 1891 Goschen was ready to fly his 'currency and banking "kites"'[10] in a celebrated speech to the Leeds Chamber of Commerce—a speech to be read in its original form rather than in his later,

---

[1] Lord Chilston, *W. H. Smith* (Routledge and Kegan Paul, London, 1965), p. 333.
[2] HD, 8 Jan. 1891. [3] Elliot, pp. 185–9.
[4] HD, 12 Nov. 1890; *The Times*, 24 Nov. 1890, in Gregory, *Statutes*, ii. 193; *The Economist*, 29 Nov. 1890, 'The Revision of the Bank Acts'.
[5] PD, 21 Apr. 1887, col. 1510. [6] HD, 18 Dec. 1890.
[7] Ibid. and 9 Jan. 1891; Hamilton to Goschen, 31 Jan. 1891, Welby 7.
[8] HD, 8 Jan. 1891. [9] Welby to Goschen, 6 Jan. 1891, Welby 8.
[10] HD, 30 Jan. 1891 and the diaries generally.

tidier, version.[1] Its familiar themes were bankers' reserves and the gold reserves, its proposals three. First, commercial bankers should keep bigger cash reserves and should publish the details more frequently. Second, he aired the possibility of a fiduciary issue of one-pound notes and of ten-shilling notes backed by silver, thereby to reduce the domestic circulation of gold and to concentrate more in the central reserve. Third, the gold partially backing the one-pound notes would constitute a second gold reserve; in emergencies, instead of uncertain reliance on suspension of the Bank Act to release gold from the Issue Department, this reserve would be made available, that is the fiduciary issue would be increased, under conditions yet to be specified provided that the foreign exchanges were or seemed likely to become favourable.

There was widespread approval of Goschen's cries of concern over the narrow escape in the preceding November and of the two leading lessons from it which formed his themes: the need for larger banking reserves and for larger gold reserves. The details were variously criticized. There was puzzlement over the second reserve proposal, which in that form was to be dropped as a means of giving flexibility. The Home Office made inquiries in some dozen districts of the country, some at least through factory inspectors, and reported adverse reactions to the note proposals.[2] That for silver ten-shilling notes, which attracted only those who saw it as the silver edge of a bimetallic wedge, was dropped. The one-pound note was on balance not rejected outright in the country as a whole or by the bankers, and was retained. The biggest and most enduring impact was from Goschen's attack on bankers' low and declining ratios of cash to deposits, and from his demand for higher bank reserves and more publicity of accounts.

The appearance of illogicality[3] in this stress upon higher, excess, cash reserves in banks when the potential weakness in 1890 had been in the country's international reserves, fades against the background of prolonged concern over the strain that low bank liquidity was felt to have placed upon the Bank

---

[1] The speech was reported in *The Times*, 29 Jan. 1891, and republished as a separate pamphlet.

[2] Welby 7.

[3] Sayers, *Lloyds Bank*, pp. 27, 225, 237; Audrey M. Taylor, *Gilletts, Bankers at Banbury and Oxford* (Clarendon Press, Oxford, 1964), p. 210.

of England. The confusion resulted rather from equating than from relating the two types of reserve. Lidderdale had long experienced the bankers' misunderstanding and suspicion of what they thought the Bank did with their balances; moreover, in the contemporary banking structure increased reserves meant primarily Bank balances for the limited number of clearing banks (against the largest of which Goschen concentrated his attack), but they meant increased cash and inter-bank deposits for the much more numerous and still extremely important non-members of the clearing bankers' group. Hence, in stressing the duty of all bankers, and not just of the Bank, to help ensure adequate international reserves, Lidderdale expressed indifference as to whether bankers increased their reserves 'in Till or in the Bank of England' as he told a leading country banker. To one persistent and erratic critic he declared that

No demand whatever has been made upon the Bankers, as a body, to keep larger balances at the Bank of England. Individual bankers may have been stirred up, but what Mr Goschen demanded —a demand supported by the Bank of England—was that larger available cash reserves should be kept *somewhere.* . . .

'An increase in cash reserves is absolutely necessary', he told yet another correspondent, but 'where these shall be kept is a secondary consideration.'

XI

The Leeds speech delivered, Treasury and Bank prepared to seek the bankers' support. Lidderdale pressed Goschen with detailed arguments for a strong line. He should tell the joint-stock banks that there would be legislation to compel publication of weekly accounts; their co-operation over one-pound note issues to concentrate more gold in the Bank would be matched by the flexibility proposal to ensure relief in emergencies; and, if necessary, he should threaten them with compulsory reserves with a fine for falling short. From A. S. Harvey, who with Currie ran Glyn, Mills and Currie's bank, the Treasury asked advice and was told to avoid legislation, but to recognize the Bank's weaker position in the money market, and to strengthen it by co-operation between Bank and bankers on rates.[1] Goschen followed Harvey rather than Lidderdale;

[1] HD, 30 Jan. 1891; Fulford, pp. 220–4.

finding 'considerable jealousy as to the Bank of England' he sought to 'contribute to a more conciliatory policy'. He met the bankers in formal interview and doubtless informally in club and Parliament. The London joint-stock bankers jibbed at weekly figures and eventually most of them provided monthly ones from July 1891; the country bankers hung back and promised quarterly figures.[1] London bankers acquiesced in one-pound notes, but existing private issuers did not, and offered the familiar suggestion of a general right of issue, this time in one-pound notes and against gold; Goschen's willingness to consider this, as procuring the extra gold and sparing the Bank unpleasant trouble and possible expense, indicated the fluid state of his intentions even three months after the crisis.[2]

Despite his scepticism of diplomatic approaches to bankers, whom he saw as 'a stiff-necked & rebellious race each caring only for his own corporation',[3] Lidderdale consciously risked his personal popularity after the crisis to forward Goschen's scheme.[4] He had to struggle. So blurred was contemporary vision of the monetary system that in May 1891 he had to explain to no less a leading banker than Bertram Currie that bankers' balances might be created by the Bank (by market operations) rather than directly by the bankers themselves; and he pleaded with Currie to 'try to believe that I care more for the safety of the general position than even for an increase of profits'.[5] Lidderdale was driven to desperation, as he confided soon after to his business partner. Bankers had not long maintained higher balances after the crisis; they had competed rates down in the market and gold away from the Bank to 'leave us to our fate'. Of forty-six bankers 'only three showed a fair increase, the rest a distinct falling off in balances' and he feared that continuance along these lines would bring 'a great financial disaster'. He persisted, however, and called in the joint-stock banks, probably in May 1891, to ask them to support rates and thereby the Bank's efforts to attract gold which would be required to

---

[1] Report of meeting of committee of Country Bankers' Association, 18 Feb. 1891, Welby 7.
[2] Smith was to meet Welby of the Treasury to discuss his proposal: Welby 7.
[3] Clapham, p. 344.
[4] '... instead of loading him with praises, they would be "cussing" him as an unnecessary meddler ...', HD, 1 Feb. 1891.
[5] Fulford, pp. 213–17.

repay the Exchequer bonds given against the Russian gold. Although only a handful really co-operated, gold did come; the effort soon fizzled out, but before long the bankers were collectively recognizing that responsibility for the reserve which Lidderdale had sought, and raised their balances to markedly higher sustained levels. Even so, from Howard Lloyd, general manager of Lloyds at Birmingham, came widely held views that the Bank was competing commercially, by implication unfairly, together with the usual suspicions about bankers' balances: all of which Lidderdale sought, somewhat unconvincingly, to refute.

Beyond these semi-public endeavours, Goschen and Lidderdale concentrated on firm proposals to precede legislation, on the central themes of increased central gold reserves and elasticity in the fiduciary issue for emergencies. Goschen had hoped to produce a plan by Budget time,[1] but it took all summer. It is clear that, though Goschen was later to ridicule suggestions that it was 'a Bank of England job' (to secure it more profits), Lidderdale's influence justified Hamilton's epitaph on it as 'really more his than Goschen's' plan, though certainly not for narrow ends.[2] Immediately after the Leeds speech he had reported the impracticability of the second-reserve idea, and urged one-pound notes as the only way to raise gold reserves; elasticity at high rates likely to keep the exchanges favourable 'would be the real Second Reserve'. In long correspondence and in personal discussion the Governor helped to shape the proposed changes in the 1844 Act around these points, although the ultimate compromise did not satisfy him. The revised plan was for one-pound notes, initially like other Bank notes, within existing fiduciary limits; once the Issue Department gold had reached a certain figure, more could be issued, on a one-fifth fiduciary basis (instead of the one-third of the earlier proposal). The fiduciary element could be further increased when the Issue Department's reserves had risen further (by the four-fifths gold backing), but such extra issues, intended for emergencies, would attract a progressively higher Bank Rate. The combined effects would raise the existing ratio of gold to notes before the flexibility condition could operate, thereby reassuring any who might fear for the ultimate convertibility of notes. Goschen threw in a bimetallic bone by stating his willingness to implement the

[1] HD, 9 Jan. 1891.   [2] HD, 26 Jan. 1892.

pledge of 1881 to operate the provision that one-fifth of the Issue Department reserve might be in silver.

Lidderdale asked all Bank Directors for comments upon the near-final draft of the formal letter embodying these proposals which Goschen was to address to him when the scheme was publicly launched. He reported fifteen directors for and eleven against the scheme, adding 'Do you expect enthusiastic support from the Bank to anything? We are not a very youthful body of men, though wonderfully youthful in spirit,—considering.'[1] Goschen arranged to visit the Bank to talk with the dissentients. Outside, the ground was to be prepared by 'coaching' appropriate people, and Lidderdale tried to coach Goschen on a strong line with the bankers whom he was to inform of the contents of his speech in advance:[2] if he could not promise them lasting peace in exchange for supporting his proposals, perhaps he could warn them that non-co-operation might earn far worse treatment from 'a Popular Ministry'.

By December 1891 Goschen was as ready as he was ever likely to be with a scheme upon which he himself 'was not very "sweet" '.[3] Lidderdale was gloomy about the note proposal, and even as the plan reached the public, pleaded for a less circumscribed form of discretionary issue. Goschen, however, by now feeling that he had been somewhat overborne by Bank and Treasury, was 'not prepared to say at present that the Bank could have quite that unlimited discretion to define emergency which you desire . . .'. To Lidderdale's almost anguished retort —'Is there any reason to suppose that the Bank of England is so much less prudent than the Bank of Germany, that we need an extra tight hand over us?'—he soothingly replied that '. . . the German Bank directors are very little trusted. The Gover[nmen]t keeps the tightest possible hand on them. Their position is not one of independence'; and he stressed the general desire to hedge around closely any extension of issue powers.

XII

Goschen delivered the revised plan masterfully before the London Chamber of Commerce in December 1891.[4] His hearers

---

[1] Bank Directors' comments, with a few omissions, in Welby 8.
[2] Notes of meeting, 1 Dec. 1891, Welby 7.   [3] HD, 19 Nov. 1891.
[4] The version used here in *Bankers' Mag.*, Jan. 1892. See also *The Times*, 3 Dec. 1891.

may have been pardoned puzzlement at its complications, despite which it left unspecified the crucial terms for relaxation of fiduciary restraints.[1] Early reactions were unenthusiastic, apart from the Stock Exchange's brief marking up of Consol prices on the proposal for enlarged fiduciary issues.[2] The daily press began by treating the scheme considerately and somewhat cautiously. At the week-end, *The Statist* welcomed elasticity; *The Economist* pointed out that the plan would increase gold in the Issue Department, not where it was needed—in the Banking Department—and that in any case flexibility in issue (which it approved) made larger reserves unnecessary.[3]

Very soon, hostility emerged from three decisive directions. First, Gladstone gave his public their lead when he slated 'a quack measure' in a professed slip of the tongue that in fact repeated his privately expressed contempt for the earlier Leeds speech.[4] Next, *The Times* gave some 29 column inches of close type to a calculated attack by a probably influential correspondent:[5] the proposals were individually unnecessary and collectively inconsistent and half-hearted. He stressed an aspect (which Goschen had admitted) that dominated public uneasiness: one-pound notes would increase the central reserve by less than the amount of gold displaced, the balance doubtless going for export, so that the country's over-all gold supply would be weakened. Gold in the pockets of the people—an emotive phrase Goschen had set rolling in unintended directions—had advantages as an emergency reserve, and its removal would lower national prestige. *The Times* itself in a leader[6] first thundered at Gladstone for delivering a 'gratuitously offensive description' from a railway platform: he had with that provided the only reason for sympathy with Goschen. It recalled Gladstone's earlier encouragement of and promise of support to Goschen in reforming the 1844 Act and for one-pound notes (Gladstone explained privately his opposition not to one-pound

---

[1] Cf. H. S. Foxwell, 'Mr. Goschen's Currency Proposals', *Ec. Journ.* ii (1892), 139–56.
[2] *Daily News*, 4 Dec. 1891.
[3] *Statist*, 5 Dec., and *The Economist*, 5 Dec. 1891.
[4] *The Times*, 10 Dec. 1891; HD, 10 Dec. 1891; Fulford, p. 213.
[5] 'Cambist', *The Times*, 15 Dec. 1891. *The Times* has not been able to trace the writer's identity.
[6] *The Times*, 17 Dec. 1891.

notes as such but to any notes not backed by gold).[1] *The Times* made telling points. Public opinion, to which Goschen was sensitive, was unfavourable; there was a heavy legislative programme for the last session of Parliament; in any case, his Leeds speech had succeeded over publication of bank accounts; not least, the run-up to a general election was a bad time—it envisaged Sir William Harcourt, the 'shadow Chancellor' as he would have been known today, rousing the electorate as he waved in one hand a filthy one-pound note with which Goschen planned to rob the poor man of the gleaming sovereign he waved in the other.

Third, the bankers were sceptical. A swift newspaper sample of some dozen banks in London yielded support only from a well-known merchant banking advocate of silver, though one or two foresaw attractions in one-pound notes as an easy means of disposing of banking hoards of light gold coin.[2] The Bank of England learned of discouraging local views, including those of bankers, from branch Agents;[3] bankers feared the clerical costs of handling one-pound notes, a view which Hamilton suspected underlay the hostility of the Association of Country Bankers, and which infuriated Lidderdale. He was all for exposing their selfishness.[4] Early in 1892 the Institute of Bankers circularized a questionnaire to its Fellows in the United Kingdom, and received replies from 110 bankers, including a number from Scottish, Irish, and Australian banks. Opinion was not heavily divided on one-pound notes; was nearly unanimous that they would make gold leave the country; very strongly favoured amendment of the 1844 Act, but equally strongly saw no general need for Goschen's plan.[5]

Some advance was made, however, if only towards a better atmosphere for central banking. Two banking leaders visited Lidderdale to apprise him of their colleagues' views and to propose a strengthening of reserves without legislation, by co-operation between Bank and bankers.[6] This foreshadowed, in its first point, subsequent developments, and in its second

[1] HD, 22 Jan. and 10 Dec. 1891.   [2] *The Daily Graphic*, 5 Dec. 1891.
[3] Reports from eight Agents, six of which are Welby 7.
[4] Lidderdale to Welby, 3 Dec. 1891, and memo. by Hamilton, 10 Feb. 1892, Welby 7.
[5] *Journ. of Inst. of Bankers*, xiii (Mar. 1891), 150–2.
[6] F. Seebohm's memorandum in Welby 7.

and third themes to be popular with bankers, but not with the
Bank, up to 1914. The Bank should use its right to reduce
the fiduciary issue gradually, to provide a reserve of notes; the
bankers would match this by setting aside assets in some form,
perhaps in special deposits; and there should be joint agreement
on the conditions under which the Bank should use its fiduciary
rights.

From the Treasury Welby made a lengthy, occasionally im-
passioned plea to the stubborn Gladstone.[1] Gold reserves had
long needed to be augmented, not necessarily because they
were normally low but because other countries' gold policies
limited England's ability to draw gold from abroad in an
emergency. This was 'no new doctrine for I think it has been
urged upon us by the best authorities from Bagehot downwards'
and Treasury spirits sank, he told his old chief, 'as year after
year goes by and no progress is made'. Hamilton saw *The Times*
leader as a piece of grave-digging for the plan, and felt that
decent burial was the best hope.[2]

Within a fortnight of the speech, Goschen's 'friends in the
Press' were recommending him to take his punishment.[3] Lidderdale saw disappointment ahead,[4] but helped Greene with
letters to *The Times* under the pseudonym 'X' in a fruitless
attempt to rally support.[5] It was no use. The City, once
Goschen's stronghold, was deserting him; Nathan Rothschild
could scarcely contain his hostile feelings towards the plan.[6]
Seven weeks after the speech, Goschen's original audience
recorded views that were on balance adverse.[7]

As the governmental machine flagged and its impending
electoral defeat was being predicted,[8] Goschen retreated. Perhaps neither his hesitancy nor his sensitivity nor his awkward
political situation should attract major blame; he was only
the most conspicuous victim of the ultimate awe which repeatedly protected Peel's masterpiece from reform. In summer
1892 Gladstone returned to office; Goschen's successor, Sir
William Harcourt, accepted the stress on bankers' reserves, but
in general favoured Gladstonian orthodoxy. He tugged at the

[1] 16 Dec. 1891, Welby 7.
[2] HD, 19 Dec. 1891.
[3] *Daily News*, 18 Dec. 1891.
[4] HD, 26 Jan. 1892.
[5] *The Times*, 14 and 25 Jan. 1892.
[6] HD, 24 Jan. 1892.
[7] *The Times*, 22 Jan. 1892.
[8] HD, 11 Mar. 1892.

Bank and drifted further away from it.[1] Lidderdale's successor, the somewhat rigorous Powell, did not bother to conceal his contempt for Goschen's scheme.[2]

XIII

It is arguable that, even without Goschen's hesitant methods, reactions to the crisis were unpromising for centralizing monetary reform. The unanimity of relief had yielded to misgiving about the guarantee: were the joint-stock guarantors, including the Bank, entitled thus to hazard their shareholders' funds, possibly for a long period?[3] The ultimate success of the reconstruction of Barings was far from obvious. Hence, possibly the initial hesitation of some guarantors, especially any with fingers already burned. Nor were the two principals optimistic. Goschen's immediate rejection of government participation in a guarantee had been coloured by nightmares of a 50 per cent. loss;[4] his own brother, whose firm did participate, at once wrote off 25 per cent.[5] Expectations that securities would be unloaded during the liquidation depressed markets; and it was reported that the West End social life of Lord Revelstoke (the partner blamed for the crisis) so enraged the Stock Exchange that it was 'ready to lynch him'.[6] Eight months after the crisis guarantors were said to be insuring themselves against loss which Rothschild thought might be 25 per cent.,[7] and people pondered the old dilemma of the relative advantages of a 'clean' solution in bankruptcy and of dragging, costly, liquidation.[8] Lidderdale remained hopeful, feeling the need for 'a fairly free hand sufficient time' as late as March 1892 when about to 'pass the

[1] HD, 16 Apr. 1892; 31 Jan. 1893; 20 Sept. 1893—'Harcourt would like to break away from the Bank as much as possible'.

[2] *The Times*, 17 June 1892, reporting Powell's comment at a Special General Court of the Bank: 'With regard to £1 notes, he hardly thought that Mr. Goschen knew his own position (A laugh)'.

[3] *The Economist*, 22 Nov. 1890, cit. Gregory, *Statutes*, ii. 197–8; HD, 12 Nov. 1890.

[4] Elliot, pp. 170–2: Goschen foresaw the loss of half of the £1 million help Lidderdale sought from the government.

[5] HD, 18 Dec. 1890.   [6] HD, 28 June 1891.

[7] HD, 28 July and 6 Sept. 1891.

[8] HD, 28 July 1891, reporting a leading stockbroker's view, and 14 Jan. 1894, a later comment by Lord Randolph Churchill.

Chair' at the Bank;[1] but the possibility of a call on the guarantors had not entirely faded by early 1893.[2] No doubt the critics were too impatient in such a delicate business.[3] There were, however, allegations that the Bank had intervened in special rather than in general public interests; one obviously inaccurate accusation, that the Argentine Committee (to steady foreign investments) formed *before* the guarantee seemed a possibility, had been designed less for the general interest than to help the guarantors, brought a stern private letter from Lidderdale to *The Economist*, which retracted.[4] In these circumstances, the Bank not surprisingly had to struggle to extend the guarantee for a further two years in 1893.[5] When it was finally wound up early in 1895, 'Never again' was the reaction.[6]

The fear that, like too easy a suspension of the Bank Act, the technique of a guarantee for a single firm in trouble might create a precedent was understandable. Even as it was being announced, the Bank was propping up Murrieta's, regarded as a sound Anglo-South American house. The Bank advanced over half a million pounds in four months to March 1891 when it called a halt. A year later, somewhat abruptly losing patience, Lidderdale demanded an end to delay in repayment and precipitated the winding-up of what was now a miserable concern; the Bank's legal enforcement of its claim publicized the affair to the world.[7]

More generally, City and banking attitudes to the Bank quickly reverted from crisis gratitude to normal resentment of its commercial competition. Having risked his prestige to support Goschen, Lidderdale was well aware during 1891 of his increasing unpopularity; this arose from his over-optimistic forecasts about the Baring liquidation and conceivably from his relentless lecturing of bankers—certainly Harcourt, reporting City chatter and no friend to the currency plan, saw the Governor's support as a drag on it.[8] Worse blows were to come for

---

[1] HD, 31 Mar. 1892.　　　[2] HD, 21 Jan. 1893.　　　[3] Clapham, p. 337.
[4] *The Economist*, 18 Mar., pp. 318–19, and 25 Mar. 1893, p. 354.
[5] Clapham, p. 338.
[6] *The Economist*, 15 Sept. 1894, p. 1190; *The Times*, 14 Jan. 1895.
[7] *The Times*, 12 Dec. 1891; HD, 16 Mar. 1892; *The Economist*, 15 Sept. 1894, p. 1126.
[8] 'I am not surprised at what H[arcourt] has heard. The Bankers have been sore with Lidderdale almost from the first. He has lectured them and has rather boasted of the language to them. The City is ungrateful and rather stupid'—Goschen to

the Bank before the guarantee was unwound. In October 1893 its widely known Chief Cashier of twenty years' standing departed in disagreeable circumstances, which indicated unsatisfactory auditing.[1] Harcourt, something of a bully and now Chancellor, dressed down the Governor and Deputy-Governor,[2] and the financial writers had a fine time. So disturbed was serious opinion that even the journal of the British Economic Association (now the Royal Economic Society), over whose foundation Goschen had presided within a week of the Baring crisis, carried a searching critique from an anonymous member in whose judgement the Editor expressed confidence.[3] For a year or so, the Bank remained a routine hack subject in sections of the press, which other newspapers copied.[4]

XIV

Clearly, the Baring crisis did not directly foster central banking, 'the essence' of which 'is discretionary control of the monetary system'.[5] It did, however, stress the control problems to be solved and, in demonstrating incontestably the dependence of the monetary system on the central reserve, it facilitated the Bank's eventual recognition as a central bank. The crisis indirectly helped to shape central banking in at least two other ways. First, the search for strength through amalgamation and branching concentrated control in a few London hands, simplifying potential co-operation between banks and Bank. Much of the growth of bank deposits in England and Wales between 1892 and 1913 occurred in the group of sixteen large London joint-stock banks (gradually reduced by internal consolidation

Hamilton, 27 Dec. 1891, HP; Harcourt's remarks in HD, 22 Dec. 1891. Goschen, loc. cit., guessed Currie to be Harcourt's source.
[1] Clapham, pp. 358–63.
[2] HD, 12 Nov. 1893.
[3] 'The Recent Criticism of the Bank of England', *Ec. Journ.* iv (1894). The author cannot be identified, but Professor E. A. G. Robinson suggests that it could have been John B. Martin.
[4] e.g. 'A Paralytic Bank of England', *Investors' Review*, Jan. 1894, and comparable discussions of a yellow press variety in later issues of this journal, widely reported in the daily press. 'Is the Bank of England irresponsible?' asked the *Financial Times*, 22 Mar. 1895. The Bank had its reasoning defenders: e.g. *The Times*, 8 Jan. 1894; *St. James's Gazette*, 6 and 8 Jan. 1894, and two articles on 'The Bank of England and its Critics', 25 and 27 Nov. 1896.
[5] Sayers, *Central Banking*, p. 1.

to ten) which published regular statements.[1] Second, the leading banks appear to have increased their cash reserves and,
seasonal fluctuations apart, to have kept them stable on a
month-to-month basis. Aggregate cash reserves remained in
the 12–13 per cent. zone between July 1891 and June 1899, and
around 16 per cent. from June 1902 to June 1914; individual
ratios, although differing between banks, were also quite stable
during these periods. Admittedly the terms 'cash reserve' and
the broader concepts of 'liquid assets' varied between banks
and over time; admittedly the old evil of window-dressing was
widely alleged to have extended; but the crucial point is that
excess reserves seem to have risen. At first these were mainly in
balances at the Bank, which rose by about 75 per cent., some
three times as much as the possible rise in bank deposits between 1890 and 1899.[2] Further rises in excess reserves were
claimed in 1909 and 1910, and Sir Edward Holden of the London, City and Midland Bank (now the Midland Bank) asserted
in 1909 that two-thirds of bankers' balances at the Bank were
excess reserves.[3] This can scarcely have been general. There
were small rises in the annual averages in 1907 and 1908 which
had disappeared by 1910; otherwise, from 1901 to 1913 they
did not stray far from the level of £23 million, which was the
Bank's private estimate of the minimum upon which banks
could comfortably work. Gold accumulation probably made
much of the running from 1899, when the outbreak of the Boer
War enlivened anxieties about gold reserves, and the Chancellor of the Exchequer urged the banks to help the Bank by
keeping gold reserves. This probably underlay the subsequent
rise of reserves to the 16 per cent. plateau; if this change were
deliberate and the product of collusion, then the bankers' committee of 1899 on gold reserves, which never reported, may not
have been idle.[4]

[1] Much of this paragraph is based upon the unpublished dissertation of my
colleague, Dr. C. A. E. Goodhart, to whom I am greatly indebted for permission to
consult it: *The Determination of the Volume of Bank Deposits, 1891–1914.*

[2] Bank deposits are not precisely known, but those given in Mitchell and Deane,
British Historical Statistics, p. 447, and closely discussed by Goodhart, appear to
give zones of approximation that are as narrow as we ever seem likely to have.

[3] Holden in letter to *Statist,* 20 Mar. 1909; Sir Felix Schuster, reported in *The
Times,* 27 Jan. 1910.

[4] Sir Michael Hicks-Beach at the Mansion House, 29 June 1899, cit. Goodhart,
p. 160; Clapham, p. 380.

These developments failed to bring bliss to the monetary system. Unease persisted over bankers' and Bank reserves, and these questions were paralleled if not overshadowed by growing yearning for a huge hoard of gold separated from ordinary banking operations, with an eye to potential panics and to war preparations.[1]

Serious strains on the gold reserves throughout 1905[2] were followed by a vintage year for reserve nerves. To control the market, the Bank borrowed heavily from banks, including clearing banks, in late 1905 and early 1906, as it had done on at least two previous occasions (in 1899 and 1903).[3] Subsequently, thoughts turned to permanent improvement of reserves. A number of clearing bankers, though not a deputation, visited or wrote to the Bank to co-ordinate such support for the future.[4] Asquith, the new Liberal Chancellor, aired the need for greater reserves, for fuller and weekly publication of the details, before the assembled bankers at a Mansion House dinner in June 1906; silence was the reaction to this part of his speech. Such publication, he continued, would make window-dressing impossible. He rejected the ideas of legislation and compulsion with the touch of one who contemplated them.[5] In fact the Bank had already proposed, with Treasury prompting or at least with its collaboration, that there should be legislation to compel publication of bankers' minimum cash reserves on a weekly basis. J. Spencer Phillips, chairman of Lloyds Bank, echoed Bank thinking in his presidential address to the Institute of Bankers in November that year. A number of London banks did not publish or publish very fully; country bank statistics were infrequent, defective, and indicated much lower cash reserves than the big

---

[1] Clapham, pp. 379–82, 413–15. Amongst the discussions: Sir Robert Giffen on 'Necessity for a War Chest', address to Royal United Service Institution, *Army and Navy Gazette*, 26 Mar. 1908; E. Crammond, proposing a 'National Gold Reserve Association' to which all banks and the government would contribute gold, reported *Standard*, 3 Nov. 1910; Crammond, to London Chamber of Commerce, on 'Gold Reserves in time of war', *Financial News*, 14 Mar. 1911; Holden, address to his bank, *The Times*, 30 Jan. 1914.

[2] Clapham, pp. 383–4.

[3] Borrowing in Dec. 1899 and Mar. 1903, offers (presumably formal after discussions) by bankers in Jan. and July 1906, Holden offered gold, which at his price was refused, 6 Mar. 1912. These Bank records amend Clapham, p. 380, 386, and R. S. Sayers, *Bank of England Operations, 1890–1914* (King, London, 1936), p. 37.

[4] Clapham, p. 385.   [5] *The Times*, 21 June 1906.

London banks were keeping. He therefore favoured compulsory publication, if possible on a weekly basis. Such powerful support came too late, as he was soon to learn privately from the Bank. Bank and Treasury shrank from compulsion because it would lead to banks' sales of Consols, which were already having a bad time; such sales were 'the last thing' the Chancellor wanted. The Chancellor, doubtless under prodding from Hamilton, was said instead to be contemplating Goschen's scheme of 1891 for drawing in gold by the issue of one-pound notes; but the Bank hobbled this, too, by recalling the earlier opposition to it. A further possibility was to force bankers' hands by revealing their balances at the Bank; but the Bank saw such requests, like those from Palgrave, as designed less to prod the bankers than to bait the Bank with the old fallacies about bankers' balances requiring the Bank to hold large reserves. To the demand for this and other detailed information about the Bank's business, the Governor objected that it was 'of a highly inquisitorial nature', unnecessary, and unhelpful; information about bankers' balances was likely to be seriously misinterpreted and, not least, concerned banker-customer relationships which the Bank could not reveal, barring a parliamentary order, without their customers' permission. His successor let it be known in 1907 'that more than one of the leading Joint Stock Banks would strongly object to publication'. It was, of course, always open to banks—as a Bank Director later pointed out—to publish their own individual holdings at the Bank.[1]

Once more, as so often in the post-1844 history of the English monetary system, each potential solution discovered another problem. By early 1907 Asquith had abandoned legislative intentions for the old rut of hoping for mutual agreement between bankers.[2] Bankers did not in fact agree sufficiently. One solid leading banker, with some justification, blamed the press for much of the alarm, but his assertion that bankers would meet any real need for reserves without any outside pressure overlooked the irresponsible bankers. It also neglected the persisting distortion of window-dressing behind which many bankers not deemed irresponsible in other respects were widely believed

---

[1] F. Huth Jackson, Presidential address to Institute of Bankers, in *Financier and Bullionist*, 11 Nov. 1909.
[2] PD, 21 Feb. 1907, col. 1053, and 22 Mar. 1907, col. 1279.

to be concealing the true facts about their reserve positions[1]—although the greater importance of liquid assets as a whole might be held to justify the cocking of this particular snook at the cash reserve superstition. A further difficulty was that country bankers claimed that their business was so different as to justify different standards, and they objected to monthly, let alone weekly, statements; one of their distinguished leaders, unintentionally imputing inefficiency to them, declared that publication would drive them into the arms of the big banks.[2]

The boom of 1905–7 and the crash of 1907 in the U.S.A. reinforced fears about gold reserves. There was now to be little relaxation in discussions about increasing reserves, where to keep them, and how to manage them. Outstanding features were Committees of London Clearing Bankers on Gold Reserves appointed (or revived) in 1907 and 1912, and committees, reports, and discussions by the London Chamber of Commerce and the national Association of Chambers of Commerce.[3] Leading clearing bankers such as Holden, who sometimes reported on possible gold movements to the Bank, were becoming aware of international pressures as their business expanded. After six changes of Bank Rate in 1906 and seven in 1907 some continuing business cries were heard for higher reserves to permit more stable rates: an inconsistency, since 'stability' was often coupled with 'low rates', and also an impossibility in Britain's open economy.[4] In general, the stress was on accumulating a hoard rather than on managing gold reserves, though protestations of faith in Bank Rate's power to draw gold did not come exclusively from the Bank; and advocacy of elasticity in Bank of England issues came from the responsible press and even from

[1] Goschen, *Essays and Addresses*, p. 128; Goodhart, *Bank Deposits*, pp. 92–93, 116–20.

[2] R. Beckett of Leeds, speaking at meetings of the Association of Chambers of Commerce, *Financial Times*, 21 Sept. 1910 and 15 Mar. 1911.

[3] Bankers' Committees: Clapham, p. 414, and *The Times*, 5 Apr. 1913. The Committee was still sitting at the outbreak of war. Chambers of Commerce: *Financial Times*, 15 Feb. and 11 Mar. 1908, 3 Mar. 1909, and 20 Sept. 1910; *Statist*, 31 July 1909.

[4] 'Traders and the Bank Rate', *Financial Times*, 3 Mar. 1907; 'Inquiry into the Effects of Dear Money on Home Trade', *The Economist*, 23 and 30 Nov. 1907, cit. Ford, *Gold Standard*, pp. 44–46; Report of *Ass. of Ch. of Com.*, Banking and Currency Comm., *Financial Times*, 3 Mar. 1909; Schuster to his bank, reported *The Times*, 27 Jan. 1910.

the multi-minded Chambers of Commerce.[1] The major inspira-
tions of these pressures were the old fears of domestic or external
panics with which only gold could deal, together with the
increasing anxiety about the supposed role of gold in readiness
for war.

Few recognized the change that the Baring crisis had brought
in the status of the Bank towards the rest of the monetary
system. It was rather the attitude of many bankers to the Bank
which had insufficiently changed. There was still suspicion of
the Bank, that it was competing commercially, and that it was
using bankers' balances for this purpose instead of protecting
them with earmarked reserves. Thus, Schuster of the Union of
London and Smiths' Bank, a relentless advocate of higher
reserves and for co-operation with the Bank, wanted a second
reserve of gold separate from ordinary balances at the Bank,
to be supervised jointly by the Bank and bankers.[2] Holden
preferred banks to accumulate their own reserves out of reach
of the Bank; and so did some others.[3]

XV

The urge to have a 'war chest', the monetary parallel of
Dreadnought construction, overlaid banking considerations
with political and nationalistic emotions. The example of the
German war-reserve of gold in Spandau, Berlin, separate from
the Reichsbank's gold—the *Juliusturm*—bewitched many;[4] the
significance for German war preparations of the mark's weakness during the Agadir crisis of 1911 and of the subsequent

---

[1] The *Statist* persistently urged elasticity. See, e.g., 7 Aug. 1909, 8 Feb. 1913.
The Association of Chambers of Commerce advocated it: *Financial Times*, 3 Mar.
1909, 21 Sept. 1910, 15 Mar. 1911.

[2] Clapham, pp. 366–7, 380, 389–90.

[3] Discussion at Institute of Bankers, *Financial News*, 16 Jan. 1907; Schuster, rep.
The Times, 27 Jan. 1910.

[4] Giffen, 'War Chest', *Army and Navy Gazette*, 26 Mar. 1908; 'Finance and
National Security', *Standard*, 3 Nov. 1910; Crammond, to Lond. Ch. Comm.,
Financial News, 14 Mar. 1911; 'Lombard Street and a First Class War', *The Times*,
29 Feb. 1912; Holden to Manchester Statistical Society, *Financial Times*, 24 Oct.
1912; *Standard*, 15 Mar. 1913—the government should have a national money
box for the Chancellor of the Exchequer's savings; *Financial News*, 8 Apr. 1913, on
the gold scramble; Holden, urging a Royal Commission to investigate the nation's
gold reserves, address to bank, *The Times*, 30 Jan. 1914.

almost sacrificial efforts to remedy it were noted.[1] Goschen publicly and, for that matter, Welby privately had buttressed their arguments in 1891 with 'league tables' of national holdings of gold, and this dubious device intruded into later discussion to obscure sterling's real situation as thoroughly as the gold-frightened Goschen had obscured his own earlier analysis of Britain's short-term creditor position.[2] A cynic might note that the countries which the monetary jingoists cited for envy, on account of their gold reserves, did rather poorly in wars.

How was the extra gold to be provided? In the absence of legislation and of sufficiently close understanding with the Bank, bankers felt obliged to accumulate their own gold. Verbal evidence is of substantial increases by 1912 and J. H. Tritton of Barclays quoted from a Mint Report in 1914 to allow the inference that bankers had increased their gold holdings substantially in 1907–8 and again (after a drop in 1910) in 1911–13.[3] Publications of bankers' gold holdings had been prematurely expected in 1913;[4] Holden promised to and duly did publish his bank's in 1914.[5] Apart from these pressures from banks, there was a persistent demand that gold reserves should be kept against the deposits of savings banks:[6] a demand as equally rejected by Bank and government, who saw it as a means of shifting from the banks a burden which they, as the providers of cheques, the main means of payment, ought to bear.[7] One-pound notes also attracted support,[8] but much the most insistent and, for central banking, most threatening demand was for

---

[1] C. Rist, *Les Finances de guerre de l'Allemagne* (Payot, Paris, 1921), ch. 1; *Statist*, 10 May 1913; *The Times*, 24 Jan. 1914.

[2] Goschen in Leeds speech; Welby to Gladstone, 16 Dec. 1891, Welby 7; Crammond, rep. *Financial News*, 14 Mar. 1911; *Standard*, 30 Aug. 1913; *Financial News*, 16 June 1914.

[3] Letter to *The Times*, 26 Jan. 1914.

[4] F. A. Bevan of Barclays, member of Bankers' Committee on gold reserves, *Financial News*, 5 Aug. 1913.

[5] Clapham, pp. 414–15.

[6] Ibid., p. 387; Chambers of Commerce, rep. *Financial Times*, 11 Mar. 1908, 3 Mar. 1909, and 20 Sept. 1910, and *Statist*, 31 July 1909; Holden, letter to *Standard*, 11 Aug. 1906, and to bank, rep. *The Times*, 30 Jan. 1914; Crammond, *Financial News*, 14 Mar. 1911; *Financial News*, 8 Apr. 1913.

[7] F. Huth Jackson on 'Gold Reserves' at Leeds, *Yorks. Daily Post*, 12 May 1914; Asquith, PD, 19 Nov. 1906, col. 398.

[8] e.g. from Holden, letters to *Statist*, 14 July 1906, and *Standard*, 11 Aug. 1906; letter from Sir Samuel Montagu, merchant banker, to *The Economist*, 21 July 1906; Ass. Ch. Com., *Financial Times*, 3 Mar. 1909.

a reduction or abolition of the fiduciary issue. It was argued, rather questionably, that such reduction was contemplated by the 1844 Act; it would give reserve elasticity, by the amount of the fiduciary issue without suspending it. Variations on this popular theme included proposals by at least two leading bankers to the Bankers' Committee in 1913, in whose activities the Bank participated, for bankers to share in this burden by paying in gold as the Bank reduced the fiduciary issue.[1]

The Bank of England's attitude to these problems naturally fluctuated with the biennial change in Governors, but a broad pattern of a dual policy emerges. First, it tended to swim with the current. It continued to stress the need for balances at the Bank as the best means by which bankers could ensure better gold reserves,[2] but it came to admit by 1914—strictly one of the Directors admitted, but he would hardly have spoken out of turn on such a matter—a case for the reduction of the fiduciary issue.[3] Indeed, ever since the shock of 1866 it had kept its overall gold holding much closer to its net note circulation, and from 1893 the former was always in excess of the latter; it had done this in only a dozen of the Bank's preceding 199 years, and six of these had been since 1866. In effect, the Bank was neutralizing the fiduciary element.[4]

Secondly, whilst nodding to contemporary prejudices, the Bank followed a central banking path. Higher cash ratios helped, but did not ensure control of the money supply; and banks' views of liquid assets were changing, especially as bills replaced Consols in the liquidity spectrum shortly before 1914.[5] The Bank's spokesmen tried to teach bankers that their and the Bank's actions were complementary: there was a single market. It refused to share its responsibility directly with bankers, but trod a delicate path to encourage co-operation, for

[1] The persistent Holden in letters to *Statist*, 14 July 1906; *Standard*, 11 Aug. 1906; *Statist*, 20 Nov. 1909; and to bank, rep. *The Times*, 30 Jan. 1914. D. Drummond Fraser, 'The Problem of the Gold Reserve' to the Manchester Statistical Society, rep. *Manch. Guardian*, 16 Nov. 1911. Chambers of Commerce, *Statist*, 31 July 1909, and *Financial Times*, 3 Mar. 1909, 20 Sept. 1910, 15 Mar. 1911.
[2] F. Huth Jackson, *Yorks. Daily Post*, 12 May 1914.   [3] Ibid.
[4] Mitchell and Deane, *British Hist. Stats.*, pp. 444–5; cf. Drummond Fraser, Gold Reserve, *Manch. Guardian*, 16 Nov. 1911. Professor Frank Paish recalls his father, Sir George Paish, telling him before 1914 that the Bank sought to keep its Banking Department Reserve at a level sufficient to cover the fiduciary issue.
[5] Goodhart, *Bank Deposits*, pp. 181–2.

which many clearing bankers were anxious. Contacts between individual bankers and the Bank were by no means infrequent before regular quarterly meetings were instituted in 1911.[1]

Within the 1844 restraints, the Bank developed considerable technical ingenuity, although the weapon of Bank Rate predominated increasingly after 1907.[2] If we admit Bank Rate to have been a uniquely successful policy in somewhat unique historical conditions, it may be appropriate not to lay all the stress on sterling's strong external position as the basis of London's ability to attract gold; the accumulation by the banks of excess reserves must have helped to increase the effectiveness of Bank Rate for which Lidderdale had yearned. One thing the Bank did not do was to develop international monetary cooperation. Bimetallism was languishing; the closing of the Indian mints to silver in 1893 had eased Britain's principal concern with the depreciated metal[3] and fresh discoveries had eased the strain on gold. Interesting proposals, with a modern flavour, were afloat for international pooling of reserves before 1914, but political considerations stressed more national approaches.[4]

By 1914 it could be argued that the Bank had acquired mastery of the market, but it was scarcely less significant that gold was king, with the effective disappearance of the fiduciary issue stiffening the rigour of the 1844 Act. Gold to meet a war crisis and a gold basis for war finance were regarded as essential. The muddle of the 1914 crisis, the very brief suspension of the 1844 Act, the issue of notes under the Treasury's name instead of that of the Bank (which had prepared much better ones), and the charade throughout the war of maintaining the 1844 Act in operation despite the vastly expanded Treasury note issue: all fit easily into the context of the pre-war gold agitation. The Cunliffe Report of 1918, with its trumpet call for a return to the dominance of gold, resumed the trend and earned the enthusiastic headline 'Back to Sanity'.[5] Ten years later, when

---

[1] Clapham, pp. 413–14.
[2] See Sayers, *Bank of England Operations*, *passim*.
[3] A. J. Balfour, PD, 30 July 1903, cols. 894–5.
[4] F. Garelli, *La Coopération monétaire depuis un siècle* (George et Cie., Geneva, 1946), esp. chaps. 1 and 3. Proposals for an 'International Council of Bankers' to have gold reserves ready at key points: *Financial Times*, 2 Mar. and 12 June 1914.
[5] *The Economist*, 2 Nov. 1918, p. 618.

the House of Lords debated the second reading of the Currency and Bank Notes Bill to complete the re-establishment of the gold base—a debate appropriately introduced by Lord Peel— the government unexpectedly found itself driven into a corner. The bill provided for a reduction of the now expanded fiduciary issue; that was acceptable. The bill also, however, at last introduced provision for expansion into the 1844 pattern; this provoked strong criticism from the House, and Peel had to battle for it as something unlikely to be used.[1] Meanwhile, as during the period 1890–1914, the realities of the monetary situation had to be managed in the politicians' framework for it. War finance had vastly and permanently enlarged the public sector, creating both greater necessity and greater scope for Bank intervention but, in a changing environment, less and less in an independent guise. The incredible tussle with the government over the Bank's gold in Canada in 1917[2] registered the State's priority in monetary management, which the events of 1931 were to seal in peacetime. By 1937 the Governor could say with reasonable accuracy, 'I am an instrument of the Treasury'.[3] To all these developments the Baring crisis gave some impetus in helping to fashion that instrument. Curiously, perhaps, the excessive stress on bankers' cash did not die its official death until 1952, when the Bank of England's annual report and the government's *Economic Survey* bracketed it with liquid assets as a whole.

[1] PD, House of Lords, 7 June 1928.
[2] Sir Henry Clay, *Lord Norman* (Macmillan, London, 1957), pp. 101–5.
[3] Ibid., p. 437.

J. E. WADSWORTH

Banking Ratios Past and Present

B ANKS in Britain did not have to worry about the precise
disposition of their assets or balance-sheet ratios until
quite recent times. Private country bankers and, for that
matter, the new joint-stock banks of a century and more ago,
simply kept in their tills their own notes, with an indeterminate
amount in gold and silver coins to pay out when required, for
example to meet notes presented and to provide small change.
They regarded balances with their London agents, possibly
fortified by holdings of bills and investments in Consols or 'the
Funds', as providing safeguards against the dread misfortune
of a run. In London, however, such bank 'reserves' took the
form of Bank of England notes and balances there. True, of
itself the keeping of cash and 'reserves' led to the emergence of
an early form of liquidity ratio, sometimes even above the 28
per cent. of liabilities (now, of course, deposits) that we know
today. But it was not maintained with the current close attention to a minimum proportion and definition of components,
and there was nothing to correspond with the strictly observed
cash ratio, or still less to the use of such conventions in the
official regulation of monetary conditions to which we have
become accustomed. Again, the restriction of advances by a
'ceiling'; the transfer of special deposits at a required percen-
age; and concern with the proportion to deposits of advances
and of 'own funds', that is capital, published reserves and undivided profits, are likewise troubles for bankers of this century,
and mostly of our own period.

Even the simple safeguard of an adequate 'reserve' against
individual bankers' own note issues of long ago was not widely
observed, nor were such 'reserves' kept closely to a particular
proportion of liabilities. But when transport was uncertain and
rumours rife, unless banks kept reasonably liquid they were
vulnerable, as the many failures showed. Dr. Pressnell, in

discussing the history of the liquidity ratio,[1] refers to the practice of some early country bankers of keeping as much as 30 to 40 per cent. in 'liquid' assets against liabilities, a practice traced back as far as the eighteenth century and regarded as justifying the description of a ratio of one-third. But, to judge by surviving specimens, balance-sheets of smaller banks often revealed in private an entire disregard for ratios sometimes professed in public. In those days reserves of liquidity were there to use, not just to hold, and no self-respecting banker has ever regarded liquid assets as something to be kept at an unvarying level or proportion, unless forced so to do by monetary regulation or following a firmly established convention. In balancing the scales between profitability and safety, a minimum would be kept in barren cash. Such reserves as were maintained quite frequently included long-term government securities, in a 'basket of assets', to use Pressnell's phrase, for in those far-away days the ready marketability and steady price of Consols endowed them with a high degree of liquidity.

More remarkable still—at any rate in England—was the practice among provincial banks of lending by way of advances and discounts amounts to a total exceeding deposits, plus, likely enough, notes issued and capital as well.[2] Indeed, early joint-stock banks sought support from investors by the dangerous offer of loans against security of the bank's own shares, to the extent of half or two-thirds of individual holdings of capital,[3] while a century ago a country bank's resources would often be enlarged by loans from other banks or by rediscounts, a means of increasing funds adopted on occasion by specialized banks today. Above all, save for the partners of a particular bank, nobody knew the extent of its 'reserves', or how they were held.

It was the publication of figures that operated as a powerful influence to extend sound practices more widely and to sow the seeds of change. The new joint-stock banks springing up in London during the early thirties began by publishing annual

[1] L. S. Pressnell, 'That Liquidity Ratio', *Journal of the Institute of Bankers*, June 1959.
[2] Crick and Wadsworth, *A Hundred Years of Joint Stock Banking* (Hodder and Stoughton, 1936). Many examples are given in extracts from bank balance-sheets in chapter appendixes. (Further references to this volume will be cited as 'C and W').
[3] Ibid., pp. 120, 177, 214.

accounts. In this they were distinctive, for private banks did not print any statements at all, and provincial joint-stock banks rarely published more than annual figures for capital and profits.[1] For these even the occasional balance-sheets appearing in minute books were at that time compressed to the point of unintelligibility. The Coventry Union Banking Company provides an example[2] in its entry for 30 June 1858, when only one omnibus item appears on the assets side, reading 'By amount of Cash and Bills on hand, also value of Bank Property, Money in the Funds and accounts owing to the Bank'. However, the Bank of England itself was required by the Bank Charter Act of 1844 to issue the weekly Bank Return, and in the legislation a shadow of the one-third rule appeared in that the limitation on enlarging the Bank's own fiduciary note issue was set at not more than two-thirds of lapsed private-bank note issues. Only a few years earlier the Bank had described its adherence to ratios in the 'Palmer rule', requiring the holding of one-third of its liabilities in gold when sterling was steady. Whether the proportion was in fact observed or appropriate is not here discussed; what is remarked is the further evidence it gives of the reiteration of the one-third proportion as a rule of thumb in quite different banking situations.

Structural and constitutional changes that from this time onwards swept across the banking scene brought pressure towards improved liquidity and towards the publication of figures. Yet right down to the end of the last century bank assets as recorded in published accounts were not often distinguished under identifiable descriptions. Barely a hundred years ago, in a detailed analysis of banking figures, John Dun complained that it was 'impossible to attain perfect consistency in arranging the assets under various heads'.[3] He spoke of 'cash and surplus funds', meaning legal tender gold and silver coins and notes of the Bank of England, notes of other banks, government and other securities, and 'money placed in a readily available position

---

[1] The Joint Stock Banking Code of 1845 (7 and 8 Vict. c. 113) required new banks to publish monthly statements of account, but this and other conditions were regarded as so oppressive that few new banks were formed until after the legislation was repealed in 1857.

[2] C and W, p. 92.

[3] *British Banking Statistics* (London, 1876), pp. 80–85. John Dun was the general manager of Parr's Bank from 1865 to 1902.

outside of the business of the bank'. If we exclude securities, these items can be regarded as reasonably close to the liquid assets of today. Nevertheless, there was no general observance of a proportion to liabilities by individual banks. In a broad sense the one-third rule—if it can be so described—reappears, at any rate for groups of banks. For these the average ratio of cash and surplus funds to liabilities was between 25·4 per cent. and 38·0. For individual banks, however, the spread was much wider, ranging from 7·7 per cent. to 62·2 among provincial banks. One large joint-stock bank operating a branch system, but not itself issuing notes, held coin and notes amounting to five per cent. Note-issuing banks would, of course, regard their own unissued notes as available for till money, but by this time private issues were restricted and were rapidly disappearing.

The banking system was evolving a fresh and firmer structure, as private banks were absorbed ever more swiftly by joint-stock banks, and the joint-stocks began to join together to form large institutions. In part this illustrated the advantages of the joint-stock system in banking, since as transport systems developed, they could gain not only economies of scale but also the benefits of the spread of risks and of wider areas for collecting deposits. A further benefit was a saving in liquid assets. A country bank would safeguard its own liabilities with local liquidity and also by holding balances with a London agent; in turn, the London agent would maintain a suitably liquid position against its deposits, including those of country banks. With amalgamation, the bank-to-bank balances would disappear; country and London offices would represent one aggregate of deposits, calling for appropriate liquidity.

A remaining disadvantage was that the early joint-stocks were, in constitution, large partnerships, with the private fortunes of members or partners liable if the institution failed. So the next change was the introduction of limited liability. Existing joint-stock banks did not generally adopt limited liability in 1858 when it was first made available to them, and even if they had done so the members would have remained liable for notes issued. The reluctance of the banks to change was largely because they believed that the public valued the safeguard of the unlimited liability of their members for all debts of the bank.

It was also because if registered with limited liability they would have to publish a statement of assets and liabilities twice a year and exhibit this in every branch. However, new banks adopting limited liability form began to be established, and this of itself brought about an extension of publication of balance-sheets to add to those issued by joint-stock banks in London. As Bagehot noted, these London banks had already suffered unfavourable comment by reason of comparisons of the proportions of the reserves they held with that of the Bank of England. By the time of writing, he was able to confirm the practice of the banks of putting 'reserves' to work: they were no longer held so largely as balances at the Bank of England but kept as to a 'main part . . . on deposit with the bill brokers or in good and convertible interest-bearing securities. From these they [the banks] obtain a large income.'[1]

After the Overend Gurney crisis of 1866 and the failure of the City of Glasgow Bank twelve years later, the advantages of limited liability became more evident, but banking objections remained. A way out of the dilemma was found by George Rae.[2] He suggested the simple form of 'reserved liability', whereby part of each share was callable only in the event of failure, a system that was introduced in 1879 and became widely adopted over the next few years. Here was another cause of the extension of the publication of bank balance-sheets. Incidentally, Rae was an eloquent advocate of giving attention to banking ratios and surely must rank as a pioneer in practising his precepts in this field. He introduced schedules giving ratios for principal assets as part of the management statistics in his own bank in 1875, 'with a view to raising the standard of liquidity. . . . Until that time loans and bills had almost invariably exceeded deposits, but thereafter the relative weight of advances was reduced, and the proportion of bank funds invested in gilt-edged securities increased.'[3]

With fairly extensive information thus becoming available,

---

[1] Walter Bagehot, *Lombard Street* (John Murray, London, 1870), 14th edn., pp. 240–1.

[2] He lived from 1817 to 1902 and was managing director and chairman of the North and South Wales Bank. Among his publications is *The Country Banker*, and in the 1885 edition he refers to the one-third 'financial reserve' against liabilities to the public (Letter XXIX).

[3] C and W, p. 190.

The Economist in October 1877 added to its half-yearly banking supplements the well-known statistical tables, thus amplifying the annual reports and other information on British banks. Even this most useful series, which improved as the years went by and publication of bank figures became more and more general, was far from comprehensive, as well as unsatisfactory in other ways. The difficulties that had confronted Dun in his pioneer effort were all too evident here, and aggregate figures could be assembled, if at all, only under headings so general as to be virtually useless for clear understanding. A penetrating examination of the series[1] reaches the conclusion that 'any analysis which . . . depends upon a careful study of the portfolio distribution of banks and upon the causes of changes in their asset holding can only find this data unacceptable'. A few years later a further move towards publication of banking figures was once again prompted by the threat of a financial crisis. In 1890 the important bank of Barings was saved from gathering difficulties by a banking consortium, and the situation then disclosed gave rise to severe criticism of banking reserves, especially by Mr. (later Lord) Goschen in his famous speech at Leeds in 1891, drawing attention to the general lack of information, and, where the figures were known, to the low percentage of cash to the liabilities of banks. Thereafter some private banks began to issue annual balance-sheets, but far more influential was the inauguration of the practice of publishing regular and frequent banking statistics by the leading joint-stocks. Twelve (later thirteen) of the large joint-stock banks began publication of monthly statements of account,[2] and although these covered less than one-half of the aggregate deposits of banks in England, the new practice began a fresh epoch in monetary arrangements.

The issue of monthly figures brought two consequences of major significance: first, attention was directed to cash, as distinct from liquid assets more widely defined; and second, the frequency of publication made it possible to follow the banking situation as it developed over the year. From the first emerged

[1] C. A. E. Goodhart—unpublished thesis on 'The Determination of the Volume of Bank Deposits, 1891–1914' (Trinity College, Cambridge, 1963), p. 107.

[2] R. H. Inglis Palgrave, 'Bank Balance Sheets', *Journal of the Institute of Bankers*, Mar. 1907.

the notion of the proportion of cash to deposits as a measure of banking strength and, once this began to be held at an established level, and then allied itself with the second consequence, the way was open for the closer regulation of monetary conditions through the banking system. As the banks became 'ratio conscious',[1] the grip of the authorities on the banking and monetary system was greatly fortified. It was to reach its full force as the amalgamation movement, already in full swing, gathered the banks in England into a few large units and brought the banking structure to its modern form, a process virtually completed just after the end of the First World War. In 1921, when all the clearing banks began to publish monthly figures, then based on averages of their weekly positions, a comprehensive view of the English banking situation was at last presented.

This was of the first importance, because at that period the monetary analysis generally accepted by the authorities, and reflected in their policy, regarded the multiplier process as stemming from the cash base of the banks. It was 'cash' that was varied by open-market operations, and 'cash' which regulated the level of deposits, thus acting as a spring-board for credit creation.[2] Hence the pervasive influence of the monthly figures, though these still had to become consistent in definition and in composition as between the banks. Hence, too, the new-found importance of the cash ratio, though this had yet to crystallize hard and clear, with window-dressing eliminated. It was a monetary analysis that was to find expressions in other countries as well, but here and elsewhere this had to await the end of the novel financial arrangements of the Second World War. Long before then a noteworthy development in money-market instruments had taken effect on bank liquidity and ratios in the United Kingdom.

Nearly a century ago the Government sought advice from Walter Bagehot, then editor of *The Economist*, as to the best method of attracting short-term finance. His suggestion of the

[1] C and W, p. 39.
[2] Committee on Finance and Industry (*Macmillan Report*), Cmd. 3897 (HMSO, 1931), para. 71: 'Since the banks as a whole maintain a cash proportion to deposits of from 10 per cent. to 11 per cent. they are, in fact, able to increase their deposits by some 10 times the cash created by the Bank of England ... the opposite process ... will reduce the cash ... and entail a reduction of their deposits.' (Further references will be cited as *Macmillan Report*.)

Treasury bill was quickly adopted and proved successful in ways more far-reaching than the simple raising of funds. True, this alone represented a major achievement—the volume reached £1,000 m. by the end of the First World War—but the significant change was that, as in subsequent years the use of commercial bills declined, they were largely replaced in the money market by Treasury bills. These became the main constituent in bank liquidity, being held by the banks for their own account and by discount houses with loans from the banks.[1] With the great increase in government borrowing, the Treasury bill became the centre-piece in monetary regulation, and great changes followed in money-market activity, to which the *Radcliffe Report* drew attention.[2]

More Treasury bills were needed when the Bank of England took over the Treasury note issue in 1928, and again following the establishment of the Exchange Equalization Account in 1932. Then came a change, with the authorities energetically pursuing a policy of cheap money, and 'funding' bills on a substantial scale. The 'bill famine', of which bankers of the time complained, was under way.[3] The banks then agreed not to tender for bills, but to obtain their needs from the discount houses and to observe minimum rates for loans to the money market, where concerted tendering by the market syndicate was soon established.[4]

Despite the importance of Treasury bills, other items also helped to fill the modern 'basket' of liquid assets, and the constituents changed over the years, as also did the practice in holdings of cash. In general, bank holdings of liquid assets had become more sophisticated and different degrees of liquidity were established. At the head remained cash, in the late nineteenth

[1] For a full account see 'The Treasury Bill: the Story of an Economist's Invention', *Midland Bank Review*, Feb. 1961. (Further references to *Midland Bank Review* will be cited as *MBR*.)

[2] Committee on the Working of the Monetary System (*Radcliffe Report*), Cmnd. 827 (HMSO, 1959). (Further references will be cited as *Radcliffe Report* and references to evidence submitted as 'Radcliffe Committee evidence'.) Para. 587 refers to 'the manifold process of cartelisation and "orderly markets", which is believed to have been deliberately fostered by the authorities between 1914 and 1925, when they were anxious to develop the market's appetite for short-term debt and believed that extremely orderly (if not dragooned) short-term markets alone could assure the necessary flow of funds into the Treasury'.

[3] See, for example, speech of Rt. Hon. R. McKenna, Annual General Meeting of Midland Bank Limited, 24 Jan. 1935.   [4] See n. 2 above.

century comprising gold coins, Bank of England balances and notes, and sometimes cheques for collection; after cash came items readily turned into cash, such as Treasury bills, money-market loans, and other bills. Other bank assets, principally advances and investments, were not interchangeable with cash, and so were low in the liquidity scale. A major change, indeed, had been the displacement of investments, primarily Consols, from their leading position among liquid assets. Right down to the beginning of this century the marketability of government stock was regarded as endowing it with liquidity characteristics surpassed only by cash itself. For most bankers Consols ranked above bills in liquidity, particularly as the large London joint-stock banks held to the practice of never re-discounting bills from their portfolios. But following the heavy fall in the market price of Consols at the outbreak of the Boer War, and public pressure upon banks to disclose the basis of valuation of their holdings, such investments were less favourably regarded. Cash holdings were then increased and the self-liquidating commercial bill acquired pride of place.

Another adjustment had been the exclusion from liquid assets of transmission items, usually cheques in course of collection on other banks, and balances with them. These had been commonly counted as part of cash or liquid assets, and often represented three per cent. or more of deposits. Since the cheques had been credited to swell the deposits of the collecting banker but were not yet debited by the paying banker, to treat transmission in items this way was at once a source of error and of double counting. For many years past the practice has been changed, and net deposits of the banks as a whole are calculated by subtracting the aggregate for transmission items from that for published (gross) deposits, but the correction cannot be made with precision in the published figures for individual banks.

The definition of liquid assets continues to be adjusted. Besides cash, Treasury bills, and loans to the discount market, liquid assets of the clearing banks have come to include short-term lending to other British banks, to money market institutions and money brokers, and to jobbers and stockbrokers. Some foreign currencies are included, as well as the banks' own holdings of Tax Reserve Certificates. Then, too, there are bank or trade bills (a marked revival in the use of commercial bills has occurred); local authority bills; holdings of Treasury bills of Commonwealth or foreign governments, and of commercial bills in foreign currencies. Generally assets are excluded that consist of claims on other members of the bank group (such as cheques in course of collection, and balances). The total for liquid items is expressed as a percentage of total deposits, both in sterling and in currency, and including the internal accounts of the banks themselves.[1]

In establishing liquidity much depends upon attitudes and practices at the Bank of England, especially in relation to the discount market. The rules to be observed as to commercial bills were described in general terms in 1931,[2] and current requirements of the Bank are made known to the market, while, naturally, the names on the bills are examined. In course of time, the discount houses became more active as dealers in short-term government debt, and when their bond-jobbing activities were officially recognized, the inclusion of these securities represented a notable addition to liquidity. As to the clearing banks, since early 1961 they have been able to include among liquid assets the re-financeable part of their medium-term export credits guaranteed by the Export Credits Guarantee Department of the Board of Trade. Incidentally, banks in Scotland have their distinctive form of liquidity: as note-issuing institutions, they replenish tills with their own notes; moreover, they count among liquid assets balances with other banks in the United Kingdom, and cheques in course of collection on them, since these are due largely outside Scotland's banking system.

As to cash, before the First World War the banks still held gold and silver coins, notes of the Bank of England and other banks, and balances with the Bank of England. As note issues of individual banks declined, these could no longer furnish till money, and it may be that with liabilities more largely in the form of deposits the need for cash in tills became greater. A bank could spread its notes far afield, as when Scottish banks sent notes to cattle fairs south of the Border, and so diminish the possibility of bulk presentation and keep up the total outstand-

---

[1] *Bank of England Bulletin*, Dec. 1962.
[2] *Macmillan Report*, para. 95.

ing,[1] but customers' current accounts turned over all the time. For quite different reasons, George Rae was arguing in 1880 in favour of reducing balances at the Bank of England and holding Bank of England notes instead, mainly in order to maintain rates in the money market.[2]

In the early part of this century some of the banks had begun to build up individual holdings of gold bullion to provide, under official encouragement, monetary reserves additional to those of the Bank of England, and the ratio of cash to deposits rose considerably. The accumulation of bullion came to an abrupt end with the outbreak of the First World War and the withdrawal of gold from private hands, including those of the banks, and cash ratios were generally reduced again when the war was over. Cash was then currency notes (they became Bank of England notes in 1928), token coins, and balances with the Bank of England. Notes on other banks had virtually disappeared and gold entirely so. But cash ratios were by no means uniform and continued to be matched to the particular requirements of individual banks. Many years later a discussion of bank liquidity in the *Bank of England Bulletin* was to draw attention to the differing needs of individual banks and the importance of keeping in mind a bank's 'likely need for cash and its potential supply of cash'.[3] Among other things, the cash requirement is influenced by the proportion of its current accounts to total deposits; the type of a bank's customers; the volume and character of overseas business; and the size of the bank itself.

During the inter-war years the situation had been reached in which bank cash was generally maintained at around 11 per cent. of liabilities, but, although this was below the ratio previously observed, bankers had none the less found a far from admirable way of lessening the cost of holding an asset that brought no return. It was the *Macmillan Report* that stigmatized the practice of a peculiar form of 'window-dressing' on the part of leading banks. Each of the large institutions selected a different day to make up its accounts, and on make-up day a bank

[1] J. E. Wadsworth, 'English Banks and Scots Invaders', *Bankers' Magazine*, Oct. 1939. See also R. S. Rait, *The History of the Union Bank of Scotland*; C. W. Boase, *A Century of Banking in Dundee* (1867). In the *Bankers' Magazine*, vol. 3 (1845), p. 17, an article says that four out of six private banks operating in Carlisle before 1810 issued Scottish notes.
[2] C and W, pp. 429–30.   [3] Dec. 1962, pp. 248–9.

would call in loans from the money market to swell its cash, re-lending them on the following morning. The loans would then be called by the next big bank, and so on, turn by turn. Thus the same liquid funds moved around 'like a stage army', to do duty for each of several banks, and the process was repeated on a bigger scale each half-year.[1]

Window-dressing was not only misleading; it must also have reduced the control of the system through the cash base, and among the changes after the end of the Second World War was its abandonment. The banks agreed to follow the practice that now obtains, namely, to make up their accounts on the same day, generally the third Wednesday in each month, and to keep to a cash ratio of 8 per cent. of deposit liabilities. Each bank, that is to say, endeavours to hold its cash ratio at precisely 8 per cent., and rarely allows it to vary by more than a decimal point or two. But whereas at the time of the Macmillan Committee the banks' holdings of cash, the 'cash base', were regarded as the fulcrum for determining the volume of deposits,[2] a quarter of a century later the Radcliffe Committee stressed the overriding importance, not of cash, but of the liquidity ratio in the monetary mechanism. The cash ratio remained significant as a means of influencing the Treasury-bill rate and of ensuring the ready interchange of bills for cash, to which the authorities—and, indeed, the banks themselves—attach great importance, but once again it became the basket of liquidity that called for special attention.

When in post-war years the use of interest rates was resumed, the liquidity ratio was brought into the family of monetary regulation allegedly by a process of adoption, though it is at least arguable that in fact it was a child of the house. For some years past the banks had been maintaining a ratio of about 30 per cent., and in monetary analysis this practice became recognized under the 'new orthodoxy' as the true hinge for monetary regulation. In 1951 the Governor of the Bank of England indicated that a liquidity ratio of between 28 and 32 per cent. would be expected of the banks in ordinary conditions, though exceptionally a low point of 25 per cent. might be countenanced. By 1955 he was insisting on a minimum of 30 per cent., and in 1957 the same Governor told the Radcliffe Committee that he

[1] *Macmillan Report*, para. 368.   [2] Ibid., para. 71.

had left the clearing banks in no doubt that 'they should not allow their liquidity ratios to fall significantly below 30 per cent.'[1]. In 1963, however, the ratio was lowered officially to 28 per cent., though it is not, and never has been, closely observed from day to day, as is the cash ratio, but instead is regarded as a minimum, as a floor. Thus the liquidity ratio of a large bank may be expected to be well above 28 per cent. towards the end of the year, when the seasonal drain of deposits to meet tax payments is ahead, and to have fallen close to the official minimum in March, when the outflow of funds has reached its flood. The Bank of England likes to speak of the ratios as established by the clearing banks, and as developed by them, among the prudent practices of past generations of bankers. This claims rather too much of history, as we have seen, and takes little account of evolution in banking affairs and monetary conditions; in fact, bankers told the Radcliffe Committee that they would be comfortable with somewhat lower ratios for cash and liquidity.[2] It is because ratios at the present level have received the accolade of Bank governors that they have become official regulators; for this purpose, it is not the particular level at which they stand that matters, within an acceptable range, but the way in which they are observed by the banks.

As developed in the fifties the operation of the liquidity ratio is by no means rigid. When liquidity is full, as from April onwards, the banks have a certain margin of flexibility in the disposition of their assets, even when credit is officially restricted. If the authorities seek to increase net holdings of government securities outside the banking system, by one or other of the various methods available, the banks may be able to use their 'excess' liquidity to avoid the full force of such action and to delay, for a time, some part of the consequential reduction in their deposits and advances. Before long the policy of the authorities is likely to prevail, though it may be further delayed if the banks are able to turn to protective action of another kind.

After cash and quick assets, liquidity is supported and

---

[1] *Radcliffe Report*, para. 429, and Radcliffe Committee Evidence, Question 1754.
[2] Leading bankers said that they would be prepared to operate below 30 per cent. (then the minimum) but would wish to take action if the ratio fell to 25 per cent. (Evidence, Question 3742.)

R

reinforced by investments; holdings of government securities, if no longer included among liquid assets, play an important part here as in other directions. First, investments represent a residual use of funds: when advances rise, investments can be sold to make room for lending; when advances fall, surplus bank funds move into investments. Second, they are so managed as to provide a regular refreshment of cash, to serve as a cushion to soften the first impact of heavy blows of credit policy.[1] As a result of official policy in the Second World War and early post-war years, the banks held an unduly high proportion of fairly long-dated securities, and a significant refinement in investment practices followed the resumption of interest-rate policy in 1951. Thereafter the fall in bond prices was far steeper and longer lasting than in the Boer War disturbances, and eventually book values of investments at figures below market prices came to be recorded in some bank balance-sheets. Inevitably, the banks turned to bonds of shorter term, but they also began to rebuild their portfolios in such a way as to hold bonds with maturity dates spread over the years ahead as evenly as practicable. With investments 'in echelon', as the practice came to be called,[2] a liquidity cushion was provided, since cash holdings would be reinforced as bonds matured from year to year and losses would be minimized on necessary sales. A similar practice had obtained with bill holdings, when these were arranged, in ordinary conditions, with maturity dates to provide cash as required.

The financial distortions of the war years, followed by the traumatic experience of the early fifties, thus transformed bankers' views until investments came to be regarded as risk assets alongside advances—a far cry indeed from the one-time leadership of Consols among liquid items, ranking second only to cash! With advances at the end of hostilities absorbing less than one-sixth of deposits of the clearing banks, the rest was lent to the government in one form or another, Treasury Deposit Receipts alone—a special war-time form of direct and enforced government borrowing from the banking system—accounting for well over two-fifths of banking resources. Eventually Treasury Deposit Receipts were funded, again at the behest of the

---

[1] *Radcliffe Report*, paras. 143, 506. *MBR*, Nov. 1959, p. 7.
[2] *MBR*, Nov. 1959, p. 7. The term was used in discussions somewhat earlier.

government, and even then the banks remained exceptionally liquid. This was partly because advances continued to be restricted by official controls in the form of requests, usually called 'directives', requiring the banks to confine lending to particular categories of borrowers. Meanwhile deposits had expanded under inflationary war-time finance to reach over twice the pre-war level, and the growth continued.

As with the holding and funding of Treasury Deposit Receipts, so on other occasions the investment policies of the banks were directly regulated by the authorities. This was in addition to the continuing and growing interest of the authorities in influencing the long-term rate, not simply because of market requirements in handling the enormous volume of government debt, but also because of the general effects upon lenders of movements in bond prices, effects that had come to be recognized as playing a major part in regulating monetary conditions. In some circumstances the investments of the banking system seem to have been regarded as included, when occasion required, within the *masse de manœuvre*[1] of marketable debt held by public departments, and so under the control of the authorities for the support of official policy. At any rate, the process of official influence over bond prices had made great progress and considerable emphasis was placed on it in the *Radcliffe Report*.[2]

Before then some of the war-time monetary controls had been dismantled, and others were being changed. In 1958, when the banks were released for a time from controls over their lending policy, advances leapt ahead, partly under the stimulus of bank initiatives in introducing fresh forms of lending. To provide funds for advances, investments were sold heavily, and soon the proportions at which both should stand were under consideration. The chairman of a large bank implied in 1960[3]

---

[1] *MBR*, Feb. 1958, p. 3.

[2] Para. 982: 'In our view debt management has become the fundamental domestic task of the central bank.'

[3] A. W. Tuke, chairman of Barclays Bank, in his annual statement to shareholders: 'Allowing for a liquidity ratio of about 30 per cent, and speaking in round figures, we should like to see our advances eventually fluctuating, as our customers' needs rise and fall, between 45 per cent and 50 per cent, which would leave about 20 per cent. for our investments. . . . If, however, our advances ever stood at 60 per cent or even more, we could have only 10 per cent, or even less, in investments, and as they are our third line of defence, it seems to me that that

that he would not like to see investments fall below 20 per cent. of deposits, or advances climb higher than 45–50 per cent. In fact, it was not long before advances had risen well above 50 per cent. and investments had fallen to 12 per cent. Perhaps he was looking back nostalgically to a working-rule of the inter-war years, the 30:70 distribution of assets, that is, with liquid assets at 30 and advances plus investments absorbing the remainder.[1]

With 'directives' gone, as it turned out only temporarily, the authorities sought a fresh means of regulation, and devised the system of special deposits, bringing yet another ratio to the banking scene. The system was said to have been selected as the least objectionable among a number of suggestions, the banks agreeing to it after consultations, though later it was disclosed that the 'consultations' were derisory in character.[2] However, it seems that, at the time, bank managements welcomed the disappearance, as they supposed, of 'directives', and buoyed themselves up with the belief that the new instrument of special deposits would never be used. In fact, both assumptions were soon proved to be wrong: special deposits were called in 1960, and shortly afterwards 'directives' returned as well! Special deposits have been as high as 3 per cent. for banks in England and 1½ per cent. for Scottish banks. They were wholly returned to the banks for a time but subsequently were called again; in July 1966 they were raised to 2 per cent. in England, and in Scotland to 1 per cent.

It is worth examining a little more closely the method of operation of this newcomer among banking ratios. Special deposits are called from the banks as a proportion of each bank's deposits to be placed with the Bank of England. They receive interest at a little below bill rate, but are not counted among the liquid assets of a bank. At the time of introduction, the Bank of

would be quite inadequate.' Thirty years before, F. Hyde, managing director of the Midland Bank, said that his aim was to keep about '12 per cent. of our assets in the form of investments. That leaves us with approximately 55 per cent. that we can lend.' Macmillan Committee, Evidence, Question 871.

[1] *MBR*, Feb.–Mar. 1939: 'Less well recognized or understood, however, is the observance of another ratio besides the cash ratio—also important if less rigidly observed—which we may describe as the "30:70 Ratio".'

[2] A. W. Tuke, to the Radcliffe Committee—Question 13054—'We were told that this was what was proposed, and allowed to express our views, but it all happened in twenty minutes. We did not discuss alternatives.'

England described special deposits as 'a general control of credit, used periodically in the same way and after the same sort of consideration as Bank rate',[1] a description that could have brought little comfort for bankers, who could not fail to have in mind that Bank rate is always with us, and in recent years has run at high levels. In effect, the system acts as a liquidity ratio varied by mandate, though the Bank of England prefers special deposits, on the grounds that a liquidity provision ought not to be used also as a regulatory mechanism, nor should the arrangement 'appear to be designed principally as a device for government financing'.[2] However, as we have seen, by this time the liquidity ratio had long been adopted as an instrument of monetary regulation, while special deposits are in fact turned over to the Exchequer by way of Treasury bills. Since special deposits are provided by the banks in cash, usually in instalments over a number of weeks, the transfer inevitably bears upon working ratios, possibly involving a further injection of cash from the central bank as needed. In these conditions liquidity ratios may well tend to sink closer to the floor of 28 per cent.

The Chancellor of the Exchequer, speaking of the first call for special deposits, was as far from recognizing the further consequences as the central bank had been. He said, 'this device is an alternative to making a request [i.e. issuing a directive] to the banks', and went on: 'I have given the banks a reasonable time in which to adjust their existing commitments to the effect I want to see, which is a moderation in their advances. That being so, and the fact that the initial deposit that I have asked for is a deliberately moderate one, will influence them in the direction of moderating their advances rather than selling gilt-edged stocks. What they do will be entirely up to decision by the banks concerned.'[3] In fact, the banks found themselves obliged to follow a policy precisely opposite to that indicated by the Chancellor: they continued to sell investments, if at a somewhat slower rate, to meet the demands for advances. The Chancellor then had to eat his words about the system as an alternative to 'a request' and soon reintroduced 'directives'. In the Budget

[1] Radcliffe Committee Evidence, vol. 1, part 1, sub-section 13, para. 38.

[2] *Bank of England Bulletin*, Dec. 1962, p. 255. It should be emphasized, also, that special deposits do not form part of bank cash, nor are they included among liquid assets.

[3] *Hansard*, 28 Apr. 1960, col. 399.

of 1967 the then Chancellor announced a second attempt to use special deposits as a main instrument of credit regulation. He removed the 'ceiling' placed on bank advances, to which reference is made below, and said that 'the special deposits system will be used in future in a new and more flexible manner . . . as a routine adjustment to conditions as they develop. The object will be to maintain a continuous control over bank lending.'[1] The selective directive on bank lending was, however, continued.

Here, then, is an intention to bring the special-deposits system closer to a variable liquidity ratio, probably with directives as a further measure of control when required. There are other differences, too. Special deposits are not only a compulsory pre-empting of loanable funds, but also for the banks an asset that is frozen ice-hard. No term is set for repayment of them, and ordinarily they cannot be encashed. They are less liquid even than war-time Treasury Deposit Receipts, though, like them, they are in essence a forced loan to the government. As we have seen, special deposits shortly after being introduced proved inadequate for the task of restraining advances; directives then returned, but this time with a sharp twist in the method of application that brought yet another ratio to be observed, for a period, by the banks.

Generally the requests to the banks had asked them to conduct their lending activities in harmony with government credit policy, commonly mentioning categories of borrowers to be given priority, such as those concerned with exports, and indicating borrowing that was to be discouraged, as, for example, in 1961 lending for personal and professional borrowing, for hire-purchase finance, and for speculative building and property development. In addition to such selective or qualitative restrictions, a quantitative curtailment might be specified. In September 1957 the banks were requested to see that the average level of advances during the following twelve months should not exceed that of the previous twelve. In 1961 and 1964 the banks were required to reduce the rate of growth in lending, but the directive of May 1965 was much more precise, and introduced another ratio as part of monetary regulation. Individual banks were required to see that their lending to the

---

[1] *Hansard*, 11 Apr. 1967, col. 100.

private sector did not exceed 105 per cent. of the figure at March 1965 for the ensuing twelve months, after allowing for seasonal fluctuations, a limitation that was continued until April 1967. Both 'private sector' and 'seasonal corrections' presented difficulties of interpretation that could result in marginal uncertainties, but the general notion was clear and in practice effective.

A 'ceiling' on advances maintained during a period when prices were rising represented a reduction in lending in real terms; nor was this the whole of the restrictive consequence. The new corporation and selective employment taxes applied at this time changed the fiscal burdens upon companies and the timing of tax transfers to the Exchequer over the year. By mid 1966 in most banks advances were pressing hard on the permitted maximum and it was feared that when the incidence of the new taxes came in the autumn a further rise would be unavoidable: advances would have to burst through the ceiling or a rash of business failures would occur. In the event, the severity of the July measures checked business confidence and the level of advances turned down: the ceiling was removed in the Budget of 1967. But the situation of mid 1966 had exposed the dangers that might have to be faced in the operation of such a rigid form of control. Moreover, the ceiling on advances in periods of growth could hardly fail to operate so as to contain business within its existing patterns, notwithstanding the needs of business development.

A difficulty for banks in the United Kingdom in observing the ceiling or of any form of quantitative regulation of advances results from the overdraft system, a long-established and well regarded method of lending in British banking. The usual arrangement is for a limit to be agreed with a borrower upon his current account, representing the amount up to which he may overdraw it. Generally a borrowing account will swing from credit to debit over the year, for seasonal or other reasons, and this in itself is often seen as evidence of a satisfactory account. Or an overdraft may increase steadily until repaid by long-term borrowing, or the limit may stand unused until the anticipated business need for it occurs. As a result the banks have commitments to lend far exceeding the total of advances outstanding at any time, and these can be called upon simply by the customer's drawing his cheque, without prior advice or consultation. In a specialized field, medium-term export credits are arranged for substantial amounts to be available for several years ahead. Thus at a time of pressure the banks may become unable to resist a rise in advances, without refusing virtually all new borrowing, should borrowers generally seek to utilize more fully the limits placed at their disposal in easier conditions. In fact, the proportion of the total for advances outstanding to commitments to lend has tended to rise when credit is restricted, but not, so far, to an embarrassing extent.

Other working ratios are not related to monetary controls, but are none the less of importance to bankers. They have to watch the proportion of the bank's 'own funds' to deposits, and, for clearing banks, this ratio fell by the end of the hostilities to less than one-half of the pre-war level of about 6 per cent. As the weakness in gilts developed, and as advances rapidly grew, it was necessary to look again at the unusually low proportion of capital, published reserves, and undivided profits taken together, more especially as further capital was required for investment in branch development, mechanization, and the introduction of computers. Hence the process of enlarging capital, partly from internal funds, that restored proportions to about the pre-war level.

Apart from the published figures of the banks are their inner reserves. These are not disclosed, but it has been indicated that substantial inroads were made upon them when the prices of bonds declined steeply in the mid fifties.[1] Since then, no doubt, individual banks have taken every opportunity of rebuilding these defences. As we have seen, the need to do so has been evident in the post-war experience of investments as risk assets, but it has also to be remembered that besides increases in their capitals, bank dividends have risen. Hence, larger inside funds are regarded as necessary to avoid untoward fluctuations in dividends. Then, too, the possibility of substantial bad debts is always present, and for generations past the banks, in years of high interest rates, have sought to make provision for the

---

[1] Lord Franks, then chairman of Lloyds Bank, said that three of the clearing banks, within a period of twelve months—Sept. 1954 to Sept. 1955—experienced a swing in the market value of gilt-edged portfolios of £44 m. in one case, £47 m. in the second, and £33 m. in the third. (Evidence taken before the Company Law Committee, 9th day, Question 3082, p. 594.)

lean years that are sure to follow. These long-established practices have been called into question by the National Board for Prices and Incomes, which in 1966 was charged with the task of examining bank charges. In that year, too, the Board of Trade was empowered to require disclosure, in the published accounts, of companies formerly granted exemption, and the position of the banks, as among exempted undertakings, is under consideration. One consequence of both inquiries is the possibility that fresh ratios will come to the forefront in assessing the banking situation.

When Britain's banking system reached its modern structure the authorities were able to use it as a channel for regulating monetary and economic conditions, because the necessary information was made available through the monthly figures and because the system had become sufficiently compact for it to be quickly responsive to official policy. In the mechanics of credit policy, too, cash was regarded as the lever for monetary action, but thereafter, under the 'new orthodoxy', the emphasis was placed on liquid assets generally. Hence the increased importance of the cash and liquidity ratios in British banking arrangements, though other influences, too, were at work. During the last war the authorities adopted the practice of providing cash to meet the demands of the public,[1] so destroying the regulatory force of the cash ratio, and the ensuing steps involved the authorities in influencing directly the investment and lending policies of the banks, with further controls over advances. But these have not been based on statutes, as are the ratios and regulations required to be observed by banks in some other countries; instead, the method has been one of 'suasion', with requests backed, if necessary, by frowns and private murmurings from the authorities. Yet here the distinctive character of Britain's practice should not be over-emphasized. When the Bank of England passed into public ownership just after the end of the Second World War the authorities were given considerable powers over the commercial banks. These could always be invoked, and, if thought necessary, exercised in

[1] 'The Bank of England remains . . . passive in deciding the amount of cash: the cash is simply fitted to the total of bank deposits coupled with the requirements of the public for circulation.' (R. S. Sayers: 'Determination of the Volume of Bank Deposits: England 1955–56', *Banca Nazionale del Lavoro Quarterly Review*, Dec. 1955.)

secret.[1] The banks are conscious of this situation. They recognize that they are confronted with a pistol that, if never produced, is known to be in the pocket of the Chancellor and fully loaded. As they have emerged, banking ratios make up a formidable group of controls, even without the 'ceiling' on advances. No doubt the cash and liquidity ratios could be lower, and some economy in cash and liquid assets could be achieved. Probably greater precision would result from calculating the ratios on the total for customers' current and deposit accounts alone, rather than on the published figures including 'other accounts', though this would lead to disclosure of the extent of 'other accounts' for individual banks. Even so, the new ratios, if these were to be arranged, would be likely to be close to those that have now obtained for so long, and the change would not be a major one.[2]

Moreover, the authorities have recognized in post-war years that the full rigour of orthodoxy in interest rate and monetary policy is not politically acceptable. Hence the reliance upon the direct regulation of bank lending. When this position is reached, the further questions go deeper and ask whether it is sensible to maintain in their present form conventions and ratios that were established in different conditions for different purposes, and to apply these in the much more sophisticated monetary and banking situation that has developed. Once banking practices are turned into an official requirement, liquidity is no longer there for use; it is ossified at the fixed ratio and only the excess held above it is available. Besides, in the process of adapting business practices to monetary requirements, methods of application tend to become convoluted and indirect, and the various forms of regulation bring further rigidity where flexibility would be an advantage. It would not be difficult to find ways of simplifying the intricacies of existing arrangements for monetary regulation and possibly getting rid of some ratios, as well as providing greater flexibility in the operation of

---

[1] The Bank of England Act, 1946: 9 and 10 George VI, c. 27, Section 4 (3) and (4).

[2] National Board for Prices and Incomes, *Bank Charges*, Cmnd. 3292, para. 69: 'There is evidence that the required cash ratio of 8 per cent is greater than the banks require for clearing purposes, while the required liquidity ratio of 28 per cent is higher than the clearing banks consider necessary for commercial purposes. Just as the liquidity ratio has already come down from 30 per cent to 28 per cent, we judge that the commercial pressures of the clearing banks for further reductions in the ratios will continue.'

them and of the levels at which they are required to be maintained.[1]

Another consequence is that the attention that has to be paid to the ratios tends to fix our eyes upon aspects of the banking and monetary situation that are of diminishing importance. The safety of the great banks and the satisfactory provision of the money supply are not really in question. It is the swift growth of non-bank financial intermediaries and of the 'parallel' money markets that is changing the banking environment; the ratios to be watched are not only those showing the disposition of banking resources, or of profits in relation to funds employed, but also those indicating the efficiency and effectiveness of the country's banking and monetary arrangements. For some time past bankers have looked with particular care at indicators that compare growth in their own industry and in the country as a whole, and have seen as significant such ratios as those of deposits and advances to the gross national product, and of banking turnover in relation to indexes of general business activity.

[1] See, however, *Radcliffe Report*, para. 505: 'The case for maintaining these restrictions [the cash and liquidity ratios] appears overwhelming.' The reason given is the importance to the authorities of influencing interest rates undisturbed.

C. R. WHITTLESEY

Rules, Discretion, and Central Bankers

I N a brief essay on central banking Professor Sayers once
began by saying that 'the essence of central banking is discretionary control of the monetary system' and ended by
observing that 'we are doomed to disappointment if we look
for rules applicable to all times and places. We have central
banks for the very reason that there are no such rules.'[1] The
quotation as it stands, it should be noted, is directed against
universal rules. It does not reject the use of rules that are limited
in time and place.

On the opposite side of the debate over Rules versus Discretion in Monetary Policy we find a somewhat similar repudiation of the other extreme. In his article bearing almost that
title Professor Simons was unequivocal—firm as he was in
stressing the virtues of rules—in specifying the necessity of
governmental action.[2] And Professor Friedman, who carries
on the Simons tradition, has 'recognized that government has
an important role to play'.[3]

It might seem that the controversy is only one of degree. But
major differences remain. Reconciliation is unlikely on either
the role of rules in the exercise of discretion by central banks or
the degree of discretion that should be allowed in the observance
of rules. And always there is the uncomfortable question of
whether the economist can admit the imprecision which discretion seems to imply without diminishing his stature as a
man of science. It might be supposed that all that was significant on the subject had long since been said. Whether said or

[1] R. S. Sayers, *Central Banking after Bagehot* (Clarendon Press, Oxford, 1957),
pp. 1, 7.
[2] H. C. Simons, 'Rules versus Authority in Monetary Policy', *Journal of Political
Economy*, Feb. 1936.
[3] Milton Friedman, *A Program for Monetary Stability* (Fordham University Press,
New York, 1959), p. 4.

not, the subject has clearly not been disposed of, as the ardour with which its ramifications are discussed clearly attests.

The controversy over rules and discretion flourishes, in large part, because of failure to make clear what is meant by rules. Two distinct concepts are recognizable. 'Rules' may refer, on the one hand, to guides or regulations which serve to govern the operation of the economic system including the actions of the monetary authorities. A provision for increasing the money supply by a fixed rate each year would be a rule in this sense. So also are fixed reserve or liquidity ratios. They constitute rules, moreover, regardless of whether the particular provision is laid down by legislation or is assumed voluntarily. In order for rules to influence policy, they do not have to be of a formal legislative or statutory character. Among the most influential rules we have today are the standard objectives towards which monetary policy is directed, such as stable prices, full employment, and sustainable economic growth.[1]

The other connotation commonly attached to Rules has to do less with the conduct of current operations than with the structuring of the system itself. The gold standard is an example of a rule of this sort (about which more will be said later). So also is the 100 per cent. Reserve Plan. Flexible exchange rates would be a further example, though they might be construed alternatively as simply the opposite of the first example given, the gold standard. The banning of discount operations and the proposal for eliminating all intermediate Treasury obligations and maintaining only the two categories of Consols and currency are among the more extreme rules that have been suggested at one time or another. Capitalism itself, with the major institutions and practices corollary to it, constitutes a rule in the most basic structural sense.

It is to be noted that rules of this sort may relate to methods as well as to structural forms. A commitment to confine open-market operations to bills only, a provision authorizing one form of consumer credit control and prohibiting another, the requirement of a prescribed and unchanging ratio of reserves or

---

[1] Perhaps one should also include economic principles, provided they are adhered to firmly enough to influence policy decisions. The quantity theory has certainly qualified as a rule of this sort at different times, and other such examples might be given.

liquid assets, are all rules of this character. They relate not to applying particular methods but to determining what measures are allowed.

The purpose of a rule in either the guiding or structuring sense is to preclude, or at least circumscribe, discretion. The exclusion may relate to acting in an unauthorized manner, or to acting at all. It is important, on the other hand, to recognize that while rules are antithetical to discretion, the inverse does not hold true: discretion is not antithetical to rules *per se*. With discretion it would be possible to adopt a rule or rules at any time that it seemed wise to do so. And, what is more to the point, it would be possible to adopt a better rule when one became available or when the former rule was found to be lacking.

Indeed, discretion not only allows rules but presumes them. Whenever discretion is exercised, it is done, we must suppose, in a responsible manner. This signifies that it is exercised for what seem to the authorities to be good and sufficient reasons. These good and sufficient reasons are rules in the sense referred to above, namely, that they influence policy and therefore the operation of the economic system.

The issue of Rules versus Discretion is typically presented as a choice between non-intervention and intervention. In that form, the respective positions are badly misrepresented. What is overlooked is that formal statutory rules of the sort ordinarily under discussion do not come into being, or at least do not become operable, spontaneously. It is reasonable enough to call attention to the intervention that is inherent in the continuing exercise of discretion. But it is wholly unreasonable to disregard the intervention that would be required to place in operation the rules intended to supplant discretion.

To institute rules such as are most frequently mentioned by supporters of the Rules position would call for governmental intervention considerably more drastic—in terms, certainly, of public acquiescence—than anything proposed by those favouring Discretion. On the one hand we may have, for example, the introduction of a 100 per cent. Reserve Plan; on the other, a continued use of the prosaically familiar discount mechanism, which is the sort of thing customarily advocated by supporters of central bank discretion.

Mild but continuing intervention of the sort to which we are accustomed is not easily calibrated with intervention which might put an end to that particular intervention, but would do so by a radical change in existing institutional forms. A rule might reduce intervention in the long run, but at the cost of massive intervention in the short run. To say that the intervention required to introduce a proposed rule should not be ignored is not to defend the *status quo*. Nor is it to measure intervention simply in terms of deviation from present conditions, for these may already embody a substantial degree of intervention. Critics of the relatively modest reliance on authority embodied in Federal Reserve action today are themselves to be criticized for overlooking the resort to authority that is implicit in the means which are offered for replacing that system with one that would require significantly less.

Nor can it safely be assumed that intervention would end with the establishment of a particular monetary rule. A provision for increasing the money supply at a fixed rate would seem to require intervention to provide another rule defining just what should be considered to be money, and still another specifying how the increase would be introduced. When would the need for intervention to establish supporting rules come to an end? Would it stop short of a situation in which the economy had more to fear from the certainties of rules than it formerly had from the uncertainties of discretion?

The adoption of a statutory rule of the sort generally in mind is itself a discretionary act. Thus the proponents of a rule for ending discretion must first call upon discretion for getting the rule into effect. The nature of such a discretionary move calls for closer inspection: it would be one taken with respect to an unknown future; it would probably be by a body whose qualifications were chiefly political; and it would be to create a law which would operate in an environment where the knowledge and experience that gave it birth would grow daily more remote from the conditions to which it applied.

The discretionary action which the critics of the rules position have in mind is of a different sort. It is action undertaken by civil servants chosen for their specialized knowledge and with a reasonably rich background of experience to draw upon. They would have the support of a staff of highly trained experts. The action would be directed to meeting concrete situations at a time when relevant considerations were as clearly perceived as was possible, except in retrospect.

We are faced, then, with no simple black-and-white alternative of intervention and non-intervention. The choice is more likely to be between intervention in the form of discount policy and open-market operations more or less as we know them and intervention in the form of establishing an untried (no evil in itself) system for, let us say, expanding the supply of money at a specified annual rate. Money would apparently be defined once and for all, and the rate would be specified, we are led to believe, for all eternity. A question immediately arises: If we are asked to believe that our chosen representatives lack the intelligence to exercise reasonable discretion, how can we assume that they have the intelligence to formulate rules that would make discretion unnecessary? The ambitious, enduring, rules that would eliminate the need for discretion would have to be devised by human beings no less fallible than those who are called upon to administer the simpler, more modest, rules implicit in discretion itself. And the order of intelligence and foresight demanded would be not less but far greater.

The case for Rules is overwhelming, if we accept the assumption of ideal rules and incompetent and arbitrary administrators. It is conclusive for Discretion if we accept the assumption of all-wise administrators and all-foolish rules. At any point between the extremes the conclusion must be qualified and indefinite. Yet it is only this intermediate zone that is relevant to the world that is and can be expected to be.

To favour Rules is not to favour all rules. In practice, perhaps, it is to favour the rule of the proponent's own choosing. And by the same token, to favour Discretion is to be in favour of that sort of discretion which its supporter has in mind. Advocates of Rules are not a united group, any more than are the supporters of Discretion. In point of fact, the sponsors of any particular rule are likely to be among the most determined critics of some competing rule. The strongest opposition to a 100 per cent. Reserve Plan or the rule of increasing the money supply at a fixed annual rate could be expected to come from defenders of the gold-standard system, and vice versa. On the whole, the split between advocates of Rules and Discretion is relatively mild compared with that between advocates of opposing rules.

In the abstract the issue can be debated in terms of Rules and Discretion. But in the concrete it is more likely to run in terms of What Rules and Whose Discretion. This has long been true and no doubt will continue to be the case. Professor Fetter has pointed out that the inclination of the classical economists toward *laissez-faire* was strongly influenced by 'their distrust of discretion by a Government dominated by an aristocracy and by a Bank run by a "company of traders" '.[1] On the other hand, Walter Bagehot defended the role of the Bank of England as lender of last resort, 'although this was all contrary to the teachings of political economy',[2] and was willing to rely on the discretion of the Bank—operating, however, with the aid of a rule which he suggested.

A significant difference in attitude is to be discerned in the two periods to which the remarks of Fetter and Bagehot relate. The Bullion Report is explicit in its repudiation of the ability of monetary authorities to regulate the money supply in a satisfactory manner: 'The most detailed knowledge of the actual trade of the Country, combined with the profound science in all the principles of Money and Circulation, would not enable any man or set of men to adjust, and keep always adjusted, the right proportion of circulating medium in a country to the wants of trade.'[3] The flow of commerce coupled with free convertibility was counted on to assure the correct adjustment of money throughout the trading world. But 'if the natural system of currency and circulation be abandoned, and a discretionary issue of paper money substituted in its stead, it is vain to think that any rules can be devised for the exact exercise of such a discretion'.[4]

In Bagehot's eyes, on the contrary, it was the discretion not of the monetary authorities but of the bankers that was open to question. His observation that 'money will not manage itself' is almost invariably quoted—out of context—as denying the possibility of an automatic monetary system. The actual

---

[1] F. W. Fetter, *Development of British Monetary Orthodoxy, 1797–1875* (Harvard University Press, Cambridge, 1965), p. 143.   [2] Ibid., p. 283.

[3] Edward Cannan (ed.), *The Paper Pound of 1797–1821* (King, London, 1919), p. 52.   [4] Ibid., p. 53.

reference, however, is to the laxity of bankers in managing the private resources entrusted to their care. His remarks constituted an attack on the conduct of private and not of public administrators.[1] They have to be construed as criticizing sole reliance on the free play of market forces.

It would be an over-simplification to say that the classical, early nineteenth-century, *laissez-faire* tradition survives in the position of the Rules advocates. Nevertheless, the trust shown in relatively simple methods of regulating the money supply is similar, and so is the confidence in the working of an undirected market mechanism. The advocates of Discretion tend to share views expressed by Bagehot as to the relative virtues of individual (and collective private), as contrasted with official, discretion. The difference is less a matter of inherited ideas, perhaps, than it is of outlook and temperament. But the point remains that what we find, mainly, is disagreement as to what rules and whose discretion should prevail.

It is the destiny of central bankers to be exposed to a highly critical audience. From David Ricardo to the present day economists have had a conspicuous place in that audience. This signifies that discretionary monetary policies have not lacked review. The operation of Rules, on the other hand, can hardly be said to have been subjected to comparably critical scrutiny. Particular monetary standards, including the gold standard, have, it is true, been examined con as well as pro. But systematic analysis of the working of the various monetary rules with which we have had experience is notably deficient; and where the information is available it has not ordinarily been made part of the debate concerning Rules versus Discretion.

The lack is unfortunate. For the relevant comparison is either with rules which we have actually had or with what might reasonably be expected to be the experience with rules that are most likely to be adopted. The standard of comparison we are typically offered, however, is with some proposed rule or set of rules which the advocate happens to fancy. But germaneness to the argument is inseparable from the order of probability that the particular rule in question will be adopted. And this, needless to say, is a test that is seldom considered.

[1] Walter Bagehot, *Lombard Street* (Scribner, Armstrong & Co., New York, 1873), pp. 18–20.

What we usually find is an attitude of hard-bitten realism toward discretionary policies on the one hand, and a personalized, Utopian view of Rules on the other. This observation has nothing to do with the relative merits of the rules proposed: the merits of some of them are unquestionably high. But it is a further reminder that what is ordinarily under discussion is some particular rule and not the general case for Rules. And it is a warning, too, that the evidence on which the case *for* Rules largely rests, as contrasted with that *against* Discretion, is almost wholly conjectural.

An appeal to historical evidence, even if it were attempted, could not be expected to decide the issue. But it is worth observing that, of the monetary rules actually adopted that come first to mind, hardly one can be said to have functioned with marked success. That holds for the Palmer Rule, the Bank Act of 1844, the eligibility requirement, the provision tying Canada's Bank Rate to the bill rate, and even the gold standard itself. Many similar examples could be given; examples of successful rules are much harder to find. This is not to imply that the record of Discretion is a particularly happy one either, but it is an observation to be borne in mind when the deficiencies in that record are under discussion, as they so often are.

Experience with the Act of 1844 is worth noting for the moral to which it points. The lengthy controversy among bankers and economists over the Banking and Currency Principles had been resolved in favour of a rule providing that changes in the quantity of Bank of England notes should take place only against the exchange of gold at a one-to-one ratio. Within a short time, a serious liquidity problem developed. Bankers and others, fearing that the rigidity of the law would force contraction of the money supply or prevent needed expansion, began to reduce lending and hold on to cash. The crisis was met by what amounted to temporarily suspending the Bank Act. The experience was repeated in 1857 and 1866. At times the mere possibility of suspension was sufficient to relieve fears and overcome the stringency without the necessity of issuing additional currency.

What, in effect, happened was that the adoption of a strict monetary rule led to a financial crisis, which was resolved by discretionary action suspending the rule. The source of the difficulty was a Rule; relief lay in the exercise of Discretion. The rule resulted in rigidity; flexibility was achieved through discretion. The lesson seems clear, but a number of questions remain. Would the situation have corrected itself, perhaps with better long-run effect, if the rule had been strictly enforced and no concession made to contemporary fears? Did such interim success as the rule enjoyed result from a growing expectation that it would be relaxed in time of crisis? Would conditions have been even worse if discretion had been relied upon from the start rather than only after crisis conditions had been allowed to develop? To raise the questions is not to suggest definite answers but to indicate the difficulty of finding them.

The gold standard is our most familiar and probably still the most influential monetary rule. Its history, lengthy and documented as it is, leads to no firm conclusion as to whether it is superior either to other rules or to no rule at all. But the fact that it survives in one form or another in so many countries suggests that the weight of opinion is in the affirmative on both counts.

The operation of the gold standard, particularly in the present century, has been characterized by continuous change and experimentation. The fact that the gold standard as it exists today bears so little resemblance to the classical pattern that developed in the nineteenth century signifies that this particular rule has survived only in conjunction with continuing change in the underlying rules by which it operates. For actually the gold standard is not a single monetary rule but the name we give to a wide assortment of rules, some written and some unwritten, for maintaining an established relationship with gold. And the evidence suggests that the gold standard has survived, in its present modified form, only because repeated and sometimes violent shifts within the body of constituent rules have provided the requisite adjustability to changing conditions.

There may, of course, be those who would argue that it would have been better to adhere to a strict gold standard of the classical type. But economic purists who attribute shortcomings to departure from original specifications have still to explain how the practical operation of a rule can be judged apart from the manner of its observance.

Whether the gold standard is looked upon as an anchor

which prevented discretionary monetary policy from being blown to the winds or as a barrier to much smoother sailing is likely to remain a matter of personal opinion. The same may be said of experience with other monetary rules. But at least it is reasonable to ask that the evidence should be tested as searchingly against one conclusion, whether that be Rules or Discretion, as against the other.

That experience with monetary Rules has tended to be viewed somewhat leniently and experience with Discretion rather severely would perhaps be disputed as a partisan judgement. What is less open to question is that the case for Discretion has been stated mainly in terms of the need to adapt to constantly changing conditions. Experience with sudden, unpredictable disturbances, as contrasted with changes of a more lasting character, has received relatively little attention in the context of the Rules–Discretion controversy. And it is here that the experience of recent years is particularly suggestive.

The early 1960s furnished a series of events that illustrate both the sort of monetary disturbances that may arise and the kind of discretionary innovations that can be developed to deal with them. In the autumn of 1962 the confrontation with Russia over missile bases in Cuba threatened to create an explosive situation in international money markets. Steps were immediately taken by the leading central banks to pool resources, provide whatever support might be required to meet abnormal demands, and allay fears of a major financial crisis. The assassination of President Kennedy a year later was met by a similar display of central bank co-operation. And a year after that, severe pressure on sterling led to the greatest combined effort to provide financial support that had ever been witnessed.

These *ad hoc* discretionary measures may have failed to provide a lasting solution. But they saved the day; and it is difficult to believe that any system of rules would have served as well. It is not unlikely that in the course of time various rules will be devised to assist in meeting similar disturbances in the future. But experience offers little hope that those rules or any others will provide, by themselves, adequate safeguards against the new and different disturbances which will surely be encountered.

Behind the persistent hankering for Rules there is the vague feeling that their use signifies a government of laws rather than men, and is therefore somehow superior to other ways of conducting our society. But what strict reliance on the rule of the automatic gold standard, for example, chiefly ensured was that we should confront our most critical tests in a manner that was inept and *ad hoc*. For when a major crisis came the system broke down and we were left to improvise as best we could. In the end we were left with a government of men after all. What was sacrificed because of insistence on a rigid rule was the experience that might have been gained under less inhospitable conditions; this and the aid and comfort of milder rules and guides which might otherwise have been put into effect.

To an even greater extent, perhaps, support for Rules is based on the thought that in this way we shall make the practice of the arts of central banking more scientific. The pressure is the greater because it comes at a time when the methods of the hard sciences are having a transforming influence on the soft sciences. Today the use of quantitative measurement, computers, and mathematical refinement is no more open to question among economists than it is among engineers. In such a setting it is all too easy to forget that the ultimate decisions in the social sciences, assisted though they will be by the methods of pure science, must continue to be human decisions. The same can be said, of course, of applying the results of physical science, as in treating a cold, building a bridge, or reaching the moon. A war fought by computers alone would be lost as surely as one fought without them.

The virtues of imprecision are no more to be denied than are the inadequacies of exactness. Because reactions which involve human response are inexact, the methods of the hard sciences, which deal with reactions of physical elements, are not necessarily sufficient. On the contrary, they may be extremely dangerous: the precision with which the results are likely to be clothed can be unwarrantably persuasive. To be fully confident of results that contain a small margin of error can be worse than having a less definite conviction regarding results which are more approximate. The looseness of more general conclusions is a protection: it provides a warning that they must be administered with, let it be said, Discretion!

Scorn heaped on economists for their impatience 'to get on with the job of reaching ambiguous conclusions' is misdirected. Let us suppose that no single outcome, no one course of action and reaction, is certain, as is bound to be the case where some of the elements that enter in are not predetermined. Then the only valid conclusion is one that is ambiguous: allowance must be made for possible changes among the determinants. To wait for a genuinely unambiguous conclusion would, in a changing world, be to defer action for ever. To assume an unambiguous conclusion and proceed inflexibly toward it could lead to frustration or worse.

Whatever the courses open to the central banker faced with uncertainty, the starting-point is honest recognition that uncertainty does exist. If a decision is to be reached and action taken, somewhere along the line judgement has to enter in. The fear of being suspected of relying on misinformation, non-information, or personal bias makes for hesitation in acknowledging that judgement is not merely indispensable but inevitable. Judgement enters, indeed, even into recognizing that a decision has been reached. Wisdom lies not in denying the importance of personal judgement but in admitting its usefulness while not forgetting its limitations.

Strategy is still human strategy, however much it brings rigorous scientific procedures to its aid. The ultimate role of the natural sciences is technique. The ultimate role of social science is judgement. Pure science does not make decisions. It can only make decisions better. Whether the strategy is military, governmental, social, or economic—whether, indeed, it is all of these together—behind and beyond all that physical science can provide must be judgement that is at one and the same time perceptive and positive. In the end it is the contriver of human judgements who is the master, and it is the purveyor of scientific method who is the servant.

The current preoccupation among central bankers is to measure ever more minutely and precisely. Speech after speech by leading officials reflects the deathless hope that by more intensive and sophisticated study we shall eventually discover how it is that monetary policy really works. The underlying premiss is that how policy really works is there to be discovered. For this to be true monetary reactions must conform to a predictable pattern. And this is to assume that somewhere, waiting to be uncovered, are those ultimate rules, good for all time and place, which Professor Sayers has warned us not to expect.

The central bankers of our day have been diligently asking what *is*. No sensible person would oppose, in principle, honest efforts to extend the boundaries of knowledge and understanding. But there is another line of thought that has been sadly neglected. A question they should have been asking all these years is what thoughts the central bankers should be thinking if Sayers is right—as we know in our hearts that he is. How, for example, should the Federal Reserve proceed if there are no sure linkages and never will be? What constructive actions are indicated or can be devised in situations where the exact outcome of a particular policy or set of policies must always remain uncertain?

Like the Maine farmer who already knew how to farm better than he was doing, the central banker has the present knowledge, one feels sure, to be a much better central banker than he is. It is hard to believe otherwise than that greater gain would have resulted from equal effort spent on obtaining information more quickly (and acting on it more promptly and with greater originality and skill) than has been derived from much of the energy that has gone into acquiring additional knowledge and carrying it to greater and greater lengths of refinement.

To say this is to argue that preoccupation with the pursuit of ever greater knowledge and precision may well have slowed the hand of monetary policy. It may have created not only gratuitous lags but absolute blockages. It may have done so through the invitation to delay that is consequent on delusive contemplation of the limits of present knowledge and of the fuller wisdom to come, as well as through the diversion of highest skills.

What has been in shortest supply among central bankers is not a working knowledge of how monetary policies work. It is imagination and venturesomeness in drawing on knowledge and administering powers we already have. Success depends on the refusal of central bankers to be immobilized from constructive action by inordinate fear of being found wrong. Insufficient attention has been given, certainly in the United States, to discovering both new methods and more effective ways of applying old methods. Central banking has surely been the least innovative of man's important occupations.

The middle 1960s gave signs of a softening of the hard crust of convention, a change not unrelated to the appointment of a number of highly qualified younger economists to the Board of Governors. At one point of perilously constricted credit (or so leading bankers at least believed) the Board brought relief by announcing a new departure in discount policy: the promise of relatively easy discount facilities for banks which would exercise care in the screening of business loans. What the move amounted to was an ingenious hybridization of familiar discount procedures with use of the directive, long and successfully employed abroad but always viewed with suspicion in the United States.

In other ways, also, the Board, long deprived of major selective instruments of credit control, discovered new possibilities in the more selective applications of existing powers. Moreover, the cloud of secrecy that traditionally shrouds the thoughts and deeds of central bankers was pierced by a number of unconventional proposals from newer members of the Board—rather to the dismay, it has been told, of older colleagues in the System. And it was reported that the time within which certain strategic information becomes available was reduced, in one case from a month to a week and in other cases from a week to a day. We are left to wonder whether the credit for this accomplishment belongs to computers, or to a tightening of procedures that had been needlessly slack all along; and perhaps to ask what other possibilities of improvement may still remain.

If linkages were stable and certain, even though at present obscure, we could hope that Rules might one day take over from Discretion. But specific causes are few while general influences are many, and ultimate resort to discretion is inescapable. Scientific skills can assist. The search for rules must continue. For these are the means of guiding the authorities and relieving them of needless burdens. But scientific endeavour and the search for definitive rules will have served us badly if they lead us to neglect the human ingredients on which the exercise of discretion depends. To forget this is to overlook that which makes economists most useful to central banking. And it is to forgo that which makes central banking most interesting to economists.

DAVID WILLIAMS[1]

The Evolution of the Sterling System

THE use of domestic currencies for international transactions is quite rare; some, indeed, would call it a privilege; it might, with justification, be better called an accident. Certainly, the conditions which give rise to an international currency might be regarded as unusual, as they rest, basically, on the ability of a country to effect a massive and sustained export of capital and the willingness and ability of 'foreigners' to absorb capital imports—either in the form of holding foreign currency assets or merchandise imports from the capital-exporting country or some combination of the two. It is not often, and, if often, not for long, that conditions (institutional as well as economic) are propitious for the growth of an international currency. This chapter attempts to outline the evolution of sterling as an international currency within the context of the extraordinary internationalization of both the British economy and its financial system from the middle of the last century.

THE PRE-1914 PERIOD

Organization

The international use of sterling arose because British merchants were accustomed to transact their international trade by means of the sterling bill of exchange. But the emergence of sterling as an international currency, in the sense that it was used by non-residents to denominate and transact their international business with other non-residents, began on a large scale only from the early 1860s and followed closely the expansion abroad of British financial institutions and the rapid improvement of communications consequent upon the invention of the telegraph.

[1] The views expressed in this article are personal; they do not necessarily represent those of the International Monetary Fund.

For much of the earlier part of the century a large proportion of British external trade had been financed and cleared effectively bilaterally with its trading partners, and to that extent sterling was the dominant currency in international finance as Britain was the dominant trading country.[1] From about 1860, however, a number of factors fundamentally altered these bilateral-type clearing arrangements. The demand for sterling facilities to finance a rapidly rising level of international trade grew as international trade patterns became focused increasingly on Britain. Broadly, the United Kingdom ran heavy payments deficits with Europe and North America but large surpluses with, in particular, the sterling countries of India and the Far East. The line of clearance of debts almost inevitably passed through London, and debts were, consequently, cleared largely in sterling. It was also becoming convenient, largely because of the pattern of settlement of the international debts of the Empire as a whole, which was centralized on London, for non-Empire countries to clear debts between themselves in London against sterling. In other words, London attracted non-Empire business because, in the first place, of the scope and rapidly rising rate of the Empire's international transactions.

The growing use of sterling in world trade was given a further boost by the establishment of organized commodity markets in London—particularly markets dealing in industrial raw materials and food. To some extent London was a natural centre for these markets, as the United Kingdom was the world's largest importer of food and industrial raw materials. Further, many of the leading products were produced within various territories of the British Empire and these looked to Britain as their natural sales outlet. London took advantage of its geographical and political position, including its policy of undeviating free trade, to become the world's largest wholesale market. It strengthened its international economic position by becoming also the leading carrier (and insurer) of international commerce, as a result of the extraordinarily fast growth of the British merchant fleet between 1865 and 1900.[2] The

---

[1] S. B. Saul, *Studies in British Overseas Trade, 1870–1914* (Liverpool, 1960), Ch. III.

[2] 'The share of British shipping was greater than the share of British trade and in 1912 British ships carried about 52 per cent. by value of world trade. . . . Of the British fleet, some three-fifths only was employed in British and Empire trades, the

concentration of shipping and marine insurance services in London, as with the commodity markets, extended the practice of denominating international prices in sterling. In addition, the growing volume of Britain's foreign investments, a very large proportion of which was in the form of long-term securities denominated in sterling, induced foreigners to accumulate sterling in order to meet sterling obligations in London.[1]

In short, the economic weight of the United Kingdom in world commerce, the economic advantages of a politically far-flung Empire pursuing a policy of free trade, the efficiency of her international service industries, such as shipping and insurance, and the increasing flow of capital exports, all tended to extend the international use of the pound sterling, both within the Empire and beyond. Nevertheless, the 'new multilateralism . . . required a new system to ease the flow of payments'.[2]

The new system, which would in time account for sterling's financing about 60 per cent. of world trade and would permit the taking up of nearly £4,000 million of long-term securities from foreigners between 1860 and 1913,[3] was achieved through a rapid internationalization of the London capital and money markets and an expansion in the rate of growth in the number of banks established in London for operation abroad (particularly in the primary producing areas of the world). To some extent, the two vital extensions of the British financial system abroad were consequent upon each other.

The London capital market became oriented early in the nineteenth century towards foreign investment. This reflected not only the foreign origins of many of the rapidly rising merchant bankers who maintained and expanded their foreign connexions and provided long- and short-term financial resources abroad, but it also reflected the comparatively small use of the capital market to finance domestic investment.[4] The institu-

balance being employed in indirect trades.' (S. G. Sturmey, *British Shipping and World Competition* (London, 1962), p. 22; see also p. 34).

[1] T. Balogh, *Studies in Financial Organization* (Cambridge, 1947), pp. 233–4.
[2] Saul, op. cit., p. 44.
[3] E. V. Morgan and W. A. Thomas, *The Stock Exchange, its History and Functions* (London, 1962), pp. 88 and 94.
[4] 'It was not until near the end of the nineteenth century that large numbers of commercial and industrial firms became public limited companies.' (Morgan and Thomas, op. cit., p. 79). Professor Paish has estimated that 'of net investment at home . . . (before 1914) . . . not more than £30 million or so out of a total of

tional machinery of the market that was built up for domestic purposes was fairly easily adapted for, and, indeed, became dominated by, issues on foreign account. The London market was dominated by the issue of bonds for domestic purposes, and this technique became a particularly suitable and appropriate form of financing international investment. To the extent that the typical British investor preferred to hold bonds as the main instrument of portfolio investment, by far the most readily available source of new and comparatively high-yielding bonds on the London market was through foreign issues.[1] Indeed, the degree of internationalization of the market is vividly illustrated in that 'By 1913 foreign stocks and shares quoted in London had a nominal value of nearly £6,800 million, 60 per cent. of the value of all quoted securities'.[2]

As with the capital market, so, too, did the London discount market become an integral part of the working of the international banking system. The initial internationalization of the discount market was due largely to the general acceptance of the bill of exchange as a medium for international transactions. The bill of exchange was the main means of financing domestic trade up to about 1850. The discount market had, however, become the centre of bill financing in the course of the first half of the nineteenth century, by its readiness to accept short-term funds employed in the discounting of bills of exchange. This unusual intermediation was extended abroad by the acceptance of foreign deposits and, more remarkably, by the readiness to discount bills of exchange[3] relating to foreign transactions.

The comparative smoothness of the development of the bill of exchange as an international 'currency' depended, however, on the development of an international banking system which would command the confidence of the London discount market.

£150 millions or more—was financed through the capital market . . . [while] . . . almost the whole of net foreign investment can be taken as represented by new long-term issues on the London market, which at their peak reached an annual total of about £200 millions.' (F. W. Paish, *Studies in an Inflationary Economy* (London, 1962), p. 223).

[1] For an interesting discussion of the predilection to acquire bonds, see A. J. Brown in *The Yorkshire Bulletin of Economic and Social Research*, May 1965, p. 56.

[2] Morgan and Thomas, op. cit., p. 97.

[3] See Balogh, op. cit., pp. 167, 174; also W. T. C. King, *History of the London Discount Market* (London, 1936), p. 280.

It was the international banking system centred on London which provided the institutional framework of the 'new multilateralism', and it was indeed the heart of the operation of the sterling system of the pre-1914 decades.

Commercial banks had been established in London with the specific purpose of operating abroad as early as the 1830s. The first bank floatations were largely for Australia and the Far East.[1] After 1852, however, with the relaxation of the chartering procedure of overseas banks and the introduction of limited liability, a flood of floatations occurred with a view to setting up banks overseas.[2] In addition, colonial banks established branches in London throughout the period (particularly after 1870) and, after the end of the Franco-Prussian War of 1870–1, European banks likewise established branches and agencies in London on a very large scale indeed. The total number of overseas and foreign banks in London grew continuously: by the end of 1842 the total amounted to about 10; by 1851 to about 25; by the end of 1867 to about 60 (the toll taken by the 1866 crisis was fearful); by 1889 to about 105, and by the outbreak of war in 1914 to more than 135.

It is not known how much sterling credit (long and short) was typically advanced to the rest of the world in the decades of rapid growth of the international banking system and of the London capital market after about 1880; it is, however, certain that the role of British banking was crucial, as an institutional mechanism, in fostering economic development over a large

---

[1] A. J. S. Baster, *The Imperial Banks* (London, 1929), Ch. III and Appendix II, pp. 266–8.

[2] On the basis of details on the establishment of banks, provided in the *Bankers' Almanac and Yearbook* (London, 1966–7), pp. g940–g1004, and in Baster, op. cit.; W. T. C. King, op. cit., pp. 264–5 and 280; and W. E. Clarke, *The City in the World Economy* (London, 1966), pp. 30–44, it would seem that the rate of establishment of overseas banks with head offices in London was something like the following:

Period	Total
1830–42	11
1843–51	4
1852–67	50
1868–89	29
1890–1914	31

It should be noted, however, that many of these banks failed soon after their establishment.

part of the world. Though the overseas banks were established to finance international trade, most of them carried out a great deal of local financing, particularly in the older territories of European settlement, like South Africa, Australia, New Zealand, and Latin America.[1] Indeed, the amount of credit extended by British banks in the overseas territories, in addition to those countries' borrowing in the London capital market, was of critical importance, almost irrespective, over the short run, of the state of international trade. Professor Joslin's description of British overseas banking in Latin America is of general applicability: 'To carry out commercial banking operations overseas, the branches were given fixed capital and sought deposits in local currency . . . they were able to increase the profitability of these transactions by issuing notes; and then used the resources at their disposal to make loans and overdrafts, and to discount promissory notes and bills. . . . Not the least important of their services was the provision of credit for international trade.'[2]

The extension of British banks into the domestic banking business of foreign countries was, in some cases, extremely high: 'In 1914 the British banks controlled approximately a third of the deposits of the Brazilian banking system and over a quarter in Argentina and Chile.'[3] The situation in the Colonies and Dominions (except Canada) was, of course, even more heavily weighted towards London banks. In most cases well over half of the local business was in the hands of the London-based banks, or, as in Australia and New Zealand, a large proportion of domestic deposits there were owned by British (especially Scottish) residents. Even when the 'Anglo' banks themselves were not dominant—e.g. in India—the local banks were heavily dependent on the London market or on the local British banks.

[1] The international branch (and agency) network of the colonial joint-stock banks with head offices in London increased from over 1,000 in 1880 to nearly 3,000 in 1914, and their total assets rose from £160 million in 1880 to £493 million in 1914.

[2] D. Joslin, *A Century of Banking in Latin America* (London, 1963), pp. 19–20; see also S. A. Henry, *The First Hundred Years of the Standard Bank* (London, 1963), pp. 32, 34; Dr. Balogh's observation, 'In pre-1914 days the London bill represented the only modern banking instrument in most overseas countries on the basis of which credit could be obtained at modest banking cost', stresses the international significance of London banking (op. cit., p. 178); also King, op. cit., p. 282.

[3] Joslin, op. cit., p. 110.

Only in North and Central America and Western Europe was British commercial banking not a dominant element in the domestic monetary structure, and even in North America the indirect reliance on the London money market was substantial.

Exchange rates and currency control

The financing of international trade and economic development was the rationale of the sterling system in the fifty years before 1914. Though sterling was the basis of the system, it operated, up to about 1870, in uneasy equilibrium, as there was recurring instability of exchange rates (and monetary conditions) even within the politically unified parts of the system, owing to the fact that some exchange rates were fixed in terms of gold and others in terms of silver, and a considerable part of the world (mainly South America) experienced fluctuating exchange rates. This instability was often reflected in rampant speculation and frequent collapse of monetary institutions operating in the developing areas. Britain had adopted a gold standard in 1819, most of the older Colonies (Australia, New Zealand, Canada, and, after a long and unique history of inconvertible paper currency, South Africa) also accepted gold coin as unlimited legal tender, and they were, in effect, also on a gold standard. The flexibility of exchange rates between London and these countries was left to the arbitrage operations of commercial banks—hence giving a form of gold exchange standard—and exchange rates tended to remain comparatively stable within the gold points.

Most of the remainder of the Empire was, however, on an effective silver standard—i.e. silver coins circulated locally without limit. By the late 1870s the exchange-rate problem with the silver-using countries (outstandingly India, Malaya, and, later, West Africa) was becoming acute. The silver-using countries were being flooded with silver coin (as the metallic value was declining relative to its internal exchange value), for which they needed to pay in rapidly appreciating gold, or by issuing sterling drafts on London at steadily worsening exchange rates. The downward fluctuations in the silver exchange rates with London were awkward for those governments which, like the Government of India, had extremely large and regular payments to make in London in sterling.[1] Further, the continued depreciation of the exchange rate was having adverse effects on the development of trade with the gold-standard countries, and particularly with Britain—the most important supplier of imports for the silver-using countries. The need for a unified and stable exchange-rate system was becoming urgent.

The pressure to stabilize exchange rates in terms of sterling in the silver-using countries of the Empire led inevitably to the control of local currency issues, and this, in turn, led hesitantly and inadvertently to the introduction of a currency or sterling exchange standard. The essence of that standard—and its later institutional manifestation in the form of various currency boards—was for countries to hold external assets to the full extent of local currency issues, and to establish complete external convertibility of the local currency with sterling at a fixed exchange rate. In the case of India, exchange-rate stability was achieved by introducing gold sovereigns convertible into rupees at a fixed rate, but, more relevantly, the Indian Government was prepared to support the rupee rate in London and the sterling rate in India also at fixed rates. The gold standard, consequently, evolved into a sterling exchange standard. In Malaya the same purpose was achieved by introducing a new currency. The new notes were to be backed by gold (at a rate of M $60 = 7 sovereigns) but allowance was made that notes could be issued locally against TT in favour of the Crown Agents in London at fixed rates. The formal gold standard again never became operative, Malaya operated an exchange standard, and, a number of years later, adopted the sterling exchange standard and a currency-board system of control.

The most important formal institutional development was a result of changes in the West African currency system. This was largely a British silver coin system. Silver was, however, of

---

[1] The rate of depreciation of silver in terms of gold and sterling is shown by the following: the selling rate of Council Bills and Telegraphic Transfers (TT) on India fell from 1*s*. 10·35*d*. in 1873 to 1*s*. 7·52*d*. in 1882 to 1*s*. 2·98*d*. in 1893. In that year the rupee rate was stabilized by the government, selling unlimited bills on India at 1*s*. 4·8*d*. per rupee as a maximum rate and maintaining a practice of not selling below 1*s*. 3 29/32*d*. In the case of the Straits Settlements the exchange value of the silver dollar (i.e. the old Spanish and Mexican silver dollar) fell from 4*s*. 1*d*. set in 1870 (as the rate for the payment of British troops) to 2*s*. 2 1/6*d*. in 1896 and to 1*s*. 6 5/8*d*. in 1902. See F. H. H. King, *Money in British East Asia* (London, HMSO, 1957), p. 11. The Malayan dollar was eventually stabilized at 2*s*. 4*d*. in 1905.

only limited legal tender in the United Kingdom and, therefore, not automatically convertible into gold at the face value of the coins. The exchange rate was, consequently, subject to fluctuation which would depend largely on the inflow of silver coins into Britain from West Africa.[1] In 1912 a Committee of Inquiry recommended the introduction of a West African currency (eventually notes as well as coins) which would be fully backed by a reserve of gold and readily realizable sterling securities, and which would be fully convertible at a fixed rate. The sterling exchange standard system was thus formally adopted.

The West African Currency Board was the forerunner of a very extensive system of currency boards established throughout the Colonial Empire in the inter-war and the 1945–52 periods, this being the means by which exchange rates were stabilized and interconvertibility of currencies was guaranteed. In many respects the currency-board techniques, from the local point of view, were similar in their effects on the economies in which the Boards operated to those intended by the passage of the Bank Charter Act of 1844 on the working of the British monetary system.[2] But from the point of view of the sterling currency system as a whole the backing to its currency was very largely fiduciary (the remainder being largely the gold reserve of the Bank of England). The fiduciary element itself represented development capital raised in the United Kingdom by the overseas territories, and also assets held in the London money and capital markets by the overseas territories for use in the sterling system as a whole. In this way, there was a considerable pooling of resources of the sterling system, and it gave the system as a whole a measure of elasticity that no individual part could achieve on its own.

The adjustment process

By the eve of the First World War the sterling system had become a complex but highly institutionalized system for facilitating international financial transactions. It has long been a

[1] For the currency situation in West Africa before the currency-board system see J. B. Loynes, *The West African Currency Board, 1912–1962* (London, 1962), pp. 7–12.

[2] With the exception that the Bank Charter Act of 1844 permitted a small fiduciary backing to the currency; this was generally not the case in Colonial currency arrangements.

source of inquiry, and controversy, of how and why the international monetary system—of which the sterling system was the key element—functioned comparatively smoothly between, say, 1870 and 1914. Most authorities have placed a great deal of emphasis on the fact that the United Kingdom, as the largest exporter of capital (both long and short), was able to 'control' the pace of overseas economic development by regulating the flow of capital export, and hence shifted the burden of adjustment of its own balance-of-payments difficulties to the primary producing countries. Such arguments suggest, indeed rest upon, a system of *stable* relationships between changes in the credit situation in the London market, changes in the lending policies of the overseas monetary institutions, and changes in the level of economic activity of the overseas territories. In practice, the system worked under conditions of substantial economic and financial instability, which was not necessarily induced by changes in financial conditions in the centre country.

The suggestion of automatism induced by credit changes in the London market, despite the deep penetration of British banks in the overseas territories, seems contrary to the working of the rapidly evolving and highly volatile overseas economies in the latter part of the nineteenth century. Indeed, the overseas monetary institutions reacted primarily to changes in local conditions. They were essential risk-takers and their risk-taking ebbed and flowed, over the short run, in the light of profitability and changing economic prospects in the overseas territories, rather than in immediate adjustments to changes in liquidity in the London market.[1] But there was as little, or as much, reason for the overseas banks in London to cut off credit automatically to their customers in Latin America, Africa, or Australia in times of 'strain' as for the domestic banks similarly to respond to their customers in Birmingham, Manchester, or

---

[1] For example, Joslin, op. cit., p. 112, with regard to Latin America: 'Bank rate had its significance in determining the ease with which British bankers could advance credit both for the conduct of trade and to domestic producers the only major instance in which the effects of a high bank rate can be traced in Latin America was in 1907.' The recent history of the Standard Bank has no important example of credit being restricted because of a tightening of monetary conditions in London; in fact, the contrary is suggested; see Henry, op. cit., pp. 44, 101, 133. Professor S. J. Butlin in *Australia and New Zealand Bank* (London, 1961), 'The Baring crisis in November 1890 shows little effect on the flow of private capital . . .' (p. 280; see also pp. 281–2).

Newcastle. Indeed, a considerable amount of evidence suggests that British bank credit overseas was cut off too late rather than too early in terms of local developments, and therefore the reaction of the London banks to local over-extension could be said more often to deepen a local crisis than to induce one. Nevertheless, the London capital and discount markets did react in rather complex and different ways to changes in economic and financial conditions at home and overseas.

The discount market provided, however, a reasonably effective self-regulating mechanism on the operations of individual overseas banks. Basically, there was a limit to the amount of paper which Head Office or the London Office of the overseas bank could absorb from its overseas branches. The limit was determined by its own capital and reserves held in London and by its borrowing powers in the London market—either in the form of overdraft limits with other London financial institutions, or by rediscounting its bills in the open market, or by collecting British deposits. Broadly, the aim was to balance the need for finance locally with the availability of funds in London, without straining the liquidity of the London office. This balance was, however, frequently upset. But the London market was extremely sensitive to unusual increases in the volume of bills rediscounted by particular banks or for particular trades or countries. Changes in overseas banks' liquidity positions in London were, therefore, fairly quickly noted by their activities in the open market, with consequential changes in credit availability for them and in the price of their credit in London. Moreover variations in credit availability in London would, usually, be sufficient incentives for the banks to curb their overseas operations. In this sense it could be said that the discount market acted as a 'safety valve' for the whole system.

Overlending by the London capital market to any one country or type of industry was also brought to an end by the increasing unwillingness of investors to absorb new long-term foreign securities of particular borrowers. The disenchantment of investors, however, usually followed, rather than led, a deterioration in economic conditions in the borrowing country, which brought with it default on principal and interest.

Overcommitment by the London banks and markets to individual borrowers was, then, usually checked by reasonably efficient market reactions which led increasingly to reduced availability of credit. Quite often, however, problems resulting from general overlending arose, which led to widespread, and sometimes severe, strains in the London markets. The strains arose mainly because periods of high levels of international economic activity usually meant for Britain high levels of domestic economic activity. Consequently, over the short run, the London money and capital markets were subject simultaneously to both external and internal pressures for funds. Over the short run, the capital–export problem was essentially a gold problem, in the sense that rising incomes—both at home and in the gold-using countries of the Empire and North America—pulled gold into circulation, with consequent pressure on the Bank of England's reserve. This was met by increasing interest rates in the money market.[1] By this means, London was able to attract funds from the gold-standard countries of Europe.

It was this ability to attract short-term funds from the European gold-standard countries through the interest-rate mechanism that probably accounted for the fact that the balance of payments of the United Kingdom was in continuous over-all surplus between 1850 and 1913.[2] On the other hand, the volume

[1] The position *vis-à-vis* the United States was rather more complicated. As with the United Kingdom, the United States tended to gain gold (and other funds) in times of domestic economic expansion and lose gold at times of domestic contraction. As a considerable number of United States contractions of incomes coincided with expansions elsewhere, the gold outflow from the United States must, on a number of occasions, have had a stabilizing effect on the level of world liquidity. So far as trade balances (and, presumably, the current account as a whole) were concerned, the United Kingdom normally improved its trade balance at times of domestic expansion, whilst the United States (and many of the primary producing countries) experienced exactly the opposite. The monetary effects of these interacting movements would, of course, tend to be cyclically stabilizing abroad but procyclical in the United Kingdom. There is also some evidence of complementarity, on the 'long swing', between the United States and the United Kingdom economies, in particular, as it affected United Kingdom capital exports. For a recent discussion of the United States balance of payments in the nineteenth century see J. G. Williamson, *American Growth and the Balance of Payments* (Chapel Hill, 1964); for an analysis of the balances of trade of the United States and the United Kingdom see Ilse Mintz, *Trade Balances During Business Cycles: U.S. and Britain since 1880*, Occasional Paper 67 (N.B.E.R., New York, 1959), esp. pp. 54–55 and 76.

[2] A. H. Imlah, *Economic Elements in the Pax Britannica* (Cambridge, Mass., 1958), pp. 70–75; indeed, there were only three recorded deficits in almost a century. This situation, of course, does not imply that the United Kingdom did not lose gold abroad, rather that monetary movements were sometimes adverse with the

of international liquidity tended to increase with the rise in international incomes and interest rates, as some countries (in particular the European gold-standard countries) were prepared to substitute gold for claims on London over the short run, whilst London maintained a considerable amount of its overseas lending (though at rising interest costs) if overseas conditions were propitious. London thereby increased its short-term indebtedness to Europe (hence, the familiar cry about 'foreign balances' in control of Lombard Street at times before 1914), but advances and discounts granted by the overseas banks and the outflow of long-term capital also created what would now be statistically recorded as 'international liquidity'. Gross claims would technically have been built up on London through the creation of assets abroad by the overseas banks.

There was no 'shortage' of international liquidity during the pre-1914 gold standard, because there were few impediments to the growth of financial resources organized within a private banking system which was becoming increasingly international in scope. The growth of international liquidity depended largely on commercial considerations and practices. Nevertheless, it is very probable that the sterling component of international liquidity fluctuated, on the one hand, with changes in the level of income in the United Kingdom relatively to income in those primary producing countries which were closely linked by trade and development with the United Kingdom; and, on the other hand, with changes in the level of interest rates in the United Kingdom relative to interest rates in Europe. In this way changes in international liquidity arose from changes in both the asset and the liability sides of London's international transactions. There is no justification for regarding the asset side as having been the more sensitive to changes in interest rates in London.

It seems rather unlikely, therefore, that international shifts of short-term funds (the basis for changes in the level of international liquidity) could be regarded as an effective stabilizing element in the adjustment process mechanism. A rise in incomes in the overseas territories induced not only an outflow of funds

gold-using countries which led to an outflow of gold; losses of gold could have occurred even where the balance of monetary movements was in favour of the United Kingdom.

from London, but a rise in interest rates which attracted funds from elsewhere, thereby inducing a rise in the level of international liquidity. A fall in incomes in the overseas territories tended to reduce the demand for short-term funds, which led to a rise in overseas balances in London or repayment of debt to the London banks, and hence contributed to the fall in interest rates in London. This, in turn, led to an outflow of gold to the gold-standard countries, thereby inducing a fall in the level of international liquidity. The efflux of funds from the primary producing countries, as with the rise in interest rates in London, has been frequently used in the argument that the United Kingdom 'pushed' the burden of adjustment on to the primary producing countries. But the liquidation of London assets abroad was, in most cases, a result of the depression of income overseas, not its cause. The volume of international short-term funds largely adjusted itself to the level of world incomes, and the rate of its creation depended not only on the growth of world trade, but on the relative interest-rate structure between London and the main money markets of the gold-standard countries.

Over the longer run, payments imbalances were eliminated by changes in the level of economic activity rather than accommodated by 'equilibrating' short-term capital movements. Between about 1870 and 1914 the British economy expanded only when the world economy was also in an expansionary phase. It was also during phases of world economic expansion that the great waves of British overseas investment occurred, and these the United Kingdom effected, over the longer run, with seeming ease.

To a considerable extent the continuation of capital exports by the United Kingdom depended on the overseas territories' absorbing British goods and services, and this in turn depended not only on their general level of economic activity but on the state of the local investment cycle. As Professor A. J. Brown has noted, '. . . it is realistic to think of an independently initiated rise of activity (abroad) drawing in both more British goods and more British capital, the ratio between the two varying widely from one case to another'.[1] British income, its foreign trade,

---

[1] 'Britain in the World Economy, 1870–1914', in *The Yorkshire Bulletin of Economic and Social Research*, May 1965, p. 53.

and its foreign investment frequently moved together over the cycle, the flow of funds from the United Kingdom being a permissive factor in the growth process.[1] Nevertheless, if the capital export was rather greater than could be accommodated by the rising current-account surplus, which usually accompanied rising domestic activity in the United Kingdom, long-term interest rates rose, and this tended to reduce not only the volume of capital exports, but also the level of domestic economic activity.[2] Overlending was thereby fairly quickly brought under control. On the other hand, if the overseas countries 'overborrowed', i.e. foreign loans did not produce, in reasonable time, a rise in their export receipts or produce sufficient foreign exchange earnings to meet debt obligations in London, there was usually a crisis locally and growing difficulties in raising funds in London (both short-term and long-term), which then led to local domestic depression.[3] In brief, the successful continuation of international investment by the United Kingdom, and world economic growth, depended on rising international trade.[4] In those cases where the capital transfer was not effected (by both the lending and the repaying country) by a rise in export receipts the ensuing balance-of-payments difficulties inevitably resulted in depression of domestic economic activity.

THE POST-1918 PERIOD

Structural changes

The pre-1914 sterling system was based to a large extent on a colossal flow of capital from the United Kingdom, of which the flow of long-term capital was of particular importance. Further, the rapid extension overseas of the British banking mechanism not only greatly facilitated the rise in international trade, which was itself in part a consequence of British overseas investment, but also extended the system of multilateral payments that came

---

[1] R. Nurkse, *Equilibrium and Growth in the World Economy* (Cambridge, Mass., 1961), pp. 288–90; see especially the footnote on p. 280.

[2] Brown, loc. cit., p. 58: '. . . we had sufficiently numerous and severe slumps to prevent any chronic balance-of-payments problem.'

[3] Compare Butlin, op. cit., p. 37; Joslin, op. cit., pp. 156–9; G. C. F. Simkin, *The Instability of a Dependent Economy* (Oxford, 1950), p. 163.

[4] 'Trade was an engine of growth transmission as well as a means of improved allocation of existing resources.' Nurkse, op. cit., p. 284.

to be based on London. The mechanism of adjustment between the various parts of the sterling system revolved essentially around the complementarity of the flows of long-term capital, overseas economic development, the growth of international trade, and the swiftness and flexibility with which the financial institutions—mainly the London capital and discount markets and the British overseas banks—reacted at times of changes in trade and income. The costs of the balance-of-payments adjustments were comparatively high in terms of economic instability, though they were thoroughly successful in maintaining an almost unparalleled stability in international monetary relations.

During the inter-war period, and even more since 1945, the United Kingdom has been in no position to generate a large and continuous export of long-term capital. It is unlikely, in any case, that the United Kingdom could have continued indefinitely exporting almost half of its domestically generated savings, as it had done in the decade before 1914, without causing irreparable damage to the structure of the British economy itself. But the deterioration that has occurred since 1920 in the current account of the balance of payments—reflecting largely losses on visible exports in the inter-war period and on net invisible earnings since 1945—has left a surplus that has generally been too small to accommodate the capital needs of countries which had, before 1914, been closely dependent on the London capital market for a large proportion of their development funds. The 'shortage' of savings apart, it seems likely that the conditions which made the London capital market a crucially important cog in the working of the sterling system before 1914 (namely, the ability of the borrowing countries to sustain their domestic economic growth and foreign borrowing through increased foreign trade, particularly with the United Kingdom) would have passed. The traditional form of United Kingdom capital exports—largely bond issues, the proceeds of which were used to build up essentially infrastructure projects—were appropriate for a particular, early, form of international economic development which was strongly oriented to increasing and cheapening the output and export of agricultural and industrial raw materials. That phase of international economic development was likely to change with the almost inevitable spread of industrialization. Indeed, changes in the structure of international investment since 1914 have, of themselves, been so substantial that the practical problems of effecting the transfer smoothly have greatly increased with the spread of industrialization, and almost irrespective of changes in the domestic industrial structure of the capital-exporting country.[1] The increases in trade which follow extensive overseas investment by the United Kingdom nowadays are likely to be competitive with, rather than complementary to, United Kingdom exports.

The comparative shortage of capital within the United Kingdom for overseas development, and, perhaps more relevantly, the different 'real returns' that British overseas investment now bring to the United Kingdom economy, with the consequent greater burden of effecting the capital transfer, have tended to exaggerate the significant shifts which have, in any case, taken place in the pattern of trade between the United Kingdom and the overseas territories. This pattern has changed partly as a result of changes in commercial policy, but also partly because of the acute shortage of capital that characterizes those countries which have been politically the closest to the United Kingdom, and which account for most countries defined as being within the overseas sterling area. And the shortage of capital in the overseas territories has undoubtedly been reflected in, if in fact it has not been a main contributing factor to, the comparatively slow rate of growth of the sterling area as a whole.[2] In addition, the exigencies of two wars, prolonged depression after one war, and acute balance-of-payments difficulties in the United Kingdom after the other (these in conjunction with the overriding desire of the primary producing countries to diversify their economies and to expedite their economic growth through industrialization), have fundamentally changed the basis of the sterling system as an integrated trading arrangement. The sterling system no longer has the

---

[1] This is not, of course, to deny that changes in the industrial structure of the United Kingdom did not occur with sufficient speed and on a scale appropriate to maintain its international competitiveness in the light of the great shifts in international trade that accompanied the spread of industrialization.

[2] Though the statistics of GDP for many individual sterling-area countries are deficient, it would seem that the average annual rate of growth of GDP of the sterling area was approximately 3·7 per cent. between 1955 and 1965. This is considerably less than the world average rate of growth of nearly 5 per cent. over the same period.

dominant characteristics of a closely knit and complementary trading association. The chief significance of this development, despite the introduction of Imperial Preference in the 1930s as an attempt to maintain the *status quo* with regard to trading relations, is that the financial arrangements which, over time, were built up to serve and expedite international trade, particularly between the United Kingdom and, to a large extent, bilaterally, with the other constituent parts of the system, are becoming less relevant as those trading patterns change. In this respect it is fairly easy to understand the expansion of British overseas banks in Europe at the same time as the banks in the formal sterling-area system are becoming increasingly compartmentalized into national banking structures; United Kingdom international trade is tending to follow the same pattern.

In brief, the complementarity of the growth in overseas investment and international trade, which to some extent 'self-financed' the burden of international indebtedness, did not survive the First World War and has been weakened further in the post-1945 period. Also, the inability of the United Kingdom to continue its role as supplier of plentiful amounts of capital for the rest of the system has led to a considerable weakening in the cohesion of the system, particularly in the light of the continued dearth of capital in the overseas sterling-area countries, which have tried to compensate for the shortage by various changes—institutional and other—in their economic relations with the United Kingdom. The most obvious symptoms of weakness in its position in the sterling system have been the emergence of the United Kingdom after 1945 as an extremely large short-term debtor on international account, and her comparative inability to maintain strong influence over the flows of short-term international capital.

As was pointed out earlier, changes in short-term capital flows before 1914 were largely complementary, and probably of secondary importance, to changes on the long-term capital account and in the working of the system as a whole. Since 1920, particularly in the late 1920s, and again since 1945, particularly since 1958, short-term capital movements have become not only a dominant element, but have often assumed a destabilizing role in the working of the sterling system. The 'burden' of 'managing' sterling as an international currency has increased as the comparative importance of long-term capital outflows—and the effect they have had on overseas economic development—has diminished. Indeed, the external short-term financial position of the London market has become the fulcrum upon which the sterling system now largely turns, rather than, as formerly, on changes in the flow of long-term capital exports. This change has, however, been compounded by a host of institutional changes within the sterling system which have weakened further the dominant role of the London capital market at the centre of the system.

The sterling balances

The outstanding characteristic of the sterling balances—i.e. United Kingdom net short-term liabilities in sterling to non-residents—has been their enormous growth since about 1914.[1] The growth in the sterling balances has reflected, *inter alia*, changes in the mechanics of international payments, changes in the domestic monetary arrangements of the sterling area territories, and the extent to which the United Kingdom not only financed a considerable part of its overseas war-time expenditures by the issue of short-term sterling liabilities, but also maintained its role as an exporter of long-term capital.

The requirements of international commerce arising from the use of sterling as a means of financing international trade, and the convenience for foreigners in investing their surplus assets in some domestic money market, were, and are, the reasons for the existence of the sterling balances. It is, however, difficult to trace the origins of the sterling balances and to explain, particularly for the pre-1914 period, how short-term claims

---

[1] The emphasis in this section on the net external short-term debtor position of the United Kingdom is not to deny the extraordinary importance of the gross value of credits outstanding, which in part determine the volume of short-term liabilities. The importance of the creditor position needs to be stressed particularly in relation to the pre-1914 period, when it was likely that the United Kingdom was a net short-term creditor on external account. The latter position arose not only from the large volume of overseas bills outstanding but also from the reputedly large volume of British deposits in the overseas banks in London, and from domestic banks extending credit to United Kingdom customers who operated mainly abroad. Since 1914, however, gross liabilities have far outstripped the rise in gross overseas credits, and the mechanism of control within the sterling system has consequently become more complicated.

were created against the United Kingdom, with the implication of balance-of-payments 'deficits' that such creation implies.[1] The most likely explanation of the growth of the sterling balances in the pre-1914 period lies in the area pattern of British and Empire overseas surpluses and deficits (including long-term capital exports from the United Kingdom) and the manner in which they were financed. The United Kingdom ran deficits with Europe and North America, financed partly in gold and partly in claims on itself; on the other hand, it is likely that Europe needed to hold balances in London to clear its deficits with the countries of the Empire and Latin America. The United Kingdom, however, ran surpluses with the Empire, which were financed by extending credit but also by receiving gold on a large scale from the producing countries within the Empire. The balance of monetary movements could then have been adverse to the United Kingdom itself.[2] The chief significance of this pattern of settlements is that United Kingdom surpluses (and, therefore, credits) arose with areas where the banking system was largely British and where virtually all financial transactions of the Empire were centralized in London; the United Kingdom deficits (and, therefore, debts) were with those areas where British banks were least well established, which led to a formal creation of claims on London that could be liquidated for gold, depending on international interest-rate differentials and other factors. As a consequence of the pattern of Empire transactions with the rest of the world, the United

---

[1] There is, perhaps, no automatic link between the level of international liquidity (as represented by foreign exchange holdings) and the condition of the balance of payments of the country whose currency is being held by foreigners, other than a formal *ex post* accounting identity. In reality, the important operative factor with regard to the creation of international liquidity is likely to be how all countries' payments imbalances are financed, irrespective of whether a country is a reserve centre or not. In the pre-1914 period it is likely that the United Kingdom financed a considerable proportion of the international debts of the Empire as a whole from the rapidly rising output of the South African gold-mines, and thereby limited the creation of claims against itself in non-Empire countries. In the post-1945 period the sterling balances have frequently moved with, not inversely to, the British basic balance of payments; and, given the dominant importance of the London money market before 1914, they might well have done so then. See C. P. Kindleberger, *Balance of Payments Deficits and the International Market for Liquidity*, Essays in International Finance, No. 46 (Princeton, May 1965), pp. 11–12 and 24–25.

[2] 'The main settlements with both Europe and America . . . ran through the Far East.' Saul, op. cit., p. 60.

Kingdom probably tended to increase its claims on the Empire and incur liabilities to the rest of the world. This, however, caused little difficulty, in that the outflow of capital from the United Kingdom (largely to the Empire countries) was accommodated partly by a countervailing inflow of capital but also by sales of gold produced within the Empire, sold in London for sterling, and then, in large part, re-exported by the United Kingdom. But it is impossible to separate the then overseas Empire banking system from the domestic British banking system, and, to that extent, it is somewhat arbitrary to speak, with regard to monetary movements, of a United Kingdom balance of payments. Under the conditions prevailing in the decades prior to 1914 it is likely that the United Kingdom balance of payments was in surplus whilst claims were able to be built up on non-residents. A large build-up of sterling balances by individual countries from purely balance-of-payments surpluses was, however, usually curbed by their demand for imports and gold (often to meet the needs for increased domestic circulation); hence the importance of the Bank of England's operations in the gold market between 1890 and 1907, and the significance of London as the main international gold market.

The significance of changes in the geographical patterns of international payments increased as the bill of exchange—the basis, though not the sole total, of London's short-term claims on the rest of the world—became a less convenient instrument of international finance. Consequently, the role of foreign deposits in the London market grew in importance as debts in London were cleared increasingly 'through fluctuations in the size of sterling balances held by foreign . . . (and overseas) . . . banks in London'.[1] In an important sense, the long-term growth of 'sterling balances' after 1900 was mainly a reflection of the growth of commercial banking in the world, and the convenience of settling international debts in cash and holding surplus funds for this purpose in a money market which offered

---

[1] Saul, op. cit., p. 43. The same point has been made by Professor Triffin: 'Surpluses and deficits between Britain and its Empire . . . merely led to a reshuffling of British bank deposits, rather than to an overall expansion or contraction in their amount and to correlative gold inflows or outflows.' Robert Triffin, *The Evolution of the International Monetary System: Historical Reappraisal and Future Perspectives* (Princeton, 1964), p. 6.

a plethora of investment opportunities. These considerations still apply.

The holding of cash balances by foreigners, instead of their incurring debt, inevitably alters the short-term debtor-creditor position in an international money market. It is only one short step in this process for governments and central banks to hold their external reserves in the form of claims on a foreign centre (particularly if they have large financial commitments to that foreign centre), or, as was common over much of the sterling system (given the requirements of the currency boards and the techniques of the sterling exchange standard), to hold them in the form of claims on overseas London banks, which also represented, to a considerable extent, the domestic banking system of the overseas territories.[1]

With the growth of central banks in the British Empire during the inter-war period there occurred considerable switching of sterling balances from the banking system to 'official holders', a process which continued on a much larger scale during the war and in the post-1945 period. The expansion of the currency-board system in the inter-war period and up to about 1950, in addition to the fact that they were operating under generally rising domestic price levels (hence increasing the local need for currency), also swelled the volume of 'official' sterling balances. To a considerable extent, therefore, the emergence of sterling as an 'official' reserve currency is, in many cases, the result of the institutional monetary arrangements which bound together the territories of the former British Empire, and which became formalized as part of their domestic monetary arrangements as those territories achieved political independence. The virtual ending of the currency-board system has, as yet, had comparatively small effects on the level of 'official' balances, as local currencies in many of the newly independent sterling-area countries are still partly 'backed' by foreign, largely sterling, assets.

More importantly, the growth of the sterling balances since 1914 has been due to the two world wars. Britain's net

---

[1] Professor Bloomfield has estimated that at the end of 1913 gross official holdings of foreign exchange amounted to almost £200 million (1913 exchange rates), of which 'a very large proportion' were in sterling. A. I. Bloomfield, *Short-term Capital Movements under the Pre-1914 Gold Standard* (Princeton, 1963), p. 14; see also p. 8.

short-term creditor position fell by over £500 million in the First World War and the gross liabilities at the end of the war might well have been of the order £500 million.[1] The sterling balances rose by about £3,000 million (net) in the Second World War.[2] Though the series on overseas sterling holdings is not strictly comparable, recorded *net* short-term foreign liabilities of the United Kingdom rose from a minimum of about £300 million at the end of 1918 to about £800 million at the end of 1937 (the peak of the inter-war period), to £3,567 million at the end of 1945, and to £3,547 million at the end of 1966 (excluding holdings by international organizations).[3]

Since 1945 the sterling balances have not increased. There has been, in fact, a secular tendency for them to fall, particularly during the 1960s, which, in contrast to the 1950s, has been a period of heavy over-all balance-of-payments deficits by the United Kingdom. This trend contrasts spectacularly with the trend of foreign holdings of United States dollars, which have increased nearly fivefold since 1945. The sterling component of international liquidity (i.e. gold, reserve positions in the International Monetary Fund, and official foreign exchange holdings) was, at the end of 1966, only 13·8 per cent. of the world total; this compares with 20·5 per cent. of the total for 1955 and 26·3 per cent. of the total for 1948. This is an extraordinarily large and rapid rate of decline in the comparative importance of sterling in the international monetary system,

[1] This 'represents the contraction in London's net short-term creditor position, private sales of securities and repayments to private lenders . . . there must have been a contraction in short-term credits of £250 mn. to £300 mn.' E. V. Morgan, *Studies in British Financial Policy, 1914–25* (London, 1952), p. 343. Morgan also suggests that foreign holdings of 'Special Deposits' were between £100 and £150 million in the spring of 1919 (ibid., p. 334); if we assume that gross liabilities of £200 million outstanding in 1914 remained in the market (though the foreign ownership of the balances would have changed), and also put a minimum figure of £150 million of London balances built up by the overseas banks of Australia, New Zealand, Egypt, India, and Argentina, then £500 million of gross short-term sterling liabilities seems a reasonable minimum.

[2] 'Reserves and Liabilities 1931 to 1945' (Cmnd. 8354, Sept. 1951), and Bank of England, *Quarterly Bulletin*, vol. iii, No. 4 (Dec. 1963), p. 276.

[3] It should be noted that there was an important break in the series in 1962, which, by excluding overseas holdings of long-term government securities that had formerly been included, reduced the sterling external liabilities by £370 million, or from £3,501 million (old series) to £3,131 million (new series revised); see Bank of England, *Quarterly Bulletin*, vol. iii, No. 2 (June 1963), pp. 98–105 and ibid., Dec. 1963, pp. 264–78.

particularly as the post-1945 evolution of the international monetary system has taken the form of creating international liquidity mainly through additions of foreign exchange holdings. Indeed, though sterling is regarded as a reserve currency, with the supposed ability to finance automatically its external deficit, the working of the sterling system since 1945 suggests no automatic relationship between the United Kingdom balance-of-payments deficit and the volume of its short-term external liabilities. The overseas sterling area (OSA)—or the scheduled territories as formally defined by the Exchange Control Act 1947—is the rump of the pre-1914 sterling system. These countries have had the closest commercial, financial, and political relations with the United Kingdom over a long period of time. They still largely centralize the bulk of their international reserves in London, and rely most heavily on the sterling banking system, which links all the members with London, for financing their international trade and providing a considerable proportion of their domestic banking services. Balances held within the system are now largely a matter of commercial practice and convenience. Nevertheless, the fall in official holdings of sterling has been quite marked: from £2,252 million (old series) in 1951 to £1,726 million (new series) in 1966.[1] Private overseas holdings of sterling (net) rose from £333 million in 1951 to £641 million in 1966, which, given the rise in the value of international trade over the period, must be regarded as an exceptionally small increase; and, indeed, the private OSA holdings of sterling as a proportion of their international trade (excluding OSA trade with the United Kingdom) were only two-thirds of the 1954 ratio.

There are a number of reasons for this prolonged decline in OSA official reserves. Some, like the depression of prices of primary products in the 1950s and early 1960s, affected all of the developing countries (of which a large proportion are in the sterling area), and were part of the general fall in international reserves of this group of countries. A number of sterling countries, however, have diversified their international reserve holdings partly into United States dollars and, more substantially, into gold. It is difficult to measure exactly the extent of

---

[1] The period prior to 1951 could be regarded as essentially the post-war reconstruction period and subject to unusually severe financial strains.

the diversification of OSA official reserves, but between 1950 and 1966 it would seem to have amounted to the equivalent of about £360 million.[1] A far more important reason for the decline of sterling reserves held by the OSA countries is, however, that many of them have embarked upon large-scale programmes of rapid economic development, which has involved the heavy use of external assets, with consequent pressure on the level of sterling balances. The overriding need for development finance has, in fact, been an exceedingly important consideration in the profound institutional changes which have occurred in the OSA countries and have affected the operation of the sterling system.

Perhaps the most significant change has been the introduction of exchange controls and increased centralization of foreign exchange assets held by central banks and by governments. Formerly, external assets were held in the banking system and transferred, when needed, to various parts of the sterling area, or held as liquid assets in London. The pre-1945 sterling banking system was little affected by national boundaries in its international operations. Latterly, however, the former flexibility of the banks has been severely curbed, with the result that the international banks need to rely more heavily than previously on their own capital resources, or match more closely their assets and liabilities in each of the territories in which they operate. This development has affected the principle of pooling the resources of the sterling area, and has also led to the centralization of foreign exchange assets, which are used more in accordance with the needs of domestic economic development than with the convenience of international commerce.

The evolution of the British Empire into a Commonwealth has been associated with a certain degree of monetary nationalism, or, at least, attempts at monetary insulation in the interests of furthering domestic growth under more stable economic conditions than hitherto. The establishment of central banks in sterling-area countries has played a crucial role in this process. They have usually taken over the function of the currency boards—namely the issue of local currency against the deposit of

---

[1] Gold and short-term United States dollar holdings rose from approximately $900 million in 1950 to $1,850 million in 1966.

sterling securities held in London—and, in the process, they have generally lowered the ratio of external assets to local currency. This, in turn, has tended to reduce the level of OSA investments in London, and, again, led to a loosening of the traditional joint support to sterling operations that had arisen from the system of pooling resources.

The establishment of central banks has made easier not only the implementation of local exchange controls but brought greater autonomy over domestic monetary matters. Through the establishment of local money markets and the encouragement or requirement that financial institutions which operate locally (though they might be international institutions) should retain a part of their resources in local assets, the new central banks have had an immediate and powerful effect on the growth of local monetary institutions. The establishment of local money markets permits the local banks to balance their regional operations locally rather than through London, and for this operation banks need to maintain and use balances locally. Further, local money markets are frequently developed for the purpose of financing government short-term operations, which provides a further inducement to hold locally a considerable proportion of 'surplus' short-term funds that would, formerly, have been held in London. In the last resort, central banks can and do immobilize foreign commercial bank assets by requiring them to observe minimum local asset ratios.[1]

In brief, the chief significance of the establishment of a central banking system within the OSA has been the introduction of a multi-centred discretionary element in influencing the flow of funds between the local economies and the central money markets. The use of monetary policy in its widest sense in OSA territories has been geared not only to economize on the holdings of foreign assets, but to the attempt to compartmentalize and partly insulate economies which were initially developed as part of a wider whole, and thereby experienced often violent economic fluctuations over which they had little control. The banking arrangements of the sterling system which were based on the financing of international trade are slowly being converted to serve the requirements of local long-run economic development, and thence partly to compensate for the shortage

[1] Bank of England, *Quarterly Bulletin*, vol. iii, No. 4 (Dec. 1963), see esp. p. 270.

of capital, not only in the United Kingdom, but also in the sterling system as a whole.

Despite the controlled use of sterling assets by many of the OSA countries, their balances in London would have fallen considerably faster if it had not been for the substantial outflow of long-term capital from the United Kingdom to the OSA countries in the form of development aid, foreign direct investment, and comparatively long-term export credits. This long-term capital outflow (excluding export credits) amounted to over £3,250 million between 1952 and 1966.[1] To a considerable extent, therefore, the comparatively stable level of short-term claims on the United Kingdom has reflected the volume of capital exports by the United Kingdom during the post-war period.

Though the sterling area is, from the point of view of the United Kingdom, an exchange-control concept for outward movements of United Kingdom funds, the distinction between sterling-area and non-sterling-area holdings in London is of some analytical significance. Externally held sterling is convertible at fixed exchange rates, irrespective of types of holders. Not only, however, were balances held by non-OSA countries considerably more volatile in the post-war period, but they had also fallen by 1966 to about three-quarters of the total outstanding in 1945. There has been a fairly massive liquidation (on a net basis) of short-term sterling assets by the non-sterling area in the post-war period. Indeed, the liquidation would have been larger during the 1960s but for periodic, and at times substantial, overseas official support (excluding operations by the international organizations) given to the United Kingdom. Perhaps even more significant is the fact that by 1966 the United Kingdom had become a net creditor to the 'other' (private) non-OSA holders of sterling, a standing to be contrasted with its net debtor position of £906 million in 1960. This extraordinarily large turn round has been due both to the overseas liquidation of sterling and, more importantly, to a large rise in sterling credits granted abroad. The increase in non-sterling-area credits is a reflection of the shift that has occurred in British international trade since the late 1950s (which has needed to be financed by increased British overseas credits), and one which

[1] *Economic Trends*, No. 104, June 1962, and No. 155, Sept. 1966.

reverses the pre-1914 pattern, when the United Kingdom was essentially a huge net creditor of the essentially sterling-area countries and a net short-term debtor to the rest of the world.

Indeed, with regard to both OSA and other holders of sterling (excluding the international organizations), the gross volume of overseas holdings of sterling now seem unlikely to exceed, to any great extent, total overseas sterling obligations to the United Kingdom. There has been, in other words, a substantial long-run strengthening of the United Kingdom external monetary position through the export of long-term capital—the speculative raids of the first half of the 1960s notwithstanding. If capital exports from Britain had been lower, the level of sterling balances would have been lower. On the other hand, it would seem that, again over the long run, long-term capital exports by the United Kingdom have tended to generate short-term external liabilities. In that respect the working of the sterling system bears some resemblance to the pre-1914 position, when the control lever of the United Kingdom balance of payments was operated by controlling long-term capital exports.

In contrast with the pre-1914 system, however, London has found it difficult to attract short-term funds from the non-sterling world to any great extent, or for any length of time, simply on general investment and commercial criteria. Perhaps the most obvious reason for this is that foreign short-term investment in sterling has been affected by continuing bouts of weakened confidence in the performance of the United Kingdom economy as a whole, and also, at times, because the structure of interest rates in the United Kingdom has not been pushed sufficiently high, compared with interest rates in other money markets, to compensate for the weakening of confidence. This can, perhaps, be partly explained by the different combination of economic policy instruments used by the United Kingdom since 1945 in the light of the different and more comprehensive aims of economic policy after 1945 as compared with pre-1914.

Secondly, the post-war rise in world trade has not been fully shared by the sterling-area countries, so that the need for non-sterling countries to maintain balances in London to clear their sterling debts has been less than if sterling-area trade with the rest of the world had grown more quickly. The London money market since 1945 has been by-passed, to some extent, by non-sterling-area countries because of their diminished need to finance their international trade in sterling, particularly in relation to the sterling area, but also because of the comparative cheapness and ready availability of United States dollars as an alternative source.[1]

In addition, the capital resources needed to finance rapidly increasing world trade, particularly as international financial needs have tended to lengthen in terms of maturity, have had to be met increasingly by the United Kingdom itself at a time of acute domestic shortage of capital. This has led frequently to a heavy strain on the balance of payments and, indeed, some speculative abuse of the sterling resources which had been made available.[2] Consequently, the international use of sterling has periodically been limited by exchange and other controls, with the result that more freely available United States dollar resources have increasingly supplemented sterling as a trading currency—not least in the spectacular expansion of the Euro-dollar market in London since the autumn of 1957.

Conclusion

It has been argued in this paper that the sterling system was built upon a base of colossal exports of capital by the United Kingdom over many decades before 1914. This was one of the foundations upon which was produced a great rise in international trade during the nineteenth century, and this, in turn, was the main reason for the expansion overseas of British banks and the adaptation of the British money and capital markets for international operations. The shrinkage both in the size of the system and in its relative importance in the international

---

[1] Estimates of the extent of world trade financed by sterling are, of course, extremely rough, but it is generally thought that sterling financed about 50 per cent. of world trade immediately before and after the 1939–45 war, about a third in the early 1950s, and, on a rather conservative estimate, about a quarter in 1965—British Banking Survey 1966, *The Economist*, 18 June 1966, pp. x–xvi. This fall has occurred despite the large increase in the overseas banks' network of branches to about 6,000 offices.

[2] In this respect the Budget speech of Apr. 1967 suggests a significant reversal of policy with regard to expanding the role of sterling as an international currency: see the Chancellor of the Exchequer's statement that 'Britain does not wish to extend the use of sterling as a reserve currency', House of Commons, *Parliamentary Debates*, No. 720, 11 Apr., col. 979.

monetary system can be traced to the fact that the flow of capital exports has dried up to a considerable extent, particularly since 1945. The generally low level of international reserves of the sterling-area members is an important indicator of the acute shortage of capital that characterizes almost all its members. Institutional changes in the OSA countries—particularly the establishment of central banks, the liquidation of the currency boards, and the implementation of exchange controls—have also been based partly on the need to acquire foreign exchange to finance local long-run economic development. The London capital market, historically a large and sensitive financial engine for overseas economic development, has needed not only to be applied to domestic purposes, but is also, perhaps, less suitable and able nowadays to meet the new and large overseas demands for development capital.

The difficulties of maintaining a large capital export by the United Kingdom are not, however, institutional, but rather the results of the pressing needs of capital investment at home and the increased burden of effecting the transfer of capital abroad without putting a direct strain on the British balance of payments and the level of its international reserves. The strain of effecting long-term capital transfers seems to have increased as the former complementarity between foreign investment and a higher volume of international trade resulting from foreign investment has been substantially modified (particularly as a considerable proportion of British foreign investment has been for local economic development).

The sterling system is now based mainly on international banking arrangements, which finance at short term a large, though decreasing, proportion of world trade. But financing world trade also needs a considerable and rising amount of capital resources, which British financial institutions alone cannot easily generate. It is probable that those institutions relied formerly on being able to draw on the resources of the whole sterling area (and elsewhere) to support their operations. This possibility is now much less, and for that reason I have argued that though the principle of pooling reserves has continued, the habit of pooling capital resources (both short and long) is being lost. Indeed, as the sterling banking system becomes more closely integrated with the many, and diverse, countries in which it operates, the basis of the system is being changed from one of financing trade to one of accommodating local long-run economic development, with consequently heavy strains on the operation of the entire system.

The strains resulting from the multifarious demands for capital, and the diminished competitiveness of the London money market in attracting and, indeed, holding, foreign funds in sterling, has had substantial effects on the level and composition of the sterling balances—in many respects the most significant indicator of the role of sterling as an international currency. The factors determining the volume of sterling balances are complex and difficult to explain with exactness, as they involve not only an assessment of the external impact of the comparatively weakened economic position of the United Kingdom itself, but also of the substantial institutional changes that have occurred in the OSA countries themselves. In the decades before 1914 the sterling balances tended to increase not only secularly with the continuous rise of overseas sterling obligations to London, but also cyclically as a result of variations in London interest rates *vis-à-vis* the rest of the world and, in particular, *vis-à-vis* Europe. The volume of international liquidity was thereby adjusted to the current level of international economic activity, which itself was held within bounds by limits on the process of domestic credit creation (and its export), and by the effects of economic fluctuations.

During the inter-war period, however, the volume of sterling balances seemed to have been far more influenced by the comparative advantage of London as an investment centre (on interest-rate grounds or as a hedge against exchange controls and exchange depreciation). In contrast, during the post-1945 period it would seem that the comparative stability of the OSA balances has been due to two forces operating in opposite directions: the tendency for overseas balances in London to fall under the pressure of the need for development finance, which has been considerably offset by the large outflow of capital from Britain to the developing countries. On the other hand, London has clearly lost its long-run attractiveness to non-OSA countries as a repository for surplus short-term funds—except in so far as their balances match their short-term obligations in sterling. To a very considerable extent, the volume of sterling balances has become dependent on the volume of capital receipts that foreigners receive from the United Kingdom.

Since the level of sterling balances has been largely determined by capital-account considerations, by far the quickest way to liquidate those balances is for the United Kingdom to curb its outflow of capital. Such a policy could, however, cause substantial strains on the OSA members and weaken still further the working of the sterling system, unless non-sterling capital could replace sterling capital in ever-increasing quantities. The comparative shortage of capital within the system is being partly alleviated, however, by the growing and already extensive use of foreign-owned—and non-sterling-dominated—capital resources. The active growth of the Euro-currency market in London since 1957–8, following the ban on the granting of sterling re-finance credits to non-residents in September 1957, and the subsequent incorporation of foreign currency assets and liabilities into the domestic banking system, is significant, in that foreign capital is being used for both international and domestic purposes. It might well be that the next stage in the evolution of the sterling system will be the extensive use of foreign currency resources within the institutional framework which was built up long ago to serve the international financial interests of Britain, but which might also suffice, given the capital resources of others, to serve a wider interest.

J. S. G. WILSON

The Art of Developing a Capital Market

THERE has been much talk in recent years about the desirability—and some of the ways—of developing capital markets; also of fostering firmer links between them. Where capital markets do not yet exist, a pre-condition is the establishment of a minimum financial infra-structure, such as a reasonably well developed commercial and savings bank system, some facilities for medium-term lending, a number of insurance companies, pension funds, and a stock exchange. While it is rather too simple a view to describe the infra-structure itself as constituting a capital market, it does provide the necessary basis. In the present context, the existence of a minimum financial infra-structure will generally be assumed.

I

It is useful to remind ourselves of certain fundamentals. First, because resources are scarce in relation to ends, choice is of the essence of the problem. Second, to the extent that we resort to the price mechanism, the basis of our decisions will be a comparison of cost and monetary return. Third, one possible choice is whether to consume today or defer part of our consumption until tomorrow. Although in general we produce in order to consume, we—or our successors—may be able to consume more in the future if we are prepared to consume less today. That is the purpose of investment. And if we are guided by market criteria, we shall choose those investment projects that offer the highest net returns, due allowance being made for risks of all kinds. Fourth, since nothing is certain, all investment activity must be based on a complex of expectations. Much, therefore, depends on the information available to the potential investor, on his judgement, on his confidence in that judgement, and on his attitude to risk. Finally, with both domestic and international investment, decisions may well be influenced by extra-economic criteria, especially by considerations of social policy.

So much for fundamentals. In order to invest, it is necessary to command the appropriate resources, and this, in a monetary economy, means a continuing access to finance. For it is the availability of financial capital that makes possible acquisition of the real capital essential to production. It is with the provision of financial capital and its allocation to alternative uses that a capital market is concerned. Assuming that income is sufficient to allow a margin for saving,[1] the most obvious source of financial capital is the flow of funds originating in private and corporate savings, supplemented perhaps by budgetary surpluses on government account. Not every ingredient in this flow is permanently available for long-term investment. Accordingly, there must be some mechanism, if funds are to be fully utilized, to facilitate the withdrawal of funds as well as their medium- or long-term commitment. This also is an essential function of a capital market, one of whose tasks is to provide the means whereby securities (i.e. claims to financial capital) can be bought and sold.

By means of capital markets, the holdings of those, including financial intermediaries, wishing to withdraw funds by selling securities can be absorbed by those who wish to invest funds by buying securities (supply and demand being equated by appropriate price fluctuations). In addition, there will be movements of funds and shifts in demand between the several sub-markets for securities, and this will establish a degree of consistency between one price and another. This same complex of markets can be used for floating new issues, thus providing financial capital, usually on a long-term basis, for initiating new economic enterprises, or maintaining and developing those already in existence.

If we abstract from credit creation, which may sometimes be the best way of stimulating investment activity (as in an economy with under-employed real resources), funds available for new capital issues can come only from corporate and private

---

[1] In the less developed countries it may first be necessary to stimulate growth of income to the point where it will exceed the minimum level at which saving becomes possible.

savings.[1] Much corporate saving is virtually automatic. So is a great deal of saving by individuals, because it is institution-alized in the form of premium payments to insurance companies, payments on mortgage loans, provision for superannuation, etc.

The automatic character of so much saving means that the level of income is likely to be a more important determinant of the volume of saving than market rates of interest, though changes in interest-rate differentials may have an important effect on the choice of the means of saving. Fiscal considerations are also highly relevant. In these circumstances, modifications of the institutional machinery and the overcoming of conserva-tive social attitudes may well prove more effective in eliciting new savings than raising the level of interest rates.

Nevertheless, rates of interest retain a measure of economic importance. The structure of interest rates measures the mar-ginal inconvenience of parting with different degrees of liquidity for a specified period. Likewise, it remains broadly true that this structure of rates serves as a kind of sieve in allocating total available resources to alternative uses. Within the private sector this is done by comparing the expected rate of profit with the relevant rate of interest.

In making these calculations, most businessmen, because of uncertainty, tend to act 'bearishly'. Many can only be induced to invest if they believe they can recoup their money in two or three years. Although the useful life of an asset may be much longer, the probability of obsolescence is another important reason for the short 'time horizon'. Hence, the prospective rate of profit and the general 'state of confidence' are likely to exer-cise a more active influence than rates of interest as such.

At the same time, expectations and the 'state of confidence' are themselves the product *inter alia* of current and expected future price experience, of which the prevailing level and struc-ture of interest rates is an important part. Further, because the rate of interest is still regarded as one of the most 'strategic' prices in the economy, current and expected levels of interest rates exert an important psychological influence on the for-

---

[1] New issues, it may be noted, absorb but a fraction of the total funds available, most of which are reinvested by corporations and firms in their own businesses, either to replace outworn or obsolete equipment or to finance growth and expansion.

mation of business opinion. Moreover, the current level of interest rates will usually reflect the extent to which finance is likely to be available, and this is a highly relevant consideration when investment projects are being planned. In many ways, 'availability' rather than the rate of interest provides the framework of the sieve through which all projects that come to the market must pass.

When a firm finances an investment from internal sources, one might expect businessmen to pay some attention to market rates of interest, debiting their internal accounts with a notional rate for the use of own funds, based on the alternative opportunities forgone as a result of employing these funds inside the business, instead of investing them outside, due allowance being made for different degrees of risk. In fact, notional rates of interest seem seldom to be applied (and, where 'conventional' rates are employed, they are rarely as high as current or expected market rates). Even when the expected rate of return is lower than that obtainable in other firms or industries, profits will often be ploughed back into the business because of the fiscal advantages, the need to grow, and the desirability of retaining some degree of financial autonomy. But, in consequence, part of the supply of funds that might have found its way into the new issues market will now have been absorbed by individual businesses before becoming more generally available, and rates to market borrowers may therefore be higher than would otherwise have been the case. As a result, some investment projects that promised relatively high yields may be starved of the financial resources necessary to implement them. Hence, to the extent that the capital market proper is by-passed and firms are prepared to invest in anticipation of prospective returns that are lower than the highest available rate elsewhere (due allowance being made for different degrees of risk), an optimum utilization of economic resources is unlikely to be realized.

II

Capital market activities will also be influenced by a variety of social considerations. The government or its agencies may intervene from time to time to supplement, to influence, or even actively to regulate the distribution of investible funds. In these cases, the available investible resources will be allocated through the medium of a combination of market mechanisms and official intervention. Thus, the availability of funds to certain favoured sectors may be supplemented by establishing specialized financial intermediaries, by directing savings towards privileged users, by furnishing 'guarantees' to buttress the credit-worthiness of the borrower, or by regulating either domestic access to foreign funds or the availability of domestic funds to foreign borrowers. Again, self-financing might be encouraged by generous depreciation allowances or accelerated amortization provisions. Interest rates might be subsidized for approved purposes. Fiscal concessions might favour certain forms of financing (e.g. bond or share issues) or certain uses of funds (e.g. for housing). Likewise, restrictive action might be applied to investment demand (e.g. by credit controls, decisions affecting budgetary expenditure, controls imposed on local authority spending or on expenditure by the nationalized industries, the issue of fewer building licences, and so on).

In this context, too, one might mention the volume of investible funds frequently absorbed by the public sector, which may seriously interfere with the possibilities of growth in the private sectors. This is not to deny the importance of social priorities and of social investment, or the inadequacy of market criteria as a basis for determining how much shall be invested in schools, hospitals, housing, roads, and other social amenities. What is implied is that (a) resources are scarce; (b) social priorities must take this into account; and (c) both the social investment programme and its related time scale must be spelt out in some detail, so that those who plan investment programmes in the private sector should have a continuing knowledge of the framework within which they are expected to operate.

Although the relevant social considerations may vary to quite a significant extent from one country to another, it is important to emphasize that they are part of the environment within which a capital market has its being. Also, it is largely as a result of introducing social considerations that the policy-makers face a real dilemma when it comes to the choice of an appropriate level and structure of interest rates. As a basis of policy, there would seem to be three main possibilities:

(a) A highly regulated interest-rate structure with the object of pursuing a low-rate policy (Norway may be quoted as a leading example, and even there the control has been by no means complete);[1]

(b) Relatively free capital markets, which because of the pressure of demand sometimes experience higher rates of interest than the authorities are prepared to countenance (e.g. Denmark in 1965 and, to a lesser extent, Western Germany); and

(c) A policy that falls somewhere in between and that attempts to influence interest rates to a rather greater extent than under (b), while eschewing the degree of regulation postulated under (a), the object being to relate the level of rates fairly directly to the current requirements of the economy; even so, certain rates may be actively subsidized or regulated to ensure that particular forms of economic activity are accorded the priorities that society is thought to demand.

The nature of the dilemma is best elucidated by considering in greater detail the third of the policy options, which in a sense is an amalgam of the other two. Depending on the current state of the economy, it may be appropriate sometimes to raise the general level of interest rates, sometimes to reduce it. But if a country persistently pursues a low-rate policy at times when the pressure of demand for funds is considerable, it can only do this provided it is also prepared to regulate directly the allocation of funds between their several possible uses. In these circumstances, extra-market criteria must be invoked; necessarily these will be arbitrary in character and will reflect chosen social priorities. Moreover, there are limits to what direct regulation can achieve, and, once the pressure begins to build up beyond the levels of tolerance, either leakages (e.g. black markets) begin to develop, or a political demand for some modification of the low-rate policy may emerge. Alternatively, if it is decided to allow market processes to operate freely, at times when the pressure of demand is high, interest rates also are likely

---

[1] As a result, in the unregulated non-priority sector, interest rates have tended to drift upwards; this has attracted funds away from priority lending, which it was intended to 'protect' by keeping down the relevant interest costs.

to rise. Moreover, the increase in rates will affect the whole range of economic activity, and, to the extent that high interest rates do exert a restrictive influence, activities such as the provision of housing are likely to suffer quite as much as those thought to have a lower social priority. In these circumstances the authorities are apt to become concerned and to lose some of their enthusiasm for the virtues of the free market. In various ways they then begin to intervene to ensure that specific social priorities are in fact met, and the operation of the market mechanism becomes less free. This is the dilemma: at both extremes, circumstances may force a departure from accepted policy, and the tendency therefore is for more and more countries to follow a pragmatic approach based on a relatively free working of the price mechanism, though subject to the constraints of a social framework based on priorities that in their very nature are arbitrary.

III

The main purpose of this essay is to explore the means of developing broader and more active capital markets, with the object of achieving greater flexibility in market rates and yields and a more effective utilization of investible funds. It is intended to concentrate on the domestic aspects of this problem; the author has already attempted elsewhere to deal with some of the complications of internationalization.[1]

In developing a capital market, the essence of the problem is how to convert savings into actual investment. In varying

---

[1] See J. S. G. Wilson, 'The Internationalisation of Capital Markets', *The Three Banks Review*, June 1964, reprinted in *Monetary Policy and the Development of Money Markets* (London, 1966). Quite apart from normal business and political risks, some of the obstacles to greater integration of capital markets include the existence of different national currencies; sometimes, the fixity (rather than the possible instability) of their exchange rates; limitations on the freedom to transfer capital to (and therefore to invest in) other countries; fiscal differences (not only in the level of taxation but also in its structure); variations in legal requirements (especially in the field of company law) and ignorance of what is required; the tendency for existing price rigidities to become embedded, and therefore difficult to shift (internationalization implies greater all-round price flexibility); the lack of co-ordination in economic and monetary policies; the existence of vested interests (of all kinds); and so on. All of these will impede the shiftability of funds: and on the freedom to move funds from one country to another without excessive cost the possibilities of integrating capital markets must ultimately depend.

degrees, market imperfections or impediments to the free flow of funds remain a problem in all countries. In some, the institutional machinery is more efficient than in others, but, even within the most sophisticated of market structures, difficulties may be experienced from time to time, blockages may occur, or the flow of funds in certain directions may be retarded. Sometimes it is a case of improving the working of existing machinery; sometimes, of setting up new institutions or providing fiscal inducements to change. Always there remains the problem of how best—within a particular environment—to translate savings into investment. Whether the mechanism employed is a direct equation of corporate saving (resulting in the generation of cash flows) with industrial investment (by means of self-financing) or an equation achieved through the operations of the securities markets, one is concerned in both cases with the same basic process. It is fruitless to maintain (as some do) that there is no real dearth of savings in this or that country—the problem remains: how to canalize the flow of funds towards, and to translate it into, actual investment. There is also a risk factor to be considered. When banks (and other financial intermediaries) accept funds from the public (e.g. by way of deposit), they offer in return (and contractually) a degree of liquidity and security. But, in the process of transforming short-term funds into investments (through the agency of a bank loan or a 'participation'), they are incurring a risk (this is in the nature of their business), and, in the event of a loss, it is the financial intermediary that will be liable.

Reference has already been made to the problems that tend to arise as a result of self-financing, viz., the probability that at least some funds will be absorbed in ventures that promise lower expected yields than are being currently offered by enterprises that are prepared to approach the capital market with new issues at competitive rates. From the point of view of developing a capital market, one must accept as a datum that there will continue to be some degree of emphasis on self-financing. Although it is difficult to conceive of optimal limits to the amount that might be undertaken, business firms themselves tend to think in terms of a minimum resort to internal sources of finance, if only because many firms equate self-financing with a capacity to grow without losing their 'independence'.

In the present context, this has clear implications. If one is to develop a broader and more active market in negotiable securities (bonds and shares), there must be an inflow of savings for new issues to tap, but if firms insist on financing from internal sources a relatively large proportion of their investment programmes, it is apparent that fewer new issues will be on offer. Likewise, the flow of savings into the securities markets will be less. Moreover, if this sector of the capital market is starved of funds and firms are obliged from time to time to seek external finance, there is a danger that they will become over-dependent either on the banks or on foreign loans, which will inhibit further the development of a healthy domestic market in securities. It is not that self-finance should be actively discouraged, since this might result in a sharp reduction in the total flow of savings. Indeed, in some countries there may be a case for more self-financing, so that firms can grow to the size that will enable them to tap the new issues market. It is rather that in economies that are already highly industrialized there is a case for pursuing a 'neutral' policy towards self-finance (i.e. neither active encouragement nor discouragement). Pursuance of the goal of economic growth suggests the wisdom of drawing investible funds from both sources—from corporate savings that will be employed primarily in self-financing, and from financial intermediaries and the general public through the agency of new issues of bonds and shares.

IV

On the assumption that a firm will usually seek to satisfy at least some of its capital requirements from external sources, it will have to consider (*a*) the extent to which it can and will depend on debt or on equity capital; and (*b*) the desired term structure of any such debt. Under the first head, it will be concerned with the problems of capital 'gearing'; under the second, it may find it difficult to match its needs with the maturities of debt on offer, and the position may be further complicated by the problem of the 'shifting temporal gap'.

In general terms, the appropriate balance that should be maintained between that part of a company's resources that derives from equity capital holdings and that representing debt will be related to the degree of risk that applies to the enterprise in question—the greater the risk, the stronger the case for equity financing. A further consideration will be the tax advantage of resorting to debt rather than to equity finance; in an age of inflation, too, the burden of debt becomes less with the passage of time.[1] Hence, there are likely to be advantages in increasing the ratio of debt to equity. On the other hand, whether one borrows from a bank or through the market against an issue of bonds or debentures, there are limits to the amount of debt accommodation that lenders will countenance, even in the case of a reputable and well established public company. These limits may be elastic, but lenders will insist that the owners of the borrowing company should maintain at all times a sizeable and related equity interest. Moreover, the several forms of debt will generally be regarded as alternatives. If a company has borrowed heavily by issuing bonds, it is unlikely that its bankers will be willing lenders for large amounts; and, if its bank loans are at a high level, it will be difficult for a company successfully to make large new bond or debenture issues.

Matching financial needs with the maturities of debt on offer is greatly assisted both by the specialized financial institutions (e.g. for medium- and long-term lending) and the generalized lending facilities of the commercial banks. Yet, despite the built-in flexibility of many of these institutions (and especially of the latter), in many countries there is still some concern about 'gaps' in the term structure. Indeed, partly in consequence of this flexibility, there may also be evidence of the related problem of a 'shifting temporal gap'. Identification of this phenomenon resulted from the author's field inquiries during the summer of

[1] At the same time, the dangers of inflationary distortion must not be overlooked. If the effects of inflation are not taken into account, the rate of profit of a business can be substantially overstated in the accounts, leading to mismanagement of a company's capital resources, with major consequences for its future viability (e.g. the incomplete recovery of resources invested in the past, an insufficiently informed assessment of the need for modernization, unrealistic pricing decisions, or unintentional distribution of capital to shareholders or employees). Where historical cost is the basis of amortization policies, the effects of inflationary erosion may go unnoticed. Unless assets are revalued periodically, not only will inflation result in a substantial understatement of the real capital resources employed but there will be a related financing problem when replacement ultimately becomes necessary. This will be particularly acute where the company's assets have considerable longevity (e.g. ships). The remedy is clear—the annual revaluation of all company assets.

1965.[1] In London, for example, there has sometimes been a gap within the 5 to 10 year range; on other occasions, it seemed to lie within the 7 to 15 year range. Likewise, in the United States, there is evidence to suggest that there may be a gap somewhere in the 5 to 15 year range (depending on the banks' attitudes to term loans, it may at times be concentrated in the 12 to 15 year range). In some countries there may still be an institutional gap to be filled (e.g. in the medium-term area, as in Denmark), but, where there is a 'shifting temporal gap' largely occasioned by changes in the degree of willingness of institutions to make term loans even to credit-worthy customers, this suggests that the gap is not merely a matter of institutional inadequacy.

To a significant extent, the shifting gap in available maturities is a function of changing expectations relating (*a*) to the general state of the economy; (*b*) to liquidity/availability considerations (these concern both lenders and borrowers); and (*c*) to possible changes in the level or structure of interest rates. For example, if, because of the state of the economy, lenders (such as banks) begin to feel less liquid, they will tend to shorten the average term for which they lend (this will be true whether they make formal term loans or lend by way of overdrafts that are not now allowed to 'run on'); if borrowers find funds with different terms more or less 'available', they will consider shifting their demand from sources that are less available to those that are more available. In this context, and despite the more vulnerable position that may result,[2] it may well be easier (if permitted) to shift towards the short end, and, by renewing a number of short borrowings, to secure accommodation for the longer term rather than to borrow long for the purpose of financing short-term requirements. But borrowing short could become increasingly expensive, and, if one expects rates to rise, it may pay to borrow long at a moderately high rate and to use the short-term markets for the purpose of lending out occasional surpluses of funds. Necessarily, the costs of moving into and out of the relevant markets must also enter into the calculation.

---

[1] For a summary of the evidence see 'Some Aspects of the Development of Capital Markets', *Banca Nationale del Lavoro Quarterly Review*, No. 79, Dec. 1966, pp. 281–3.

[2] The existence of a 'shifting gap' places an additional limit on the extent to which capital gearing (i.e. resort to debt finance) is possible and safe.

It is clearly undesirable that every 'gap' should immediately be filled by setting up a new institution or facility. In some countries there is far too great a tendency to proliferate facilities as the 'easy way out', politically if not financially. There is much to be said—especially where the financial infra-structure is already established—for using more effectively the existing institutions.[1] If every conceivable gap is to be filled, there is little left for the art of financial management to achieve.

In marshalling the economic and financial resources available, it is desirable that from time to time companies should be obliged carefully to consider both current investment expenditures and their plans for growth by being forced to make a formal application to a market institution and to apply the objective tests of market criteria to the investment programmes proposed, whether it be by accepting the discipline of a higher interest rate or of reduced availability of finance.

Moreover, if companies wish partially to avoid the inconvenience of the 'shifting gap' and have a growth programme that is really soundly based and sufficiently tempting to investors, the remedy is in their own hands—they can go to the market for equity finance. Although they will still be subject to market tests, an issue of new shares will provide them with capital on a 'permanent basis' (the alternative—and this is really the only way to avoid the dictates of the market—is to build up the company's equity by self-financing; indeed, this is its attraction).

V

Nevertheless, even where an established financial infrastructure exists, the development of a broader and more active capital market may require (*a*) breaking down the conservatism both of potential market borrowers and of investors; (*b*) over the longer run, provision of a range of facilities as nearly as possible calculated to satisfy the needs of both sides of the market. These objectives are intimately interrelated; so, too, must be the solutions. Educational propaganda may assist in moderat-

---

[1] On occasion, it may be necessary to supplement the resources of particular institutions (by increasing their capital or by raising their borrowing limits, so that they can attract additional funds by issuing bonds on the open market). Rarely should it be necessary to establish a new institution; usually a 'gap' can just as readily be filled (and much more economically) by extending (or adapting) the functions of an institution already operating in a related field.

ing the conservatism, but the parties must also be tempted into the market by the facilities on offer. On both sides of the market there must be a willingness to experiment and emphasize on greater flexibility.

Many of the problems that face users of capital—both small firms and large—derive from their excessively conservative attitudes. For example, in a family firm there is often a disinclination to 'go public' or, if formally a public company, to place new issues of shares on the open market for fear of losing control over policy and sacrificing 'independence'—even if this means forgoing growth. The preference therefore tends to be for self-financing or debt-finance. If the market is approached, only industrial bonds or debentures may be offered to the public. Clearly, there are limits to the possibilities of financing by debt creation (in whatever form). This is the problem of maintaining a correct 'gearing' between total debt and the equity interests of the shareholders. There are also dangers—over-dependence on borrowed moneys is the surest way of losing control over policy decisions, unless one can successfully sustain such a rapid rate of growth that profits will provide a sufficiently regular generation of cash virtually to convert the debt component in the financing programme into a revolving fund. In this way a measure of independence can be retained.

Yet the conservatism is by no means one sided. Even if the issues were available for purchase on the open market, it is questionable in some countries whether there would be a demand for them from the investing public. This is probably more true of equities than of industrial bonds. Hence the attempt is often made (sometimes successfully) to build a bridge between debt and equity financing by issuing 'convertible bonds'. But the basic difficulties remain: (*a*) the continued preference of many private investors for highly liquid earning assets (e.g. savings bank deposits); (*b*) the disinclination, even in some countries of institutional investors, to invest in equities, on occasion in industrial bonds. The remedy for the first would seem to be a concerted programme of educational propaganda (in collaboration with the stock exchanges and other financial institutions) and an increase in the number of securities that are offered in relatively small unit amounts; and, for the second, propaganda, fiscal encouragement, and, where necessary, permissive legislation to encourage a progressive increase—up to a specified limit—in the proportion of equities (and industrial bonds) held in their investment portfolios by institutions like insurance companies, pension funds, and savings banks. Moreover, in order to maintain institutional interest, an active secondary market in securities must exist. If institutions are to be ready holders of large quantities of securities, these must not only be saleable on a regular basis but also in a market that is sufficiently active to minimize the risk of substantial loss due to inadequate turnover.

VI

What, next, are the institutional changes most likely to assist in broadening a capital market and creating an environment within which an increase in turnover is probable? To this end a range of facilities must be developed that will, as far as possible, satisfy the requirements of both sides of the market. So far as supply is concerned, i.e. the offer of securities for purchase, what seems to be required is not only a greater volume of new issues but also a wide range of maturities and a good industrial spread. To a not inconsiderable extent, achievement of these objectives would be assisted by greater resort to institutions like the French *banques d'affaires* or the British Industrial and Commercial Finance Corporation and similar organizations, whose functions are at least partially pump-priming in character (e.g. by resorting to interim loans and taking up 'participations'), with a view to creating in due course a supply of new marketable securities (when the investment has had a chance to demonstrate its profitability and can be floated off as a new issue, part of which can be sold to the general public, either through the banking system or on the open market). The original 'participation' will then have been liquidated and the process can begin all over again. In countries where such facilities do not exist there is a case for establishing appropriate institutions using similar techniques, suitably modified (where necessary) to accord with local requirements.

Two very important respects in which such institutions could assist in broadening the market and help to develop the demand for shares, both by individuals and institutions (like unit trusts), would be (*a*) by encouraging more medium-sized businesses to 'go public', thereby greatly enlarging the number of shares listed on the several stock exchanges; and (*b*) by ensuring that the individual share units are issued in relatively small amounts, so that the modest investor will be able to spread his purchases (if he so desires) over a relatively wide field. In order to create the economic basis of a more attractive security (e.g. by creating a firm capable of securing some of the economies of scale), two or more related businesses of medium size might on occasion be merged to form a larger company. This could be encouraged in such cases by favourable tax rates on interest or dividends, though subject to limits on the concessions offered. For the rest, what the investing public is likely to want is a wider range of maturities (which may also be a means of reducing the significance of the 'shifting temporal gap'); greater flexibility in terms of issue is another technique that might be used to persuade the public to buy.

Basically, there are only three types of marketable securities that can be issued to the general public—shares, bonds (or debentures), and convertible bonds—but there is considerable room for experiment in offering a variety of maturities and related terms of issue; in addition, much more use might be made of the convertible bond and of issues (whether of shares or bonds) made up of smaller individual units. When it comes to institutional investors, the scope is wider. For example, more emphasis might be put on private placements, whereby debt issues are taken up directly by the ultimate lenders (insurance companies and pension funds). Term loans are somewhat similar. Although they represent virtually a non-marketable security, it does cater for the institutional investor who demands a definite date of maturity that will fit in with his own schedule of projected out-payments.

In considering the relative attractiveness of issues of bonds or shares, the tax advantages usually enjoyed by the former helps to explain why it has often been difficult to encourage a growth in equity investment and greater activity in share transactions on the stock exchanges. In this context the Norwegian fiscal experiment is highly relevant—for a period of seven years (and subject to certain conditions) companies are allowed a deduction for the purposes of company tax (as with interest on a bond) in respect of dividends up to 5 per cent. distributed on new share capital issued, thereby making it as attractive to raise capital by issuing shares as by issuing bonds, with the advantage that shares represent risk capital 'permanently' available to the company concerned.

Share issues might also become a more attractive investment in certain countries if less were ploughed back by way of self-finance or by building up 'hidden reserves', and a higher proportion of profits was distributed as dividends. In any event, where the creation of hidden reserves is common, company accounts fail fully to reflect the operational results of the business concerned, and paucity of published information may subsequently make it difficult for a company successfully to approach the market with a new issue.

VII

If now we can assume the offer of a reasonably attractive range of securities, how might we expect to encourage greater activity on the demand side? This can be done (*a*) by adopting measures to stimulate an increased demand for securities, both by the general public and by institutional investors; and (*b*) by developing (where necessary) an active secondary market, so that securities can readily be bought and sold, and in some volume.

Where members of the general public are already accustomed to hold part of their wealth in a wide range of earning assets, including marketable securities, further broadening of the demand might be achieved by increased advertising and educational propaganda. Nor should the efficacy of advertising as a stimulant be underestimated.

An additional means of interesting the small or conservative saver more especially in equity investment is by setting up unit trusts. By this means—and especially when their operations are linked to a contractual savings plan—the small saver might be tempted away from placing his money with a savings bank, building society, or savings and loan association and be encouraged to invest his savings in 'units' that can be redeemed if he so desires. Meanwhile, through the unit trust, he will have an indirect interest in industrial and commercial investment (including equities, and therefore a hedge against inflation). There is also a spread of risks that in a well-run unit trust provides him with a reasonable degree of protection against sudden loss of capital and/or income. In other words, he can benefit from the investment decisions of a sophisticated professional management and hold a security with a reasonably high degree of liquidity, usually with some built-in safety as well. If the number of securities quoted on the local stock exchange is limited, unit trusts can even overcome this (provided the authorities are agreeable) by investing a proportion of their funds in well established foreign concerns, thereby assisting (if only in a small way) the integration of the several national capital markets into a larger whole. If a little 'pump-priming' were necessary in the setting up of a unit trust, the authorities might consider the possibility of either a State unit trust, or (where the electorate is averse to State participation) a major unit trust sponsored by the leading commercial banks in a country. Nor need the established savings institutions fear unduly the suspected threat to their own traditional forms of business, since the probability is that the unit trusts will elicit additional savings both from old and new sources, and the operations of these institutions are likely to become supplementary rather than competitive. It is also a means of developing greater market activity, since a unit trust—whether seeking income or growth—will necessarily reshuffle its portfolio from time to time and by buying and selling will help to increase stock-exchange turnover.

Quite apart from the presence or absence of unit trusts, in a number of countries there is still a great dearth of institutional investors. In particular, insurance companies and pension funds often seem to be quite small. Where this is due (as in Western Germany and Austria) to the existence of a good social insurance scheme, there may be little prospect of encouraging any significant growth in this sector.

By way of contrast, where (as in Sweden) a National Pension Fund exists or (as in Norway) a National Pension Scheme is being launched, this will tend to have two effects. Certainly it helps to widen the scope of institutional demand, but it also tends to concentrate it largely in the hands of one authority, and this has obvious dangers. The managers of such funds clearly carry a heavy responsibility and it is difficult to conceive of their being able to formulate a policy that could in any sense be regarded as 'neutral'. With such a big block demand (absorbing in Sweden up to 50 per cent. of all new bond issues), the great danger is that the market may become 'skewed'; instead of a large number of separate individual demands, there is now a semi-monopsony and rather less interplay than previously obtained between the conditions of supply and demand. On the other hand, at times when the demand may be inclined to flag this same semi-monopsony may become a major stabilizing influence. Presumably, in matters concerning debt management, there would be regular consultations between the managers of such funds and the country's central bank.

However, where there is still ample scope for greater institutional investment on private account, it may be possible to influence the ways in which insurance companies, pension funds, and savings banks invest their funds, and to encourage larger investments in industrial bonds and equities—by moral suasion or by permissive legislation to enable such institutions to invest a higher proportion of their funds in bonds and shares. Again, it is a matter of breaking down conservative attitudes—in terms of the savings at their disposal, the security purchases of these institutions are often quite low and their choice of investments unadventurous and traditional.

Whether one is attempting to stimulate the private or the institutional demand for securities, a potent consideration will be the extent to which a secondary market in such assets already exists. Investors will not always want to hold securities to ultimate maturity; their demand for securities will therefore tend to be enhanced if they know there is a ready market available, in which they can sell for cash or (if they so desire) purchase alternative securities. This is what the existence of a secondary market implies. It provides opportunities for shifting or converting assets into liquid form. If such a market does not exist, there is a clear case for encouraging its development, in order to stimulate both market activity and, in the longer run, a growth in the demand for bonds and/or shares.

This can be done in a number of ways. Fiscal imposts on share and bond transactions, as well as fees and commissions (i.e. the costs of shifting), might be kept at minimal levels. Equally, firms might be encouraged to satisfy their longer-term financial requirements by making new issues of bonds or shares and reducing longer-term bank accommodation. In some countries there may also be a case for opening up the capital market to a larger number of underwriters, thereby exposing those currently in the field to increased competition, with the possibility of greater flexibility in terms and rates. On the other hand, savers might be encouraged to invest more positively and to divert their savings (say) either to unit trusts or to the insurance companies, both of which institutions are already geared to making a proportion of their investments through the agency of the stock exchanges. Alternatively, savings banks might be encouraged to invest a proportion of their funds in industrial bonds, if not in equities.

So far as direct private investment through the capital market is concerned, there is little one can do about shares, but in the case of government and semi-government bonds the emergence of a secondary market could be assisted by offering higher rates and, if necessary, by tax concessions. For the rest, it is a matter of giving every encouragement to the institutional investors, since it is they that are most likely (in pursuit of profit) to be concerned periodically to re-shuffle their portfolios, and in that way to provide the turnover that is of the essence of a secondary market.

In summary, there can be no effective broadening of a capital market if institutions merely hold securities indefinitely in their portfolios. One needs to develop not only an appetite for new securities (by the general public and institutional investors) but also a desire periodically to buy and sell existing securities, thereby increasing the turnover of the market and fostering the emergence of a flexible and consistent structure of rates and yields. The aim is to promote a basis for informed portfolio management, such that institutions will seek to hold those securities that offer either the best current returns or the best prospects of future return. In an uncertain world, not everyone can be right in his judgements, but given the fullest possible information and operational experience, there will be an increased probability that market prices will reflect the underlying real earning trends and prospects of the concerns and industries to which the securities traded in relate.

INDEX

Absentee landlords (Ireland): and transfer problem, 65, 66, 67–68.

Accord, Treasury–Federal Reserve (U.S., 1951), 47.

Adjustment hypotheses: and monetary theory, 97 ff.

Adjustment mechanism: and fixed rates of exchange, 119 ff., 123, 124; and sterling system, 278–9.

Adjustment policies: and domestic policy goals, 27, 31, 33, 34, 37, 44–45, 46, 113, 114, 120–1; and external imbalance(s), 26 ff., 113 ff.; and rules of behaviour, 32 and n., 35, 45; and transfer problem, 63 ff.

Advances (of U.K. banks), 242–4, 245, 246–8.

— 'Ceiling' on, 247–8.

Africa:

— Commercial bank expansion, 153 ff.

— External reserves, 161 ff.

— Monetary authorities in, 160 ff.

— Monetary expansion in, 158, 161 ff.

Agadir crisis, 224.

Aggregate demand functions, 87.

Aggregate-demand policies, 38, 44.

Amalgamation movement (of banks, U.K.), 235.

Appiah, A., 151 n.

Arbitrage:

— Interest, 41.

— Operations, 272.

Argentina, 193–5.

Argentine Committee, 201, 218.

— Securities, 193–5, 201.

Ashworth, W., 193 n.

Asquith, H. H., 221, 222.

Association of Country Bankers, 190, 215.

Autumn drain, 196.

Autumnal pressures, 189.

Bagehot, W., 175, 181 n., 182, 184, 192, 196, 199, 216, 235–6; and banking reserves, 185, 187, 188, 233, 257–8.

Balance of payments, 38, 40, 41–44, 46, 113 ff., 279, 280, 281.

— Adjustment policies, 26 ff., 119 ff.

— Adjustment problems, 113 ff.

— Africa, 158–9, 166.

— and financing policies, 121 ff.

— and income changes, 67, 124.

— and incomes policy, 127–8.

— and real adjustment policies, 121, 126 ff.

— and transfer problem, 63 ff.

— Deficit(s), 37, 38, 41, 43, 46, 115, 118 ff.; of United States, 119, 124.

— of United Kingdom, 113, 277, 282, 288, 289, 294, 295.

— of United States, 81–83, 113, 119, 124, 128.

— Surplus(es), 37, 38, 41, 43, 46, 114–15, 118 ff.

Balance sheets (of banks), 231, 233–5.

Ball, R. J., 89 n.

Balogh, T., 268 n., 269 n., 271.

Bank accounts, publication of, 189, 208, 209, 211, 215, 221–3.

Bank Charter Act of 1844, 168, 170–1, 172, 174, 177, 178, 182, 184, 186, 189, 200–1, 204, 208, 215, 218, 226, 227, 231, 259, 274.

Bank deposits, 179, 180, 219–20.

Bank notes:

— Issues; and reserves (U.K.), 229 ff. *passim.*

— Restriction on issue of (Canada), 137–9.

Bank of England, 1, 3, 28 n., 169, 172, 176, 179–80, 181, 182–4, 185–90, 191–2, 194, 195, 211, 223, 225, 228, 231, 236, 249, 257, 277, 286; and Bank Return, 231; and Banking and Currency Principles, 259; and Baring crisis, 195–207, 217–19, 224; and central banking, 226–8; and commercial banks, 170, 175, 180, 189, 190, 191, 192, 210–12, 215–16, 221–2, 226–7; and Government, 180, 225, 228; and lending at Bank Rate, 7–9, 11–18, —statistics of, 19–23, 24–25; and liquidity, 238; and monetary reform, 177, 208, 210–13, 215; and money market, 168, 179, 180, 189, 190, 192, 210, 221, 227; and one-

— One-pound, 173, 174, 176–7, 208, 209, 210, 212, 214–15, 222, 225.
— Private, 174, 176, 183, 211.
— Scottish, 176.
— Silver backed, 178, 208–9.
— Ten shilling, 178, 209.
Nurkse, Ragner, 29, 280 n.

Obsolescence, 300.
Ohlin, Bertil, 79.
Olley, R. E., 145 n.
Open-market operations, 28 n., 86, 187, 235, 253, 256.
— in U.S., 47, 48, 50, 51, 53, 56.
Overdraft system, and 'ceiling' on advances, 247–8.
Overend Gurney crisis (1866), 233.
Overseas banks, 270–2, 275–6, 278, 280–1, 286, 294.
Overseas investment, 266, 268–71 *passim*, 275, 279, 280–2, 283, 292.

Paish, F. W., 226 n., 268 n.
Paish, Sir George, 226 n.
Palgrave, R. H. I., 183, 189 n., 222, 234 n.
'Palmer rule', 231, 259.
Panics, 177, 181, 182, 183, 185, 188, 190, 200.
Paris markets, 181, 199, 205.
Parliament, 171, 211.
Parnell, Sir Henry, 69.
'Participation', 305, 311.
Patron, M., 199 n.
Peel, Lord, 228.
Peel, Sir Robert, 169, 171, 173, 175, 207, 216.
Penalty rates, 53–54, 55–56.
Pension funds, 311, 314–15.
Permanent consumption, 96 n.
Permanent income, 91, 92, 93, 94, 95, 96, 97, 98–101, 102, 108, 109.
'Permanent prices', 91.
Permanent saving, 96 n.
Phillips, J. Spencer, 221.
Pigou, A. C., 74 n., 85.
Policy goals, and adjustment policies, 27, 31, 33, 34, 37, 44–45, 46, 113, 114, 120–1.
Portfolio management, 314, 316.
Post Office Savings Banks, *see* savings banks.
Postal orders, 177.

Powell, D., 217.
Pressnell, L. S., 229–30.
Price-adjustment transfer theory, 67, 69, 71, 72, 79.
Price, B. B., 167 n., 187.
Primary securities, 131.
Private placements, 312.
Provincial Notes Act, 1866 (Canada), 138.
Publication of banking statistics, 188, 189, 221, 222, 230–1, 233–5.

Quantity theory, 253 n.

Radcliffe Committee (U.K.), Report and Evidence, 5, 156 and n., 236 and n., 240, 241 and n., 242 n., 243 and n., 244 n., 245 n., 251 n.
Rae, G., 175, 176 n., 182, 189–90, 233, 239.
Rait, R. S., 239 n.
Rate of profit, 300, 301; and inflation, 307 n.
Real estate, lending against security of, Canada, 137, 139.
Regular money, 4.
Regulation A (U.S.), 49.
Reichsbank, 28 n.
Reluctant adjustment, process of, 120–1, 122, 128.
Reserve currency; and confidence, 117.
Reserve-currency country(ies), 115, 116, 118, 119.
— United Kingdom as, 116, 266 ff.
— United States as, 45, 82, 116, 119, 294.
Reserve requirements:
— Canada, 134, 137, 138, 150.
— U.S., 47, 56, 61.
Reserve Plan, 100 per cent., 253, 254, 256.
'Reserved Liability' Act, 189.
Reserves (cash):
— Africa, 158–60.
— Canada, 134, 138.
— United Kingdom, 229 ff. *passim*.
— United States, and demands for loans, 56–57; and member bank borrowings, 49–50; excess, 47.
Revelstoke, Lord, 195, 202, 217.
Rhodesia:
— Capital flight from, 156.

PRINTED IN GREAT BRITAIN
AT THE UNIVERSITY PRESS, OXFORD
BY VIVIAN RIDLER
PRINTER TO THE UNIVERSITY